THE P

THE POWER OF BLACK MUSIC

**Interpreting Its History
from Africa
to the United States**

Samuel A. Floyd, Jr.

Oxford University Press

New York   Oxford

Oxford University Press

Oxford   New York
Athens   Auckland   Bangkok   Bombay
Calcutta   Cape Town   Dar es Salaam   Delhi
Florence   Hong Kong   Istanbul   Karachi
Kuala Lumpur   Madras   Madrid   Melbourne
Mexico City   Nairobi   Paris   Singapore
Taipei   Tokyo   Toronto

and associated companies in
Berlin   Ibadan

Copyright © 1995 by Samuel A. Floyd, Jr.

First published in 1995 by Oxford University Press, Inc.,
198 Madison Avenue, New York, NY 10016

First issued as an Oxford University Press paperback, 1996

Oxford is a registered trademark of Oxford University Press

Library of Congress Cataloging-in-Publication Data
Floyd, Samuel A.
The power of Black music : interpreting its history from Africa
to the United States / Samuel A. Floyd, Jr.
p. cm.   Includes bibliographical references, discography,
filmography, and index.
ISBN 0-19-508235-4
ISBN 0-19-510975-9 (Pbk.)
1. Afro-Americans—Music—History and criticism.
2. Music—United States—History and criticism.
ML3556.F65   1995   780'.89'96073—dc20   94-21

Since this page cannot legibly accommodate the acknowledgments,
pages v–vi constitute an extension of the copyright page.

1 2 3 4 5 6 7 8 9 10

Printed in the United States of America
on acid-free paper

Text

Musical Examples

Example 1: Adzida Dance, from *Studies in African Music* by A. M. Jones.
Copyright © 1959 by Oxford University Press.
Reprinted by permission of Oxford University Press, Inc.

Example 2: *Runagate, Runagate* by Wendell Logan, set to poem by Robert Hayden.
Reprinted with permission of MMB Music, Inc., St. Louis.
Copyright © 1989. All rights reserved.

Examples 3 and 4: "For You There Is No Song" by Leslie Adams.
From *Anthology of Art Songs by Black American Composers*, compiled by Willis C. Patterson.
Copyright © 1977 by Edward B. Marks Music Company.
Reprinted by permission of Edward B. Marks Music Company.
Text from *Collected Poems of Edna St. Vincent Millay*, edited by Norma Millay Ellis.
Copyright © 1981. Reprinted by permission.

Example 5: "Dancing in the Sun" by John W. Work, set to poem by Howard Weedun.
Reprinted by permission of the composer's family.

Example 6: "Soliloquy" by John W. Work, set to poem by Myrtle Vorst Sheppard.
Reprinted by permission of the composer's family.

Example 7: "A Red, Red Rose" by George Walker, set to poem by Robert Burns.
Reprinted with permission of MMB Music, Inc., St. Louis.
Copyright © 1975. All rights reserved.

Example 8: "Faithful One" by Robert Owens, set to poem by Langston Hughes.
Copyright © 1969.
Reprinted by permission of Orlando-Musikverlag, Munich, Germany.

Example 9: "Velvet Shoes" by Hale Smith, set to poem by Elinor Wiley.
Copyright © 1974 by Edward B. Marks Music Company.
Reprinted by permission of Edward B. Marks Music Company.

Examples 10 and 11: *Two Songs for Julie-Ju* by Noel DaCosta, set to poems by George Houston Bass.
Copyright © 1977 by Edward B. Marks Music Company.
Reprinted by permission of Edward B. Marks Music Company.

Example 12: "A Song Without Words" by Charles Brown.
Copyright © 1977.
Reprinted by permission of the composer.

Example 13: "A Death Song" by Howard Swanson, set to a poem by Paul Laurence Dunbar.
Copyright © 1951 by Weintraub Music, a division of Music Sales Corporation (ASCAP).
Reprinted by permission.

For

Theora

Barbara

Wanda

Cecilia

Sam III

Acknowledgments

For their contributions to the inspiration and support I needed to undertake this project, I would like to thank James Winn, director of the Institute for the Humanities, University of Michigan, whose fellowship support allowed me to explore the implications of critical theory to black music inquiry; Richard Crawford, professor of music at the University of Michigan, whose friendship, sharp and scholarly eye, and helpful criticism made my introductory article in this area better than it otherwise would have been; Orin Moe, my remarkably well-read friend who called my attention to Peter Kivy's four books on the philosophy of music and Lawrence Kramer's work on musico-literary analysis; and Bruce Tucker, guest editor of an issue of the *Black Music Research Journal,* for inviting me to submit the article in which many of these issues were first raised, for contributing to the identification of one of the seminal ideas in that piece, and for reading portions of the present work. It was Bruce, a former colleague at Fisk University and now a freelance writer, who encouraged me to write *The Power of Black Music* from a personal perspective. Rich Crawford, Marsha J. Reisser, and singer William Brown read the entire manuscript and offered corrections and valuable content and editorial suggestions. William Komla Amoaku critiqued chapter 1 and offered valuable suggestions; Calvert Bean, Orin Moe, and Mark Tucker, all of whom serve on the editorial board of *Black Music Research Journal,* read chapter 9; composer T. J. Anderson read and critiqued chapters 7 and 8; and Eileen Southern read the manuscript's early chapters. Chapter 10 profited from Douglas Dempster's astute comments on the philosophical issues I discuss there. Early in my research, Horace Boyer provided me with recorded examples of certain performances of gospel music, which proved helpful, and information about the Boyer Brothers' recordings; his brother James provided me with a recording that had proved otherwise impossible to obtain. Country-music scholar Charles Wolf directed me to DeFord Bailey's recordings, and record collector Roger Miscewicz provided recordings of the blues pieces I discuss in chapter 9. My discussion in chapter 5 of the Chicago flowering of the Negro Renaissance was aided greatly by the assistance of Virginia McLaurin, of the Vivian Harsh collection of the Carter G. Woodson branch of the Chicago Public Library System. The librarians at the Columbia College Library were extremely helpful, especially Paula Epstein, who not only did not tire of my constant requests for help but went further than I would have expected in locating hard-to-find citations and materials. And the fine staff at the Center for Black Music Research performed in superb fashion, providing research and material needs on consistently short notice; my thanks go especially to Suzanne Flandreau, Marcos Sueiro, and Richard Barnes. The untiring work of Deborah Coney, my former secretary in the dean's office at Columbia College, in acquiring books and articles for me, was indispensable and is very much appreciated. My brief stint as a Fellow of the National Humanities Center, in Research Triangle Park, North Carolina, made it possible for me to bring my work to completion well before my submission deadline. Special thanks are due Dominique-René de Lerma, who over the past twenty years has generously shared with me, and with numerous others, information in his files and an extensive database of names of black composers and the titles of their compositions. Susan Allan deserves thanks for editing early drafts of each of the book's chapters, and Chris Rohmann for his masterful editing of the final draft. Finally, my thanks go to Sheldon Meyer, my editor at Oxford, who encouraged the development of this book and helped facilitate its completion.

My research was assisted immeasurably by Eileen Southern and Josephine Wright's *African-American Traditions in Song, Sermon, Tale, and Dance, 1600s–1920: An Annotated Bibliography of Literature, Collections, and Artworks* (1990), an extremely valuable research tool that will immeasurably facilitate the advancement of scholarship in the field of black cultural expression in the coming years.

Contents

THE POWER OF BLACK MUSIC

Introduction

The calves follow their mothers. The young plant grows up near the parent stem. The young antelope leaps where its mother has leaped.
Zulu proverb

We carry with us the wonders we seek without us: there is all Africa and her prodigies within us.
Sir Thomas Browne

I am a member of perhaps the last generation of African Americans whose parents and grandparents were intimately familiar with Br'er Rabbit, Legba, the Signifying Monkey, Stackolee, John the Conqueror, and other black folk characters and practices. My generation grew up hearing the tales of these and other African and African-American folk figures, and we actually saw the practice of some of their superstitions. My generation also had the good fortune of regularly hearing great songsters who trudged the streets of neighborhoods singing a cappella or accompanying themselves on guitar. I remember most poignantly Mr. B., a blind seller of boiled and "parched" peanuts who peddled his wares by singing street cries and blues as he walked the streets of my neighborhood in Lakeland, Florida, in the 1940s and very early 1950s. And each winter until I graduated from high school, in 1953, I saw the Silas Green from New Orleans show, which featured one of the great-

3

est of tent-show bands, tremendous blues singers, and much signifying and fronting by interlocutors, end men, comics, and skit players.

It was also my good fortune to have been introduced early to the performance of blues, jazz, and rhythm and blues through my high-school band director, Lawrence Pope, who was as much at home with Franz von Suppé's *Poet and Peasant* overture as he was with the music of Louis Jordan, Jimmy Lunceford, and Dizzy Gillespie. With my mother hoping that I would become a concert pianist and my band director and friends serving as models and peers along the jazz and R&B routes, I was able to achieve a good balance of musical tastes and practices that remained with me throughout my entire intellectual and musical development. Little did I know then that hearing the early folk tales and sayings, seeing the practice of black folk superstitions, and learning about and playing black music would later inform my scholarship and ignite an African cultural memory that had remained unconscious for many years. The feeling of having such a cultural memory inform and ignite the intellect is powerfully gratifying; it confirms the validity of new knowledge and new ideas as no amount of rational thought will or can. In pursuing and developing the narrative of this book, I found myself constantly checking the correctness of conclusions—however intellectual, rational, and reasonable they may have been—against the subjective criteria of that cultural memory, which I found to be highly reliable, as incidents, stories, and activities long forgotten returned to my mind and fit as perfectly as a peg into a hole I had measured to be filled. In the course of writing, I found such confirmations highly satisfying, aesthetically gratifying, and intellectually invigorating.

More recently, my scholarship has been informed by, among other things, my extensive reading of biographical and autobiographical studies of black musicians in compiling *Black Music Biography: An Annotated Bibliography* (Floyd and Reisser 1987). The biographies and autobiographies of major figures as diverse as Sidney Bechet, Jimi Hendrix, and William Grant Still have given me significant insight into the lives of these musicians and the extent to which those lives were formed and motivated by African cultural memory and its mythological and interpretive values. These works also confirm and validate the influence of the values, transformations, and contributions of black musicians on and within American culture.

While on fellowship study at the University of Michigan's Institute for the Humanities, I became interested in black literary theory, and I quickly perceived that this field of study had implications for the study of black music. After reading three rather introductory studies, I came across Henry Louis Gates's *The Signifying Monkey: A Theory of African American Literary Criticism* (1988), which convinced me of the usefulness—indeed, the indispensability—of black literary theory for inquiry into black music and for black-music scholarship in general. *The Signifying Monkey* also revived a belief and assumption that I had held since 1987—that Sterling Stuckey's *Slave Culture: Nationalist Theory and the Foundations of Black America* (1987) could serve as the basis on which a mode of inquiry into black music could be effectively developed. On rereading both Stuckey and Gates in this light and becoming convinced of the soundness of my conclusions, I broadened my research and began work on an article that would come to be titled "Ring Shout! Black Music, Black Literary Theory, and Black Historical Studies" (Floyd 1991), which, in turn, led to the planning and eventual writing of this work.

In this book, I offer an approach to the study of black music consistent with and grounded in the music itself. *The Power of Black Music* pursues the implications of "Ring Shout!" substantially expanding and adding depth to the various ideas presented there. It is not a traditional music history, but an interpretation of the origin and development of African-American music and musical culture. It is not all inclusive and is not meant to be. In this regard, only those figures and events important to the realization of my purpose have been treated in this book, regardless of their importance in the history of African-American music. *The Power of Black Music* is based on the assumption that African musical traits and cultural practices not only survived but played a major role in the development and elaboration of African-American music. The debate and interpretations surrounding the theories of survivalism, syncretism, and nonsurvivalism—posited by Herskovits (1947), Waterman (1948, 1952), and Jackson (1933, 1943), respectively—are not relevant to this study. But I should point out that although some scholars continue to differ in their view that one of these theories is more valid than another, most accept the compromise position (Hornbostel 1926) that Africans took the music of whites in the New World and transformed it through their own performance practices. My position in this book, however, is more in line with the survivalist theory, but my assumptions are quite different. In the pages that follow, I will demonstrate that African survivals exist not merely in the sense that African-American music has the same characteristics as its African counterparts, but also that the musical *tendencies*, the mythological beliefs and assumptions, and the interpretive strategies of African Americans are the same as those that underlie the music of the African homeland, that these tendencies and beliefs continue to exist as African cultural memory, and that they continue to inform the continuity and elaboration of African-American music. I have tried here to address the absence of a thorough and specific aesthetic for the perception and criticism of black music; to suggest a viable, valid, and appropriate way of inquiring into the nature of black music; to suggest a basis for discourse among intellectuals on musical difference; and to help break down the barriers that remain between "high art" and "low art." In short, this book is meant as a vehicle of rapprochement between vernacular and classical, formal and folk, academic and popular ways of knowing, attending to, and criticizing music. I have kept musical notation to a bare minimum because my intention is to write an interpretation of black music and its criticism that can be read, appreciated, and interpreted not only by music scholars but also by scholars in other disciplines, as well as by any interested reader.

In *Slave Culture,* Stuckey (1987) presents as his central tenet the hypothesis that "the ring shout was the main context in which [transplanted] Africans recognized values common to them" (16)—that is, the values of ancestor worship and contact and of communication and teaching through storytelling and trickster expressions and various other symbolic devices. He explains that the shout was a distinctive cultural ritual in which music and dance were merged and fused, that in the ring the musical practices of the slaves converged in the Negro spiritual and in other African-American musical forms and genres. In this way, the ring helped preserve the elements that we have come to know as the characterizing and foundational elements of African-American music: calls, cries, and hollers; call-and-response devices; additive rhythms and polyrhythms; heterophony, pendular thirds, blue notes, bent notes, and elisions; hums, moans, grunts, vocables, and other rhythmic-oral declamations, interjections, and punctuations; off-beat melodic phrasings and parallel intervals and chords; constant repetition of rhythmic and melodic figures and phrases (from which riffs and vamps would be derived); timbral distortions of various kinds; musical individuality within collectivity; game rivalry; hand clapping, foot patting, and approximations thereof; apart-playing; and the metronomic pulse that underlies all African-American music.[1]

In the world of the slaves, the ring shout fused the sacred and the secular, music and dance; it continued the African and African-derived tendencies to eschew distinctions between religion and everyday life, between one performance medium and another. From the ring emerged the shuffling, angular, off-beat, additive, repetitive, intensive, unflagging rhythms of shout and jubilee spirituals, ragtime, and R&B; the less vigorous but equally insistent and characteristic rhythms of "sorrow songs" and blues; and all the musical genres derived from these and other early forms. All were shaped and defined by black dance, within and without the ring. Movements that mirror the rhythms of all the African-American music genres can be seen in the ring and in dances such as the breakdown, buck dance, and buzzard lope of early slave culture, through those of the Virginia essence and the slow drag of the late nineteenth century, to the line dances of more recent days. The concept of Dance, Drum, and Song has long been considered central to the black cultural experience,

---

1. These characteristics and practices have been documented by a number of scholars over the decades, including, for example, Allen, Ware, and Garrison (1867), Ballanta-Taylor (1925), Burlin (1918), Charters (1961), Ekwueme (1974), Lomax (1970), and Oliver (1970). These observations have been summarized and interpreted most recently from a scholarly standpoint by Reisser (1982) and from an empirical point of view by Wilson (1983).

and it is clear that the entire musical content of the ring can be subsumed under it. The presence in the ring of Dance, Drum, and Song, and its cultural indispensability to the ring, make it possible for Stuckey's hypothesis to be seen as a conceptual frame in which all African-American musical analysis and interpretation can take place.

The inspiration for Gates's hermeneutics, as developed in *The Signifying Monkey,* is Esu-Elegbara, the mythical African "classical figure of mediation who is interpreter of the culture," "guardian of the crossroads," "master of style," and connector of "the grammar of divination with its rhetorical structures." Esu, one of the African pantheon of gods, is also a trickster figure. His African-American descendant—his "cousin," so to speak—is the Signifying Monkey, a symbol of antimediation in black vernacular culture in the United States (Gates 1988, 56). Both of these tricksters—Esu and the Signifying Monkey—provide keys to the interpretation of black vernacular culture. For our purposes, as for Gates's, Esu will stand for discourse on African-American "texts" and the Signifying Monkey for the rhetorical strategies by which we read African-American musical genres.

In the black narrative tradition, the concept of "Signifyin(g)" can be traced to its origins in tales about the Signifying Monkey in African-American vernacular culture, where it is, as Gates (1988) puts it, "the black trope of tropes, the figure for black rhetorical figures" (51). Signifyin(g) is figurative, implicative speech that makes use of the tropes of "marking, loud-talking, testifying, calling out (of one's name), sounding, rapping, playing the dozens, and so on" (52). One rather obvious mode of Signifyin(g) is found in the "toasts" of African-American culture—the long, complex, metrical, and multimetric epic poems that include "The Signifying Monkey," "The Titanic," "Squad Twenty-two," "Shine," "Stackolee," "The Great McDaddy," and other such tales (Labov et al. [1979] 1981, 341; Mitchell-Kernan [1979] 1981, 331).

For Gates, the vernacular is used to read and inform the formal, since the former contains the very critical principles by which the latter can be examined. So the vernacular tradition actually Signifies (comments) on the black literary tradition and can also be used for the development of critical strategies for black literary inquiry. Similarly, African-American music can be examined through the same vernacular tradition, with the rhetorical tropes of verbal provenance replaced with those of its own genesis. In this way, the calls, cries, hollers, riffs, licks, overlapping antiphony, and various rhythmic, melodic, and other musical practices of the ring—since they are used as tropes in musical performances and compositions—can serve as Signifyin(g) figures. In studying the use of these devices in black music, we come to see that these figures Signify on other figures, on the performances themselves, on other performances of the same pieces, on other and completely different works of music, and on other musical genres. We come to see that jazz improvisations are toasts—

7

metaphoric renditions of the troping and Signifyin(g) strategies of African-American oral toasts. In other words, musical Signifyin(g) is troping: the transformation of preexisting musical material by trifling with it, teasing it, or censuring it. Musical Signifyin(g) is the rhetorical use of preexisting material as a means of demonstrating respect for or poking fun at a musical style, process, or practice through parody, pastiche, implication, indirection, humor, tone play or word play, the illusion of speech or narration, or other troping mechanisms.

As this book progresses, I use Gates to read Stuckey, Stuckey to read Gates, and Stuckey and Gates to read the formulations of disparate others, including Peter Kramer, J. H. Kwabena Nketia, Francis Bebey, Olly Wilson, John Dewey, and Albert Murray. I have used all the foregoing to "read," in more or less detail, sound recordings of dozens of performances and compositions of black music, including classical works, jazz performances, ragtime pieces, R&B performances, and gospel renditions. In the course of these readings—throughout the book's first eight chapters—the outlines of an aesthetic theory evolves and is given form in chapter 10. This theory has been shaped by the readings themselves, by previous formulations of my own (see, e.g., Floyd 1978), and by my earlier encounters with other writings, including John Cage's *Silence: Lectures and Writings* (1961), Grosvenor Cooper and Leonard B. Meyer's *The Rhythmic Structure of Music* (1960), Aaron Copland's *Music and Imagination* (1967), Gordon Epperson's *The Musical Symbol* (1967), Susanne Langer's *Philosophy in a New Key* (1979), Edmund Gurney's *The Power of Sound* ([1880] 1966), Eduard Hanslick's *The Beautiful in Music* ([1854] 1957), Leonard B. Meyer's *Emotion and Meaning in Music* (1956) and *Music, the Arts, and Ideas* (1967), and Houston Baker's *Modernism and the Harlem Renaissance* (1987).

I have already used the term "cultural memory" several times, and I will use it throughout the book. My adoption of this term was inspired by Jason Berry's employment of it in his article "African Cultural Memory in New Orleans Music" (1988). In this book, I will use it to refer to nonfactual and nonreferential motivations, actions, and beliefs that members of a culture seem, without direct knowledge or deliberate training, to "know"—that feel unequivocally "true" and "right" when encountered, experienced, and executed. It may be defined as a repository of meanings that comprise the subjective knowledge of a people, its immanent thoughts, its structures, and its practices; these thoughts, structures, and practices are transferred and understood unconsciously but become conscious and culturally objective in practice and perception. Cultural memory, obviously a subjective concept, seems to be connected with cultural *forms*—in the present case, music, where the "memory" drives the music and the music drives memory. Sidney Bechet (1960), for example, says that there "was something happening all the time to my people, a thing the music had to know for sure. There had to be a memory of it behind the music" (103). In speaking of his grandfather Omar, who died a slave as a young man, Bechet says, "Inside him he'd got the memory of all the wrong that's been done to my people. That's what the memory is. . . . When a blues is good, that kind of memory just grows up inside it" (108). The music "taught me a whole lot about Omar's trouble in a way I couldn't have known about until I'd had some trouble of my own" (104). He continues, "If you're any good musicianer, its Omar's song you're singing" (202). For Bechet, although he did not see or experience it, slavery was a "memory": of New Orleans's Congo Square, where Omar had participated as a musician and dancer; of slave intrigue; of the violence, love, happiness, and sadness of Omar, his cohorts, and his descendants; of New Orleans jazz funerals, dances, and picnics, in which Bechet performed as a clarinetist; and of his later experiences outside New Orleans. He elaborates further:

> I met many a musicianer in many a place after I struck out from New Orleans, but it was always the same: If they was any good, it was Omar's song they were singing. It was the long song, and the good musicianers, they all heard it behind them. They all had an Omar, somebody like an Omar, somebody that was *their* Omar. It didn't need just recollecting somebody like that: it was the feeling of someone back there—hearing the song like it was coming up from somewhere.
>
> A musicianer could be playing it in New Orleans, or Chicago, or New York; he could be playing it in London, in Tunis, in Paris, in Germany. I heard it played in all those places and a many more. But no matter where it's played, you gotta hear it starting way behind you. There's the drum beating from Congo Square and there's the song starting in a field just over the trees. The good musicianer, he's playing *with* it, and he's playing *after* it. He's finishing something. No matter what he's playing, it's the long song that started back there in the South.
>
> It's the remembering song. There's so much to remember. (202)

For Bechet, African-American music, with its "feeling of someone back there," with its "remembering song" "coming up from somewhere," was expressive of cultural memory, and black-music making was the translation of the memory into sound and the sound into memory. And it is so for many black musicians, for they have always been highly sensitive to the efficacy, powers, and imperatives of the cultural memory. For Berry (1988), as for me, however, the memory goes back beyond Omar and the slave experience in America to Africa, and the musical retentions and performance practices of African-American music helped and still help to preserve this memory, recalling the mysteries of myth and the trappings of ritual long after they are no longer functional. Perhaps mental tracings have been left, passing from descendant to descendant and preserving the memory as residue. Whatever its nature and process, cultural memory, as a reference to vaguely "known" musical and cultural processes and procedures, is a valid and meaningful way of accounting for the subjective, spiritual quality of the musical and aesthetic behaviors of a culture.

One of my central arguments and proofs in this book is that Stuckey's ring-shout hypothesis can serve as the frame in which Gates's theory can be applied. Another is that a compelling cultural and musical continuity exists between all the musical genres of the African-American cultural experience—a continuity that can be seen in and traced from the musical characteristics of the ring into the most recent music making of black Americans. A third argument I make throughout the book is that all African-American-music making is driven by and permeated with the memory of things from the cultural past and that recognition of the viability of such memory should play a role in the perception and criticism of works and performances of the music. Finally, I argue and demonstrate that from the proofs and conclusions from all of this, the outlines of a theory of the interpretation of black music can be derived, a theory that can be applied to the perception and effective criticism of black music.

Chapter 1 briefly explores aspects of African expressions in religious, musical, and narrative contexts and sets the stage for our understanding of how these expressions were transformed, in a new land, into African-American music. Treated here are the Africans' idea of God, their pantheon of lesser gods, their ancestor beliefs, the roles these beliefs play in ritual, and the relationship of these beliefs to Dance, Drum, and Song. Chapter 2 discusses how African musical traditions survived the Middle Passage to become syncretized with European music on the North American continent while retaining their most important cultural traits and characteristics. The focus here is on the ring shout and its music, on music outside the ring in the form of black folk song and instrumental music, on black dance as it relates to black music, and on the African-American songsters and bluesmen of the core culture.[2] Chapter 3 treats the syncretization of African and European music in the New World, exploring works and performances of black musicians of the nineteenth century and at the turn of the twentieth. Emphasis is on the spiritual, blues, ragtime, and other nineteenth-century folk forms; the beginnings of jazz are also explored.

Chapter 4 is devoted to the beginnings of African-American modernism in the 1890s, the origin and development of Pan-Africanism and black nationalism, and the seeds of the Negro Renaissance. It explores the dyadic nature of the culture and the conflicting attitudes of the period's black cultural leaders as they would come to affect the music and investigates the relationship of

---

2. I ran across the term "core culture" more than ten years ago in a source whose title and author I no longer recall; nor do I recall that unknown author's precise definition of the term. I use it in this book to refer to that portion of the black population that has remained closest to its mythic and ritual roots, whose primary cultural values and interests lie *within* that community, and whose concerns for racial integration appear to be secondary to its concern for individual and community survival and the perpetuation of African-American cultural and social behaviors and institutions. It is in this population that the cultural memory is strongest and most abiding.

these conditions to the rise and practice of Signifyin(g) in urban black America. The spirit and significance of Esu pervades the first four chapters, with the venerable *orisha* emerging in chapter 3 as Legba, guardian of the crossroads and grantor of the privilege and gift of interpretation for the early bluesmen. The spirit and significance of the Signifying Monkey pervade the chapters that follow, with the interpretive qualities of Esu and the rhetorical values of the Signifying Monkey merging to form a frame of reference for the interpretation and criticism of musical Signifyin(g).

In chapter 5, I discuss the music of the Negro Renaissance, paying special attention to its major flowerings in Harlem in the 1920s and in Chicago in the 1930s and 1940s. Since I have thoroughly treated the Harlem Renaissance elsewhere (Floyd 1990b), I place more emphasis in this study on the Chicago movement. Chapter 6 examines the concert-hall tradition, beginning with the music of William Grant Still and that of other black composers within the context of the Americanist, neoclassical, and avant-garde ideas of the 1920s through the 1940s, and setting the stage for discussion of the works of black composers of the 1950s through the 1980s. I treat concert-hall performances as the rituals they are, and Eero Tarasti's book *Myth and Music: A Semiotic Approach to the Aesthetics of Myth in Music* (1979) serves as an important source for my discussion of myth as the basis for that ritual. Tarasti's study posits "the idea of reconstructing myth and mythical communication," explores "the hypothesis of an 'unconscious'" that works of art "are capable of reflecting," and claims that, in composing music that suggests the primitive, for example, the artist reconstructs not primitive art, "but rather the unconscious" (62, 63).

Chapters 7 and 8 are surveys, quasi-chronological accounts of musico-aesthetic developments that took place in the United States during the periods 1950 to 1962 and 1963 to 1989, respectively. Chapter 7 focuses on the continuing evolution of African-American music in the face of the reactionary musical currents of the 1950s. I am especially interested here in how the political, social, and aesthetic currents of the time affected the continuing growth and simultaneous stagnation of black music in the United States. Ideas and events related to the New Critics, neoclassicism, the Paul Robeson case, and other such influences are discussed. Chapter 8 is devoted to the exploration of the explosive multiplicity of styles spawned by this new awakening, in forms of jazz, gospel, and R&B, and in concert-hall activity. In chapter 9, two major tropes of black music are treated: the spiritual and the blues, represented by the "chariot trope" and the trope of the "riding train," respectively. The use of these two tropes in a variety of musical performances is explored as a way of demonstrating the power of musical troping and its pervasive use in black music.

In chapter 10, which is devoted to the treatment of black music as a Signifyin(g) symbol, I apply the precepts and concepts discussed in preceding chap-

11

ters and evolve an approach to the criticism of the music. Treated here are music as symbol, music as *Signifyin(g)* symbol, the notion of black music, and the valuation of black music. In recognition that Stuckey's hypothesis and Gates's theory cannot by themselves provide and sustain musical philosophy and analysis (which is what this book ultimately is about), chapter 10 also explores and adopts some of the theoretical formulations of musical and philosophical scholars whose thought is pertinent to the subject of this book—most notably Peter Kivy, Lawrence Kramer, and Mark Evan Bonds. Kramer's book *Music as Cultural Practice, 1800–1900* (1990), an interdisciplinary approach to the uniting of poststructuralism and critical historicism, treats the relationship of music to text, representation, and cultural practice. Although devoted to works in the Western European tradition, Kramer's work parallels Gates's in that both rely on tropes and troping and both insist that the interpretive criteria of critics come from within the works they examine. Kivy's books on musical expression and representation exhibit the best and most advanced thinking in the philosophy of music. These include *Sound and Semblance: Reflections on Musical Representation* (1984); *Sound Sentiment: An Essay on the Musical Emotions* (1989), which includes the complete text of his 1980 study *The Corded Shell: Reflections on Musical Expression;* and *Music Alone: Philosophical Reflections on the Purely Musical Experience* (1990). Bonds's *Wordless Rhetoric: Musical Form and the Metaphor of the Oration* (1991) treats musical form as orational metaphor. Although his discussion examines discourse related to composition and analysis of large-scale form in the eighteenth and nineteenth centuries, his focus on grammar and rhetoric has implications for the criticism of black music. All these works have significant bearing on my theory; Kivy's ideas, in particular, have several points of convergence with the position taken by me and by those on whose work I build. By way of conclusion, chapter 11 muses on the journey I have taken in writing this book, shares thoughts about the meanings of many of its ideas, and theorizes about the future of black-music scholarship. It draws conclusions about the work as a whole and about future research in the field.[3]

The African proverbs that serve as epigraphs to the chapters are culled from Jan Knappert's collection *The A to Z of African Proverbs* (1989). Proverbs, part of the daily conversational experience in all of Africa, are "true expressions" of African philosophy, Knappert confirms. These "short expressions of wit, containing the wisdom of past generations in condensed form," express "the essence of African wisdom" and "reveal the unity of mankind and the universality of our human emotions, thoughts and problems" (2, 3). In African

---

3. Work currently in progress overlaps the 1980s and covers the period 1980 to 1991.

proverbs the entire realm of human experience is condensed, making them excellent for teaching, for soothing emotions, for social control, and for helping us adapt to a variety of conditions and circumstances. In addition, they are "poetic commentaries on human life and society" (10). As epigraphs in this work, they are combined with quotations from European and American writings to illuminate, from the perspective of both continents, the central ideas of the chapters they accompany.

Many musicians and composers worthy of treatment have not been discussed in this book. The reasons for these exclusions lie in the criteria I set up at the outset of this project: to discuss only those composers and musicians who serve the purpose of my narrative, since the artists themselves are not the focus of this work; to discuss (of necessity) only those musical works available commercially in recordings or in scores; and to select examples to be cited for their quality as well as their relevance. In the final analysis, selection has been subjective, for the writing of this book has been a highly personal experience. I have written this book not to chronicle black composers' contributions to American culture but to discover and elucidate what makes this black music so powerful and moving and to share my explorations and conclusions with others who may want to know what I have come to know and believe.

CHAPTER **1**

African Music, Religion, and Narrative

The objective of African music is . . . to translate every-day experiences into living sound . . . to depict life, nature, or the supernatural.
Frances Bebey

We cannot love that which we do not know.
Guinean proverb

In spite of the quite apparent importance of African religion to the understanding of African ritual and its musical derivatives, music scholars have neglected to pay significant attention to it. The reasons, I suppose, are several, including the fact, perception, or assumption that the myths and legends of ritual are not compatible with the positivistic element in musicological scholarship and the assumption that, since African cultures are many and diverse, there is no single concept of African religion, and thus a study of them all would not be productive. Within the framework of the mode of inquiry presented in this book, however, familiarity with African religious practices is essential. The best source of this knowledge appears to be the work of John S. Mbiti ([1969] 1990), on whose formulations the discussion in this chapter will largely rely.

Mbiti's descriptive, comparative, and interpretive approach to the study of African religion brings together in one conceptual framework the diverse beliefs, elements, and characteristics of the more than three thousand African ethnic groups, each with its own religious system. Mbiti ([1969] 1990) observes that in spite of this diversity, "there are sufficient elements which make it possible for us to discuss African concepts of God as a unity and on a continental scale" (30). He stresses that in spite of the variety of religious beliefs that conform to the values and needs of the various linguistic groupings of African peoples, fundamental concepts of some basic elements are common throughout the continent. It is for this reason, Raboteau (1978) tells us, that "similar modes of perception, shared basic principles, and common patterns of ritual were widespread among different West African religions" (7). Thus it is proper and useful to speak of *an* African religion.[1]

In all African societies, "without a single exception, people have a notion of God . . . a minimal and fundamental idea about God" (Mbiti [1969] 1990, 29). Like the Christian God, the African God is known as a High God, a Supreme God, a father, king, lord, master, judge, or ruler, depending on the society doing the naming (or, in some matriarchal societies, Mother, although the image of God as Father is not limited to patriarchal societies). God is a Creator and Provider who reigns in the sky or heaven and over heaven and earth, the two having originally been "either close together or joined by a rope or bridge" (52). Africans are expected to be humble before him, to respect and honor him. This image of God is "the only image known in traditional African societies" (48).

In traditional African culture, there was no formal distinction between the sacred and the profane realms of life, or between the material and the spiritual; thus there was in traditional Africa no word for "religion" because the Africans' religion permeated and was the basis for all aspects of life, including education, politics, harvesting, hunting, homemaking, and community welfare. Since religion permeated the everyday life of African peoples, the great number of religious beliefs that existed were not systematized into dogmas, but appeared as ideas and practices that governed everyday life in the various communities. All African peoples recognized God as the One, although in a majority of cosmologies other divinities also existed, some of whom were closely allied with him. In a few cases, dual and trinitarian concepts prevailed (Mbiti [1969] 1990, 35–36). But whatever the case may have been, Africans, on the whole, worshipped God, the One.

A pantheon of lesser gods, "mythological figures of a spiritual nature" (Mbiti [1969] 1990, 77), existed in many African societies. They were timeless fig-

1. In the discussion to follow, I will use the past tense in referring to African beliefs and practices. Although the present tense is used quite properly by Mbiti and others on whom I will rely for information, my choice of the past tense for this discussion was made in the interest of historical sense, to create a sense of chronology and succession between traditional Africans and the early African Americans. In quotations, however, I will leave the writers' use of tense unchanged.

ures who sometimes acted as intermediaries between God and the people. Known in the Yoruba tradition as *orisha,* these spiritual divinities can be seen as "archetypes of the collective unconscious" (Gonzáles-Wippler 1985, 13). Unlike the High God, the lesser divinities were "constantly concerned with the daily life of the individual and the affairs of society as a whole" (Raboteau 1978, 8). Among the African pantheon, Olodumare was senior, known as "God, the creative force of the universe"; Orulna was the diviner and symbol of wisdom; Ochosi was "the divine hunter"; and there were numerous others, the most prominent being Esu (Eshu, Legba, Esu-Elegbara, Eshu Elleguá), "to whom a special first offering was made at the beginning of ceremonies so that he will open the way, and to ensure that as divine trickster he will not disrupt the proper order and decorum of the service" (Raboteau, 19), for as an "incorrigible prankster, he sometimes causes havoc apparently for no good reason" (Gonzáles-Wippler, 117). These and many other African divinities attended to human affairs, arbitrarily created ill or good will, helped or hindered, informed or limited knowledge, and interacted with one another. Africans praised and made sacrifices and offerings to them and established cults in their honor. The African gods—*orisha* (Yoruba), *abosom* (Ashanti), *vodun* (Fon), *alose* (Ibo)—were sometimes considered to be spirits, since they dwelled in the nonmaterial, or spirit, world. They were, in a sense, semiphysical and semispiritual, for some of these divinities were anthropomorphized by some peoples and became "*real beings*" (Mbiti, 76). But however they were viewed, these *orisha* played a central role in African religion and thereby affected all aspects of African life.

Divinities were not the only inhabitants of the spiritual world. The living-dead and ordinary spirits dwelled there as well. Although the dead were no longer physically a part of the community, they were part of human society as long as they were remembered and their former associates kept contact with them; for although the departed were immediately cut off from human society, they died only gradually, as their memory faded in the minds of those who knew them. Death was a gradual process, with the deceased becoming living-deads at the moment of their physical death. The Senegalese poet Birago Diop says,

> Those who are dead are never gone
> They are in the brightening shadow
> And in the thickening Gloom
> The dead are not beneath the Earth
> They are in the quivering Tree
> They are in the groaning Wood
> They are in the flowing Water
> And in the still Water

They are in the Hut,
They are in the Crowd;
The Dead are not Dead.

(quoted in Bebey [1969] 1975, 126)

Traditional Africans believed that ancestors, after their deaths, were born again, at some future time, in those who descended from them, with "resemblance between a grandchild and his deceased grandfather [as proof] that the latter has been reincarnated in the former" (Raboteau 1978, 12). Therefore, in the African metaphysics, "elders of the community do not 'die,' but upon physical death are reborn into the spiritual realm as ancestors." Similarly, "the spirits of the ancestors [eventually] take physical form in the new babies that are born to the community. Babies are therefore not 'new,' but represent the timeless regeneration of the human" (Richards 1980, 8). Once the memory of a departed person has faded entirely—that is, when all who knew him have died—he is an ordinary spirit: "He is no longer remembered by name, no longer a 'human being,' but a spirit, a thing, an IT" (Mbiti [1969] 1990, 83). In the spiritual world, ordinary spirits occupy a position below the divinities and the living-dead.

Spirits and the living-dead were sometimes referred to collectively as "the ancestors." By whatever name they were called, they were not worshipped, as it is sometimes claimed. Mbiti ([1969] 1990) instructs that it is not proper to speak of Africans "worshipping the ancestors," for "Africans themselves know very well that they are not worshipping the departed members of their family" (8–9). Africans certainly venerated their ancestors, but they did not worship them. Heeding Mbiti's admonition, therefore, I will use the terms "spirits" and "living-dead" to replace the much-abused and uninformative term "ancestors."

Spirits, "the depersonalized residue of individual human beings," were the conveyors of prayers, sacrifices, and offerings to God. It was *with* these spirits that an African worshipper rejoiced, for

> he rejoices not alone but with his kinsmen, his neighbors and his relatives whether dead or living. . . . People report that they see the spirits in ponds, caves, groves, mountains or outside their villages, dancing, singing, herding cattle, working in the fields or nursing their children. Some spirits appear in people's dreams, especially to diviners, priests, medicine-men and rainmakers to impart some information. These personages may also consult the spirits as part of their normal training and practice. (Mbiti [1969] 1990, 79, 80)

Africans relied on spirits for catharsis, confessing their troubles to them as a means of seeking relief. Like the gods, the spirits could intervene in human affairs, aid and abet, and intercede with the gods on behalf of their descen-

17

dants. This African belief in life after death differed from that of Christian religion, because the emphasis in the former was on the here and now and not on a future heaven or hell, and in it, as we have seen, "no line is drawn between the spiritual and the physical" (4). Furthermore, salvation and redemption are not part of the African religious conception.

But in some African societies, at least, the living sometimes did long for life as an ancestor, as revealed in the funeral chant of the Basotho, as reported by a European observer:

> We stayed outside,
> We stayed for the sorrow,
> We stayed for the tears.
> Oh, if there were a place in heaven for me!
> That I would have wings to fly there!
> If a strong cord came down from the sky,
> I would tie myself to it,
> I would climb up above,
> I would go live there.[2]
>
> (quoted in Zahan [1970] 1979, 48–49)

This longing—apparently prevalent among the Bantu, according to Zahan—contained elements of African and Christian religions (for example, the notion of a "heaven"). But the description does not otherwise contradict the Africans' religious beliefs.

The most common acts of worship or veneration among African peoples were sacrifices (that is, the killing of animals in order to present them, in part or in whole, to God, to supernatural beings, to spirits, or to the living-dead) and offerings (the presentation of other food, material items, and blood to God, to spirits, and to the living-dead). According to Mbiti ([1969] 1990),

> The items for sacrifices include cattle, sheep, goats, chickens, dogs and even human beings. Items used for offerings include foodstuffs like fruits, maize, millet, nuts, cassava, vegetables, leaves, honey and eggs; beverages like porridge, milk, beer, wine and water; and other things of a miscellaneous nature like the dung of the hyrak, cloth, money, chalk, incense, agricultural implements, ornaments, tobacco and cowrie-shells. Blood is also offered by a number of societies. Thus, almost everything that man can get hold of and use is sacrificed or offered to God and other spiritual beings, by one people or another. As a rule, there are no sacrifices without prayers: sacrifices and offerings are the silent responses, prayers are the verbal responses. (61)

2. This lament is remarkably similar in spirit to the Negro spiritual, and I shall examine its implications for the development of that genre in chapter 2.

Such sacrifices and offerings were made to ensure favor for the community with respect to aspects of daily life, not for reward in the future or in the after-life. But it was believed that ancestors punished descendants who were delinquent in offering sacrifice, so veneration of the ancestors was important (Raboteau 1978, 12).

Sacrifices and offerings were sometimes, but not always, accompanied by prayers; but short, extempore, direct prayer was a common act of worship among practically all African ethnic groups, with long and more formal prayers being less common. Prayers were made to God, to the living-dead, and to other spirits in time of need or in recompense. According to Davidson (1969), the precedent for prayer lay in the expectation that the elders of a community or family would intercede with the deities in time of need or offense. As an example, he cites this Karimojong prayer for remission:

OFFENDER Father, father, let me be. Help me. Leave me alone. I will not do these things again, truly. I will not repeat them.

ELDER Very well. Have you believed?

OFFENDER I have.

ELDER Do you still argue?

OFFENDER No, I have believed. (88)

For the traditional African, the practice of religion involved two or more celebrants (Mbiti [1969] 1990, 60), so individuals were assisted by human intermediaries—priests, elders, rainmakers—and by the gods, all bridges to God, who helped worshippers make contact with the Maker.

This was the African's corporate faith, which had no liturgy and no creed. It was a utilitarian, practical faith, although also spiritual (Mbiti [1969] 1990, 67). Traditional Africans came to God in particular circumstances with sacrifices and offerings—through the divinities, spirits, the living dead, and human intermediaries—and they came in Dance, Drum, and Song.

The religious beliefs of Africans were externally manifested in ritual, through which they worshipped God and venerated their ancestors and ordinary spirits, calling on the divinities to assist them in making such contact. The formal trappings of ritual and its supporting mythologies—including the God Creator, the lesser gods, the spirits, and the living-dead—came together in communal ceremony. Of Dance, Drum, and Song, dance was the most central to ritual. It was believed in some African societies that "ritualistic dancing can increase and generate *ache* [àshe] or life force in the individual" (Gonzáles-Wippler 1985, 12). The Yoruba believed that *àshe*—a dynamic, malleable en-

19

ergy, a life force that can be put to good or evil use—was "the true nature of things," that *àshe* was received "directly from the orisha through propitiation and invocation" (12). And here is the source of the spirit possession common to African ritual: "This generated power is tapped directly from the orisha to whom the individual dedicates the dance. The power is said to increase particularly during the trance states of possession, when an orisha is said to take over the conscious personality of a believer" (12).

The same can be said to hold true in most African societies, since spirit possession is common among nearly all African peoples (Mbiti [1969] 1990, 80). In most African societies,

> the *orisha* [or] *vodun* are called to take possession of their devotees by the songs and the drumming of the cult groups, each of the gods having his or her own songs and rhythms. When "mounted" by their gods, the devotees dance to the accompaniment of songs and music the distinctive steps revelatory of their gods. (Raboteau 1978, 15)

Huet (1978) explains why: "While the possession dances are being performed, the 'horse of the genie' [he whom the spirit or god rides] has possession of the code of conduct of gestures, attitudes, and conduct of the genie, and his acting will ensure that the incarnated spirit is recognized" (16). And González-Wippler (1985) explains further that during such possessions, "the individual displays all the characteristics ascribed to a particular orisha, as well as unusual precognitive abilities, uncanny powers, and superhuman strength, all natural attributes of an archetype formed of pure psychic energies directed into a specific channel" (13). In other words, the "devotees have become mediums of their gods," miming their character in highly stylized and controlled theatrics, through dance, speech, and song (Raboteau 1978, 10–11). They have become living gods (Walker 1972, 166).

Ceremonial possession was brought about by rhythmic stimulation (drumming and chanting), energetic and concentrated dancing, and controlled emotional and mental concentration (Walker 1972, 15, 18). But it was the whole of the ritual experience that made it effective—dance, music, costumes, and, at times, storytelling. Depending on the specific society, ceremonies could be simple or complex, could take place on fixed or unpredictable dates, and could occur either in the community or in the surrounding countryside (Huet 1978, 16). In all African societies, ritual aspired to the dramatic; it sought to become ritual drama in which Dance, Drum, and Song validated and heightened conflicting and contrasting expressions and interpretations and established, built, and sustained accord. Ritual "symbolizes the principles of interdependence and reciprocity" of the human and spiritual realms, making understood the unexplainable (Richards 1980, 8). The African myth system created and nurtured this propensity for possession to the extent that states of trance and altered consciousness were achieved by members of the society as a matter of course. Sometimes the onset of these sacred, blissful, altered states, although brought on principally by drumming, were aided by the ingestion of hallucinogens (Walker 1972, 160; Zahan [1970] 1979, 17).

The formal trappings of ritual included Dance, Drum, and Song in the form of mass dancing (concerted movement performed by large crowds), team dancing (linear, circular, semicircular, or serpentine), or small-group dancing (two, three, or four people). By far the most common, however, were the ring dances (Nketia 1974, 225). The ring—symbol of community, solidarity, affirmation, and catharsis—was common to many African societies. Keil (1979), discussing the ring in Tiv culture, points out that "the circles of men's and women's dances, in which virtually all young people take part, are the best organized and most enjoyable events in Tiv life. The unifying pulse of the drummers at the center and the encircling audience define a middle ground in which individual actions complement each other perfectly" (21). Ring dances were widely and frequently performed in most, if not all, parts of Africa.

So were processions, themselves ritual in nature. According to Nketia (1974),

> A procession may go at a normal walking pace or a hurried one. It may also be a dancing procession, in which special movements form the basis of the forward progression. There is not always a correlation between the pace of the music and the pace of the procession; indeed, each might move independently, except where the idea of marching or dancing to music inspires the performance. The pace of a procession may be set by the spectators who cluster around the performers and move along with them, or by a member of the performing group itself. (233)

Included in these, of course, were funeral processions, where the music, according to Bebey ([1969] 1975), "can be as gay and tumultuous as a marriage feast," since "mourning in African society is both a physical and an emotional act and the sound of the trumpets or drums in no way diminishes for the African [his] sincerity." For the African, "the concept of life and death transcends physical notions of noise or silence" (126).

But dancing in African societies was not limited to religious ritual. Nketia (1963), for example, tells of the "dancing ring" in Akan communities, in which participants express their "reactions to attitudes of hostility or co-operation held by others towards" them, "show deference to a superior [or] gratitude to a benefactor or . . . assume an air of importance in the presence of rivals, servants, and subjects" (163–164). In the dancing ring, participants also mime and interpret the rhythms of drummers for entertainment and mime the dramatic actions of storytellers. Especially attractive rhythms are accompanied by shoulder and head movements, foot stamping and hand clapping, and vocal shouts from spectators, dancers, and singers—all of which "animate the per-

21

formances" (166). Nketia tells also of the expectations of the dancers as they step into the ring (164). Young children imitate the steps and movements of adult dancers, moving "along the fringes of the ring and behind it" (165–166). The activities that took place, and still do, in the Akan dancing ring—as they did also in those of other African societies—have implications for the origin of the "second line" of New Orleans jazz funerals, for the origin and nature of scat singing in early and later jazz, and for the nature of "shouting" in African-American ring ritual and its derivatives. And it all sprang from myth:

> Living myths are not mistaken notions and they do not spring from books. They are not to be judged as true or false but as effective or ineffective, maturative or pathogenic. They are rather like enzymes, products of the body in which they work; or in homogeneous social groups, products of a body social. They are not invented but occur, and they are recognized by seers, and poets, to be then cultivated and employed as catalysts of spiritual (i.e., psychological) well-being. (Campbell [1969] 1990, 6)

The Africans' religious system of God, lesser gods, spirits, and the living-dead was a complex of imaginative beliefs, narrations, and symbols that served fundamentally and meaningfully as the basis for their culture. It was a symbolic field through which the nature of existence was observed and venerated, and it was kept alive through the artistry of ritual. African myth was the authority and support for African law, morality, and community. It explained the origin of the world and ratified, rationalized, and justified African community, social, and political systems. It accomplished these things through symbolic narrative. The law and practice of sacrifice, for example, symbolized relationships between human beings and spirits—the reciprocal interdependence in which human beings took nourishment and sustenance from the spirits and were obliged to return some form of these to them. Sacrifice was symbolic of, a metaphor for, this interdependence: it is why, for example, blood sacrifices are made to trees before they are cut down. These acts and rituals are, as Campbell (1986) puts it,

> productions of the human imagination. Their images, consequently, though derived from the material world and its supposed history, are, like dreams, revelations of the deepest hopes, desires and fears, potentialities and conflicts, of the human will—which in turn is moved by the energies of the organs of the body operating vicariously against each other and in concert. Every myth, that is to say, whether or not by intention, is *psychologically* symbolic. Its narratives and images are to be read, therefore, not literally, but as metaphors. (55)

Myths are also hypotheses—tentative assumptions about the nature of being—that societies attempt to test in the course of life and living. Seen in this way, the African myth system can be taken as a way of coping with the exigencies of life, not as "willful extravagancies" or "naive superstitions," but as reasonable hypotheses, warrantably assertable narratives propounded by human beings who preceded us in time and whose notions of being have been corrected by the experiences of those who came after them (Frazer 1922, 264).

Meanwhile—and in the absence of convincing evidence to the contrary—for Africans, Olumare, Orunla, Elegbara, and Ochosi were metaphors for and symbols of creation, wisdom, caprice, and provision, respectively, among other things. God was a metaphor for and symbol of the generosity, sustenance, abundance, privations, insufficiencies, caprice, and authority of nature; and spirits and the living-dead were metaphors for the temporariness, regeneration, and inevitability of life. The entire myth system is a metaphor for, a symbol of, and, at the same time, a hypothesis about the nature of being itself. But "a mythology is not an ideology. It is not something projected from the brain, but something experienced from the heart, from recognitions of identities behind or within the appearances of nature" (Campbell 1986, 17); its purpose is "to bring us to a level of consciousness that is spiritual" (Campbell 1988, 14). It is the recognition, function, and mystery of the myth that leads us to refer to African life and culture as "spiritual"; African mythology is a symbol of the spirituality of African life, and, conversely, the term "spiritual" is a symbol of African mythology. African life and community were rife with ritual, which was preserved and nurtured through what we in the Western world know as art. In ritual, Africans expressed their worldview and symbolized intercourse between the material and spiritual worlds through Dance, Drum, and Song.

Inevitably, myths are transformed into legends and tales and become bearers of cultural and social wisdom—the stuff of folk narratives. In the fireside, bedside, ritual, and pastime tales of Africans are seen remnants of ancient tales of creation, need, solution, caprice, trickery, and all the other assets and foibles of the gods, of spirits, of God, and of human beings. But the folk tales are a form of instruction and entertainment, not of myth, and they are measured by their success as innocent amusements. They are not necessarily to be either believed or understood. "The Pig's Nose and the Baboon's Rear," for example, explains in an amusing way the respective territorial domiciles of the baboon and the pig, at the humorous expense of both:

> Long ago, the pig and the baboon used to live together on the hillsides. One day, it was very cold and a cutting wind was blowing. As the pig and the baboon sat in the sun trying to get warm, the baboon turned to the pig and said, "This wind is enough to wear the end of one's nose to the blunt point." "Yes," answered the pig, "it's really enough to blow the hairs off one's buttocks and leave a bare, dry patch." "Look here," said the baboon, getting cross, "you are not to make personal remarks!" "I did nothing of the kind," retorted the pig, "but you were rude to me first." This started a quarrel, and they came to the conclusion that neither cared for the other's company. So they parted, and the

baboon went up on to the rocky hill, while the pig went down to the plains, and there they remain to this day. (Abrahams 1983, 193)

African stories come out of a quite distinctive oral tradition, and their allusions are central to their telling and requisite to their full understanding. Unfortunately, the stories that have come down to most of us have come by way of printed anthologies. The material is thus transmitted through the *written* word—and an edited one at that, the purposes of such editing being (1) to make the stories' difficult features easy to understand and (2) to eliminate features that are not readily understandable by individuals from outside the storytellers' culture. But storytelling is a performance art, and much is lost in both the transcription of the oral tale and the subsequent editing of that transcription. And much is lost in the selection process itself, since anthologies contain only those stories that informants choose to share and those that may have been accidentally overheard and recorded (Abrahams 1983, xiv–xv). So the collection, selection, and publication processes have determined much of what Western society has received from the African storytelling tradition. In spite of these shortcomings, however, the stories to which we have access can tell us much about the nature and importance of stories in African society. We know, for example, that African tales come in a variety of guises and have a variety of purposes. There are moral tales, domestic tales, stories of praise, and stories meant to entertain. Among these last are the trickster tales, which are of primary and most direct concern for this study.

In Africa, Trickster is a childish, selfish, scheming, outrageous, and annoying figure who usually takes the form of an animal—most often a spider (the venerable Anansi Kokrofu), a hare (or rabbit), a fox (or jackal), or a monkey— and can change form to fit the occasion. Trickster lives in "nooks" and "crannies" and at crossroads, occasionally entering the affairs of humans to commit mischief. (In the African myth system, Trickster is epitomized by Esu, whom we have already encountered in the African pantheon.) In animal trickster stories, Anansi, Rabbit, Monkey, or some other animal enters a situation in order to upset its normal harmony and create dramatic contrast; his subsequent antics inevitably lead to a rather chaotic situation that is eventually resolved through some form of accommodation. But Trickster can also be found, for example, "on the eve of battle when the warriors have withdrawn from their families and are ritually forbidden to go unto their wives before the clash, slaking his lust to the full in a village of husbandless women" (Goss and Barnes 1989, 104). In the trickster tales, we observe deception, narrow escapes, revenge, much vitality on the Trickster's part, and dramatic oppositions and resolutions. The following tale, "Why Monkeys Live in Trees," will illustrate:

Listen to the story of the bush cat.
The bush cat had been hunting all day, and had got nothing. She was tired. She went to sit down and rest, but the fleas wouldn't give her any peace.

She saw a monkey passing. She called to him, "Monkey, please come and flea me" (for that is what friends do for each other). The monkey agreed, and while he was picking out the fleas, the bush cat fell asleep. Then the monkey took the tail of the bush cat, tied it to a tree, and ran away.

The bush cat awoke. She wanted to get up and leave, but she found her tail tied to the tree. She struggled to get free, but she could not do it, so she remained there panting.

A snail came along. "Please unfasten my tail," cried the bush cat when she saw him. "You will not kill me if I untie you?" asked the snail. "No, I will do nothing to you," answered the bush cat. So the snail untied her.

The bush cat went home. Then she said to her animal friends, "On the fifth day from now, announce that I am dead, and that you are going to bury me." The animals said, "Very well."

On the fifth day, the bush cat lay down flat, pretending to be dead. And all the animals came, and all danced round her. They danced.

The bush cat sprang up all at once. She leaped to catch the monkey. But the monkey had already jumped into a tree. He escaped.

So this is why the monkey lives in the trees, and will not stay on the ground. He is too much afraid of the bush cat. (Abrahams 1983, 158)

And here is a trickster tale about Esu, related by González-Wippler (1985):

Two friends loved each other like brothers and vowed that nothing and no one would ever come between them. Such a statement would naturally be a challenge to Eleggúa, who can disrupt any relationship no matter how close it may be. He therefore decided to put this great friendship to the test. To that effect, he dressed himself in a garment that was red on the right side and black on the left. Thus attired he walked between the two friends.

Seeing Eleggúa pass by, one of the men remarked to the other on the handsome black suit the orisha had been wearing. The second man looked at his friend in disbelief.

"Are you color blind?" he asked in mocking tones. "That man was dressed in red!"

Naturally this happened because one man had seen the side of the suit that was red, while the other had seen the black side. This simple difference of opinion was enough for the two formerly inseparable friends to start an argument which grew to such proportions that they were soon at each other's throats. The quarrel stopped there, but the two friends parted as enemies and never spoke again. (177)

This trickster story is tame, by any African measure, and it is rather short; but it does illustrate to some degree the nature and character of African trickster tales. And its telling does prepare us for the stories and toasts we will encounter later with the African-American trickster figure. But it should be noted here that the trickster tales are told not just for humor, but to instill discipline and ingrain fear, a sense of accomplishment, pride, and humility. In at least one African society, Surinam, versions of the Anansi trickster tale were

25

told during burial ceremonies to amuse the spirit of the deceased, for the dead, who are reported to be susceptible to humor and excitement, like trickster tales.

These stories are intimately related to the nature of African music. In the trickster tales, we find several features that appear in African storytelling and that they "share with the other African performance traditions": indirection, argument, and opposition, as well as "overlap, apart-playing, and interlock" (Abrahams 1983, 20), all of which will concern us later.

Myths generate legends, which have a historical basis that is embellished by imaginative and fictional elements. Focusing on extraordinary occurrences, legends occupy a station somewhere between myth and historical narrative. The heroes of myth often become the subjects of the legends, so it is not surprising to see characteristics of the gods in legendary heroes. Unlike myths, however, which are the stuff of African metaphysics, legends treat everyday living; they are didactic and tutorial. Myths, tales, and legends serve as inspiration and material for both African music and the ceremony and ritual of which that music is a part. With this notion in mind, we return to the ring.

The activities that took place in the ring were strictly regulated; the dances and the music were institutionalized, and the behavior of the participants was policed by dance chiefs, chief and assistant drummers, line leaders, crowd controllers, and other regulators, each of whom played specific and important roles. The choreography, music, tales, and participants, then, were focused toward the primary objective of the ceremony (Huet 1978, 12; Keil 1979, 247). In this controlled environment, Dance, Drum, and Song, together with the reciting of myths and sometimes the donning of masks, resulted in a "complicated network of elements" that reinforced the unity of the community, transcending daily life (Huet, 13). And "the effects of the drums are heightened by the simultaneous rhythmic stimulation of other sensory receptors because the participants are dancing, singing, and moving together in close proximity in a ceremonial atmosphere in which possession manifesting the presence of the gods is expected" (Walker 1972, 147). Regulated Dance, Drum, and Song was central to the order and success of ritual.

My concern here is primarily with Drum and Song, the musical components of ritual. Understanding Drum and Song as a unit is central to the proper study of the transformation of African music into African-American music, with its own elaborations and its own social, cultural, and aesthetic underpinnings. The main barrier to studying African music is similar to what in the past prevented the study of African religion. This is the assumption that since cultural practices differ widely among more than three thousand African ethnic groups, it would be futile to try to describe or characterize something called "African religion," and that to even attempt such study would be naïve. Indeed, such attitudes themselves have come to be considered naïve, as Mbiti's ([1969] 1990) study demonstrates: despite this diversity, there are underlying similarities among all African religions. For music, scholars such as Nketia (1974),

Bebey ([1969] 1975), and others have demonstrated the same. Alan Lomax (1975), for example, has demonstrated that across black Africa there exists an

> extraordinary homogeneity of African song style. . . . When most Africans sing they are non-tense, vocally; quite repetitious, textually; rather slurred in enunciation; lacking in embellishment and free rhythm; low on exclusive leadership; high on antiphony, chorally; especially high on overlapped antiphony; high on one-phrase melodies, on litany form; very cohesive, tonally and rhythmically in chorus; high on choral integration or part-singing; high on relaxed vocalizing; and highest on polyrhythmic (or hot) accompaniments.
>
> This relaxed, cohesive, multileveled, yet leader-oriented style, is distinctly African. It dominates African song from the Cape of Good Hope to the Straits of Gibraltar and west into the American colonies, and is the source and symbol of African cultural homogeneity. (46)

In sum, Lomax found that "the common stylistic thread that unites all Africans is repetitious, cohesive, overlapping or interlocked, multi-leveled, and hot," that "song style functions as a suitable symbol for and reinforcement of social norms," and that "the erotic content of Pygmy song was of service to an expanding economy that needed manpower for its growing lineages" (48, 49). African song in general is erotic because "fertility and sexual prowess are central values in African life"; African dances are "designed to educate boys and girls for their adult sexual roles in a polygynous world" (49). Lomax's survey shows that prominent in African culture is

> the use of bodily polyrhythm, in which the trunk and the pelvis of the dancer and the hands and sticks of the drummers steadily maintain two separate and conflicting meters. This twisting pelvic style (and its reflection in hot rhythm) infuses African work and play with a steady feed of pleasurable erotic stimuli. . . . The non-complex structure of text and tune and the multi-leveled structure of Pygmy-Negro performance style afford added incentives for group participation, opening the door for anyone to make a contrastive and complementary personal contribution to the whole sound. Where the whole society is needed to accomplish heavy, monotonous hand labor in intense heat, we find a communication style maximally inviting, encouraging and eroticizing participation by all present. This style was continued under slavery and now forms the baseline for the entire Afro-American tradition. (50)

Lomax's conclusions are provocative, and their implications will be explored in the chapters that follow. For now, however, let them suffice as descriptions and partial explanations of African musical style, while we take a look at what other scholars have noticed about African music.

Olly Wilson (1992a) has observed in African music what he calls a "heterogeneous sound ideal" that results from "the timbral mosaic created by the interaction between lead voice, chorus, rattle, metallic gong, hand clapping, various wind or string instruments, and drums, which exist in greater or lesser **27** degrees of complexity in almost all African ensemble music" (331). He goes on to say that the heterogeneous sound ideal is reflected in vocal music as well. The "extraordinary unaccompanied singing of the Dorze people of Ethiopia is characterized not only by polyphonic and canonic textures, but also by the usage of a wide range of vocal timbres that help define its stratified musical structure" (332). What Wilson is referring to here is, of course, Africans' overwhelming preference for timbres that contrast rather than blend and their adoration of the resulting "tonal mosaic" as ideal for their culture. Together, drum, rattle, bell, voice, and hand claps not only contrast but commingle—harmonize, in their own way—in a heterogeneous fusion that is unequivocally African. Such exclusive focus on this kind of mosaic was carried into the diaspora and is the sound ideal of the ring; it sonically defines ring music.

Adding Wilson's heterogeneous sound ideal to Lomax's discoveries further documents a concept of African music and expands our understanding of it. But there is more. A number of scholars have commented on the verbal and melodic basis of African rhythm. Bebey ([1969] 1975), for example, tells us that in African music, the "prime motive of the instruments is to reconstitute spoken language" (115). Nketia (1974) says that "although rhythm is the primary focus of drumming, some attention is paid to pitch level, for the aesthetic appeal of drumming lies in the rhythmic and melodic elements." (137–138). And Wilson (1992a) maintains that "the pre-existing repertoire of drum patterns used by master drummers in many African cultures is based on musical patterns derived from selected genres of oral poetry" (330). The rhythm-motives of the drums and the pitches therein, together with the contrasting timbres of the instruments, result in Wilson's "mosaics of tone color and pitch," a realization of the "heterogeneous sound ideal" (331).[3]

All the rhythmic processes to which I have referred are controlled by the time line, which Nketia (1974, 131–138) describes as an externalized pulse, usually manifested in hand clapping or in the rhythms of an idiophone such as a bell. The time line is an integral part of the music itself and is therefore usually more complex than a simple accompanying pulse; it is usually "additive or divisive . . . embodying the basic pulse or regulative beat as well as the density referent." It is against the time line that the other instruments play the multilinear rhythms that yield the exciting interlocking, cross-rhythmic, and polyrhythmic configurations of African music. What Nketia calls the "time line," Jones (1959) terms "background rhythm," pointing out that it is most

3. The effectiveness of pitch changes in African drumming is especially evident in the dance drumming recorded by John Miller Chernoff on *Master Drummers of Dagbon* (1984), particularly on "Lua," "Kurugu Kpoa," and "Zuu-Waa." The last cut is also a good example of polyrhythmic and cross-rhythmic drumming. The recording *Songs and Instrumental Music of Tanganyika* in Decca's Music of Africa series is also a good source of examples.

frequently played by a clapperless bell called the *gankogui:* "the foundation *par excellence* of the background rhythm section—which usually plays steadily and continuously right through a dance" (1:52–53). Jones gives the following example of a background rhythm (or time line):

Gankogui

Clap

Resultant

GO-dzi GO-GO dzi GO - dzi   GO - dzi.

Jones (1959, 1:54) points out that the practice of having an idiophone lay the foundation rhythm of a musical performance is common in West Africa and goes on to describe how the other foundation instruments relate to the rhythm of the time line. His transcription of an Adzida Dance (2:112–133) is illustrative, particularly in its first section (Club Dance) where the instruments enter one after the other (Example 1). In this case, the *high atoke* (gong) sets the time line, but in subsequent sections, the *gankogui* takes it (for the complete transcription, see 2:112–167). The multilinear rhythms in such performances, played in a heterogeneous instrumental environment of "sonority contrasts," result in what Nketia (1974) calls "little tunes" (137–138). I shall return to these concepts again as we traverse the transformation of African music into African-American music and its development.

I have made much of the ritual context of African music, but ritual was not the traditional African's only avenue for self-expression and communal expression through music. Play, sport, work, relaxation, the everyday events and vicissitudes of life, and other periodic interactions of living were accompanied by and expressed in musical forms ranging from the simple to the complex. Songs of satire, love, praise, play, mockery, insult, celebration, morality, patriotism, war, nonritual dance, and exorcism were all part of the African musical experience and were performed vocally and instrumentally, the last on a large variety of idiophones, aerophones, membranophones, and chordophones. In these media, traditional African music made use, variously, of a musical vocabulary that included melodic monophony, heterophony, and polyphony; parallel thirds; "tongue clicks, suction stops, explosive endings, throaty gurgles"; overlapping call-and-response events; and "hand-clapping

29

EXAMPLE 1. Adzida Dance, excerpt.

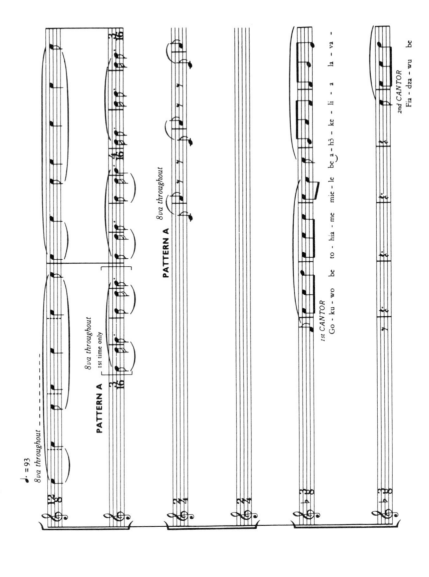

with off-beat syncopation" (Kebede 1982, 45, 50, 131).[4] Styles ranged from the simple monophony of Watusi warriors to the complex melodic polyphony of the Pygmies of Central Africa. African song is related to African calls, in which "peasants melodically call to each other to announce an emergency or news considered important to villagers, to fix a time to go to market, to organize a work gang to farm the land of a sick neighbor, and just to convey greetings to a friend. Calls travel long distances, echoing over mountains and hills" (130).

Scholars seem to agree that the aim of African music has always been to translate the experiences of life and of the spiritual world into sound, enhancing and celebrating life through cradle songs, songs of reflection, historical songs, fertility songs, songs about death and mourning, and other song varieties. Singers of songs, accompanied and unaccompanied, made use of "a mellow tone to welcome a new bride; a husky voice to recount an indiscrete adventure; a satirical inflection for a teasing tone, with laughter bubbling up to compensate for the mockery—they may be soft or harsh as circumstances demand" (Bebey [1969] 1975, 120). Such expression and communication was facilitated by the fact that African music emerges from

> the intonations and rhythmic onomatopoeia of speech. . . . African voices are used to echo the speech and thoughts of the people as faithfully as possible without embellishment. Their technique is a quest for truth. An African singer will stutter if he is singing about a stammerer or will literally attempt to tie his tongue in knots when he has something difficult to say. He cups his hand over his ears to discover unusual sonorities and reproduces them with a dexterity that amazes and delights his listeners. The African singer alternates head and chest voice like a game of hide-and-seek in a labyrinth of rhythm. Every note that he sings is a reflection of life itself and his technique is amply suited to his role of depicting life. His voice recreates a world of laughter and pain, mockery and praise; and it throws open the gates of time to reveal a glimpse of the future. (129, 132)

Nketia (1974) agrees with Bebey, pointing out that Africans "treat songs as speech utterances," inspired, perhaps, by "the importance of the song as an avenue of verbal communication, a medium for creative verbal expression which can reflect both personal and social experiences," by the influence of the verbal texts themselves, and by the prospect of enhancing musical expression through prosodic analogies (177, 178). This accounts, to some degree, for an African performance style characterized by "rapid delivery of texts, explosive sounds or special interjections, vocal grunts, and even the whisper"

---

4. As Komla Amoaku counsels, "You cannot separate any of these from that all-encompassing world view that does not separate the sacred from the profane, no matter how simple or complex the music" (personal correspondence). For more on Amoaku's African views and scholarship, see Amoaku (1975).

in their musical performances (189). It also accounts for the African's expectation that a musician would make up texts extemporaneously and then set texts to tunes and tunes to words. And this expectation and practice also characterized instrumental music, in which mnemonics were used for teaching and memorizing rhythms and nonsense syllables were employed as "verbal scores" (188). Nketia even speculates that multimeters and additive rhythms were "derived from the treatment of speech rhythms in vocal music" (188). He also calls attention to the use of "speech surrogates": "clan name or praise poems may be played on drums, or the lead trumpeter of a trumpet ensemble may call the names of members of the ensemble in his introductory solos" (235). And through all of this, the traditional African musician was concerned strictly with the artistic merit of his performance, not with the technique he used to render it. He paid little attention to technique, since it was "very much a matter of individual taste" (Bebey [1969] 1975, 132).

The musical artistry of Africans supported their ritual in a profoundly mystical universe, a universe in which African peoples sought union with the invisible—God, lesser gods, spirits, and the living-dead—a universe in which "the use of euphemism, symbol, allegory, and secret" were a normal part of the oral expression of society (Zahan [1970] 1979, 114, 154). Understanding this universe is important if one wishes to understand African music either for its own sake or as the antecedent of African-American music. Elements of African myth and legend reside in, are supported by, and parallel those of African Dance, Drum, and Song. These elements and relationships will serve as points of departure and reference, guides to inquiry and analysis, and foundations for the development of a new critical theory of African-American music, as we traverse the transformation and development of the transplanted African musical tradition.

In concluding this chapter, I would like to address briefly the communal context in which Dance, Drum, and Song took place in traditional Africa. Dance, Drum, and Song was inseparable from the traditional communities in which it existed—communities in which social and cultural conformity and egalitarianism prevailed, in which extraordinary individual achievement and the failure to live up to one's social obligations were interpreted as hostility toward the community (Davidson 1969, 66). Simultaneously, however, the artistic boundaries of the community, even within its highly controlled ritualistic system, were stretched by the creativity of individual members of the community, particularly by the master drummers and by the venerable griots, who were virtuosi on a variety of musical instruments. The coexistence of these apparently contradictory processes—discouragement of exceptional achievement, on the one hand, and the veneration of it, on the other—was possible

33

because of the prevalence of what Davidson has described as a sense of "controlled freedom" in which "an inner tension and creativeness . . . emerged in artistic triumphs that were morally inspired" (66–67, 68). This controlled freedom took place within a moral order in which daily interdependence was the normal state of affairs. It was, in Davidson's words, a "robustly collective" society. Based on collective responsibility, it was a society in which exceptional individual achievement was expected to serve the community. This was its moral imperative. The moral order was maintained through the telling of tales and myths and through ritual; it was enforced by chiefs, elders, secret societies, and the general community.

Clearly, traditional African communities, insofar as they conformed to the general description outlined here, were more concerned with the community than the individual and had rules whose primary purpose was the protection of the society. Musical innovation did take place in these nonindividualistic communities, and these innovations were easily assimilated into the prevailing system. The reason for this easy absorption was that innovations were not subversive; they were made on the verges of existing performance practices. It is in this context that a critical system evolved, as evidenced by the fact that

> dancers were celebrated not because they knew the steps—practically everyone knew the steps—but because they danced them supremely well. Drummers were admired for the rhythms they could hear and play, rhythms so complex that an unskilled listener like myself cannot even recognize them. . . . There was an exacting scale of achievement; and the criteria were aesthetic. (Davidson 1969, 163)

And it was against such a scale that individual competition took place, with rhyming games and other competitions prevalent in communal African societies.

In traditional African society we thus find a complex, flexible, and dynamic religious and aesthetic system based on intricate moral and artistic beliefs and practices, all governed by societal structures and procedures. The religious system included ideas that we recognize as both monotheistic and polytheistic, with the former subsuming the latter. It was a system that, instead of opposing good and evil, recognized a single power capable of both. It was this system, with its moral and aesthetic supports, that would most fundamentally determine the emergence and course of African-American music.

CHAPTER **2**

Transformations

You cannot escape God. You will meet him in foreign lands.
Namibian proverb

The music, yearning like a God in pain . . .
John Keats

In the late nineteenth century, George Washington
Cable watched an exhibition that took place in New
Orleans's Place Congo, later to be known as Congo
Square.[1] African slaves were engaged in their usual
Sunday recreation, performing transplanted African
dances with musical accompaniments. Cable's
([1886] 1969b) striking and informative narrative is
so engaging that I will quote from it at length:

> The gathering throng closed in around, leaving
> unoccupied the circle indicated by the crescent of
> musicians. The short, harsh turf was the dancing-
> floor. The crowd stood. . . . The pack of dark, tat-
> tered figures [was] touched off every here and
> there with . . . bright colors. . . . [There stood] the
> squatting cross-legged musicians . . . grassy plain

1. Since writing the introduction to this chapter, I have come
across information demonstrating that Cable's description was
constructed from others' first-hand knowledge of such events
(Starr 1995, 41; Turner 1956, 227–233). But I have chosen to
leave my statements as I have written them, since Cable's description, although imaginative, conforms to the essentials of actual reported accounts of such activities.

stretching around and behind, dotted with black stumps; in the distance the pale-green willow under-growth, behind it the *cyprière*—the cypress swamp. . . .

The occasion began . . . with very slow and measured [movements]; they had such [tunes] that were strange and typical. I have heard the negroes sing one . . . that shows the emphatic barbarism of five bars to the line, and was confined to four notes of the open horn.

But I can only say that with some such slow and quiet strain the dance may have been precluded. It suits the Ethiopian fancy for a beginning to be dull and repetitious. . . .

The singers almost at the first note are many. At the end of the first line every voice is lifted up. The strain is given the second time with growing spirit. Yonder glistening black Hercules, who plants one foot forward, lifts his head and bare, shining chest, and rolls out the song from a mouth and throat like a cavern, is a *candio,* a chief, or was before he was overthrown in battle and dragged away, his village burning behind him, from the mountains of High Soudan. . . . He is of the Bambaras, as you may know by his solemn visage and the long tattoo streaks running down from the temples to the neck, broadest in the middle, like knife-gashes. See his play of restrained enthusiasm catch from one bystander to another. They swing and bow to right and left, in slow time to the piercing treble of the Congo women. Some are responsive; others are competitive. . . . A smiting of breasts with open hands begins very softly and becomes vigorous. The women's voices rise to a tremulous intensity. Among the chorus of Franc-Congo singing-girls is one of extra good voice, who thrusts in, now and again, an improvisation. This girl here, so tall and straight, is a Yaloff. You see it in her almost Hindoo features, and hear it in the plaintive melody of her voice. Now the chorus is more piercing than ever. The women clap their hands in time. . . .

See! Yonder brisk and sinewy fellow has taken one short, nervy step into the ring, chanting with rising energy. Now he takes another, and stands and sings and looks here and there, rising upon his broad toes and singing and rising again, with what wonderful lightness! How tall and lithe he is. He, too, is a *candio,* and by the three long rays of tattooing on each side of his face, a Kiamba. The music has got into his feet. He moves off to the farther edge of the circle, still singing, takes the prompt hand of an unsmiling Congo girl, leads her into the ring, and leaving the chant to the throng, stands her before him for the dance.

Will they dance to that measure? Wait! A sudden frenzy seizes the musicians. The measure quickens, the swaying, attitudinizing crowd starts into extra activity, the female voices grow sharp and staccato, and suddenly the dance is the furious bamboola.

Now for the frantic leaps! Now for frenzy! Another pair are in the ring! The man wears a belt of little bells, or, as a substitute, little tin vials of shot. . . . And still another couple enter the circle. What wild—what terrible delight! The ecstasy rises to madness; one—two—three of the dancers fall— *bloucoutoum! boum!*—with foam on their lips and are dragged out by arms and legs from under the tumultuous feet of crowding new-comers. The musicians know no fatigue; still the dance rages on. (37–38)

In Cable's description, we notice the ever-present circle—the ring—of African provenance, transplanted to American soil and now playing a central role in the entertainment of Africans on a day of respite. We notice in this activity the initially slow tempo of the music—in this case, repetitious singing, which gradually increases in tempo and "spirit." Call-and-response figures and polyphony are implied in the statement that "some are responsive; others are competitive," with hand clapping and the "smiting of breasts" serving as substitutes for drum playing—forms, surely, of patting juba—all rising in "piercing" and "staccato" intensity to finally reach a sudden climax. These musical developments accompany the dancers—couples entering and leaving the ring—proud, tall, and straight African Americans now, but still with a strong cultural memory of the motherland and its rituals, of the Sudan, the Congo; proud, transplanted Africans—Yaloff, Bambara, and others—in delightful ecstasy brought on by singing and dancing the bamboula. Absent, however, in addition to the drums in this particular description, is an account of the presence of the gods through possession.

In 1867, the compilers of *Slave Songs of the United States* reported seeing shouts performed indoors, following church services:

> The benches are pushed back to the wall when the formal meeting is over, and old and young, men and women, sprucely-dressed young men, grotesquely half-clad field-hands—the women generally with gay handkerchiefs twisted about their heads and with short skirts—boys with tattered shirts and men's trousers, young girls barefooted, all stand up in the middle of the floor, and when the "sperichil" is struck up, begin first walking and by-and-by shuffling round, one after the other, in a ring. The foot is hardly taken from the floor, and the progression is mainly due to a jerking, hitching motion, which agitates the entire shouter, and soon brings out streams of perspiration. Sometimes they dance silently, sometimes as they shuffle they sing the chorus of the spiritual, and sometimes the song itself is also sung by the dancers. But more frequently a band, composed of some of the best singers and of tired shouters, stand at the side of the room to "base" the others, singing the body of the song and clapping their hands together or on the knees. Song and dance are alike extremely energetic, and often, when the shout lasts into the middle of the night, the monotonous thud, thud, of the feet prevents sleep within half a mile of the praise-house. (Allen, Ware, and Garrison 1867, xiii–xiv)

Here, again, we see the shuffling around in a ring, the upper-body dancing of African provenance, the ever-present singing accompanied by the hand clapping and thudding, repetitious drumming (of feet in this case), and the extended length of the activity. And here enters also the spiritual, the primary music of the ring for slaves in the southern United States. And even in the North, as a report from eighteenth-century Philadelphia attests, "more than one thousand of both sexes, divided into numerous little squads," could be seen dancing and singing, "each in their own tongue," after the customs of **37** their several nations in Africa (Watson 1881, 265). All over nineteenth-century North America, bands of singing and praying African Americans would meet after regular church services to pray, sing, and dance the shout.

These African rituals and their supporting myths were brought to the Americas during the years of legal slave trade (1619–1808) by way of the Middle Passage. Imported by slavers from France, England, and Portugal, Africans from Cameroon, the Ivory Coast, Guinea, Cape Verde, and Senegal were transported directly to New Orleans, while those from Angola, the Congo, Nigeria, and Ghana went to Brazil. Cuba and Martinique received natives of the Ivory Coast, Nigeria, and Ghana. But wherever African slaves were sent, they took Dance, Drum, and Song with them. Soon, however, the ritual would be denied them. Viewed as heathen ceremony, the ring was prohibited.[2] But the ring did not disappear altogether, as the descriptions of Cable ([1886] 1969b) and of Allen, Ware, and Garrison (1867) attest.

Through the ring ritual, the African performance practices discussed in chapter 1 were retained in the New World and influenced the development of music making in which African music was eventually syncretized with European practices to form a new music. Since most of the slaves brought to America were from western Africa, it was the music of this large region that came with them. From Cameroon, Dahomey, Gabon, Gambia, Guinea, Nigeria, Senegal, Sierra Leone, and the western Congo came Ashanti, Baoule, Fanti, Fon, Hausa, Jolof, Mandingo, Yoruba, and other tribespeople (Southern 1983, 3–6), bringing with them the African calls, variegated songs, and dance music that would sow, in a new land, the seeds that would blossom into an ever-unfolding extension and elaboration of their progenitors' culture. They brought with them and altered to their new circumstance the apart-playing, polyrhythms, cross-rhythms, time line, elisions, hockets, ululations, tremolos, vocables, grunts, hums, shouts, and melismatic phrasings of their homeland. They brought with them knowledge of and emotional attachment to Dance, Drum, and Song, to be performed within and without in the ring.

The ceremonies and music of the ring were looked on by most whites in the New World as "idolatrous dancing and revels" (Godwyn 1680, 33), and they were mightily criticized and suppressed in nearly all parts of the United States (New Orleans was perhaps the major exception). As time went on, even black Christians began to view shouting as savage, lascivious, and lewd. But for the new black Americans, slave and free, these "debased" dances, as they were referred to by some, were proper, culturally affirming, and justified by the African metaphysic and the necessity, as we have seen in chapter 1, for prolific propagation; that is, these dances were justified by ring ritual (featur-

2. In 1740, for example, South Carolina prohibited the playing of loud instruments such as drums and horns. In 1800, the state prohibited slaves from meeting for religious or educational purposes, thus ruling out the ring (O'Neall [1848] 1970, 26, 24).

ing the gods, spirits, and living-dead, and allowing for the rebirth of ancestors in new babies) and by the strong African values of fertility and sexual
prowess that fuel the erotic impulse. These dances, in their ritual context, enforced and reaffirmed community, discipline, identity, and African cultural
memory—an identity and a memory that the slave owners sought to eradicate
in order to make better slaves.

In this striving to maintain unity and to affirm identity in a new land, the
Christian God was substituted for the African High God—an easy transition,
since the concept of a supreme god was not new to the transplanted Africans.
This new God became central to ring ritual, with Christ substituting for all
the divinities. In ring ritual, Christ, not the *orisha,* rode the participants, and
for those slaves introduced to Roman Catholicism, "Catholic notions about
the role of Christ, Mary, guardian angels, and patron saints as intercessors with
the Father in heaven for men on earth proved quite compatible with African
ideas about the intervention of lesser gods in the day-to-day affairs of human
life, while the supreme god remained benevolent and providential but distant"
(Raboteau 1978, 23). This African–Catholic syncretism made the transition
for Africans to Western culture easier in Latin America and in some parts of
the United States, particularly New Orleans, and served as support for the continuation of African traditions in the New World. But it was Protestantism that
fueled the religion and religious fervor of enslaved and free blacks in the United
States. Protestantism, with its more direct access to the High God through
song and praise, made possible the emergence of a new song for Africans, a
new song in which they could express themselves as freely as they had in their
homeland. This new song was the African-American spiritual.

In the early days of the Africans' transformation into African Americans, the
spiritual was the most widespread, or at least the most widely known, of all
African-American musical genres. It was created by American slaves as they
participated in the process that Christianized them and as they performed their
ring rituals, striving to retain their African cultural memory. For this reason,
Stuckey (1987) tells us,

> too often the spirituals are studied apart from their natural, ceremonial con-
> text. The tendency has been to treat them as a musical form unrelated to dance
> and certainly unrelated to particular configurations of dance and dance rhythm.
> Abstracted from slave ritual performance, including burial ceremonies, they
> appear to be under Christian influence to a disproportionate extent. Though
> the impact of Christianity on them is obvious and considerable, the spirituals
> take on an altogether new coloration when one looks at slave religion on the
> plantations where most slaves were found and where African religion, contrary
> to the accepted scholarly wisdom, was practiced. (27)

39

I am not sure that the singing of spirituals in the African ceremonial context was any more "natural" than singing them in their Christian setting. But Stuckey is correct, for his purpose, in stressing the African orientation of the songs and their use in African-derived ritual. And this perspective is critical to my purpose in this book. In the circumstance of slavery, the spiritual was the transplanted Africans' primary means of expressing their current struggles and fulfillments while maintaining contact with the traditions and meanings of the past. While they contained the African characteristics of call-and-response and textual improvisation, these songs derived directly from the black experience in America. As in African song, myth, and tale, figures of speech were prominent and important, for in their use of simile, metaphor, and personification, the spirituals were also imbued with a surreptitiously rebellious spirit that reflected the militant refusal of large numbers of slaves to cooperate with the practice of slavery (Harding 1981, 199). The slaves used these techniques with ingenuity and with the drama that is central to African music and ritual, reflecting their sophisticated understanding of the struggles and the fulfillments of slave life.

The focus of the songs was on slavery and on the possibility of freedom for slaves in America. Freedom, in fact, according to Lovell (1972, 90), was the principal idea of the spirituals. Traditionally, the spirituals have been viewed as songs of conventional religious faith, but they are much more than that. In spite of their biblical references, the essence of these songs goes far beyond narrow and conventional religious boundaries. The spirituals are also folk songs of freedom and of faith in the inevitability of freedom (37). They are quasi-religious songs of longing and aspiration as well as chronicles of the black slave experience in America—documents of impeccable truth and reliability (8)—for they record the transition of the slave from African to African American, from slave to freedman, and the experiences that the African underwent in the transition:

> Oh, nobody knows the trouble I've seen,
> Nobody knows but Jesus.
> Nobody knows the trouble I've seen,
> Glory, Hallelujah!

The influence of the African heritage is evident here, for this African-American spiritual is remarkably similar, in tone and text, to the funeral chant of the Basotho we encountered in chapter 1:

> We stayed outside,
> We stayed for the sorrow,
> We stayed for the tears.

Oh, if there were a place in heaven for me!
That I would have wings to fly there!
If a strong cord came down from the sky,
I would tie myself to it,
I would climb up above,
I would go live there.

(quoted in Zahan [1970] 1979, 48–49)

Through the spirituals, slaves made the Christian religion their own; through the spirituals, they affirmed their traditional worldview (modified by the realities of slavery and the myths and rituals of Christian religion). Descriptions of the creative process by which the spirituals were made have been recounted by Levine (1977). He presents, among other accounts, a description of an incident that took place in 1926 in a prayer meeting on a South Carolina plantation, when a man got up and

suddenly cried out: "Git right-sodjer! Git right-sodjer! Git right-wit Gawd!" Instantly the crowd took it up, moulding a melody out of half-formed familiar phrases based upon a spiritual tune, hummed here and there among the crowd. A distinct melodic outline became more and more prominent, shaping itself around the central theme of the words, "Git right, sodjer!" Scraps of other words and tunes were flung into the medley of sound by individual singing from time to time, but the general trend was carried by a deep undercurrent, which appeared to be stronger than the mind of any individual present, for it bore the mass of improvised harmony and rhythms into the most effective climax of incremental repetition that I have ever heard. I felt as if some conscious plan or purpose were carrying us along, call it mob-mind, communal composition, or what you will. (27)

Such communal, improvisatory experiences sometimes resulted in a variety of voice parts—renditions ranging from as many as eight parts (Lovell 1972, 109) down to solo renditions accompanied by humming, foot patting, and bodily movement.

Spirituals are of two text types: sorrow songs and jubilees (some of the latter were used as "shout" spirituals). Sorrow songs speak of the past and present trials and tribulations suffered by the slaves and their Savior. Of these sorrow songs, W. E. B. Du Bois ([1902] 1967) wrote,

Through all the sorrow of the sorrow songs there breathes a hope—a faith in the ultimate justice of things. The minor cadences of despair change often to triumph and calm confidence. Sometimes it is faith in life, sometimes a faith in death, sometimes assurance of boundless justice in some fair world beyond. But whichever it is, the meaning is always clear: that sometime, somewhere, men will judge men by their souls and not by their skins. (261)

41

Examples of this type of spiritual are "Nobody Knows de Trouble I See," "What a Tryin' Time," "I'm Troubled in Mind," "I Couldn't Hear Nobody Pray," "Go Down Moses," "Were You There," and "Sometimes I Feel Like a Motherless Child."

Jubilees express the joyful expectation of a better life in the future. Songs such as "Goin to Shout All Over God's Heaven," "Little David Play on Your Harp," "King Jesus Is a-Listenin'," "In That Great Gittin' Up Morning'," and "When de Saints Go Marchin' In" express jubilation for present and future blessings. Two of the most stirring shout spirituals are "I Can't Stay Behind, My Lord" and "Turn, Sinner, Turn O!"

The kinship of these early spirituals to African performance practice is striking. The song "Steal Away," for example, has short phrases that repeat, grow, and make larger melodic structures and uses multimeter, pendular thirds, and descending phrase endings. It also makes use of the "implication, euphemism, symbol, allegory, and secret [that] is a part of the everyday technique of oral expression" in Africa (Zahan [1970] 1979, 114). Furthermore, any performance of "Steal Away" will conform to many of Lomax's (1975, 46) characteristics of the African song style that I quoted in chapter 1: it will be vocally non-tense, textually quite repetitious, lacking in melodic embellishment, non-complex, relaxed, cohesive, multileveled, and leader-oriented—"distinctly African," according to Lomax. In this spiritual, as in most others, we see the African retentions that effect the continuity that is characteristic of the elaboration of black music in America.

The spiritual was central to ring ritual. It was the "song" in Dance, Drum, and Song. It was sung, danced to, and accompanied by drumming, constituting the "ring shout," as it was known in the Africans' new homeland. Known also as "shout," "glory shout," "holy dance," and "walk in Egypt," this phenomenon was based on the West African practices discussed in chapter 1. It consisted of

> a circle of people moving single file (usually counter-clockwise) around a central point, to the accompaniment of singing, stamping, and heel clicking. In some instances, the participants tap (in effect, drum) on the floor rhythmically with sticks to produce percussion effects. The steps are akin to a shuffle, with free foot movement prohibited, and little versatility permitted. Sometimes, the clearly defined single file gives way to a sort of amorphous crowd moving around a central point. The tempo may build up gradually, singing interspersed with exclamations characteristic of some other Negro church services, until it reaches a tense peak close to an ecstatic breaking point. At the high point of the excitement, such exclamations as "Oh, Lord!" and "Yes, Lord!" turn into nonsense sounds and cries; seemingly wild emotional responses, they never-

theless are related to the music as a whole, and no notation which omits them can give a fair picture of what is heard. (Courlander 1963, 194–195)

It was in the ring and through the ring that the spiritual had its most dramatic use, with the ring's diverse manifestations depending on local customs and occasions. For example, in southwestern Louisiana among the Creoles of color, whom some whites call "black Cajuns," there exist performances called juré (joo-ray)—"testifying shouts"—based on African and Catholic beliefs and practices and performed by men during Lent. In a performance included in *Zydeco: Creole Music and Culture in Louisiana* (1984), a film by Nicholas Spitzer, four men, seated, perform a juré they call "Rockaway." It is almost purely African, with continuous stamping and clapping accompanying a short, repeated melody. Most of the action is in the feet, with hand claps keeping the beat. Pendular thirds abound, repeated over and over to the energetic and engaging patting and stamping. Spectators—family and neighbors of the four performers—"dance" with their upper bodies and torsos, African style.

A more common type of shout can be seen in the film *Georgia Sea Island Singers* (1963), featuring Bessie Jones. Here, a spiritual called "Bright Star Shining in Glory" is used in a ring, accompanied by the slow counterclockwise circling common to nearly all shouts (in some shouts, the circling direction is reversed). The buildup begins almost immediately, with a call-and-response pattern, a repeated four-beat melody, multimeter and cross-rhythms created by hand clapping and foot stamping (remarkably like those of the juré), and a tambourine filling all the musical space; the tempo goes faster and faster, and the end of the dance is collectively improvised in a grand, dancing out-chorus. The MacIntosh Shouters of MacIntosh County, Georgia, appear throughout the video *Roots of Resistance* (1990) in vignette performances that are remarkably similar to the juré of the Louisiana Creoles. The men are seated—one using a stamping pole—and the women are standing, all stamping their feet and clapping their hands in accompaniment to short melodic fragments in call-and-response. These performances are very recent but are clearly quite traditional, giving modern audiences a view into the African-American past.[3]

Whatever its manifestation and whatever it was called, the shout's essentials were always present in early black religious ceremony. In fact, as Stuckey (1987) assures us, the religious practices of burial ceremonies "reflected a base so broad that slaves from almost any section of West Africa could rest their religious beliefs on it, however different those beliefs in other respects" (109). For Africans, song and dance were religious affirmation; they were urgently compelled to perform music and dance as a means of keeping in contact with

---

3. For other footage of the ring shout, see *To Live as Free Men* (1940) and "Georgia Shouters" (1928–1929).

their ancestors in order to "retain their power of self-definition or [they would] perish" (Small 1987, 123). For African Americans, the spiritual was the musical vehicle within the ring for this affirmation and unity, for these songs were "masterful repositories of an African cultural spirit" (Baker 1987, 60) and, through the shout and its developments, they proved central to the maintenance and perpetuation of African cultural values.

Black churches in the North helped keep the spiritual alive in free communities. Excluded from or treated poorly in white churches, African Americans in the North founded their own congregations and maintained the spirit of the ring. In fact, the Africanisms were so strong in the praying and singing bands and in the holy dances that the African Methodist Episcopal (A.M.E.) Church sought to curb and ban them (Southern 1983, 130–131). Surely spirituals were used in these activities, certainly in the "holy dances." The evidence for this is so strong that Southern has reasoned that Negro spirituals originated not only among blacks on the southern plantations, but also among blacks in the North. She points out that these quasi-religious songs "traveled from congregation to congregation, carried by black preachers and deacons, by black watermen who worked on the boats that plied the Mississippi, the Ohio, and the Missouri rivers, and by the slaves when they were sold from one state to another" (26).

The spirituals to which the ring shout was danced employed both long-phrase and short-phrase melodies, used texts in dialect, made use of call-and-response figures, had pentatonic and modally ambiguous melodies, used typical African-derived rhythmic conventions, used conventional harmonies of primary chords, made judicious use of blue-notes, and prudently employed elision. Aside from the rhythmic excitement of the shout, call-and-response devices were the most noticeable and most frequently mentioned. Central to the very structure of the spiritual, such antiphony appears in two forms: call-and-response and call-and-refrain. In the former, "a soloist or a small group of leaders takes a lead and the whole body of the group or the chorus responds." In the latter, "group response is a standard unchanging refrain after each variable solo 'call' " (Ekwueme 1974, 136). I will refer to them both, as well as to the solo–solo version not mentioned by Ekwueme, generically as call-and-response. An anonymous nineteenth-century observer wrote down the text of a call-and-response spiritual as he heard it coming from the interior of a slave cabin.

> LEADER Old Satan is liar and conjurer too—
> REST   Oh, my Lord!
> LEADER If you don't mind, he'll conjure you—
> REST   Oh, my Lord!

ALL   Oh, my Lord is a lily in the valley,

            A lily in the valley;

            Oh, my Lord!

LEADER Old Satan wears one iron shoe—

REST   Oh, my Lord!

LEADER If you don't mind he'll slip it on you—

REST   Oh, my Lord!

ALL   Oh, my Lord is a lily in the valley,

            A lily in the valley;

            Oh, my Lord!

(quoted in B. 1880, 750)

Another nineteenth-century observer gave an account of the presence of call-and-response *figures* in the ring: "The fascination of the music and the swaying motion of the dance is so great that one can hardly refrain from joining the magic circle in response to the invitation of the enthusiastic clappers, 'Now brudder!' 'Shout, sister!' 'Come, belieber!' 'Mauma Rosa kin shout!' 'Uncle Daniel!' 'Join, shouters!' " (Christensen 1894, 155). And another saw and heard an Amen Corner in action: "The performance was frequently diversified and enlivened by several old ladies in the corner calling out: 'Amen!' 'Yes it is.' 'Bless the Lord!' 'Just so, brodder!' 'Dat's de Lord's troof!' Or making other affirmatory and confirmatory noises, gestures, or ejaculations" (Holcombe 1861, 620). These confirmatory noises, gestures, or ejaculations are, of course, a legacy of the ring, for it was there they were first manifest and there, when the ring moved inside church buildings, they were made part of black Christian worship.[4]

When the shout moved indoors, it underwent significant change. The dancing, singing, drumming, and verbal shouting were altered to fit the new circumstance—altered by the constraints of size, acoustics, confinement, and shape of the indoor dancing ground. However, many of the African practices of the ring were retained to some degree in nearly all African-American churches.

The music the slaves played and sang outside the ring included spirituals and secular song, the distinction between sacred and secular becoming more and

---

4. The importance and validity of the shout as foundation for subsequent African-American musical development is evident in the fact that since the term's probable emergence from Gullah dialect, it has been applied both to performance practices used in spirituals, hymns, blues, and jazz and to *styles of performing* in these genres (Gold 1964, 276–277; Wentworth and Flexner 1975, 473). In these genres, shout elements became tropes in the discourse of African-American–music making.

45

more a part of the growing Christianization of the African-American psyche. The songs of black boatmen and the music and songs of black social dance and amusement were all ascendant during the period of slavery. The calls, cries, and hollers of field workers and rivermen had been widespread, central, influential, and indispensable in slave culture from the beginning. All this music, in substance or in form, directly or indirectly, derived from African ritual and performance practice. This is confirmed by Lomax (1975), who has demonstrated that except in small ways, "Afro-American [song] style is virtually identical with that of the homeland" (55).

Since sound recordings of African-American calls, cries, and hollers did not appear until well into the twentieth century, we cannot with any reliability say exactly how the early ones sounded. But we can assume that they were quite similar to their African prototypes and extrapolate from early descriptions of those sounds and from the calls, cries, and hollers of contemporary traditional Africans. As I pointed out in chapter 1, Africans used calls to make announcements, arrange appointments, organize meetings and work details, and convey greetings. African-American calls and cries were used similarly, and these short, rhythmically free phrases employed all the characteristic inflections and decorative colorings of their African counterparts. There were night cries, field cries, hunting cries, and street cries, the character of each matching its function. According to Willis Lawrence James (1955), these cries can be classified as plain, florid, or coloratura. The florid cries were simply plain with decorations; the coloratura were elaborate displays "which were among the most amazing and remarkable vocal feats in folk music" (23). There were "cornfield hollers, 'whoops,' [and] water calls" (Southern 1983, 156), all sung in the typical falsetto, "hoarse, rough, or foggy" voice that is cultivated and highly valued in black culture (Courlander 1963, 24).[5] Sometimes these fragments and phrases were verbally articulate and communicative; at other times, they were wordless. But *meaning* was always present and was always communicated. According to Wilson (1992a), and I agree with him, it is in this tradition that the vocal realization of the heterogeneous sound ideal is most vividly portrayed, for the "textless single-line vocal interjections illustrate with expressive brilliance the significance of timbral nuance in black music" (334). The shifting among melodic events, hums, moans, yells, and elisions in a vocal performance results in a vocal line characterized by multiple, contrasting tone colors, rather than one that features a single, basic timbre.

Hollers were portions of yodelized song,[6] derived from Pygmy singing by way of Kongo peoples, which the slaves used to communicate across fields,

---

5. Calls, cries, and hollers can be heard on James's album *Afro-American Music: A Demonstration Recording* ([1970] 1978) and on *Roots of the Blues* (1977).

6. "Yodelized song" is Thompson's (1989, 138) terminology for a "chest/head, high/low snap across an octave."

valleys, and hollows. Calls and cries were used for closer and more personal communication. Kebede (1982) discusses the relationship between African-American calls and cries:

> Unlike calls, which are primarily used to communicate messages, *cries* express a deeply felt emotional experience, such as hunger, loneliness, or lovesickness. They are half-sung and half-yelled. Vocables are often intermixed in the text. The melodies are performed in a free and spontaneous style; they are often ornamented and employ many African vocal devices, such as yodels, echolike falsetto, tonal glides, embellished melismas, and microtonal inflections that are often impossible to indicate in European staff notation. (130)

Kebede fails to mention some other important devices found in calls and cries, but Wilson (1992a, 334) has observed ametrical rhythm, pitch reiteration, and wordless intensifiers such as "a-hum." Kebede also fails to include in his description the street cries of urban vendors. When slaves and freedmen moved into cities to sell their wares or those of their masters, the cries of the field moved to the street with appropriate textual, tonal, and expressive modifications. Street cries, however, did not express "hunger, loneliness, or lovesickness," for they had a specific and practical function. In 1879, an observer in Charleston, South Carolina, recorded the texts of several street cries:

> Big House, look out of de window!
> Now's yer time to git snap-beans.
> Okra, tomatoes, an' taters gwine by.
> Don't be foolish virgins;
> Hab de dinner ready
> When de master he comes home.
> Snap-beans gwine by.
>
> Now's yer chance! Now's yer chance!
> Dis de last time I'se gwine by yar today.
>> Strawberries!
> I'se willing to do widout dese yar strawberries.
>> Strawberries gwine by.
>
> Taters, Irish taters!
> Squash, Irish squash!
> Squash, Mexican squash!
> Protestant and Catholic
> Taters and squashes!
>
>> (quoted in L.E.B. 1879, 5)

In addition, William H. Croome (1851) collected twenty-four "designs" of black street criers in Philadelphia, including examples of cries about chimney sweeping, whitewashing, wood splitting, and the selling of crabs, ice cream, hot corn, and hominy.

Calls, cries, and hollers were reliable devices for transplanted Africans who were learning a new language, since their own languages were denied them by slave owners by prohibition and through the deliberate mixing of slaves who spoke different African languages. It was in these practical genres that African-American musical expression in the United States first crystallized as it was being spread to and within the other musical forms that were emerging.

Anansi the spider, Rabbit, Monkey, Fox, Turtle, and the other African animal tricksters were brought with Africans to the New World and, reincarnated in similar or identical form, they became central to the new tales the African Americans were telling. Most important among them, Rabbit, who holds top rank as a trickster, became Br'er Rabbit in numerous Uncle Remus tales (see, for example, Harris [1881] 1982),[7] and Monkey later became the Signifying Monkey of black urban folk culture.[8] Because they were symbols of the African Americans' ability to outwit their more powerful social and political opponents, Br'er Rabbit and the Signifying Monkey became heroes in black culture. Br'er Rabbit's ability to overcome larger, stronger, and better-armed foes through cunning is exemplified in the tale "Br'er Rabbit and Br'er Lion," in which "Rabbit is invited to offer up his life for Lion's supper and is so adept in his survival strategy that Lion dies wrestling with his own shadow" (Goss and Barnes 1989, 105). (I posit, as have others in casual conversation, that Br'er Rabbit later metamorphosed into Bugs Bunny, trickster hero of millions of Americans, white and black, child and adult.)

Like tricksters of all kinds, these tricksters of black culture, according to Barlow (1989), "habitually overcame their more formidable opponents with guile and a certain amount of bravado and by cunningly inverting the status quo of normal power relations" (22). In Barlow's view, this constituted a "sneak attack on the values of the dominant white culture," undermining its power and control to a degree that made life more tolerable, amusing, and optimistic for African Americans of the nineteenth century. The transplanted Africans also brought with them the trickster god, Esu, but now the god appeared as Legba, guardian of the crossroads, or as the Devil, who frequented crossroads in search of souls for which to trade.[9]

---

7. Harris's and other such collections of the period were edited in corrupt versions, most perpetuating white perceptions of blacks as "primitive and child-like darkeys."

8. It is clear that the Signifying Monkey toasts have their origin in African tales, as can be seen by comparing the toast "The Signifying Monkey" (chapter 4) and the tale "Why Monkeys Live in Trees" (chapter 1).

9. I will discuss Legba again in chapter 3 and the Signifying Monkey in chapter 5. For now, suffice it to note the presence and transformation of the African tricksters into African-American figures in the African-American narrative tradition.

The animal tricksters were not the only heroes about whom tales were composed by African Americans. Tales of "court, arrests, idleness, crime, and bravado" featuring the rounder, the eastman, the creeper, the badman, and other generic characters in the form of Stackolee, Casey Jones, John Henry, Railroad Bill, and other legendary heroes abounded (Odum 1925, 288, 289, 355), some of which still have currency in African-American core culture. Most of these tales found form in the secular song of southern blacks and became part of their musical repertoire; thus black folk song and folk poetry go hand in hand in one important corner of black folk culture. Tales of heroes and legends joined work songs, children's songs, dance songs, love songs, hymns, anthems, and general songs of amusement, comment, satire, and food as grist for the African American's secular cultural and aesthetic mill.[10] These early songs were made and spread by talented individuals who became known as the "songsters," "musicianers," and "music physicianers" of black culture. Songsters were makers of songs; musicianers were instrumentalists, primarily banjoists or fiddlers; music physicianers were musical itinerants who both made and played songs (259).

In 1922, Thomas Talley, a African-American Fisk University professor, published his *Negro Folk Rhymes, Wise and Otherwise,* the first comprehensive and substantive collection of African-American secular song. Hailed at the time of its publication as a masterpiece in its field, the collection consisted of "Rhyme Dance Songs" and "Negro Dance Rhymes." Talley's purpose was to show that "the Negro . . . has the rhyme-making habit and probably has always had it, and that the American Negro brought this habit with him to America . . . ; that a small handful from darkest Africa contains stanzas on the owl, the frog, and the turkey buzzard just like the American rhymes" (quoted in Wolfe 1991, 235). To prove his point, Talley inserted "a small foreign section including African rhymes" (279). Included among the "Rhyme Dance Songs," to be used specifically for the dance, is one called "The Banjo Picking," and among the "Negro Dance Rhymes" we find "Juba." These songs were performed and danced to in the ever-present circle, of course, with "those forming the circle . . . repeating the rhyme, clapping their hands together, and patting their feet in rhythmic time with the words of the rhyme being repeated." As the dancers in the circle executed the graceful dances, their feet "beat a tattoo upon the ground answering to every word, and sometimes to every syllable of the rhyme" (235). Among these rhymes were "Possum Up a Gum Stump" and "Jawbone." In all the songs, the rhymes were performed antiphonally, with the commission being given to the chosen leader as follows: "You sing the 'call' and we'll sing the 'sponse.'" Among the examples in the collection with "sponses" are "'Juba' with its sponse 'Juba'; 'Frog Went a-Courting,' with its

---

10. For texts and explanation of all varieties of black secular and sacred song, in addition to Odum, see Bontemps and Hughes (1958).

sponse 'Uh-huh!'; 'Did You Feed My Cow?' with its sponse, 'Yes, Ma'am,' etc., and 'The Old Black Gnats,' where the sponses are 'I cain't git out'n here, etc.'" (254). These songs, collected in Tennessee and other locations in the South, were survivals of nineteenth-century folk practices; many of them are still sung and danced to in rural and even in some urban black communities. Talley's collection is an intriguing reminder that Dance, Drum, and Song was alive and well in the first quarter of the twentieth century. I posit that it is still contributing to the continuity of African-American music.

Let us now take a look at the work songs and "seculars" of African-American culture. In Africa, men and women sang as they worked, and it was natural for the practice to carry over into the mandatory toil of the African slaves of North America. Early on, slave masters noticed that their slaves worked harder when they sang, and that "there was usually a *lead singer* who set the pace for the group. In fact, when slaves were auctioned, singers with the strongest voices brought top prices" (Kebede 1982, 130). Unfortunately, as with calls, cries, and hollers, there are no early examples and few contemporary descriptions of work songs extant, probably "because the travelers who wrote so many of the accounts rarely saw Afro-Americans at work" (Epstein 1977, 162). But surviving prison work songs, although they have been influenced by modern practices, do give us a good idea of how the early work songs might have sounded. And Wilson (1983) has discussed for us the utilitarian and artistic interrelationships of one dockside steamboat work song, "Katie Left Memphis,"[11] the function of which is to "facilitate the task of chopping wood" to fuel the *Katie Belle*'s travels. Wilson points out that in the singer's performance of the song while at work, "the process of chopping the wood becomes an intrinsic part of the music," wherein "the work becomes the music, and the music becomes the work" (11, 12). In Wilson's transcription score, we see the presence of pendular thirds, call-and-response between voice and axe, and counter-rhythms produced by the sound of the axe on the fourth beat in connection with other weak-beat accents against the normally strong beats of the 4/4 meter. Wilson's transcription and description of the music document the synergistic relationship between work and song and identify the use of the axe striking the wood as Drum. In the work song, the elements of Dance, Drum, and Song are present, although not part of community ritual in this case, with Dance playing a much subdued role in the movements of the arms and torso—African style—and the legs. Extrapolating from the first recorded work songs, we can conclude that the early specimens were characterized by regular meters and rhythms, contained grunts and moans as part of their expressive vocabulary, and made use of overlapping call-and-response constructions.

11. The performance Wilson describes can be found on the album *Roots of the Blues*.

There appeared in 1921 a small collection of seven ring-game songs, collected and notated by a graduate of Hampton Institute as they were performed by black children in Raleigh, North Carolina (Spenney 1921). In 1890, a New Englander had published a discussion of the texts of ring-game songs of African origin, including "Mosquito He Fly High" and "Gon on, Liza," having transcribed them as her black nurse sang them to white children (Clarke 1890). Clearly, many of these songs are African survivals, for ring games were popular among children in traditional Africa.

Game and social songs were metrically regular, made use of simple additive rhythms, and employed repetitive pentatonic melodic constructions, with accents on the off beat. And there are similarities between African and African-American game songs and children's songs. Ekwueme (1974) mentions that

> The children's games, "Ring around the Rosie" or "Bob a Needle," each with its accompanying song, have counterparts in Africa, such as the Akpakolo of Igbo children in West Africa or the funny game-song of the Kikuyu of Kenya called, "R-r-r-r-r-r an ngubiro," which is a special East African follow-your-leader version of "Ring around the Rosie." (128–129)

It is evident that African to African-American continuity is strong even in the songs of children. In the children's game songs recorded by James on *Afro-American Music* ([1970] 1978), we can hear some of this continuity. Pendular thirds, repetition of short phrases, and responsorial events are their strongest overall elements, with multimeter and elisions sometimes occurring in the melodic lines. The calls, cries, and hollers, work songs, children's songs, and spirituals all share certain characteristics. And I should add that in all these genres, "natural pauses in the melody were filled in with clapping, stomping, pattin', vocal outbursts, and, in the case of dance music, strumming or slapping string instruments, shaking rattles, and beating sticks, bones, and other percussive instruments" (Southern 1983, 201). These devices arose as efforts to fit African performance techniques to the new musical system to which the slaves were adapting and to fit the new system to African-American performance practices. They persisted in African-American music, giving it a distinctive color, character, and emotional quality and effecting an artistic continuity that is tenacious and unmistakable.

African-American folksongs could not be recorded in their heyday, but we are fortunate that examples of this music have been retained in an environment in which African-American performance practices "continued to survive in a remarkably pure form," according to Lomax (1977, 1). The Georgia Sea Island Singers, residing in the rather closed society of St. Helena Island, have preserved striking specimens. "Knee Bone" is a secular dance piece with "layers of crossed rhythms." "Raggy Levy" is an exciting black stevedore's song "made for lifting or pulling heavy weights." "The Titanic" is a ballad about the momentous sinking of the great ocean liner. **51**

The folk music of African Americans was created over three hundred years, from the seventeenth through the nineteenth century, in the slave community of North America, where transplanted Africans took their native song and adapted it to their new environment in order to express the struggles and fulfillments of their new and brutal condition. Since the median age of slaves in 1850 was 17.3 years (Lovell 1972, 40), most of these songmakers were at the beginning of their most creative years, when, I believe, they were best able to and motivated to transform African musical practices and assumptions into new forms.

Although the slaves who developed this music included individuals of exceptional talent, no records were kept of the accomplishments of these early bards; but history does record the names of some who were contributors. These were individuals who escaped from their slavery, such as "George of John Means," born in 1827 in Missouri, who "plays well on the violin"; "Sambo of Mark Jackson," born around 1736 in Virginia; "Dinah," known for her "hymnsinging" (probably spirituals); and "Charles of John Giles," born around 1740, who "played exceedingly well on the banjo." All these runaway slaves were noted for their musical abilities (Ballou 1967).

> Often these fugitives carried strange bundles and burdens. Some expropriated large sums of money from their masters' coffers; others took guns and powder. A few even ventured to ride off on horses, and a good many black musicians took their violins—forerunners of the generations who would walk the roads with guitars strapped to their backs. (Harding 1981, 37)

Expressive of the plight of the transplanted African in a new land, black song helped the slaves bridge the newly created cultural gap by serving them in their daily activities. On the early plantations, as we have seen, there were work songs, rhyme songs, songs of satire, derision, and mimicry, songs of nostalgia and nonsense, children's songs, lullabies, and "songs of play and work and love" (Levine 1977, 15). Some songs contained elements of other song types; for example, "repetitive songs designed to lighten labor or pass the time were ideally suited for the insertion of satiric or derisive lines" (Epstein 1977, 187). So while singing songs to accompany their digging, cutting, pulling, and driving, their basket weaving and grain grinding, these African Americans were constantly poking fun at themselves, their overseers, their masters, and visiting observers. Their humor was their armament in a culture in which they had little control.

African-American song—even the spiritual, in some cases—was accompanied by instruments, among which were some of African origin: banjo, musical saw, reed flutes, drums (where they were not prohibited), sticks or bones, and rattles of various kinds. Instruments were also used as timekeepers for dancing. An early transplanted African dance was the calinda, which was undergoing transformation in New Orleans in the 1880s, if not before. This transformed calinda was danced to music played on the banza (banjo). Among other existing dances were survivals from Africa and other African-American jigs and ring dances (Epstein 1977, 33–38, 44). Other, more Americanized dances were the Virginia Breakdown, Georgia Shuffle, Alabama Kick-up, Louisiana Toe-and-Heel, Tennessee Double Shuffle (Hentz [1854] 1970), and cakewalk. The buzzard lope is an African survival—a miming dance in which, of course, the buzzard is mimicked. An example of the music that accompanies such dances can be found on the album *Georgia Sea Island Songs* (1977).

When folk-made or makeshift instruments were not available to accompany song and dance, individuals and groups patted juba. "Patting juba" was an extension and elaboration of simple hand clapping that constituted a complete and self-contained accompaniment to the dance. The practice included "striking the hands on the knees, then striking the hands together, then striking the right shoulder with one hand, the left with the other—all while keeping time with the feet, and singing" (Northrup [1853] 1970, 141). This description, given by a former slave, is only one version of the practice. Given the penchant of African Americans for variety and improvisation, there probably existed numerous versions. Epstein (1977, 143) has reprinted a notated juba pattern as it was recorded in 1880 by Sidney Lanier:

Epstein quotes another contemporary observer's account of a performance that was accompanied by the words "Juber up and Juber down, Juber all around the town" (143). Reprinted in the *Black Perspective in Music* is the text of an extended juba song:

> Master had a yaller man
> Talles nigger in de land,
> Juba was dat feller's name
> De way he strutted was a shame.
> Juba, Juba, Juba, Juba— (repeat several times)
> Oh, twas Juba dis and Juba dat
> Juba killed de yaller cat
> To make his wife a Sunday hat—Juba.
> Twas Juba dis an' Juba dat,
> His wife was yaller, tall an' fat;
> He killed ole missis yaller cat
> To make his wife a Sunday hat.
>   Juba!—
> Marster had a yaller steer
> Ol's de mountin to er year,
> I tells ye dis for all er dat

53

He'd run erway at de drop o' yer hat.
                    Whoa Mark.
See 'm comin up de road
Pullin on er monstrous load,
Git out'n de way mighty spry
Or he'll tho' you to de sky.
                    Whoa Mark.
Juba driv dat ole steer
Fer five and twenty year,
Thu der rain and thu de snow
Juba an de steer'd go,
                    Whoa Mark—Juba.
When de sun was shinin bright,
Ef twas day, ef twas night,
Hear him holler loud an' strong
Mark, why don't yer git er long.
                    Golong—Whoa Mark, Juba.
By 'm by dat ole ox died,
Juba he jes cried and cried
Tell one day he ups an' die
I spec he's drivin in de sky.
                    Golong—whoa Mark—Juba.
            ("Negro Folk Songs" [1895] 1976, 148–149)

The texts, whether spoken or sung, were accompanied by versions of the rhythm notated earlier, using the technique reported by a white visitor to a southern plantation:

> Someone calls for a fiddle—but if one is not to be found, some one "pats juba." This is done by placing one foot a little in advance of the other, raising the ball of the foot from the ground, and striking it in regular time, while, in connection, the hands are struck slightly together, and then upon their thighs. In this way they make the most curious noise, yet in such perfect order, it furnishes music to dance by. (Paine 1851, 179)

Of course, patting juba is only one form of patting that prevailed in the African-American folk community, the "hambone" pat being the most popular in my own childhood and one of the few still extant:

The typical African-derived rhythms ♪♩ ♪, ♫, and ♫♫ were patted variously to diverse songs, games, and dances. Derived in part from the black music of

Latin America, these rhythms had an early influence on black music in the United States. Rhythms such as the ones just cited, including the hemiola of the hambone pat, played an important role in black music all over the Americas and had a strong influence on the folk rag (Floyd and Reisser 1984, 24–27).

In 1852, a novelist wrote about the "single, double, compound, complex, implex, wiggle and twist" steps of the slave dancers and referred to their "corn-stalk jigs and banjo dances" (Hall 1852, 22, 103). Although this description appears in a book of fiction, it is confirmed by numerous accounts that appear in travel diaries and official and unofficial reports of nineteenth-century observers. Other reports document dances such as " 'pitchin' hay,' 'corn-shuckin,' 'cuttin' wheat,' and 'spottin' (dancing with the hands and other parts of the body without moving the feet), . . . 'pony's prance,' 'the swan's bend,' 'the kangaroo,' and 'shooting the chute' " (Stuckey 1987, 65–66). Some of these dances included the "flaunting of . . . handkerchiefs" (Holcombe 1861, 626), a practice I will comment on later. These and many other black dances of the period have their counterparts or beginnings in African village life, and they served as model and stimulus for the invention and development of a large number of African-American dances with similar movements and names in the latter part of the nineteenth and into the twentieth century. They would be the foundation for the development of jazz dance.

I should say just a word here about solo dancing, epitomized in the nineteenth century by the incomparable "Master Juba" (William Henry Lane). Known for his ability to astound with his intricate steps, Juba danced the Virginny Breakdown, the Alabama Kick-up, the Tennessee Double Shuffle and all the rest of the dances of black culture with ultimate perfection. With his reputation already well established in the United States as a nonpareil of dance, Juba performed in 1848 at Vauxhall in England, where one observer saw him "tie his legs into such knots, and fling them about so recklessly, or make his feet twinkle until you lose sight of them altogether in his energy." But, the reviewer pointed out, "Juba is a musician, as well as a dancer. To him, the intricate management of the nigger tambourine is confined, and from it he produces marvelous harmonies [sic]. We almost question whether, upon a great emergency, he could not play a fugue upon it" ("Juba at Vauxhall" 1848, 77). Judging from other contemporary reports, such extravagant praise was well deserved by Master Juba. But my point in quoting this Englishman is twofold: (1) to call attention to the existence and importance of solo dancing among blacks in America, and (2) to make mention of the use of the tambourine and Juba's virtuosity on it.[12] Juba was Mr. Tambo with the Georgia Champion Min-

12. I believe that this instrument has not received the attention it has warranted in scholarly research, and that filling in the gap between Juba's use of it and its later use in the music of black Pentecostal churches has been hampered by its association with minstrelsy.

strels in 1843. He moved to England in 1848, taking London by storm, and died there in 1852 (Rice 1911, 48).

The references here to the tambourine brings us to a brief mention of instrumental music in its transition from African to African-American music. The banjo, flute, violin, triangle, drum, quills, and sticks (bones) were ubiquitous in slave culture. It is not surprising to find that this combination of instruments is perfectly suited to the realization of the heterogeneous sound ideal. The combination of these sounds creates a contrasting, not a blending, conglomerate, resulting in a sound that is ideally suited to the rhythmic, polyphonic, and tonal stratifications of African and African-American music.

Such instrumental combinations have continued to exist and have continued to be valued, sought, and utilized throughout the history of African-American musical culture. This ideal sound played a critical role in determining the nature of blues, ragtime, jazz, gospel, R&B, and all the other African-American musical genres, and it also influenced mightily the unique sound of American popular music in general. The influences have been many, diverse, and undeniable. These influences are

1. Melodic
   • in microtonal inflections in pentatonic and modally ambiguous contexts
   • in vocalizing that is variously rough, sandy, piercing, and falsetto
   • in the use of wordless sounds for their own value rather than for the communication of verbal meaning
   • in the ease of movement "from a speaking to singing mode within a musical context" (Wilson 1992a, 330)
   • in the use of ululations, grunts, hums, shouts, and melisma as integral and indispensable parts of the musical meaning
2. Rhythmic
   • in hand clapping, foot patting, and patting juba
   • in the repetition of short rhythmic motives, cross-rhythms, accented and isolated second beats, and "basing"
3. Textual
   • in the tales, ballads, stories, and toasts told in metaphor
   • in the figures of speech, implications, indirection, and personification in dialect and call-and-response

Because of the persistence of the African cultural memory of fertility and reproduction, the erotic element is frequently present, particularly in the context of dance. And since most African-American musical genres derived from the dance, erotic elements play important roles in most African-American music.

In addition, according the diary of a mid-nineteenth-century observer, the slaves imitated instruments with their voices and added "peculiar . . . musical sounds at the end of the verses" (Bodichon [1857–1858] 1972, 119). These "peculiar" sounds at the ends of verses probably grew out of the Africans' propensity to *speak* the last words or syllables of musical phrases, and that tradition is related to another African practice, elision, which results from Africans' singing mirroring the rise and fall of pitch and inflection in their regular speech (Ekwueme 1974, 133). So, obviously, the blue notes, elisions, and other melodic assets of African-American singing style did not come about by accident, but resulted from the African Americans' natural use of the cultural, physical, and musical assets they brought with them to their new homeland.

The manifestation of these elements in Dance, Drum, and Song, together with the social and religious values of the ring, the "motor-memory" and cultural memory of transplanted Africans, the exigencies of slave life in a foreign land, and the necessity of conforming to the expectations of the dominant culture created an African-American ethos, a common consciousness, a cultural unity, that is reflected also in "our language, . . . our thought patterns, our laughter, our walk" (Richards 1980, 14), and other aspects of African Americans' being. It is this ethos and this being that make black American culture distinctive, that create its aesthetic. In the pages that follow, I will identify this ethos more precisely, trace its continuing development, determine the nature and character of the aesthetic, and discuss its implications for African-American musical discourse.

CHAPTER **3**

Syncretization and Synthesis: Folk and Written Traditions

When God shuts a door for us, he will open another door.
Swahili proverb

I do not see why the devil should have all the good tunes.
Rowland Hill

In the early years of the nineteenth century, white-to-black and black-to-white musical influences were widespread, a fact documented in numerous contemporary accounts. For example, in chapter 2 I mentioned the report of a black nurse singing black songs to white children. Add to that occurrence a report (Gilman 1834) of black children singing "hymns" to white children ("Master Jesus Is My Captain" and "I'm Walking On to Jesus") and the knowledge that at slave balls, the cotillion, the quadrille, and other European social dances were danced by blacks, and it becomes clear that the prevailing musical interactions and influences in nineteenth-century America produced a black populace conversant with the music of both traditions. It is with this perspective in mind that I examine the continuing development of the old, established, and developing genres and their syncretization into new forms.

Pre-twentieth-century writers and compilers of black religious music began to publish collections of hymns and religious songs in the late eighteenth century and continued through the nineteenth. Newport Gardner (b. 1746)—a former slave who, after gaining his freedom, studied with the white singing-school master Andrew Law—conducted a singing school and composed and saw published his "Promise Anthem" (1764). We do not know much about Gardner, since he emigrated to Liberia, where he lived until his death in 1826.[1] But we do know a great deal about Richard Allen (1760–1831), who founded the African Methodist Episcopal (A.M.E.) Church and who compiled and published *A Collection of Spiritual Songs and Hymns Selected from Various Authors* (1801); in 1818, he also helped compile the first official hymnal of the A.M.E. Church. And we know something about William Wells Brown (1814–1884), who compiled *The Antislavery Harp* (1849), a collection of song texts; Edwin Hill (1845–1925), composer and music publisher, who wrote a number of religious works in the European tradition, including the anthem "Hallelujah! Christ Is Risen from the Dead" (1882) and "Easter Anthem" (1898); and John Turner Layton (1849–ca. 1915), who edited the eleventh edition of the *Hymnal for Use by the African Methodist Episcopal Church* (1897), to which Henry F. Grant (fl. ca. 1870), composer of "Jesus, Lover of My Soul," contributed two songs.

The religious songs of these composers were sung primarily by northern free black congregations made up of refugees from white churches and from southern slavery. They were intended, in part, as replacements for the shout spirituals so loved by black churchgoers, and they were also part of the arsenal of black aspirants to white culture. These songwriters and compilers eschewed the African-American musical heritage, but other writers of black religious song did not. Examples of a different outlook can be found in other works. William Henry Sherwood (active 1880s–1890s), for example, evangelist and superintendent of Sherwood's Orphan School, compiled his *Soothing Songs Hymnal* (1891) and *The Harp of Zion* (1893), which would later serve as the basis for *The National Harp of Zion and B.Y.P.U. Hymnal* (1893); and Charles Albert Tindley (1859–1933) later compiled his own songs and those of other composers in the collections *Soul Echoes* (1905) and *New Songs of Paradise* (1916). The contents of all these collections were in some way compatible and consonant with the African-American musical tradition.

In the secular world, the published vocal music of African Americans included pseudo-spirituals, "carry-me-backs," art songs, and sentimental parlor songs. Frank Johnson's "American Boy" (1837) is the earliest extant part-song by a black composer. And Johnson's "Now Sleeping Fair Maid of Love" (1822–1823) and William Brady's "Leila, Leila Cease Thy Lay" (1845) appear to be the earliest extant solo songs by African Americans. Henry Williams's "Bermuda's Fairy Isle" (1854) followed, together with a modest number of

---

1. Gardner was one of approximately twelve thousand American blacks who returned to Africa in 1822 after the founding of the Republic of Liberia. For a brief statement on African colonization and abolition, see Carroll and Noble (1988, 176). **59**

songs by others, as the century progressed. In the 1890s, the song output of black composers increased and included Will Marion Cook's "Love Is the Tend'rest of Themes" (1896) and Harry T. Burleigh's cycle *Three Songs* (1898). These pieces were all well crafted, but devoid of the "ring" characteristics so important in African-American music.

By the 1870s, pseudo-spirituals had begun to see print. Published in sheet-music form for voice and piano and designed for parlor and show performance, these imitations of the slave songs included James Bland's "Oh Dem Golden Slippers" and Jacob Sawyer's "My Lord Is Writin' Down Time" (1883) (Dennison 1982, 297, 329, 332). "Carry-me-backs," such as Bland's "Carry Me Back to Old Virginny" (1878), helped spur and sustain a theme then prominent in proslavery circles, the notion that freed slaves longed to return to the security and solace of their former homes. And there were also songs, written by both blacks and whites, that appealed to the vicious and racist attitudes that prevailed just after the Civil War. Denigrating sheet-music titles sold hundreds, perhaps thousands, of copies.

With the onset of the "coon song" craze in the 1880s, Tin Pan Alley consolidated the production and marketing of sheet music, producing such titles as Ernest Hogan's "All Coons Look Alike to Me" (1896) and "Da Coon Dat Had de Razor" (1885). Through such titles and their illustrated covers, Tin Pan Alley consistently portrayed the African-American male as a fun-loving dandy, a chicken- or ham-loving glutton, a razor-totin' thief, gambler, or drunkard, or an outrageously unfaithful husband or lover. The black female was presented in these illustrations either as a very black, fat, large-lipped mammy or carouser, or as a beautiful light-skinned "Yaller Rose of Texas," showing the white male's ostensible preference for exploiting fair-skinned females as well as the African American's indoctrination into the preference for white ideals of beauty. In the late nineteenth century, the advertising of musical products became the primary means of developing, perpetuating, and communicating the negative images of black people in American society. The coon song was the vehicle for repeating these messages in American culture. The stereotypes perpetuated by these publications linger as both conscious and unconscious images of blacks in the memory of countless Americans. As music, these coon songs were obviously counterfeit versions of black song. Generally, the tunes lacked ring traits, and the rhythms were rigidly uniform. But real African-American music continued to evolve, expressing the values of the ring and the authentic struggles and fulfillments of turn-of-the-century African Americans.

By the late nineteenth century, Dance, Drum, and Song was undergoing significant change. In the 1870s, the Fisk Jubilee Singers enthralled Europe with their renditions of Negro spirituals. But already the songs had been changed—artistically reshaped—by the refinements of the singers' training. A contemporary witness observed that

> to render these songs essentially as they had been rendered in slave-land came the Jubilee Singers. They visited most of the cities and large towns of the North, everywhere drawing enthusiasm among the people rarely before equalled. The cultured and uncultured were alike charmed and melted to tears as they listened with a new enthusiasm to what was a wonderfully new exhibition of the greatness of song-power. . . .
>
> The songs . . . possessed in themselves in a peculiar power, a plaintive, emotional beauty, and other characteristics which seemed entirely independent of artistic embellishment. These characteristics were, with a refreshing originality, naturalness, and soulfulness of voice and method, fully developed by the singers, who sang with all their might, yet with most pleasing sweetness of tone. (Trotter 1878, 258, 259)

This description contrasts with prior descriptions of spirituals and the singing of them by blacks. The songs are now "fully developed" and sung with "most pleasing sweetness of tone." And given the identity of the writer—the sophisticated and refined journalist James Monroe Trotter—the statement is certainly not uninformed. The fact is that by this time, the Jubilee Singers had adapted the slave songs to fit the vocal and expressive requirements of their European-style choral training. Trotter either did not know the difference or really believed that the way the Jubilee Singers sounded was the way the spirituals had been sung by untutored slaves. Trotter either had not seen the ring or simply did not appreciate its musical products. His musical prejudices are revealed in a statement later in his book: "I shall here make mention by name none but persons of scientific musical culture; of none but those who read the printed music page. . . . The singer or player 'by ear' merely, however well favored by nature, will not be mentioned" (Trotter 1878, 286).[2]

In the Jubilee Singers' renditions, the powerful Negro spiritual had been transformed into a fine imitation of itself. But the transformation was not complete; it was to continue, generation after generation, until audiences would no longer hear spirituals even as the Jubilee Singers themselves had first sung them, let alone as they had been sung by the slaves. Meanwhile, however, Dance, Drum, and Song was still ascendant in African-American culture, where, if the spiritual was present, so was the shout. And other syntheses were also taking place. In African-American religious life, African metaphysics had merged with elements of Christian theology to create a spiritual worldview that was different from both. The African scholar Francis Bebey ([1969]

2. Other and later accounts of the folk, entertainment, parlor, and concert-hall musical activity of African Americans in the nineteenth century are in Keck and Martin (1988).

1975) points out that the *style* of the African American's vocal expression was a direct result of this syncretic process:

> The American Negro has managed by trial and error to transform the white man's language into a singing language whose intonations resemble his ancestral tongues. The shifting of the tonic accent, the ellipse of certain syllables, and the addition of percussive onomatopoeias, not to mention the difficulties encountered in pronouncing some words correctly, have given us . . . declamatory style. (120)

The spiritual and the black declamatory style went hand in hand, simply because they both emerged from the same source: African intonations, inflections, and rhythmic conventions applied to a new language and linguistic style in the context of a new religion. In such a context, supplications and entreaties to God for deliverance and protection were common, and they were easily expressed in the call-and-response figures so common to black worship. A white folklorist describes a scene of black worship:

> [The] preacher began in a quavering voice a long supplication. Here and there came an uncontrollable cough from some kneeling penitent or the sudden squall of a restless child; and now and again an ejaculation, warm with entreaty, "O Lord!" or a muttered "Amen, Amen"—all against the background of the praying, endless praying.
>
>   Minutes passed, long minutes of strange intensity. The mutterings, the ejaculations, grew louder, more dramatic, till suddenly I felt the creative thrill dart through the people like an electric vibration, that same half-audible hum arose—and then, up from the depths of some "sinner's" remorse and imploring came a pitiful little plea, a real Negro "moan" sobbed in musical cadence. From somewhere in that bowed gathering another voice improvised a response: the plea sounded again, louder this time and more impassioned; then other voices joined in the answer, shaping it into a musical phrase; and so, before our ears, as one might say, composed then and there by no one in particular and everyone in general. (Burlin 1919, 88)

This was nothing new. Praying had been part of the Africans' religious behavior in the homeland, and the call-and-response and ejaculatory interjections described in this report were part of the African narrative and musical expressive technique. It was new only to Europeans and Americans who were uninformed about the slaves' past. This preaching, praying, and singing event was a syncretized product, born of the synthesis of African religion and Christianity, and it was to pervade all aspects of African-American culture, intruding into even the published music of the musically literate. In spite of the refining of the spirituals by trained choral and concert singers, the preaching, praying, and singing of spirituals would sound over and over again through the decades as a theme in the music of African Americans.

The spiritual was being transformed in still other ways. No longer concerned so much about the world to come and the freedom it would bring—on heaven or on earth—African Americans began to make a new song. Writing about "Negro Music" in 1892, an observer warned that slave songs were disappearing "before the triumphant march of 'Gospel Hymns'" (Tonsor 1892, 121). As I mentioned earlier, in 1893 William Henry Sherwood compiled two collections of sacred songs. Both anthologies contained many of his own hymns, including "Happy Hosts of Zion" and "Take It to the Lord." The emotional contrast between these new songs and the spiritual was marked. Sherwood's focus was on the immediate, everyday doings of churchgoers, and the character of his music was uplifting, confident, and encouraging. Also different was Charles Albert Tindley's 1905 collection, which contained songs of his composing in which he had left appropriate gaps and spaces in which performers were to continue the melodic embellishment and rhythmic improvisation derived from the African tradition. Tindley's music was more consonant with and hospitable to African-American performance practices than were the hymns of Sherwood or the earlier black songwriters, and the singers soon began to exploit the possibilities inherent in his work. The hymns written by Tindley carried a camp-meeting intensity and fervor that would inspire the later development and crystallization of the black gospel style. In the first five years of the twentieth century, Tindley wrote "I'll Overcome Some Day," "Stand by Me," "We'll Understand It Better By and By," and other hymns, and he set the stage for the emergence of Thomas A. Dorsey and Lucy Campbell.

The period of Sherwood and Tindley, spanning the years 1896 to 1920, has been designated by Boyer (1985–1988) as "the first period of gospel singing," which included the Azusa Street Revival[3] and the rise of the "Sanctified Singing Preachers and their Congregations" (13). In their music, the Sanctified and Pentecostal churches made extensive use of the hand clapping and foot stamping that descended from the shout; they also used drums and tambourines, and their own distinctive songs were heavily laced with or based on call-and-response figures. From this tradition emerged the singing preachers of the Sanctified tradition. The status of the black preacher in the core black community had emerged not out of African values but out of the legacy of the Second Great Awakening, which had sparked the Kentucky camp meetings of the 1790s and provided the permissive religious environment in which the spirituals flourished. Since this evangelical movement bestowed high social status on their preachers, blacks embraced this practice as they had other customs

3. Scholars attribute the nationwide widespread of Pentecostalism to the Azusa Street Revival, which took place at 312 Azusa Street in Los Angeles from 1906 to 1909. The church is supposed to have been founded as a racially integrated church by the Reverend Philip Seymour, who introduced into it "speaking in tongues," the "falling of the Holy Ghost," and other unusual practices (DjeDje 1989, 37; Spencer 1987a, 1).

63

of the movement they found valuable—experiences such as conversion (which paralleled in some respects the possession rites of African religion) and testifying. In the absence of the African spiritual system of God, the lesser divinities, spirits, and the living-dead, the black religious behaviors of preaching, praying, and testifying emerged to constitute the primary spiritual conduct of African Americans.

This legacy fueled the holiness beliefs and practices that were so hospitable to the birth, nurture, and development of black gospel music: Dance, Drum, and Song in the context of preaching, praying, and testifying. The Sanctified or Holiness preacher employed, as Paul Carter Harrison (1972) describes it, "Drum—the rolling vowels, foot-stomping, hand-clapping—Dance—transporting himself, at times, up and down the aisles—and Song—the pitch and modulations of his voice intoning the breath of the spirit—putting together the necessary ingredients for the ritual," affirming "the ethos of the community, and the sanctions of the life-style" (45, 220).

Other murmurings of the black gospel sound at the turn of the century were heard in the renditions of the Fisk Jubilee Quartet, spawned by the Jubilee Singers in the 1890s, and some of its imitators. From 1909 to 1927, the quartet, which included the soon-to-be-famous tenor Roland Hayes, traveled widely and recorded spirituals and other folk narrations on forty-nine Victor and Columbia sides. With its highly developed rhythmic sense and precise execution, its commendable ensemble and period vibrato, the college-trained Fisk Jubilee Quartet of the second decade of the century represented that strain of the spiritual that took on the trappings and characteristics of European choral singing and became accepted and lauded by middle-class blacks and white aficionados. Imitators sprouted and flourished, including the less refined quartets associated with churches. These groups added to what they had borrowed from the Fisk Jubilee Quartet the styles, manner, and musical traits of core-culture churches and sang in a heavily call-and-response manner (Boyer 1985–1988, 15). It was all reminiscent of the ring and recalled for tens of thousands of former slaves and other free blacks memories that remained strong and vital. The success of the gospel quartets was stunning; groups sprang up all over the South and spread the new black gospel quartet sound throughout Afro-America.

According to Kip Lornell (1988, 16), the earliest published mention of black quartet singing was made in 1851 by Fredrika Bremer, who observed approximately a hundred slaves singing in four parts. The first documented observation of one-on-a-part four-part singing by blacks was made before the turn of the century by James Weldon Johnson, who observed four youngsters harmonizing in his hometown of Jacksonville, Florida.[4] Among the earliest of the

---

4. Abbott (1992) has made a compelling case for the origin of barbershop-quartet singing in black culture.

black quartets were college groups such as those at Fisk University, Hampton Institute, and the Dix Industrial School (whose Dinwiddie Quartet became famous after it turned vaudeville in 1902 and recorded on Victor). Almost simultaneously there arose community quartets, such as Polk Miller's Old South Quartette and the Standard Quartet, the latter having recorded on Columbia as early as 1895.

"Company quartets," representing coal mines and other industrial concerns, church quartets, and other varieties sprang up in the South, multiplied, and flourished between 1900 and 1919—all singing spirituals, hymns, and songs of their own making (Lornell 1988, 18). The Great Migration brought many of these groups north, and the 1930s saw the rise of the great, fully professional quartets such as the Golden Gate Quartet and the Five Blind Boys of Mississippi. These quartets added to their already impressive repertoires the gospel songs of Dorsey, Campbell, Brewster, and others; brought to quartet singing additional and more refined, expanded, and elaborated tropes of the ring—a pumping bass, "rhythmic inventiveness, a strong sense of syncopation, and the use of . . . vocal technique such as growls, slurs, and falsetto"— and frequently presented songs that approximated sermons (21, 24).[5] These quartets inspired and opened the door for others to turn professional, spawning later notables such as the Famous Blue Jay Singers, Soul Stirrers, Kings of Harmony, Dixie Hummingbirds, and Fairfield Four.[6]

Also added to the gospel mix were contributions from the continually developing Holiness churches. Flourishing since the 1890s, Holiness churches contributed the Pentecostal fervor of holy dances, hand clapping, foot patting, and the use of instruments such as drums, cymbals, tambourines, triangles, and guitars. The quartets of the 1940s and 1950s added the organ and, in some cases, wind instruments and string bass. They brought to the ever-developing genre interruptions and punctuations made by sharp, halting, and irregular intakes and outlets of breath, sotto voce phrases, stutters, and syncopated words and syllables. In the 1920s, the Primitive Baptist Church brought style and substance to the piano accompaniments, and Holiness singer Arizona Dranes's work contributed stylistic features resulting from "a mixture of ragtime and barrelhouse techniques, with considerable rhythmic drive" (Oliver 1984, 10). Female singers such as Dranes and, in succeeding decades, Sister Willie Mae Ford Smith and Mahalia Jackson brought a committed lustiness that became a hallmark of the tradition.[7]

5. For musical transcriptions of sermons of black preachers, see Spencer (1987b).

6. For examples of the singing of several of these quartets, see the recording *Birmingham Quartet Anthology* (1980).

7. Dranes's art can be heard on the album *Songsters and Saints: Vocal Traditions on Race Records* (1984). Smith can be heard on *Mother Willie Mae Ford Smith: "I Am Bound for Canaan Land"* (ca. 1950); listen particularly to the title track, "Goin' On with the Spirit," and "Pilot Take My Hand."

Emancipation brought dramatic change to the life of Afro-America. Since praise meetings no longer needed to be held in order to justify social gatherings for blacks, social life took on a more secular character. Jook houses emerged and influenced the direction and character of Dance, Drum, and Song, with ring dances giving way to solo and couples' dances (Hazzard-Gordon 1990, 81). The shout continued, of course, retaining its sacred/secular character, but the jook was unabashedly secular, even though it was rooted in African traditions that did not recognize such a distinction: an African institution called the "party for the gods," which Africans commonly held for their deities, seems to have been the model. In these jooks, dances such as the funky butt, the buzzard lope, the slow drag, the itch, and the grind were danced to rags, to songs of legend and fable (called "ballads"), to early blues, and to prototypes of the music that would come to be called jazz. Liquor and beer were sold, and card playing and gambling were allowed. The dances were obviously of African provenance. Hazzard-Gordon points out that the itch, which became the basis for the development of jazz dance after the turn of the century, suggests Esu (Legba), since his "horse" scratched in his dance (83–84).

In the late nineteenth century, African Americans danced in and outside the ring to rhyme-dance songs, medleys of folk tunes, and spirituals. The medleys were called "rags" and their performance, "ragging" (Hughes 1899, 158). They were made by stringing together secular songs and spirituals to form more or less coherent pieces configured in the manner of A B A B C D E F, and so on. We know that these folk rags grew out of the African-American vocal and instrumental traditions, that like all the music of black culture— emerging from Dance, Drum, and Song—they made use of multimeter, polyrhythm, and melodies based on gapped scales, and that they employed folk tunes, including spirituals.

It was in the folk rag that the polyrhythms and cross-rhythms derived from Africa most obviously manifested themselves. Two-against-three and three-against-four combinations were common, and the hemiola and additive patterns of 2 + 3 and 3 + 4 were ascendant. These mixed, simultaneous, and conflicting rhythmic patterns are the source of the propulsive excitement of African and African-American drumming and general music making. To the unpracticed and uninformed ear, these additive, multimetric configurations appear to be mere syncopations, but they are not, as has been demonstrated elsewhere (Floyd and Reisser 1984, 32, 44–45). Multimetric, additive, and cross-rhythmic configurations were retained in the transition of African music into African-American music; their use defined the character and quality of African-American rhythm and remain central to its character and aesthetic power. The folk rags were performed primarily by banjo players and by bands made up of fiddles, fifes, triangles, quills, and other instruments that contributed to the heterogeneous sound ideal of the transplanted Africans.

It was this music that became the music of the jooks, but by then it had become raucous and raunchy: gutbucket, barrelhouse, rags, and blues—good-time music. The dancing and carousing that took place in the jooks were not condoned in all circles. Christianity's sacred–secular dichotomy and the frank atheism and amoralism of the jook crowd created a schism in the core culture. This breech was related to the fact that some blacks, striving for white values, approval, and acceptance, opposed the presence of jooks. These blacks held "race improvement" dances where they danced the quadrilles, cotillions, polkas, and waltzes of white society. But the musicians played for both kinds of functions and continued to syncretize the two musical styles. Apparently, the cakewalk was acceptable to all (Hazzard-Gordon 1990, 70, 75), probably because of its stately and fancy mimicking of Master and Missus at the ball. This state of affairs continued through the ragtime craze and beyond, until jazz became ascendant.

Meanwhile, quadrille and cotillion music was being performed by a large number of black bands and orchestras. The music for square dances, marches, and round dances (such as mazurkas, polkas, and waltzes) was performed by black musicians at white dances and slave balls and for the entertainment of free blacks. Having been introduced into the United States from Europe in the eighteenth century, the music for these dances reflected the social and aesthetic values of the cultures from which they emanated and in which they first functioned in America. Early on, this social-dance music had been performed by black musicians such as Sy (Simeon) Gilliat (d. 1820) and London Briggs of late-eighteenth- and early-nineteenth-century Virginia; later, many influential bands were established across the country, including those of James Hemmenway (1800–1849), A. J. R. Conner (d. 1850), and Isaac Hazzard (1804–1864) in Philadelphia, and J. W. Postlewaite (1837–1889) in St. Louis. And much of the music they played was composed by their leaders, as well as by other leading black composers of the period, including E. D. Roland (1803–1894) of Philadelphia, William Brady (d. 1854) and Walter Craig (1854–1929) of New York, Justin Holland (1819–1887) of Cincinnati, and Henry F. Williams (1813–1903) of Boston.

The most acclaimed band of the period was that of Frank Johnson (1792–1844) of Philadelphia. In addition to being a bandleader, trumpeter, and violinist, Johnson was a prolific composer, and many of his more than two hundred published compositions remained popular for years after his death. Eileen Southern (1983) suggests that Johnson was improvising in the black tradition in the 1830s; she cites a contemporary statement that refers to his "remarkable taste in distorting a sentimental, simple, and beautiful song, into a reel, jig, or country-dance" and concludes that he "stands at the head of a long line of black musicians whose performance practices made the essential difference in the transference of musical scores into actual sound" (108,

113). Herein lies Johnson's importance to this discussion. In his improvisations on American and European social-dance tunes, Johnson was making use of both sides of his heritage, contributing to the one with the other, and helping to effect the syncretism that is African-American music. Although Johnson and his black Philadelphia colleagues also played for black affairs, their clientele, I believe, was primarily white, dancing to the social-dance music of America's European settlers and their descendants.

But African Americans danced these dances, too. Characterized by the stamping, patting, and clapping that create propulsive, provocative, and offbeat rhythms, African-American dances and African-American versions of imported European dances were performed in the African tradition. The Georgia Sea Island Singers' "See Aunt Dinah" is a "song to which they swing partners, do-si-do, and circle to the right in their Saturday-night version of the Virginia reel," but its character is definitely African-American. The renditions of African-American square dancers, according to Alan Lomax (1977),

> had something in them carried over from Negro country dances. Movements and postures characteristic of the Mobile Buck and the Cake Walk, while subdued, tempered, and disguised, were doubtless present. . . . Negro set callers . . . brought to the square dances an element of spontaneity and improvision [sic] characteristic of Negro secular music in general, along with an imagery and idiom that made the calls unique. (4)

This imagery and idiom can be heard in Leadbelly's rendition of "Skip to My Lou," a typical African-American dance call. In it we can hear echoes and direct use of the pendular thirds, repetitions, short repeated phrases, elisions, and multimeter of African derivation.

It was the European *form* of these dances that was adopted by blacks, but the *content* was African, for although African and European dances coexisted easily, the slaves, according to a former bondsman, "danced the dances like the white folks danced them, and then we danced our own kind of dances" (quoted in Epstein 1977, 44). When, in 1853, one white observer saw at a slave ball "about sixty Negroes, all dancing . . . to the music of two violins and a banjo . . . a Negro . . . standing on a chair, calling what figures were to be performed in the Virginia reel," and when another saw that "Mingo with his triangle and Mose with his banjo came up from the quarters and made music for the happy belles and beaus . . . danced the cotillion and Lancers, winding up with the Virginia reel" (quoted in Epstein, 154, 158), they were witnessing syncretizations of African-American and imported European social-dance music.

In spite of several unique examples, such as Johnson's "Voice Quadrille" (1840) and Connor's "Five Step Waltz" (1840), the social-dance music written by black composers was typical of that of the early nineteenth century. Most

FIGURE 1. **Typical structure of a rag.**

Section	Intro	A		B		A		C		D	
Measures	4	‖:	16	:‖:	16	:‖:	16	:‖:	16	:‖:	16	:‖
Key .		C		G		C		F			

of the pieces are structured in march-trio or march-minuet form, both of which consist of several eight-measure sections and are through-composed. Each of the various key centers is usually associated with entire eight-measure sections and is closely related to the others. Emphasis is on the primary chords, with occasional appearance of secondary dominants and borrowed and augmented sixth chords. The rhythms are based on duple and triple divisions of the beat that accommodate a few syncopations and polyrhythms, and the melodies are based on major and minor scales (Floyd and Reisser 1980, 165–195). With the appearance of J. W. Postlewaite's "St. Louis Greys Quick Step" (1852), we see the first use of consistent sixteen-measure sections in a march by a black composer (Figure 1), a structure that "was later to become standard for marches and for classic ragtime pieces" (170). We know that this structure was familiar to black folk musicians in the late nineteenth century, since similar configurations have been found to be typical of African-American folk rags.

We do not know exactly when folk rags were first played on the piano, but there is evidence that "the legendary rag pianist John the Baptist . . . had been active in the '70s and '80s" (Southern 1983, 327). We know that, later, John "Blind" Boone (1864–1927) was playing piano rags and recorded some on rolls. So in the absence of exact contemporary evidence, we have an idea, from early piano rolls cut by Boone in 1912, of how nineteenth-century rags sounded. Boone's "Camp Meeting No. 1" and "Rag Medley No. 2," recorded and released in 1912,[8] both conform to the rag and ragging tradition of early African-American folk instrumentals. David Jasen and Trebor Tichenor (1978) assure us that since "Boone was nearly fifty at the time of his . . . recordings, his playing was probably in the style of the nineteenth century" (9). Boone's performance of "Rag Medley No. 2" has a straight bass, duple meter, and sectional organization, and contains tunes commonly used in blues and jazz around and after the turn of the century. "Camp Meeting No. 1" is structured as follows: A B A B C D C D E F; it is in duple meter, with an occasional "throbbing effect" produced by bass–treble note–chord alternation, and con-

---

8. I thank ragtime collector and scholar Trebor Tichenor for information on these and the others.

tains hymn tunes and spirituals. (In some of the voicings of the spiritual harmonies, elements of what would become the gospel piano style of the 1920s can be heard.) These recordings remind me of James Weldon Johnson's ([1912] 1989) description of a live ragtime improvisation that took place sometime before 1912:

> The barbaric harmonies, the audacious resolutions, often consisting of an abrupt jump from one key to another, the intricate rhythms in which the accents fell in the most unexpected places, but in which the beat was never lost, produced a curious effect. And, too, the player—the dexterity of his left hand in making rapid octave runs and jumps was little short of marvelous; and with his right hand he frequently swept half the keyboard with clean-cut chromatics. (99)

Boone's music was later notated to be published as sheet music. In this form, one can see in the music configurations that would later be used in classic ragtime. As early as 1892, Boone published "I Meet Dat Coon Tonight," which included two features that would become essential elements in this new form: the throbbing effect and arpeggiated sixteenth notes in the right-hand part.

This mention of the throbbing effect and the preceding discussion of the folk basis of ragtime music recall some commentary I first mentioned in chapter 2. The existence of the "straight bass" in ragtime music was vividly recounted by Julia Neeley Finck (1898), who was struck by the fact that the black performances she heard "nearly always accent the second beat in an accompaniment, and follow with a pause, producing a throbbing effect" (605). This throbbing effect, of course, is one of the defining characteristics of ragtime, although not limited to it. It is a source of the constancy and rhythmic inevitability of African-American music. The folk basis of ragtime recalls Holcombe's (1861, 626) comment about handkerchief-flaunting in nineteenth-century folk dancing, which is intriguing and provocative with regard to the naming of ragtime. Contrary to early-twentieth-century reports that ragtime got its name from its "ragged rhythms,"[9] I believe that the music was named, by its black makers, after the customary practice of the "flaunting" of handkerchiefs (the black folk called them "rags").[10] This practice of "flaunting" rags, together with the blacks' practice of calling their dancing "ragging" and giving the name "rags" to the performances of tunes to which they danced, as we learn from Hughes (1899, 158), constitute coincidences too powerful and convincing to ignore.

9. For discussion related to this, see Berlin (1980, 11–13).

10. The flaunting of "rags" while dancing was widespread in nineteenth-century Afro-America. In St. Louis, for example, the premier center for ragtime in the late nineteenth and early twentieth centuries, rags—"usually stolen from a clothes line"—were hoisted to signal a dance—thus rag time. "It was not long before the Shake Raggers' dances became known all over St. Louis" ("Origin of Ragtime" 1901, 7). Even Scott Joplin succumbed to the prevailing conventional wisdom that ragtime was so-called because of its "ragged" rhythm, saying that "it suggests something like that" (quoted in "Scott Joplin" 1907, 5).

The structural similarity between nineteenth-century marches and African-American folk songs and instrumentals helped facilitate the syncretization that would take place to create classic ragtime, which is characterized by the multimetric patterns over a straight bass.[11] The resulting polyrhythmic configurations were new to Western music, as were melodies based on gapped scales and the use of what I have elsewhere called "melodic compositional complexes" (Floyd and Reisser 1984, 47), such as ♫♪ and ♪♫. The multimetric patterns and the gapped scales clearly derive from African and African-American folk performance styles. The compositional complexes, while not seen in the music of the ring, nevertheless were used almost exclusively by black ragtimers, rarely by white imitators. The fusion of these traits with the unyielding structure of the march would result in classic ragtime music, a genre—a "mulatto text," Gates would say—possessed of an artistic power that transcended the expressive potentials of the two forms that were merged.

By the turn of the century, several "schools" or centers of ragtime existed, the most important of which were St. Louis and Sedalia in the Midwest; New Orleans in the South; and Baltimore, Philadelphia, and Washington, D.C., in the East. Holding forth in St. Louis and Sedalia were Scott Joplin, Scott Hayden, Arthur Marshall, Tom Turpin, Louis Chauvin, and others who composed classic rags and performed them in a rather controlled but vigorous style. In New Orleans, Jelly Roll Morton, Alfred Wilson, Sore Dick, Drag Nasty, and Black Pete were the masters of a style that was largely improvised, with its roots more firmly grounded in the folk-rag tradition. On the East Coast, the legendary Jack the Bear, One-Leg Shadow, and Charles Luckeyeth "Luckey" Roberts were in charge, playing a style that in a decade or two would be transformed into stride.

The ragtime of New Orleans and the East Coast had a significant impact on American music, as can be seen in Morton's career and in the eventual development of stride piano from East Coast ragtime in New York City. But it was the ragtime of the St. Louis school, led by Scott Joplin (1877–1931), that had the greatest initial impact and attracted the widest attention. Joplin formalized folk-rag procedures in 1899 when he published "Original Rags" (1898) and started the worldwide ragtime craze with his "Maple Leaf Rag" (1899).[12] Of the two, "Original Rags" is the more folksy and, in some ways, the more rhythmically complex. This optimistic, festive-sounding piece is lyrical in some strains and rhythmically complex in others. It contains the harmonic parallelism that can be found in African music, but its basic materials come from

11. The straight bass probably derived from the foot-tapping, hand-clapping trope of African-American music, in spite of its similarity to its counterpart in the American march. But the presence of the pattern in both genres made for great troping and, thereby, for easy and fluid syncretization.

12. Joplin's own piano-roll renditions of these two rags, the first he issued, can be heard on *Jazz*, vol. 2 (1953) and on the *Smithsonian Collection of Classic Jazz* (1973).

the African-American folk tradition. Joplin transforms these materials by making use of elements of the cakewalk and other minstrel practices as well as traditional piano performance techniques. As with classic ragtime generally, "Original Rags" is structured in sixteen-measure sections as follows: Introduction A A B B C C A D D E E.

Although folk elements are at its base and serve as Joplin's compositional point of departure, "Maple Leaf Rag" is more complex and sophisticated than "Original Rags" and moves farther away from the folk tradition. Joplin's published ragtime music straddles two adjacent centuries, standing firmly in nineteenth-century fashion and manner while introducing the expressions that would be utilized, modified, and eventually superseded in later years. For example, "Original Rags" is certainly a nineteenth-century product, looking, as it does, toward black folk culture; but "Wall Street Rag" (1909), in spite of its folk-rag feeling, is twentieth century in outlook, style, substance, and implication—a programmatic piece, experimental in sound and intent, with tone clusters and a subject matter (the financial district) that expresses the present and points to the future.

Interesting relations exist between ragtime music and dance. The following list of dances contained in the 1902 edition of Joplin's "The Ragtime Dance," a cycle of ten dance pieces, make it clear that the two forms were related on the level of social dance.

Ragtime Dance	Rag Two Step
Cakewalk Dance	Back Step Prance
Slow Drag	Dude Walk
Clean Up Dance	Stop Time
Jennie Cooler Dance	Sedidus Walk

The slow drag, cakewalk, rag two-step, and all the rest were popular dances at the turn of the century, particularly in black culture—the slow drag, for example, emerged from the jook houses of the rural South. This listing recalls the inextricable binding of black music and black dance in the Dance, Drum, and Song of African and African-American ring ritual and its persistence in activity outside the ring. This binding persevered in folk and classic ragtime, defining the music as black by its very presence; for in its heyday, ragtime—even in its classic form—was dance music, and it remained dance music even after African Americans turned their attention from it to a different form of dance music and music making, leaving ragtime to white imitators.

Back in slavery, Trickster had been playing a rather benign role, frolicking as Br'er Rabbit or some other animal in the ring games and rhyme dances of enslaved and free blacks. Unlike his African counterpart, in his American incarnation Trickster was more mischievous than vicious, more victim than aggressor, more helpful than destructive (Abrahams 1983, 155–156). In this more gentle role, he simply outwitted his stronger opponents when they threatened or tried to oppress him. Trickster's divine incarnation as one of the African gods did not survive the Middle Passage to North America, but he was reincarnated in some parts of the Americas in a form that contained Esu's more malevolent traits—that is, as Legba, the Devil. In Latin America, as Eshu, or Ellegua, he was associated with both Jesus and the Devil—as both originator and settler of quarrels (Jahn 1961, 63). Probably brought in this form to North America in the early nineteenth century by slaves imported from the Caribbean, this new incarnation of Esu as the Devil took hold as he emerged at the crossroads sometime in the late nineteenth century to deliver superior creative skills to black songsters, and exerted a powerful influence on the development of the blues, which would become ascendant following Emancipation.

There is a Yoruba legend about the crossroads that is relevant here:

> At a crossroads in the history of the Yoruba gods, when each wished to find out who, under God, was supreme, all the deities made their way to heaven, each bearing a rich sacrificial offering on his or her head. All save one. Eshu-Elegbara, wisely honoring beforehand the deity of divination with a sacrifice, had been told by him what to bring to heaven—a single crimson parrot feather (*ekodide*), positioned upright upon his forehead, to signify that he was not to carry burdens on his head. Responding to the fiery flashing of the parrot feather, the very seal of supernatural force and *àshe*, God granted Eshu the force to make all things happen and multiply. (Thompson 1983, 18)

It was with this leave and this power that Legba appeared in African-American culture at the crossroads. By this time, the guitar had become widely used by African-American songsters. It became the instrument of choice for bluesmen, superseding the violin and the banjo, and it also became the instrument of blues legend, as is made clear by this excerpt from an African-American tale, the events of which take place, again, at a crossroads ("a fork in the road"):

> Sit down there and play your best piece, thinking of and wishing for the devil all the while. By and by you will hear music, dim at first but growing louder and louder as the musician approaches nearer. Do not look around; just keep on playing your guitar. The unseen musician will finally sit down by you and play in unison with you. After a time you will feel something tugging at your instrument. . . . Let the devil take it and keep thumping along with your fingers as if you still had a guitar in your hands. Then the devil will hand you his instrument to play and will accompany you on yours. After doing this for a time he will seize your fingers and trim the nails until they bleed, finally tak-

73

ing his guitar back and returning your own. Keep on playing; do not look around. His music will become fainter and fainter as he moves away. When all is quiet you may go home. You will be able to play any piece you desire on the guitar and you can do anything you want to do in this world, but you have sold your eternal soul to the devil and are his in the world to come. (Puckett 1926, 554)

This African-American legend seems to me remarkably consonant with, and a logical extension of, the Yoruba myth–an embroidered and African-Americanized revision of it. In the context of African and African-American mythology, such an event can be accepted simply as being in the order of things; and in the first thirty years of the twentieth century, African cultural memory was vivid. This myth engaged the imagination of Robert Johnson, Tommy Johnson, Peetie Wheatstraw, and other bluesmen who would, in turn, perpetuate it in their life-styles and in their music. Robert Johnson became obsessed with and fatalistic about "the forces against him," eloquently expressing this obsession and fatalism in "Hell-Hound on My Trail," "Crossroads Blues," and "Me and the Devil Blues" (Barlow 1989, 49; Palmer 1981, 127). In Robert Johnson's blues, the Devil is a trickster, "the ultimate trickster," according to Barlow (49). Tommy Johnson, who arrived at a crossroads at midnight under a full moon, also met the trickster there—again disguised as the Devil—and developed an act in which he took pride in being in league with him, in "having a covenant with him" (Barlow, 41; Palmer, 113). Peetie Wheatstraw boasted of being "the Devil's son-in-law." But it is not Esu as the Devil that is the point here; it is Esu as Trickster—in his role as guardian and inspirer of the art of interpretation, as "ultimate master of potentiality" with "the force to make all things happen and multiply" (Thompson 1983, 19, 18)—who figures most importantly in this legend, for it is Esu who triumphs, bringing to American soil a new mode of musical expression based in the primal force of Dance, Drum, and Song.

The blues is a solo manifestation of the values of the ring, possessing similar cathartic, affirming, and restorative powers. For African Americans, Esu's appearance as the Devil at the crossroads affirmed African custom and tradition, an affirmation so vital to their spiritual survival that they treasured the memory of this trickster and behaved as if the legend were true long after they had stopped believing it, as evidenced, as we have seen, by the music and the statements of bluesmen such as Robert Johnson, Tommy Johnson, and Peetie Wheatstraw. Armed with the elements of the ring and the interpretive gifts of Esu, early bluesmen brought a new music into the twentieth century.

Musically, the blues probably took its most significant features from the calls, cries, and hollers of field slaves and street vendors and from the spirituals of brush harbors and church houses. It is a remarkable manifestation of some of the primary features of African and African-American song expression, making wide use of call-and-response figures, elisions, repeated short phrases, falling and pendular thirds, timbral distortions, ululations, vocables, hums, moans, and other devices typical of music derived from the ring.

The impetus, tone, and emotional quality of the blues may have come from Senegambia. Michael Coolen (1991, 3) has shown, for example, that Senegambians suffered inordinately from the slave trade, due to their convenient proximity to the Senegal and Gambia rivers, on which "slave factories" were located and where slave ships arrived to pick up human cargo. The consequent large concentration of Senegambian slaves in America, he believes, is the reason for the structural and tonal similarities between the blues and the Senegambian *fodet*, which (1) uses cyclical form, with phrases played or sung to "an alternated use of tonic and secondary tonal centers," (2) commonly has an A A B text structure, (3) makes use of a vocal practice in which the song begins on a high pitch and "gradually moves to lower pitches at the end," and (4) contains a low level of virtuosity, with the option of a "hot" performance always available (16). This description, obviously, could be applied as accurately to the blues.

As far as instruments are concerned, prototypes of the banjo and the fiddle, ubiquitous in slave culture, were in prominent use among Senegambian musicians in the eighteenth and nineteenth centuries. The model for the bluesmen may have been the Senegambian *gewels* (griots), "entertainers who play for dances, do acrobatics, tell stories, pose riddles for members of the audience to solve," and, like many African-American songsters and instrumentalists, "pride themselves on being able to provide the appropriate music for any situation" (Coolen 1991, 9). Also like the early bluesmen, the *gewels* had to do work outside music to make their living (8).

Whether or not the bluesmen took the *gewel* for their model, the model was African. The delivery and performance style of bluesmen recall Bebey's ([1969] 1975) description of African voices, which I quoted in chapter 1. The African-American bluesman, with his own unusual sonorities, rough and hoarse voice, laughter, and pain, also does his own reflecting, laughing and suffering as he goes, looking to the future:

> Woke up early in the morning : blues all round my bed (repeat)
> And the blues ain't there : they easing everywhere
>
> If I feel tomorrow : like I feel today (repeat)
> Going to pack my suitcase : get me down the road somewhere
>
> And I'm going I'm going : your crying won't make me stay (repeat)
> And I won't be there : just won't blow back anywhere
>
> If I feel tomorrow : like I feel today (repeat)
> Going to ride till sundown : tomorrow catch me there

> And its one of these mornings : honey it won't be long (repeat)
> You will call for me : and I'll be a thousand miles from home.[13]
>
> ("Papa Long Blues," in Taft 1983, 225)

Whatever their African source, early blues melodies were based on a pentatonic arrangement that included blue notes—or the potential for blue notes—on the third and fifth degrees of its scale. As the same neutral intervals are found in the music of some African societies, the blues intonation was not new to African Americans; it was new and strange only to those who were not in tune with the culture. Early blues was as free as the other African-American genres, only later becoming tamed and forced into the eight-, twelve-, and sixteen-bar frameworks that became somewhat common.

The lyrics of the blues were acquired from two primary sources: from life as the singer saw it, lived it, and survived it, and from the "traveling" lyrics of African-American culture (Barlow 1989, 4). They represent a wide expressive spectrum, spanning "proverbial wisdom, folk philosophy, political commentary, ribald humor, elegiac lament, and much more" (Baker 1984, 5), including satire; they describe social phenomena and treat romantic relationships. Unlike the spiritual—a communal testimony oriented toward the next world—the blues song is a personal statement about an individual's view of his or her current circumstances. Blues singers composed their songs by combining fragments and verses from the hundreds or thousands of formulas that were floating around in black communities everywhere, spread by the traveling songsters. Black creativity combined these fragments with African-American performance practices, transforming them into original works of musical poetry.

The blues, as they emerged during or after Reconstruction, were a way of coping with the new trials and realizations brought by freedom. There were blues songs about voodoo, estrangement, sex, protest, bad luck, deceit, war, joblessness, sickness, love, health, evil, revenge, railroading, and a variety of other life experiences, some sad, others not. These tropes express, in text and in tune, the variety of struggles and fulfillments of African-American life in their new manifestations. African Americans were no longer bemoaning their condition in the disguised lament and protest of the spirituals, which sang of escape from the tribulations of this life into the next, because following Emancipation, death was no longer a release from slavery. As the blues poet sang:

> Oh-oh: death is awful
> Oh-oh: death is awful

76   13. "Papa Long Blues" was recorded by the Memphis Jug Band on their album *Memphis Jug Band* (1928).

Oh-oh: death is awful
Spare me over, another year.
(Sackheim 1975, 25)

In common with the spiritual, though, the blues was full of implication, albeit secular:

Went to Church, put my hand on the seat
Lady sat on it, said: "Daddy you sure is sweet,
        Mr. diddie wa diddie
        Mr. diddie wa diddie"
I wish somebody would tell me what diddie wa diddie means.
(Sackheim 1975, 29)

The similarities between the blues and the spiritual have often been remarked. Harry T. Burleigh said after the turn of the century that "the blues and spirituals are first cousins" (quoted in Handy 1941, 163). And James Weldon Johnson ([1930] 1977) commented, "Indeed, the blues are as essentially folk-songs as the spirituals. In the one the Negro expresses his religious reactions to hopes of a blissful life hereafter; in the other he expresses his secular and profane reaction to the ills of the present existence" (228).

The blues recognized and represented independence, autonomy, a certain amount of liberation, and release from the oppression of slavery. According to Barlow (1989), bluesmen "acted as proselytizers of a gospel of secularization in which belief in freedom became associated with personal mobility—freedom of movement in this world here and now, rather than salvation later on in the next" (5). In black culture, this freedom of movement was symbolized by songsters traveling rural roads with guitars on their backs; it was epitomized by the railroad train. For fretting parents, the passenger car was the primary means of relocating one's family to a less hostile and oppressive environment; for songsters, the freight was a means of getting from a turpentine camp to a jook[14] miles away. They sang about these trains and imitated them with mouth harp and guitar—hence the trope of the train and train whistle in blues music. The words and the music of blues songs express both the profundities and the trivialities of the black experience in America.

Ronald Davis (1980) has provided an effective description of the lyrics of early blues songs:

Lyrics were harshly realistic and directly related to everyday life. Like the work songs, country blues was almost sung speech. The delta vocal style tended to

14. Hazzard-Gordon (1990) defines "jook" or "juke joint" as a place "of social interaction and entertainment . . . rooted in West African traditions that intertwined religious and secularized elements," where music-making, dancing, drinking, and, sometimes, gambling take place (76, 77, 79).

> be hard and unrelenting, producing rough, growling tones, although the falsetto was frequently employed for contrast. Blues singers elsewhere moaned, hollered, murmured, or declaimed. "Blue" notes were produced by sliding up to tones. The melodic range in country blues was limited, while accompaniment was simple, initially limited to tonic, subdominant, and dominant chords, used in prescribed arrangement. "Breaks" at the end of each line permitted improvisation on the accompanying instrument and time during which the singer could interject asides, such as "Oh Lawdy!" (202)

In the moans, hollers, hums, falsetto, and elisions that Davis mentions, together with the timbre of the guitar and harp—distorted by bottleneck and hand-muffling, respectively—the heterogeneous sound ideal was realized in the blues, revealing the derivation of the music from spirituals and the ring, even down to the use of "Oh, Lawdy" in a musical form that is, from the standpoint of Christianity, unabashedly profane. And the improvisatory potential revealed in Davis's description prefigures jazz and confirms the presence of melodic extemporization in the African-American musical arsenal. Of course, he says nothing about sadness or lamentation, traits that have been exaggerated—by well-meaning promoters of the black social cause and by not-so-well meaning record producers—to such a degree that it is commonly thought that the expressive range of the blues is limited to that one quality. Followers of the blues know that much of its repertoire is optimistic, some of it violent, some of it romantic, and some merely descriptive; and, while no blues recordings were made in the nineteenth century, it is logical to assume that this wide, expressive range was characteristic even then.

Having surpassed in importance and effectiveness the spirituals and the "slave seculars" of pre-Emancipation Afro-America, the blues were central to what Barlow (1989) has called "the indigenous communication system" of the culture (3). As a communication system, the blues, as had the spirituals earlier, spoke in code—a semantic code that now included euphemisms for sex such as Bessie Smith's "deep sea diver," "black snake," "ain't no more 'taters: the frost have killed the vine," and so on. But the blues also spoke a musical code in which, according to Baker (1984), "the harmonica's whoop and the guitar's bass can recapitulate vast dimensions of experience" and in which the guitar's "growling vamp" signifies something other than what it speaks of (5–6). In short, instrumental blues spoke a musical code decipherable by knowers of the culture but inaccessible to those outside it. It is this code and its interpretation that links the blues to other black modes of expression. The code itself is interpretive, traditionally taught to blues people by Esu, the African god of interpretation and connector of the people to their African past.

The blues was a new expression, created by a people coming to grips with the changes wrought by the onset of Reconstruction and the dawning of a new century. As the genre developed, certain musical elements of the ring became so prominent that they emerged as primary tropes, and other genres began to borrow heavily from it. Since the blues appears to be basic to most forms of black music, and since it seems to be the most prominent factor in maintaining continuity between most of them, we might think of it as the Urtrope of the tradition.

In the turn-of-the-century development of the poetry and music of the blues, Charley Patton (1887–1934) and Charles "Buddy" Bolden (1887–1931) were seminal figures, creating blues and jazz styles consonant with black thought and expression. Patton's recording of the "Devil Sent the Rain Blues" (1929) is a good example of his commanding presence and delivery. This twelve-bar, carefully arranged, and effectively accompanied rendition comments on restlessness, sex, and travel, with Patton making use of the elisions, blue notes, and register jumps common to ring-derived music. Bolden was known by those who heard him play the trumpet as a "rough" musician who "played nothing but blues and all that stink music, and he played it very loud" (Stoddard 1971, 16). Bolden's style probably was earthy, hard, and sensual, coming directly from blues, ragtime, and other black secular and sacred music, contrasting sharply with the society bands that were plentiful in New Orleans in his lifetime. The ring elements that stood out in his style probably drew from some quarters the same reactions as had the shout—accusations of being "barbaric, "lewd," and "lascivious." But Bolden's combining of these elements with the stylistic traits of other emerging genres may have contributed to the tremendous positive impression he had on black culture through his influence on subsequent masters of the trumpet such as Bunk Johnson, King Oliver, Freddie Keppard, and, eventually, Louis Armstrong.

As it entered the twentieth century, the blues had emerged from a long line of development that had begun on southern plantations. Robert Palmer (1981), describing blues life on and around the Dockery Plantation in the Mississippi Delta, allows a former Dockery bluesman to present a scenario that shares its essentials with scenes common all over the South in the early decades of the twentieth century:

> On Saturday afternoons everybody would go into town and those fellows like Charley Patton, Robert Johnson, and Howlin' Wolf would be playin' on the streets, standin' by the railroad tracks, people pitchin' 'em nickels and dimes, white and black people both. The train come through town maybe once that afternoon, and when it was time, everybody would gather around just to see that train pull up. They'd play around there, before and after the train came, and announce where they'd be that night. And that's where the crowd would go.
>
> They'd have a plank nailed across the door to the kitchen and be sellin' fish and chitlins, with dancin' in the front room, gamblin' in the side room, and

maybe two or three gas or coal-oil lamps on the mantelpiece in front of the mirror—powerful light. It was in different people's houses, no clubs or nothin'. (61–62)

The earliest great southern blues musicians for whom we have good documentation are Blind Lemon Jefferson (1897–1929) of the Texas tradition and Charley Patton of the Delta, both of whom were seminal figures. But there were others, too, of singular influence, of whom Leadbelly (Huddie Ledbetter [1888–1949]) and Mississippi John Hurt (1893–1966) were among the most versatile and original. They all had in common the vocal quality and variations in timbre that make the genre distinctive: the nasal, foggy, hoarse texture that delivered the elisions, hums, growls, blue notes, and falsetto, and the percussive oral effects of their ancestors. Instrumentally, these bluesmen followed the African tradition of timbral distortion: the guitar players applied bottle necks and knife blades to the strings of their instruments to modify their naturally produced sounds; the mouth-harp players produced variations in timbre and volume by alternately blowing and sucking and, with their cupped fingers and palms, covering and uncovering the air columns of their instruments. Unfortunately, there exist no examples of country blues performances before the 1920s, but recordings from that decade can give us a good idea of what the early styles sounded like.

Mississippi John Hurt's "Big Leg Blues," recorded in 1929, contains five vocal stanzas of twelve measures each, with instrumental interludes of 12, 12, 12 + 8, and 8 measures. Tonic, subdominant, and dominant chords are used exclusively, supporting a melody in which there is considerable tonic–leading-tone interplay, with descending movement and off-beats at phrase endings. The melody is of small compass, carrying a text that comments on and makes allusions to sex, rejection, and skin-color distinctions. The melody is laid over a ragtime-inspired guitar accompaniment and delivered in the typical heterogeneous texture of the blues voice, with the requisite vocables, elisions, and moans uttered in the quiet, sensual approach typical of the Mississippi Moaners.

The year before Hurt recorded "Big Leg Blues," Rubin "Rube" Lacy had recorded "Ham Hound Crave," in which an ersatz twelve-bar structure and an ostinato-like guitar accompaniment, consistent with boogie-woogie bass, form the framework onto which are set elisions, blue notes, one responsorial comment, and a text that makes reference to items of southern soul food such as chitlins and hamhocks. Men such as Hurt and Lacy were important to the establishment and elaboration of the blues and to black-culture entertainment in the 1920s. But compared with the women, they performed in relative obscurity. As we shall see, it was the female singer who had the public appeal and nonthreatening countenance and behavior requisite for success in the more intimate new nightclub settings.

In the trickster tale "Buh Rabbit in Red Hill Churchyard," collected from among black South Carolinians by E. C. L. Adams (1928), probably in the 1920s, a remarkable musical performance occurs:

> Dat mockin' bird an' dat rabbit—Lord, dey had chunes floatin' all 'round on de night air. Dey could stand a chune on end, grab it up an' throw it away an' ketch it an' bring it back an' hold it; and make dem chunes sound like dey was strugglin' to get away one minute, an' de next dey sound like sumpin' gittin' up close an' whisperin'. (172)

This remarkable description of musical animal tricksters in action, in which Sterling Stuckey (1987, 18–19) has recognized the resemblance of Br'er Mockingbird's whistled song to jazz improvisation, confirms that jazz in its beginnings was as much a rural as an urban phenomenon, flourishing economically only when it became part of the urban entertainment scene. And the fact that the activity being described in the churchyard tale is first of all a burial shout suggests that jazz has deep roots in burial-ring ritual. Furthermore, the fact that in nineteenth-century South Carolina the mourners who attended a certain black funeral were gathered "around a coffin singing songs and clapping their hands and singing lively songs on their return from the grave site" (Barr 1883, 1222) suggests that the up-tempo playing of hymns and spirituals on the return from a burial is not just a New Orleans tradition, but was practiced in other places as well and may have been widespread in the nineteenth century.

In New Orleans, as in other cities, African Americans practiced ring ceremonies, accompanied funeral processions with marching bands, and organized secret societies. Some aspects of these activities merged to help create the environment for and the character of the music that would be called jazz. And in spite of the fact that the presence of marching bands and secret societies among African Americans is usually attributed by some scholars—in conversation, at least—to European influences, they are as much African as they are European, and the primary influences on black jazzmen were most likely the African antecedents. A drawing in a book published in England in 1824 shows a marching band in Africa in ritual ceremony, with the author explaining that

> firing and drinking palm wine were the only divertissements to the ceremony of the caboceers presenting themselves to the King; they were announced, and passed all around the circle saluting every umbrella: their bands preceded; we

reckoned above forty drums in that of the King of Dwabin. (Bowdich [1819] 1966, 275)

The drawing shows at least one band with trumpets. As for the secret societies, I have already noted their presence in Africa before the slave trade, and the existence of African secret societies has long been known among some folklore scholars in the United States. For example, N. N. Puckett (1926) reports that "the chief recreations of the natives of Angola are marriages and funerals" and goes on to say that

> the African is intensely social and occasions of this sort as well as palavers, se̱ret societies and other meetings offer a chance for gathering together in crowds and making an inconceivable hubbub, which to them is as much self-gratification as self-perpetuation or any other basic societal activity. Precisely the same thing holds true with the rural Southern Negro. (77)

Puckett confirms not only that Africans had secret societies but, by implication, that the practice was transplanted from Africa to North America.

Whatever the direction of these influences, New Orleans had several black marching bands as early as 1860, all of which played parades for secret societies:

> Thomas S. Kelly's, Charlie Jaeger's, Frank Dodson's, Louis Martin's, Vinet's, Wolf's and Richardson's. The most famous of them was Sylvester Decker's Excelsior Brass Band. When the band members appeared in a parade in 1879 in their blue Prussian-styled uniforms and long-plumed hats, the *Louisianan* claimed that "everywhere they appeared their approach was heralded with murmurs of admiration." Playing at conventions, in parades, at parties, dances, and funerals, these bands created what is now known as jazz. (Blassingame 1973, 140)

This quotation underscores what is well known: that there were several black bands in New Orleans by the middle of the nineteenth century and that they played for funerals. Although Blassingame's claim that these bands invented jazz is specious, the successors of these bands at the turn of the century and later were numerous, and they did play jazz, or a precursor of it. Bunk Johnson, who was active as a New Orleans bandsman in the first decade of the twentieth century, has given an insider's account of a band's participation in a funeral:

> On the way to the cemetery with an Odd Fellow or a Mason—they always [were] buried with music you see—we would always use slow, slow numbers such as "Nearer My God to Thee," "Flee as a Bird to the Mountains," "Come Thee Disconsolate." We would use almost any 4/4, played very slow; they walked very slow behind the body.
> After we would get to the cemetery, and after that particular person were put away, the band would come on to the front, out of the graveyard. . . . And

then we'd march away from the cemetery by the snare drum only until we got about a block or two blocks from the cemetery. Then we'd go right into ragtime.

We would play "Didn't He Ramble," or we'd take all of those spiritual hymns and turn them into ragtime—2/4 movements, you know, step lively everybody. "Didn't He Ramble," "When the Saints Go Marching In," that good old piece "Ain't Gonna Study War No More," and several others we would have and we'd play them just for that effect.

We would have a second line there that was most equivalent to King Rex parade—Mardi Gras Carnival parade. The police were unable to keep the second line back—all in the street, all on the sidewalks, in front of the band, and behind the lodge, in front of the lodge. We'd have some immense crowds following. (quoted in Leonard 1987, 76–77)

And no wonder: cultural and "motor" memories of the mass, circle, and line dances of African societies and of slave culture were operative. The second line, for example, was not a new invention. As I pointed out in chapter 1, Akan children watch and imitate their elders in ring ceremonies, moving "along the fringes of the ring and behind it" (Nketia 1963, 165–166), as do the children, youth, and adults in the second line of New Orleans jazz funerals.

This mythic call to Dance, Drum, and Song in the form of parades goes back to the African processions I mentioned earlier—in this case, with trumpets and drums—and back to the burial rites of Africans and African-American slaves so beautifully portrayed by Br'er Rabbit and Br'er Mockingbird in the tale "Buh Rabbit in Red Hill Churchyard." From these ceremonies, because of the necessity of the participants to move to a remote destination, the ring straightened to become the second line Bunk Johnson described in his account; and the change from the slow dirge to the shout spiritual on the return remarkably mimics the walk-to-shout, slow-to-quick progression of the ring shout. There can be no mistaking the fact that the beginnings of jazz in the ring—as partial as it may have been—was a direct result of the transference of the structure and character of the shout to the funeral parades of black bands and community participants. What Johnson did not describe, beyond indicating that hymns and spirituals were played, is the nature of the music itself. But Br'er Rabbit and Br'er Mockingbird have already done that for us, and anyone who has ever seen the "return" portion of a New Orleans jazz funeral can vouch for the authenticity of the description in "Buh Rabbit in Red Hill Churchyard." Bunk Johnson's description was of a New Orleans event, but Eubie Blake reported identical events held in Baltimore (in Leonard 1987, 77), and the bandleader Leonard Bowden, who died in 1989 at more than ninety years of age, told me that such events also took place in Mobile, Alabama, when he was growing up there.

I do not claim here that jazz developed *only* in African-American funeral parades. Naturally, this music was performed wherever black bands played— at picnics, parties, dances, and other events. What I am saying is that the impetus for the development of this music was ritual, the ring ritual of transplanted Africans extended and elaborated through spirituals and folk rags. They converged in the ring—these spirituals and this ragtime—and awaited the blues, which joined them directly. In these early jazz funerals were found the tropes of the ring, including the heterogeneous sound ideal, which was creatively extended in the form of two rhythmic groups: the front line of cornet, clarinet, and trombone and a rhythm section of drums and tuba (which would include piano and banjo when the bands moved indoors):

> The timbral independence of these instruments is clear. The practice of collective improvisation, whereby all three front-line instruments improvised simultaneously, created a musical texture that highlighted the timbral mosaic-like quality of the ensemble. This development was highly significant because it created a new paradigm—a distinctly African-American means of realizing a fundamentally African idea. This paradigm, in turn, then spawned its own modifications. (Wilson 1992a, 336)

Clearly, the instrumentation of early jazz bands resulted from the preferences of transplanted Africans for the heterogeneous sound ideal. African Americans did not select these instruments because they represented European band sections, but because (1) they were available, (2) the musicians had experience playing them, and (3) they conformed to and could satisfy the musicians' sonic expectations. Everything I have said about Africans' and African Americans' sonic preferences supports these conclusions. The fact that the instruments were European helped to make the syncretism that resulted from their use more easily achievable. In a sense, then, the instruments were "makeshift," or "found."

The first documented jazz musician was the legendary Buddy Bolden, whom I mentioned in discussing the blues. He was a New Orleans trumpeter reputed to have had a powerful and unique sound based in ragtime and blues. We know that Bolden's band was active in 1897, that he had attained citywide fame by 1890, and that "he played all over town for different strata of black society and for every conceivable function," performing in Lincoln and Johnson parks, at Odd Fellows and Funky Butt halls, on "advertising wagons, at picnic excursions, and parties," and in other locations (Marquis 1978, 56). And we know that he and his sidemen engaged in "cutting" contests with the John Robichaux Orchestra, which did not play ragtime, blues, or jazz! Louis Jones, who was a close friend of Bolden, claimed that Bolden's band

> was the first to play the hard blues and jazz for dancing. Had a good band. Strictly ear band. . . . John Robichaux had a real reading band, but Buddy used

to kill Robichaux anywhere he went. When he'd parade he'd take the people with him all the way down Canal Street. Always looked good. When he bought a cornet he'd shine it up and make it glisten like a woman's leg. (quoted in Ondaatje 1979, [5])

In spite of Johnson's statement that Bolden's band was strictly an "ear band," there is evidence to the contrary (Marquis 1978, 106). The Bolden band members improvised, but they also read music. In his blues-tinged, ragtime-inspired, unique improvisations Bolden continued the legacy of the ring, perceived and exploited the existing means of expressing it, and at the same time must have developed ways of communicating the newly emerging values of the period between Emancipation and the turn of the century.

The erotic character of early jazz has been much remarked. This is not surprising, given the reactions of earlier observers who considered the shout to be debased (for example, Godwyn 1680, 33). It was, in fact, erotic, its eroticism based in African cultural memory and the behavioral continuity of the ring. As Lomax (1975) wrote about the Pygmy song and dance, "the twisting pelvic style (and its reflection in hot rhythm) infuses African work and play with a steady feed of pleasurable stimuli" (50) because this erotic content supports the need for fertility and sexual prowess and helps prepare young people for their polygynous life-style. The references to the twisting pelvis and hot rhythm certainly describe the infectious quality of jazz, as well as dancers' and listeners' reaction to it. It is a legacy of the African tradition, in which the style encourages and invites "eroticizing participation from all present" (50). (Perhaps Esu is at it again: he does have "great phallic powers and can give or take away virility from any man" [Gonzáles-Wippler 1985, 30].)

From my examination of the syncretic process as it occurred in nineteenth-century America, I conclude that the emerging African-American genres were not formed by the insertion of African performance practices into the formal structures of European music, as the conventional wisdom would have it, but were molded in a process that superimposed European forms on the rich and simmering foundation of African religious beliefs and practices. The foundation of the new syncretized music was African, not European.

The late nineteenth century saw the appearance of cheap, popularized printed versions of black music, prepared and published for the uninitiated and for the gain of profiteers. Ragtime, for example, became associated in the public mind with the image of a white or black piano player—decked out in a straw hat, a white or striped long-sleeve shirt with garters at the elbows, and a bow tie, with a cigar in his mouth or between his fingers—beating out vapid but toe-tapping versions of the real thing. The multimeter of folk and classic ragtime was reduced to simple syncopation, and its polyrhythms, so vital to the

85

genre, disappeared. Spirituals were replaced by pseudo-spirituals and Euro-peanized versions in which the sincere emotional quality of the former was presented as mere sentimentality. Some of the most vital qualities of black folk music were lost or suppressed, and the real thing remained outside the com-mercially profitable, far-reaching cultural marketplace.

Meanwhile, the songsters, "musicianers," and "physicianers" of the late nineteenth century kept secular folk music alive in Afro-America, as they per-formed functions similar to those of the Senegambian *gewel,* singing and play-ing blues, ballads, and social, comic, and rhyme songs for dances and other functions (Small 1987, 195). The itinerant bluesmen and other folk singers, the rag and barrelhouse pianists, the banjo and mouth-harp players, and the jug- and string-band musicians were giving early shape to African-American secular song and were playing a large role in determining the directions African-American music would take.

CHAPTER **4**

African-American Modernism, Signifyin(g), and Black Music

Watch the Chameleon: it treads ever so carefully, and it can make itself hard to see.
South African Proverb

Rationalism in order to save the truth, renounces life.
José Ortega y Gasset

In *Modernism and the Harlem Renaissance* (1987), literature scholar Houston Baker marks September 18, 1895, as the beginning of African-American modernism, and he takes as its triggering event Booker T. Washington's opening address at the Negro exhibit of the Atlanta Cotton States and International Exposition. He bases his attribution on Washington's adroitness with the minstrel mask in announcing a plan of action, acceptable to both whites and blacks, that would ensure that a large portion of the nation's black citizens would get an industrial education. Baker defines the actual minstrel mask as "a space of habitation" in which resides, among other things, the denial of the humanity of Africans and their descendants. He views the minstrel mask as a "governing object" in a ritual of *non-sense*, which mandates that blacks "meld with minstrel's contours"; it is a mask of selective memory, misappropriating from the core culture elements of common use and "fashioning them into a comic array" (20, 21). The original, actual minstrel mask was used to remind

whites of African Americans' ostensible lack of humanity, their supposed irresponsibility, and their willingness to accept ill treatment. Baker contends that it was necessary for any African American who would be heard and taken seriously by whites in the 1890s to communicate through a discursive, verbally rhetorical manifestation of the mask. Hence, Booker T. Washington's stance and his success at Tuskegee.

According to Baker (1987) the "wearers" of this metaphorical mask manipulated its figures in order to turn it and its sounds into negotiable discursive currency. For behind this discursive version of the mask, black users of it made power plays; this use of the mask was their only intellectual recourse at the time. It was a "liberating manipulation of masks" that allowed Washington to succeed, "his mind [always] fixed on some intended gain, on a [rhetorical] *mastery* . . . that leads to Afro-American advancement" (25, 31–32). In this way, he achieved "an effective modernity" (36), and his behavior was liberating. It was this mastery of the mask by Washington, Charles Waddell Chesnutt, and other turn-of-the-century black leaders that constituted "a primary move in Afro-American discursive modernism" (17).

Against the mastery of the mask, Baker (1987) sets "the deformation of mastery," a technique used by spokespersons whose entirely different rhetoric found an entirely different kind of economic support and created a different kind of liberation. Frederick Douglass, W. E. B. Du Bois, Paul Laurence Dunbar, and Richard Wright are the examples here. Their primary tool was phaneric display[1]—in this case, "the coding of African, tribal, or social sounds as active, outgoing resistance and response to oppressive ignorance and silencing" (104). A statement such as "Don't never let *nobody* hit you more than once" (Sonya Sanchez, quoted in Baker, 103) is a guerrilla tactic, a liberating strategy designed to "ameliorate desire or to secure material advantage" (105). This phaneric approach does not mask, in the sense of concealing; it displays, advertises, secures advantage, and enhances survival. It *deforms* the mask and its mastery by displaying distinguishing and subversive codes, refusing and defusing the non-sense of the minstrel mask. According to Baker, Washington's mastery was based on the fictions of minstrelsy, while Du Bois's deformation, for example, was an authentic folk exposition.

In my view, from the 1890s onward African Americans employed both strategies, using masking and deformation equally in their quest for liberation. This was the African-American modernist field of discourse. The modernist sensibility required the rejection of many of the values, techniques, and procedures of the past and the embracing of new ones, for modernism brought with it a spiritual apostasy symbolized by a new rationalism and a desire for the conspicuous consumption of art and entertainment, a rejection of myth, and a re-

---

1. Phaneric display is described as "allaesthetic" by zoologist H. B. Cott and taken up by Baker to refer to masks that advertise rather than conceal.

pudiation of the cosmic vision of African culture and cultural memory. Generally, neither the assumptions and trappings nor the cultural behaviors of African-derived ritual were acceptable to modernists; on one level, the mysteries of myth languished and rational explanations replaced them, with little immediate improvement in the black social circumstance. This demythicizing of black culture, together with the increasing separation of blacks from rural America, resulted in new tensions for African Americans who were seeking new roots and comforts. Furthermore, modernism accelerated the process of social differentiation among African Americans and brought new processes in which economic, social, and artistic success could be obtained only on the basis of skills marketable in the urban setting, through the artificial values of materialism, and through forms of creativity that were acceptable to white society. Since comparatively few blacks could meet these criteria, a cultural and social abyss was created, to be filled in part by the individual social commentary of the blues and the coping behaviors of frustrated and disillusioned African Americans.

Washington, Du Bois, and other leaders of the period did not create African-American modernism; it was a product of the social and cultural developments of the era. Emerging in urban communities in the 1890s was a small black middle class that included railroad porters, barbers, tailors, and a variety of skilled workers. The first decade of the twentieth century saw the beginnings of a black elite consisting of physicians, dentists, lawyers, publishers, morticians, preachers, and other businessmen. But the black population was still largely made up of the unskilled working class, whose social values and behaviors embarrassed many among the black elite and the emerging middle class. By 1915, both of these groups were contending that black youths should begin to "devote more of their time to literary societies, musical clubs, debating societies, and sewing circles, . . . and less to pool playing, dancing . . . and other virtue-robbing pleasures" (quoted in Landry 1987, 35). What really existed, in fact, was a three-way schism within the black community. The middle class aspired to the values of the elite, which was already embracing white culture and had separated itself from blacks of the lowest class. The elite established high-status organizations that excluded working-class blacks, even including churches in which there was to be "no shouting, emotionalism, or 'Amens' " (34). Cotillions were held for the organized entertainment of elite youths, while dance parties served the working class (171). As one eighty-four-year-old black fiddler from Tennessee remarked in the 1950s to Terry Zwigoff (1987),

> When we played for the black people it would all depend on what element we played for. Because there were the upper class, or elite, black people. We would call them "siddity," which is black chat for highfalutin', high strung, or elite. That means high brow. And you couldn't play no low-down funky blues for

89

The Power of Black Music

them neither. We'd have to play basically what we had to play for high-brow white people. (17)

Such attitudes had begun to spread across the South as elite blacks from among the Creoles of color, as well as blacks of the emerging middle class, took on what they viewed as white values and behaviors. In Memphis, for example, Furry Lewis, referring to the practice of bands marching and playing jazz in funeral parades, told Margaret McKee and Fred Chisenhall (1981),

> They don't have music like they do at funerals in New Orleans. . . . We all just goes to see him for the last time. . . . I don't think that no one—me or other musicians—are 'sposed to take a church song and make the blues out of it. I call it playing' with God. . . . You ain't got no business singing' "Old Rugged Cross" and all like that in no blues fashion and no jazz fashion and no mess such as that. (113)

Musically, the spirit of modernism is effectively summed up, I think, in a single work of the first decade of the twentieth century: Scott Joplin's folk opera *Treemonisha* (1911). Set in 1884 in rural Arkansas near the Red River, the work rejects "ignorance and superstition" and looks forward to the "raising of the race" through education. Its music aspires to the proportions of grand opera and includes an overture, instrumental act preludes, arias and recitatives, duets, quartets, instrumental and choral ensembles, choreography, and strong choral writing. Joplin's ambitions were aligned with black intellectual thought of the period, consonant with modernism and with the black nationalist thought then fueling the prevailing renaissance spirit. Joplin's primary characters are Treemonisha herself and Zodzetrick, one of the three conjurers; Treemonisha represents the forces of education and light, and Zodzetric and his companions symbolize those of superstition and darkness. Education triumphs, of course, with the libretto making the point that the intellect can lead the race away from the fetters of ignorance and to the personal and community freedoms and rewards that all Americans deserve. It is interesting that *Treemonisha* was written years before Esu would visit Robert Johnson (b. 1912) at the crossroads. Joplin, a modernist, apostatized African-American mythology; Johnson later celebrated it.

Another modernist work of the period is N. Clark Smith's *Negro Folk Suite* (1902), which signals, in part at least, the direction that African-American musical nationalism would take in subsequent years. Like *Treemonisha*, this descriptive work illustrates the possibilities of wedding European and African-American traditions. The "Orange Dance" has embedded within it the "Stevedores's Song" and is based on rhythms from British Guiana. The "Pineapple Lament," reflecting the composer's perception of the mood of Martinique, was composed in memory of the pineapple groves that were lost in the volcanic eruption of Martinique's Mount Pele in 1902. The "Banana Walk" is a

90

highly rhythmic piece that makes use of melodies from St. Helena Island, one
of the sea islands off the coasts of Georgia and South Carolina, where African
and early African-American cultures remained almost intact until the middle
of the twentieth century. This entire movement, written long before James P.
Johnson's popular "Charleston," is marked "tempo di Charleston" in memory
of the fact that "boys from the banana farms danced the Charleston for
us" during the composer's return from a trip to the North in 1902 (Smith
1925, 7).

Another work by Smith, *Negro Choral Symphony*, was published by the composer in 1917, in Kansas City, Missouri, where he was then living and teaching. My search for the work has turned up only one movement, "Prayer," for
soprano solo and chorus, with piano accompaniment (cues for harp, however,
suggest a more elaborate orchestration). This movement is reminiscent of the
spiritual, in that it is musically a kind of lament and its text is an appeal to
God for deliverance, suggesting the Old Negro rather than the New.

In sum, Smith's two works and Joplin's *Treemonisha* pay tribute to black culture while, in Joplin's case, rejecting and, in Smith's, ignoring its mythical underpinnings.

During the years between Emancipation and the rise of African-American modernism, a large part of Afro-America made a more or less gradual shift from a
cosmos controlled by black mythology and African-American community to
one dominated by individual determinism. While many were able to successfully make that shift, many others were not, and few were allowed to determine their own social and political status and future. At the same time, for
some of those on the urban landscape particularly, the ideal of community no
longer determined most of their associations, values, and judgments. This psychological alienation from cultural roots, on the one hand, and the rejection
by white society, on the other, resulted for many black Southerners in a dis-
mal gloom that was both evoked and lifted partially by turn-of-the-century
bluesmen. These factors, together with the social schisms I outlined earlier,
the disintegration of spiritual and communal life, and an inhospitable general
environment, created in many rootless African Americans a need for belong-
ing. This need was met somewhat by the outbreak of World War I, when the
opportunity to move north to jobs and new associations in urban America
brought relief. But with the beginnings of the Great Migration, a new manifestation of an older conflict arose: the very idea of hundreds of thousands of
southern blacks moving north between 1917 and 1919 spurred white resent-
ment and worsened the existing conflict. And when black participation in
World War I did not bring African Americans the freedoms they expected—

91

the attainment of which blacks had justified to themselves partially on the basis on modernist rationality—they developed a level of cynicism that would have a significant consequence: a renewed and intensified mistrust of white society. African Americans resented the refusal of white society to grant them the rights they had earned in slavery, had been granted by Emancipation, and had proved themselves worthy of by fighting for democracy in World War I. But far from conceding these claims, white people had resisted all along—through passive resistance, segregation, social aggression, and violence.[2] The resulting black cynicism was accompanied by psychological self-defense and self-empowering strategies, one of which was Signifyin(g).[3] Signifyin(g) became the tool of the human, urban trickster, whose general behavior is symbolized in the toast of the Signifying Monkey:

> Said the signifyin' monkey to the lion one day:
> "Hey, dere's a great big elephant down th' way
> Goin' 'roun' talkin', I'm sorry t' say,
> About yo' momma in a scandalous way!
>
> "Yea, he's talkin' 'bout yo' momma an' yo' grandma, too;
> And he don' show too much respect fo' you.
> Now, you weren't there an' I sho' am glad
> 'Cause what he said about yo' momma made me mad!"
>
> Signifyin' Monkey, stay up in yo' tree
> You are always lyin' and signifyin'
> But you better not monkey wit' me.
>
> The lion said, "Yea? Well, I'll fix him;
> I'll tear that elephant limb from limb."
> Then he shook the jungle with a mighty roar
> Took off like a shot from a forty-four.
>
> He found the elephant where the tall grass grows
> And said, "I come to punch you in your long nose."
> The elephant looked at the lion in surprise
> And said, "Boy, you better go pick on somebody your size."
>
> But the lion wouldn't listen; he made a pass;
> The elephant slapped him down in the grass.
> The lion roared and sprung from the ground
> And that's when that elephant really went to town.

---

2. For a good account of the vicious, crusading racism during the years 1890 to 1917, see Carroll and Noble (1988, 254, 255–256, 274–277).

3. "Signifyin(g)" with the bracketed "g" is Gates's (1988) form of the term, coined to distinguish it linguistically from standard English usage.

I mean he whupped that lion for the rest of the day
And I still don't see how the lion got away
But he dragged on off, more dead than alive,
And that's when that monkey started his signifyin' jive.

The monkey looked down and said, "Oooh wee!
What is this beat-up mess I see?
Is that you, Lion? Ha, ha! Do tell!
Man, he whupped yo' head to a fare-thee-well!

"Give you a beatin' that was rough enough;
You s'pposed to be the king of the jungle, ain't dat some stuff?
You big overgrown pussycat! Don' choo roar
Or I'll hop down there an' whip you some more."

The monkey got to laughing and a' jumpin' up and down,
But his foot missed the limb and he plunged to ground,
The lion was on him with all four feet
Gonna grind that monkey to hamburger meat.

The monkey looked up with tears in his eyes
And said, "Please Mr. Lion, I apologize,
I meant no harm, please, let me go
And I'll tell you something you really need to know."

The lion stepped back to hear what he'd say,
And that monkey scampered up the tree and got away.
"What I wanted to tell you," the monkey hollered then,
"Is if you fool with me, I'll sic the elephant on you again!"

The lion just shook his head, and said, "You jive . . .
If you and yo' monkey children wanna say alive,
Up in them trees is where you better stay."
And that's where they are to this very day.

Signifyin' Monkey, stay up in yo' tree
You are always lyin' and signifyin'
But you better not monkey wit' me[4]

(Oscar Brown, Jr., "Signifyin' Monkey," in Goss and Barnes 1989, 456–457)

For urban blacks, the strategy of this toast became a means of coping sym-
bolically with the whites' suppression and denial of their freedoms. In coping
with white resistance to racial progress, and with the hostilities then preva-

---

4. I do not know when this toast was collected or when it was first told, but I believe that
the toast of the Signifying Monkey is an urban version of the African folk tale "Why Monkeys
Live in Trees" (chapter 1), and it is probable that it became popular in urban Afro-America after the onset of modernism.

lent within the African-American community itself, African Americans did not, in the period following World War I, retreat to the solace of the Negro spiritual, which had already served its purpose and was no longer relevant to the times; nor did they become self-destructively aggressive. They *signified,* using the toast of the Signifying Monkey as their model.

The toast itself is a metaphor, a symbol for the state of things—for the American condition as seen and experienced by sophisticated urban African Americans, the new city slickers—and the Monkey's strategy is symbolic of a way of coping with that condition through trickery. In the Signifying Monkey we have a new trickster on the African-American landscape, cultivating a new language (Gates 1988, 7) in order to help neutralize the forces of oppression and exploitation. For city dwellers, the Signifying Monkey is a key mythological figure in the African American's struggle for adjustment, dignity, and equality: a trickster who will baffle, circumvent, and even subdue agents of oppression with the same wit, cunning, and guile as tricksters past. It is as if, after giving birth to the bluesmen on the eve of the Great Migration, Esu—a victim of the apostasies of modernism—perished and was reborn as a new and "citified" trickster. Esu's demise had been caused by the modernists' rejection of myth, but in his place came the more rational and acceptable slickster—the Signifying Monkey. When the virtue of rural plainness came to be seen as urban naïveté, African Americans at first used the talents and skills of the trickster as a substitute for the knowledge and sophistication they would need to negotiate the urban landscape. They began to master and to deform the minstrel mask with the disingenuousness of fronting and the phaneric display of Signifyin(g).

The device of Signifyin(g) is clearly of African origin. Recall the tale in which Esu wears a suit of black and red in order to trick two friends and destroy their relationship. This was silent, but active, Signifyin(g). The notion of Signifyin(g) is a survival and elaboration of a technique used in several animal-trickster tales of Afro-America: "Why Monkeys Live in Trees," "Why the Dog Always Chases Other Animals," "Cutting the Elephant's Hips," "How Squirrel Robbed Rabbit of His Tail," and numerous others that were collected and published in the 1880s by Joel Chandler Harris and other writers. But the term "signifying" itself—as an African-American vernacular technique—first appeared in print, I believe, in the title of the tale "The Signifying Monkey." In keeping with the prevailing spirit of renaissance, urban African Americans, I believe, resurrected the African tale "Why Monkeys Live in Trees" and transformed it into armament in a new battle for dignity and freedom.

In the trickster figure, Stuckey's (1987) hypothesis and Gates's (1988) theory converge. For Gates, Esu and the Signifying Monkey are ascendant; for Stuckey, it is Br'er Rabbit, "keeper of the faith of the ancestors, mediator of their claims on the living" (18). In the tale "Buh Rabbit in Red Hill Churchyard," as we have seen, Br'er Mockingbird joins Br'er Rabbit in a ceremony in which

> dey had chunes floatin' all 'round on de night air. Dey could stand a chune on end, grab it up an' throw it away an' ketch it an' bring it back an' hold it; an' make dem chunes sound like dey was strugglin' to get away one minute, an de' next dey sound like sumpin' gittin' up close an' whisperin'.

I quote this passage again because it vividly suggests the tropes of the ring and their inclusion in the music making of an African-derived burial ceremony. In the tale, Br'er Rabbit is interpreting the music of the rite through what is obviously improvisation. The imagery and symbolism in the churchyard are provocative: the trickster is at the burial ground, venerating the spirits and interpreting the culture through music; the instrument he plays is the fiddle, prominent in Africa, ubiquitous in slave culture, sometimes played by Esu, and profane among some Christians; Br'er Rabbit even dances on a tombstone—something Esu probably would do. Most significant, though, Br'er Rabbit is Signifyin(g), and so is Mockingbird.

In the black vernacular, Signifyin(g) is figurative, implicative speech. It makes use of vernacular tropings such as "marking, loud-talking, testifying, calling out, sounding, rapping, playing the dozens" (Gates 1988, 52), and other rhetorical devices. Signifyin(g) is a way of saying one thing and meaning another; it is a reinterpretation, a metaphor for the revision of previous texts and figures; it is tropological thought, repetition with difference, the obscuring of meaning (53, 88)—all to achieve or reverse power, to improve situations, and to achieve pleasing results for the signifier. For in Signifyin(g), the emphasis is on the signifier, not the signified. In African-American music, musical figures Signify by commenting on other musical figures, on themselves, on performances of other music, on other performances of the same piece, and on completely new works of music. Moreover, genres Signify on other genres—ragtime on European and early European and American dance music; blues on the ballad; the spiritual on the hymn; jazz on blues and ragtime; gospel on the hymn, the spiritual, and blues; soul on rhythm and blues, rock 'n' roll, and rock music; bebop on swing, ragtime rhythms, and blues; funk on soul; rap on funk; and so on. Call–Response, the master trope, the musical trope of tropes, implies the presence within it of Signifyin(g) figures (calls) and Signifyin(g) revisions (responses, in various guises) that can be one or the other, depending on their context.[5] For example, when pendular thirds are used in an original melodic statement, they may constitute a "call"; when they are

5. I am grateful to Bruce Tucker for putting me onto this idea early in the development of my ideas, when he stated that something like the Afro-American musical process of call-and-response, metaphorically speaking, might be considered as the musical trope of tropes.

used to comment on, or "trope," a preexisting use of such thirds, they can be said to constitute a "response," a Signifyin(g) revision.

A twelve-bar blues in which a two-measure instrumental "response" answers a two-measure vocal "call" is a classic example of Signifyin(g). Here, the instrument performs a kind of sonic mimicry that creates the illusion of speech or narrative conversation. When performers of gospel music, for example, begin a new phrase while the other musicians are only completing the first, they may be Signifyin(g) on what is occurring and on what is to come, through implication and anticipation. The implication is "I'm already there." And when soloists hang back, hesitating for a moment to claim their rightful place in the flow of things, they are saying, silently and metaphorically, "But I wasn't, really." This kind of Signifyin(g) allows the performer to be in two places at once; it is sheer, willful play—a dynamic interplay of music and aesthetic power, the power to control and manipulate the musical circumstance. In this way, performers combine the ritual teasing and critical insinuations of Signifyin(g) with the wit, cunning, and guile of the trickster in a self-empowering aesthetic and communicational device.

Musical Signifyin(g) refers to the rhetorical use of the musical tropes subsumed under the master trope of Call–Response: calls, cries, whoops, and hollers; call-and-response, elision, pendular and blue thirds, musical expressions, vocal imitations by instruments, and parlando; multimeter, cross-rhythms, and interlocking rhythms; and all the rest. Musical Signifyin(g) carries with it a nonverbal semantic value, a "telling effect" that "asserts, alleges, quests, requests, and implies . . . mocks, groans, concurs, and signifies misgivings and suspicions" (Murray 1973, 86). In Signifyin(g), the vernacular is used to read black formal products. In this way, Signifyin(g) is also criticism, since it validates and invalidates musical narrative through respectful, ironic, satirizing imitation and manipulation. Derived from the Signifying Monkey tales, with Esu-Elegbara as its interpreter and connector to African mythology, Signifyin(g) connects its user with the roots of black culture; for in all of Africa, Zahan ([1970] 1979) reminds us, "the use of implication, euphemism, symbol, allegory, and secret" is a normal "part of . . . oral expression" (114).

Gates (1988) makes the point that Signifyin(g), by redirecting attention from the signified to the signifier, places the stress of the experience on the materiality of the latter: "the importance of the Signifying Monkey poems is their repeated stress on the sheer materiality . . . of the signifier itself" (59). If I interpret Gates correctly, the *material* signifiers in Dance, Drum, and Song, aside from the musicians' tropings, can also be the body movements of the dancers and musicians—the performers' physical play as they perform their respective roles. These movements, together with the signifier's willful play, are "the dominant mode of discourse" (58) in the ring. This is why, in contrast to the European musical orientation, the *how* of a performance is more important than the *what*. Certainly, African Americans have their favorite tunes, but it is what is done with and inside those tunes that the listeners look forward to, not the mere playing of them. The hearing of an old or a favorite tune may carry pleasant memories, but those memories and their quality—absent inquiry—are based in preference and nostalgia. With the *musical* experience, the expectation is that something musical will *happen* in the playing of the music, and it is the *something* that fascinates, that elevates the expectation and places the hearer in a critical mode. The "something" that is expected might relate not only to the sounds that will be heard, but also to the players' movements as they perform. The movements of the instruments, the movements of an individual's limbs, torso, shoulders, head, neck, and eyes—even the wrinkling of the forehead—accompany the sonic gestures made by the musicians, the musical troping they perform on or within the tune or figure, in whole or in part, as they make the performance. These movements are the physical signifiers that are part and parcel of the black musical experience. They prevailed and still prevail in traditional Africa; they prevailed in eighteenth-century slave balls and still do in urban black America. When dancers are dancing, it is how they relate to what the musicians play and how the musicians react to their movements, gestures, and urgings that make the dance a success, for it is the dancers' physical Signifyin(g) that excites other dancers and musicians alike: a bump here, a grind there, a nod here, a dip there. Within black life, it is culturally, socially, and artistically significant—something fraught with cultural memory and, in that sense, quite meaningful to actual and potential signifiers. It is this manifestation of *materiality*, this physical realization of the Signifyin(g) mode, inside and outside the ring, that creates and makes possible intracultural, interdisciplinary aesthetic communication. It is to this materiality that we must attend if we are fundamentally to understand the music, for it is in the material manifestations of Signifyin(g) that reside many of the clues and cues to the perception of black music and its evaluation.

In "Buh Rabbit in Red Hill Churchyard," Br'er Rabbit and Br'er Mockingbird re-create the ritual with which Africans and early African Americans worshipped God and venerated the ancestors, recognized and celebrated the cycle of Being (deceased ancestors being reborn in new babies in a never-ending cycle), and paid tribute to life's nourishments through sacrifice (returning to the earth some form of human or animal residue). In the African ontology, Being was a never-ending cycle of give-and-take that involved the living, the living-dead, the spirits, the gods, and God. And it was this Being, or existence, that was symbolized in African ritual. The churchyard tale is an imaginative telling of this tradition. Br'er Rabbit and Br'er Mockingbird, in "basing" the dancing "little beasts," are playing the typical role of musicians in African-American ring ritual, expressing through their music the struggles and fulfillments of existence. The Signifyin(g) imitation and revision, indirection, figures, and metaphors involved in and implied by this musical performance by Br'er Rabbit and Br'er Mockingbird symbolize life, existence, Being; they thereby constitute a musical symbol—a *Signifyin(g)* musical symbol.

In chapter 3, I pointed out that black composers in the United States have been writing and publishing music since the late eighteenth century. For my purposes, this notated music and all that followed will be viewed as "texts," candidates for Signifyin(g) revision; and since recorded performances can be heard again and again, without change, they also will be treated as formal "texts," to be "read," studied, and revised. Any text, black or white, can be read by the vernacular, by the signifier, as evidenced by the black musical "discourse" on the white social-dance music of the nineteenth century in which power relations were significantly reversed, turning white texts into black as black musicians applied African-American rhetorical strategies to European forms. In these events, European and American dance music was trifled with, teased, and censured as it never had been before—infused with the semantic tropes and values of Call–Response. The "willful play" of the black signifiers became more important than the given melodies they played as they created call-and-response figures, cross-rhythms, elisions, smears, breaks, and stop-time figures, "telling a story" with musically dialogical, rhetorical tropes that asserted, assented, implied, mocked, and critically evaluated the possibilities of the new music with which they had made contact.

I believe that Signifyin(g) was developed in response to the black cultural apostasy that resulted from the onset of modernism, which itself was fed by factors such as the prohibitions instituted by exclusionary lawmaking after Reconstruction, the loss of the communal ethos of black culture, and the continued ill-treatment of African Americans throughout the United States. But another and different response to—or perhaps even a cause of—this apostasy was the determination of elite and middle-class African Americans to "elevate the race" by producing within it the artistic and intellectual resources and excellence that would prove them to be the intellectual and social equals of white Americans. They would accomplish this not by denying the value of their racial heritage, but by reaffirming and asserting it. This spirit of "renaissancism" (Baker's [1987] good term) was pervasive all across the United States, the Caribbean, and the Atlantic world at the time. But in New York City, renaissancism sank its roots early and deep and flowered as the Harlem Renaissance; later, a Chicago flowering would develop.

Booker T. Washington's plan of action and its acceptance by whites had raised expectations among the black populace, perhaps even helping to bring about this spirit of "renaissancism," this "*spirit* of nationalistic engagement that [began] with intellectuals, artists, and spokespersons at the turn of the century and [received] extensive definition and expression during the 1920s" (Baker 1987, 91). From the context of Baker's discussion, it is clear that he believes, as do many scholars, that although this spirit flowered and flourished in Harlem in the 1920s, it transcended both place and period, engaging the entire African diaspora for more than four decades between around 1910 and 1950. During the Negro Renaissance, spirituals, ragtime, blues, jazz, and gospel music would undergo significant development, and Signifyin(g) would play a role: the musicians would become signifiers par excellence—musical tricksters who would help define the music and the culture of the United States.

CHAPTER **5**

The Negro Renaissance: Harlem and Chicago Flowerings

I am a Negro:
Black as the night is black,
Black like the depths of my Africa.
Langston Hughes

Would ye both have your cake and eat your cake?

The cat would eat fish, and would not wet her feet.
John Heywood

The flowerings of the Negro Renaissance in Harlem (1917–1935) and Chicago (1935–1950) were spawned by Pan-Africanism, which posits the belief that black people all over the world share an origin and a heritage, that the welfare of black people everywhere is inexorably linked, and that the cultural products of blacks everywhere should express their particular fundamental beliefs (Martin 1983, vii). According to Esedebe (1982, 3), Pan-African thought seeks to glorify the African past, inculcate pride in African values, and promote unity among all people of African descent. Pan-African thinking was set off in part by the transatlantic slave trade and was intensified by the Haitian Revolution of 1804 and the onset of nineteenth-century colonialism in Africa. Pan-Africanism flourished among persons of color in Europe in the late nineteenth century when, according to Lotz (1990), "black entertainers roamed Europe from Scotland to Russia, from the Mediterranean to the polar circle. . . . Blacks—whether Africans, Afro-

Americans, West Indians, European-born, etc.—were in close touch with one another, even across barriers of language, profession, or social status" (264).

It was in this European environment that Marcus Garvey, a West Indian who moved to England in 1912, began his development as the individual who, more than any other, "introduced the ideas of an African Nationalist and the African personality . . . to the uninformed masses in the villages and streets of the African world," developing a plan for the liberation of Africans in the diaspora (Esedebe 1982, 67, 70). Late in 1916, Garvey left England for New York. There he became the self-appointed leader of Africans and their dispersed descendants by founding the Universal Negro Improvement Association (U.N.I.A.), which, by 1919, could be found established in countries in all parts of the world (75). The U.N.I.A.'s official publication, *Black World,* first published in 1918, was the organization's news and propaganda organ. The organization's tricolor flag of red, black, and green was complemented by its "African National Anthem"—the first militant Pan-African musical product, referring as it does to Ethiopia as "the land of our fathers," admonishing the oppressors to "Let Africa be free," and proclaiming that "Ethiopia shall stretch forth her hand" to freedom.[1] Garvey's primary messages were direct and forceful: salvation for blacks existed only in the African homeland, to which they should return, and blacks in the United States should purchase only from black merchants, particularly from the U.N.I.A.'s businesses.[2] In 1919, the year after Garvey's launching of *Black World,* W. E. B. Du Bois called a Pan-African meeting in Paris that was attended by fifty-seven delegates from fifteen territories, including, among others, "Abyssinia, Liberia, Haiti, the United States, San Domingo (Dominican Republic), French Caribbean, British Africa, French Africa, Egypt, and the Belgian Congo" (81). Between this gathering and 1927, Du Bois sponsored annual meetings, four of which were held in the United States, that helped keep alive Pan-African ideals.[3]

In England, black physician John Alcindor's African Progress Union Committee "included blacks born in Trinidad, Guyana, Barbados, Liberia, Sierra Leone, Ghana, and South Carolina, and was able to take a global view of the black world" (Green 1990, 61–62). This was only one of several such groups, and musicians were comfortably among them:

> In August 1919 members of the Southern Syncopated Orchestra of Will Marion Cook were present with their leader and business manager George William

---

1. The complete song text is in Esedebe (73–74). Such Pan-African patriotic songs must have come into vogue around this time. In 1915, Harry T. Burleigh wrote the song "Ethiopia Saluting the Colors" and in 1920 F. A. Clark composed and published a song called "Ethiopia," which he referred to as a "race anthem."

2. Garvey's efforts, part of the New Negro movement's early years, ended in 1926, when he was deported for mail fraud.

3. The term "Pan-Americanism" had become popular by 1897, and the first Pan-African conference was held in England in 1900.

Lattimore at a function in honor of several groups of blacks in London that had been organized by the Coterie of Friends, a student group of Caribbeans (and one Ghanaian) led by South Carolina–born Edmund Thornton Jenkins. Jenkins had been a student at London's Royal Academy of Music since 1914 and was currently teaching the clarinet there. [John Richard] Archer and Afro-American lawyer Thomas McCants Stewart mixed with South Africans and Guyanese in a room decorated with the flags of Haiti and Liberia. Jenkins, with two ladies from Cook's orchestra and vocalist Evelyn Dove, played works by Weber, Coleridge-Taylor, and himself. Dove, whose father was Francis Thomas Dove, a lawyer from Sierra Leone, was likened to Josephine Baker by Henry Champley. (156–157)

With Pan-Africanism widespread among blacks in England and with study opportunities widely available there, it is not surprising that black composers would emerge. The most notable, Samuel Coleridge-Taylor (1875–1912), was famous around the world in the 1890s. Coleridge-Taylor is marked as a Pan-Africanist by his contributions to the musical literature of the diaspora and by his interactions with other Pan-Africanists.[4] His Pan-Africanist orientation is demonstrated by his work, for example, with African-American poet Paul Laurence Dunbar, whose poetry he set to music and with whom he collaborated on the opera *Dream Lovers* (1898). His African- and African-American–oriented compositions include *Symphonic Variations on an African Air* (1906), *The Bamboula* (1910), and *Twenty-Four Negro Melodies, Transcribed for the Piano* (1905).

Through his music and by his example, Coleridge-Taylor influenced African-American composers and musicians (see, for example, Still 1975), and societies bearing his name sprang up in cities across the United States in the early years of the twentieth century. Coleridge-Taylor's friendships and professional relationships with African-American artists such as Dunbar, Harry T. Burleigh, John Turner Layton, Clarence Cameron White, Felix Weir, and Gerald Tyler were developed through transatlantic visits and written correspondence. As a composer and conductor, Coleridge-Taylor became "the prototype for a renaissance of black culture" (Tortolano 1977, 73), probably serving as a model for composers such as Robert Nathaniel Dett, William Grant Still, and Florence Price. These composers would succeed in the years after Coleridge-Taylor's death with extended works of both significant and modest musical merit—for example, Dett in 1921 with *The Chariot Jubilee* and in 1932 with *The Ordering of Moses;* Still with the three-movement suite *Levee Land* and *From the Black Belt* in 1926, and *Africa* and *Afro-American Symphony* in 1930; and Price in 1932 with the Symphony in E Minor and in 1934 with the Piano Concerto in One Movement.

4. Coleridge-Taylor's *African Suite, Danse Nègre,* and "Onaway, Awake, Beloved," the last from *Hiawatha's Wedding Feast,* are available on a record in the Black Composers Series.

The American composers whom Coleridge-Taylor influenced were all nationalists, as their works attest. In America, black nationalism—an aspect of Pan-Africanism—had been developed, debated, and written about by free blacks as early as the first decade of the nineteenth century.[5] It was publicly elaborated by David Walker and Henry Highland Garnet in the early nineteenth century and around the turn of the century by Carter G. Woodson, W. E. B. Du Bois, and others (Stuckey 1987; Tate 1988). But of all the major black-nationalist theorists, Du Bois was the only one who recognized—or at least wrote about—the importance of black music to nationalist thought. This importance is underscored in his book *The Souls of Black Folk* (1902) by the snippets of spiritual melodies and texts that appear at the beginning of each chapter, by his liberal quotations from the spirituals throughout his narrative, and by his essay "Of the Sorrow Songs." In this essay he discusses, perceptively and sensitively, the aesthetic and social value of the spiritual, focusing on the music itself, on the cultural and political contributions of the original Fisk Jubilee Singers, and on the spiritual singing of the South Carolina and Georgia Sea Islanders. Du Bois had seen and studied the ring and had heard the spirituals during his college and teaching days at Fisk University in Nashville, and he wrote about the shout, specifically, in *The Souls of Black Folk* ([1902] 1967, 190–191).

Another influential individual who recognized the importance of black music to nationalist thought was American journalist James Monroe Trotter, who, nearly thirty years before the publication of *Souls,* had documented the secular activities of black musicians in various locations in the United States. His *Music and Some Highly Musical People* (1878) was the first comprehensive survey on this aspect of American music history. Although Trotter was not a major theorist of the movement, his book is in the tradition of the "collective elevation" thrust of nationalist thought; in it, as I noted earlier, he was determined to put the race's best foot forward by treating only the accomplishments of those who could read music. Trotter's work covers aesthetics, music history, and the social contexts of more than forty-one black musical groups and figures who were then or had been active in the United States, including Frank Johnson, Justin Holland, Elizabeth Taylor Greenfield, Sam Lucas, Samuel Snaer, and others in more than twenty American cities.[6]

Musically, the spirit of the Negro Renaissance had begun to manifest itself, in the late 1890s and in the first and second decades of the twentieth century,

5. The term "black nationalism" refers here to movements in which blacks take pride in their African heritage and desire to control their own destiny and communities. It does not necessarily refer to separatist movements and thinking.

6. The appendix of Trotter's book contains sheet-music facsimiles of works by thirteen composers.

in the work of Scott Joplin, Will Marion Cook, Harry T. Burleigh, John Turner Layton, Robert Cole, the brothers J. Rosamond Johnson and James Weldon Johnson, Alex Rogers, Ford Dabney, Will Vodery, Will Tyers, and others. Of these composers, Cook and Burleigh were perhaps the most important and revered. Cook, a kind of dean of black musicians, served as musical director, composer, and producer for a number of black shows on Broadway between 1898 and 1914, including *A Trip to Coontown* (1898), *Clorindy: Or the Origin of the Cakewalk* (1889), *In Dahomey* (1902),[7] and *In Bandanna Land* (1907). His *Three Negro Songs*—"Exhortation," "Rain-Song," and "Swing Along"—reveals his strong devotion to the African-American cultural tradition as well as his training in the European concert tradition. "Exhortation" is the best example of this fusion, manifesting elements of black preaching within the context of a kind of recitative-and-aria that comprises a declamatory setting of the text in the first part of the song and a lyrical treatment of the second part. The text of "Exhortation" was written by Alex Rogers, a singer and actor who was also the chief lyricist for some of Cook's shows. He also wrote the lyrics for "Rain-Song," a swinging, crowd-pleasing, comic song. "Swing Along," a favorite of the men's choruses of the day, was borrowed for this cycle from Cook's show *In Dahomey* and became the most widely performed and famous of the three pieces in the cycle. The three songs were brought together to form the cycle in 1912 and were published by Schirmer.

Burleigh's published works and his performances of art songs and spirituals made him both an exemplar of the tradition and an influence on composers and singers. His *Album of Negro Spirituals* ([1917] 1969) put him in the vanguard of later race-preservation and -promotion efforts and provided concert singers such as Roland Hayes, Marian Anderson, and Paul Robeson with a repertoire of arranged spirituals that would serve them well. In this century's second decade, Burleigh wrote two impressive song cycles: *Saracen Songs* (1914) and *Five Songs of Lawrence Hope* (1919).

Cook and Burleigh were not the only highly significant figures of the period. The brothers James Weldon and J. Rosamond Johnson composed "Lift Every Voice and Sing" (1899), which was taken up as an anthem for the nationalist movement; Bob Cole collaborated with both of the Johnsons, together and singly, to write some of the most popular songs of the day, among which were "Under the Bamboo Tree" (1902), "The Old Flag Never Touched the Ground" (1901), and "The Maiden with the Dreamy Eyes" (1901).

Meanwhile, Ernest Hogan's orchestra, the Memphis Students (also referred to as the Nashville Students, both names serving as elliptical and exploitative references to the Fisk Jubilee Singers and their success), was introducing black secular music to America and Europe; Cook's American Syncopated Orches-

---

7. The Overture to *In Dahomey* is recorded on *The Black Music Repertory Ensemble in Concert* (1992).

tra (also known as The New York Syncopated Orchestra and the Southern Syncopated Orchestra) was developing the beginnings of "symphonic jazz" (Locke [1936] 1968, 65; Southern 1971, 345–347); and the ragtime craze of 1898 to 1917 was in full swing, with its most famous composer, Scott Joplin, publishing his opera *Treemonisha* in 1911. And James Reese Europe was organizing his 369th Regiment "Hell Fighters" band, which would take France by storm during World War I.

In New York, Europe had already organized the Clef Club, which served as a social club, booking agency, and musicians' union and controlled the music and entertainment business (Ellison 1916). Europe was supreme in New York. His recordings of "Castle House Rag," "Castle Walk," "Memphis Blues," and "Clarinet Marmalade," made in 1914 and 1918, are ambitious, exciting, and sensitive renditions of some of the popular songs of the century's second decade, reflecting social and musical changes, the beginnings of jazz dance, and the social optimism that prevailed in black society as a result of African-American modernist thought and the participation of black men in World War I. Europe was the music director for the white dance team of Irene and Vernon Castle. He wrote "Castle House Rag" in tribute to the Castle House for the Teaching of Correct Dancing, where the more staid versions of black dance were introduced to white society and where the "rules of good taste were sufficiently strict to make the new dances acceptable" (Buckman 1978, 167). "Castle House Rag" was introduced to the public by the Castles and Europe's Society Orchestra in 1914. It is a "trot and one-step," combining the one-step, the ubiquitous dance of the ragtime period, with elements of an African-American animal dance called the turkey trot. The dotted shuffle rhythms of the one-step in the first part contrast sharply with the syncopated rhythms of the second, the latter clearly revealing its African-American lineage. Europe's musical conception, based in the military march and in ragtime, made use of blues and jazz devices that he had probably heard in the various "syncopated orchestras" of Cook and Hogan and elsewhere.

The dancing of the Castles was called jazz dance. Although the music was not jazz as we know the genre today, jazz elements were made manifest in it. Europe's bands—at least the ones that were recorded—did not play jazz as we have come to know it. But whether or not Europe's band played jazz, it fairly *shouted*, with its brassy trumpets, smearing trombones, and additive and cross-rhythms, all of which can be heard on "Memphis Blues" and "Clarinet Marmalade." The prototype that Europe fostered in the second decade of the twentieth century should give him a place in the history of jazz.[8]

In the face of such accomplishments within the context of other Harlem-based nationalist activity then taking place, it was only a small step to musi-

8. For more on Europe, see Badger (1989).

cal culture-building by blacks across the United States. Unlike the European Renaissance, which took place in western Europe from the fourteenth through the sixteenth centuries and was largely fueled by the rediscovery of the Greek cultural legacy, the Negro Renaissance had no large body of written texts—no Plato or Aristotle—on which a new culture might be based. But African Americans were inspired by a growing awareness of the African civilizations that had once flourished along the Nile, Tigris, and Euphrates rivers. They longed to restore African culture to a position of respect, and they used what they knew of African and African-American folk art and literature of times past and current in an attempt to create new cultural forms. It is in this sense that the period was called a "renaissance." But the primary motive of the movement was political: if African Americans could demonstrate substantial abilities in arts and letters, then social, political, and economic freedoms would surely follow. As James Weldon Johnson (1922) wrote at the time:

> A people may be great through many means, but there is only one measure by which its greatness is recognized and acknowledged. The final measure of the greatness of all peoples is the amount and standard of the literature and art that they have produced. The world does not know that a people is great until that people produces great literature and art. No people that has produced great literature and art has ever been looked upon by the world as distinctly inferior.
>
> The status of the Negro in the United States is more a question of national mental attitude toward the race than of actual conditions. And nothing will do more to change that mental attitude and raise his status than a demonstration of intellectual parity by the Negro through the production of literature and art. (vii)

The guiding assumption was that "excellence in art would alter the nation's perceptions of blacks, [leading] eventually to freedom and justice" (Rampersad 1988, 6). Patrons supporting or promoting this belief were wealthy black and white philanthropists, publishers, entrepreneurs, and socialites who wanted to promote the aesthetic advancement of the race; assist in blacks' social, artistic, and intellectual progress; or reap financial or social gain. Among the real patrons of the movement were A'Lelia Walker, the black beauty-culture heir, who provided a gathering place for musicians and writers alike on the third floor of her Harlem residence, known as the Dark Tower; Casper Holstein, the black "numbers" kingpin, whose Holstein Prizes for musical composition were offered through *Opportunity* magazine; J. E. Spingarn, who offered a gold medal for "musical achievement in any field" (Cuney-Hare [1936] 1974, 261); David Bispham, sponsor of a prize medal of the American Opera Society, one of which was won by Clarence Cameron White for his opera *Ouanga* (1931); Julius Rosenwald, who offered prizes for creative work, apparently in any field; the Harmon Foundation, whose Harmon Awards—gold and bronze—were offered for high achievement in musical composition; the Wanamaker family, whose Wanamaker Music Contests were held under the partial auspices of the National Association of Negro Musicians (NANM); writer, photographer, and "Negrotarian" Carl Van Vechten; and the elderly and wealthy Charlotte Mason, who was the patron of writers Langston Hughes and Zora Neale Hurston.

The intellectual and artistic activity of writers, painters, sculptors, photographers, playwrights, and actors was feverish, and progressive organizations published magazines for the intellectual and political edification of black thinkers and strivers. Jean Toomer wrote the novel *Cane* (1923), Walter White wrote *Flight* (1926); Langston Hughes wrote *Not Without Laughter* (1930); and Zora Neale Hurston penned the short story "Sweat" (1926). Alain Locke edited the *New Negro* (1925). Aaron Douglas painted allegorical scenes; Archibald Motley painted *Syncopation* (1925), *Stomp* (1926), and *Spell of the Voodoo* (1928); and Palmer Hayden painted *Schooner* (1926) and *Quai at Concarneu* (1929). Eubie Blake and Noble Sissle wrote the musical *Shuffle Along* (1921); James P. Johnson wrote *Runnin' Wild* (1924); Johnson and Fats Waller wrote *Keep Shufflin'* (1928); and Donald Heywood wrote the operetta *Africana* (1933). Paul Robeson acted in *Simon the Cyrenian* (1920), *All God's Chillun Got Wings* (1923), *The Emperor Jones* (1925), and *Show Boat* (1928). The National Association of Colored People (NAACP) published *Crisis* magazine, and the National Urban League published *Opportunity*.

Musically, the idea was to produce extended forms such as symphonies and operas from the raw material of spirituals, ragtime, blues, and other folk genres. The movement's first successful effort in the transformation of folk music into "high art" was Dett's Oratorio *The Chariot Jubilee* (1921). Still's *Afro-American Symphony* (1930) was the movement's crowning achievement. There were frequent concerts by the Harlem Symphony Orchestra and the Negro String Quartet (Felix Weir and Arthur Boyd, violins; Hall Johnson, viola; and Marion Cumbo, cello), which played works by black and white composers. But the pride of the Renaissance leaders were the recital singers: Roland Hayes, Paul Robeson, and Marian Anderson had magnificent voices, and they served as exemplars for the New Negro movement. Burleigh's *Album of Negro Spirituals,* which he had begun to write as early as 1916, probably served as the initial impetus for the black-music repertoires of these and other concert singers. In 1925, James Weldon and J. Rosamond Johnson's *Book of Negro Spirituals* appeared, followed in 1926 by their *Second Book of Negro Spirituals*. Also in 1925, Paul Robeson became the first black solo artist to sing entire recitals of these songs, taking them to parts of the world that the Fisk Jubilee Singers had not reached in their tours during the 1870s to 1890s. Robeson was the son of a preacher and was steeped in black culture (Hamilton 1974, 12; Robeson 1930); he was nourished on the spiritual and on the sustenance of the ring. His biggest contribution to African-American musical nationalism was probably the influence he had on the recital artists of the period: after his 1925 concert of spirituals, nearly all black concert singers included them on their recital programs.[9]

And for entertainment, all danced the Susie Q, the lindy, the black bottom, and the Charleston at clubs such as Barron's, Rockland Palace, and the Bucket of Blood. Initially, entertainment music, including jazz, was ignored or dismissed by Renaissance leaders in favor of concert music; the blues and other folk forms (except for the Negro spiritual, which was held in high esteem) were rejected as decadent and reminiscent of the "old Negro." But many of the movement's entertainers were both amused and offended by the superior attitudes and posturings of some of the black intellectuals. So the entertainers subjected them to "Signifyin(g) revision" or "troping," commenting on them occasionally in speech, posture, gesture, and even song—for example, in Fletcher Henderson's "Dicty Blues" (1923) and in Duke Ellington's "Dicty Glide" (1929).

Ironically, however, it was jazz and the blues that provided the movement's aesthetic ambiance. Bands such as Henderson's and Ellington's were playing dance halls and floor shows; classic blues was ascendant, having first appeared in Harlem in the 1910s and now being recorded by female classic blues singers such as Mamie, Trixie, and Bessie Smith. When W. C. Handy arrived in New York from Memphis in 1918, the blues had been there for years among southern immigrants, and female professional entertainers from southern minstrel and vaudeville shows were already important in entertainment circles. These women had spent their apprenticeships and early professional careers in shows such as Silas Green from New Orleans and F. S. Wolcott's Rabbit Foot Minstrels. The Silas Green show had featured at different times future stars Ma Rainey and Ida Cox, and the Rabbit Foot Minstrels had headlined Rainey, Bessie Smith, and Bertha "Chippie" Hill. With her early start in southern tent shows, Rainey had defined the basic style for those who emerged as classic blues singers in the Harlem Renaissance, although that style was refined considerably for the sophisticated urban environment.[10] Singers such as Trixie, Mamie, and Bessie Smith, Chippie Hill, Lucile Hegaman, and Ethel Waters mastered the twelve-bar blues form and made it speak to the more sophisticated urban audiences. Bessie was dominant: her weighty voice, superb intonation, powerful emotional delivery, and subtle bending of blue notes were compelling and inimitable, setting her clearly apart from the other blues stylists of the pe-

---

9. For additional information about the intellectual and artistic ferment of the movement, see Floyd (1990a), Huggins (1971), Lewis (1981), and Locke ([1936] 1968).

10. Rainey can be heard on *Ma Rainey* (1974). A discography and information about Rainey's accomplishments are found in Lieb (1981).

riod.[11] All these women sang the blues they had heard and learned in southern jooks and tent shows, songs they had composed themselves, and songs written by professionals such as Handy. Handy's songs were not strictly in the standard twelve-bar form. They were mostly Tin Pan Alley–type songs into which the structural and expressive characteristics of the blues were carefully set and integrated. "Memphis Blues" (1912), for example, is a simple A B construction, the A section being sixteen measures in length with a four-bar extension, the B section a twelve-bar blues. "St. Louis Blues" (1914) is A B C, with twelve, sixteen, and twelve measures, respectively. In spite of these structural aberrations, however, or even partly because of them, Handy's work was both different and familiar enough to make a strong and positive impact on the popular culture of the time; his blues songs became part of the classic blues repertory.

The blues tradition, with that of the spiritual, provided the basis for some of William Grant Still's work in the 1920s and 1930s. Throughout the 1920s, he heard many blues, spirituals, and African-American secular folk songs. He absorbed the styles, made them part of his emotional and compositional arsenals, and experimented with them in works such as *From the Black Belt* (1926) while making his sketches for the *Afro-American Symphony*—the first symphony composed by an African American. That work, completed in 1930 and first performed in 1931, effectively mirrors the ideals of the Harlem Renaissance. Still realized those ideals not by using existing folk songs, but by creating stylized imitations of them, which he cast in conventional and not-so-conventional classical musical forms. Briefly, the four movements of the work can be described as bound together by an ever-prevailing "blues theme." The work's first movement begins with this trope; then a modified sonata form of this twelve-bar blues is presented in two "choruses" accompanied by a variety of riffs, walking rhythms, and call-and-response dialogues. The second theme is an ersatz spiritual. Then comes the requisite development section, where, in this case, the second theme and its accompanying figures are developed. In the recapitulation, the second theme returns first, with the first theme following on the heels of intervening riff signals; then follows a brief coda, which Signifies on the opening blues theme. The slow second movement, which begins with an introduction that tropes the blues theme of the first movement with fragments of itself, contains two themes, both tinged with blue notes and dance rhythms. Extensions, elaborations, and repetitions of the second theme appear; then the first theme returns in a statement that brings the movement to a close. The third movement is a "scherzo" in 2/4. A dance movement that appropriately employs the banjo, it features ring-based back-

---

11. For examples of Bessie Smith singing, listen to her on *The World's Greatest Blues Singer* (1970).

beats, a sprightly dance melody, an ersatz spiritual melody, approximations of the time line, and cross-rhythms. The fourth movement, slow and in triple meter, also has two themes, both of which are developed through Signifyin(g) revision; this final movement ends with a troping coda that Signifies on the work as a whole, with pendular thirds prominent and muted trumpets Signifyin(g) on classical trumpet timbres and African-American timbral distortions. Fraught with dialogical, rhetorical troping, the entire work carries considerable semantic value, to use Gates's term. The *Afro-American Symphony* is of two lineages—African-American and European—and these two lineages shine through the entirety of the work. The *Afro-American Symphony* effectively realized the goals of the Harlem Renaissance, with Still vindicating the faith of the movement's intellectuals and establishing himself as the first black composer of a successful symphony.

Stride piano was also flourishing in New York, and the amazing keyboard feats of James P. Johnson, Willie "the Lion" Smith, and Fats Waller were enthralling and stunning the cabaret-goers, house-rent-party revelers, and sophisticated white social set of the day. When Luckey Roberts (1890–1968) reigned as king of the Harlem ragtime pianists, the eastern school of ragtime was at its peak, and his "Nothin'" was "the last word in cutting contests from 1908" (Jasen and Tichenor 1978, 189).[12] Known especially for his composition and performances of pieces such as "Spanish Venus" and "Pork and Beans," the latter of which was published in 1913 and recorded by him around that time, Roberts was without equal in Harlem's gladiatorial cutting contests.

Around 1918, Roberts was succeeded as "king" by James P. Johnson, who broke with eastern ragtime and moved stride toward wide acceptance with his stunning performances, especially his recording of his own "Carolina Shout" (1921), a fast-moving, celebratory piece inspired by shout culture that was quite unlike any of the works of Scott Joplin, Eubie Blake, Jelly Roll Morton, or the other ragtime composers and pianists of the period. Willie "the Lion" Smith relates that Johnson "played a 'shout' and a shout was a stride. Shouts came about because of the Baptist Church and the way black folks sang or 'shouted' their hymns. They sang them a special way and you played them a special way, emphasizing the basic beat to keep everybody together" (quoted in Waller and Calabrese 1977, 26). Johnson had grown up in New York City's black community, where he saw southern black dances and heard southern black music as they were brought north by early black immigrants—the squares and jubas danced to mouth harps, bones, Jew's harps, and other makeshift musical instruments of the core culture (Kirkeby 1966, 36)—so he was wise to the mu-

---

12. Roberts's "Nothing'" was recorded on *Harlem Piano Solos* (1958).

sical ways of the culture. Johnson confirmed that his music was "based on set, cotillion, and other southern dance steps and rhythms"; his songs were pianistic expressions of the actual sacred and secular "shouts" he had heard and seen danced in the northern black working-class culture (Brown 1986, 22).

Yes, "Carolina" was a shout, yet it also foreshadowed the coming age of more advanced musical ideas. As an improvisational vehicle, it provided new latitude for the creative realizations and executions of the striders, the virtuoso party and cabaret professionals who would later revolutionize jazz piano with startling improvisations: newly invented melodies, rhythms, and harmonies, in seemingly endless variation, that were carried from key to more difficult key in two-handed voicings that cowed and drove away would-be carvers. "Carolina Shout" is a three-theme rag reflecting Johnson's impressions of the shout. It begins innocently enough, but quickly moves to tricky cross-rhythmic constructions that could confound a novice; and the melodic embellishments become more complex as the piece progresses. The piece is replete with Call–Response tropes: call-and-response figures, riffs, straight bass with tricky reverses that create cross-rhythms, and much imitative hand-to-hand action. "Carolina Shout" replaced Luckey Roberts's "Nothin'" as *the* cutting contest "separator." On May 13, 1941, Fats Waller recorded his version of "Carolina Shout," but did not play the cross-rhythms that are so clearly evident in the repeat of the first chorus of Johnson's performance (although he does approximate the device a little later in the piece). Waller's performance is much faster than Johnson's, however, and it displays an impressive technique.

After "Carolina Shout," Johnson, Smith, and Waller—the "Big Three" stride pianists—went on to revolutionize jazz piano, Smith with his wonderful two-hand melodic elaborations and Waller with his two-fisted, cadenza-like Signifyin(g). The lyric, expressive side of stride can be heard in other works by the Big Three—for example, Willie "the Lion" Smith's rendition of "Tea for Two," recorded much later, in an interview session. Although well past his prime at the time of this rendition, the Lion is in good form in this stride-based, inventive set of "melodic beautifications" (as he liked to describe his work and that of the other striders). He begins his performance with the verse, out of tempo (rubato) and with much melodic filigree, then moves into the chorus, which is played four times. The first "chorus" is highly embellished, with more rhythmic activity and added-note chords than the verse. The second chorus (what he calls "first dressing") is dressed with much scale-like movement in the service of melodic elaboration. The two-measure phrases of the third chorus move to ever higher keys in a series of modulations ("changing apartments," according to the Lion) that continue throughout the sixteen measures of the theme. The fourth chorus, based solidly in shout-stride, is much more energetic, with Smith's left hand laying the foundation for his extensions and elaborations of the melody and bass line.

111

With prodigious talent and technique, the Harlem striders remained ascendant until Art Tatum arrived in New York in 1931. According to a witness,

> Tatum spread his hands out over the keyboard, feeling out the instrument. Finding the tension of the keys to his liking, he nodded ever so slightly and rippled off a series of runs. He played around with effortless grace for a short time, gaining speed and tempo. A breathtaking run that seemed to use up every note on the piano led to a familiar theme—*Tea for Two*. But something strange had happened to the tune. Just as suddenly as he gave them the melody he was out of it again, but never far enough away from it to render it unrecognizable. Then he was back on it again. The right hand was playing phrases which none of the listeners had imagined existed, while the left hand alternated between a rock solid beat and a series of fantastic arpeggios which sounded like two hands in one. His hands would start at opposite ends of the keyboard and then proceed towards each other at a paralyzing rate; one hand picking up the other's progression and then carrying it on itself, only to break off with another series of incredible arpeggios. Just when it seemed that he had surely lost his way, Tatum came in again with a series of quick-changing harmonies that brought him back smack on the beat. His technique was astounding. Reuben Harris stole a look around the room. Everyone was exactly as they were when Tatum first sat down. Fats' drink halted on its way to his lips. Fats sat down as if turned to stone. A wrinkle had appeared between his eyes as he half frowned, half smiled at what he had heard. Nearby, James P. was likewise transfixed, small beads of perspiration showing on his forehead. (Kirkeby 1966, 148)

The torch had passed. In this performance—reminiscent of the Signifyin(g) symbolism of Br'er Rabbit and Br'er Mockingbird, by the way—Tatum, with his new melodic and harmonic ideas and his superior technical ability, demonstrated his inimitable synthesis of ragtime, boogie-woogie, and stride piano, revealing his debt to Waller, Earl Hines, and the Chicago boogie-woogie men (some of whom we will encounter presently). He had brought together their disparate styles and molded them into a phenomenal composite that would launch a new school of jazz piano.

The range of Tatum's art can be heard on *The Best of Art Tatum* (1983), his extraordinary talent clearly evident on "Willow Weep for Me," a performance that is both elegant and eloquent in its semantic value. This rendition reveals Tatum's style as characterized by a level of melodic ornamentation and filigree that surpasses that of the striders; by frequent left-hand, right-hand, and two-hand runs, all superlative and incomparable; by considerable rhythmic, melodic, harmonic, and tonal variety; by quasi-rubato passages; by gestures approximating blue notes and other blues and jazz devices; and by more inventiveness—melodically, harmonically, and rhythmically—than that in the striders' performances. The semantic value of Tatum's music is high, containing allusive gestures that analogously sigh, posture, gesture, and "breathe" at the end of "sentences." In much of this he takes after Hines. In his prime, Tatum did not stop with pianists; he also sought out horn players, both to cut and to interact with cooperatively. On *The Best of Art Tatum,* he plays solo on four cuts and performs as a sideman and leader in groups with Roy Eldridge, Benny Carter, Lionel Hampton, Ben Webster, Jo Jones, and others. The harmonic and rhythmic support, filigree, flourishes, and countermelodic figurations and statements he contributes establish and significantly enhance the character and quality of the entire album. Tatum's unusual rhythmic devices, fantastic runs, phrasings, and bravura conceptions are evident on "Caravan," "A Foggy Day," "Elegy," and other cuts and suggest why he was able to best any musician he ran across. If the philosophers of the Harlem Renaissance were after artistic refinement and complexity, Tatum, like Ellington, clearly realized their desires (although belatedly and within a vernacular form—which, of course, in their view, may have disqualified the accomplishment).

As the 1920s progressed, jazz became, for Renaissance leaders, the most acceptable of the secular vernacular genres. Before the Renaissance, the earliest recognized general manifestation of jazz, New Orleans jazz, had been a collectively improvised, out-of-doors music, played primarily at "parades, picnics, concerts, riverboat excursions, and dances" (Gridley 1983, 53). Drawing from the rich reservoir of the ring, it had spread quickly in the second decade of the century to most of the nation's major cities and to points in Europe (note, for example, Jelly Roll Morton's and Freddie Keppard's sojourns in California, King Oliver's permanent residence in Chicago, and the European tours of Sidney Bechet with Will Marion Cook's Southern Syncopated Orchestra).

In the Renaissance period, the challenge of maintaining in jazz the continuity of this African-American aesthetic expression within the framework of new and expanding technical resources as well as restraints was first faced, seriously and effectively, by Fletcher Henderson. New York's large dance halls required larger bands than the honky-tonks, nightclubs, and smaller halls that employed small jazz and society units. So Henderson devised a way to accommodate eleven pieces, initially, to handle the expanding requirements of the genre in its new setting. Henderson and his arranger, Don Redman, began making arrangements that would exploit the instrumental resources of a big band yet retain some of the flexibility and spontaneity of the small jazz ensemble. They accomplished this by placing the winds and brasses in contrast to each other, by employing composed riffs to create continuity and generate propulsive force, and by setting occasional solos against all of this. This process and structure started a new line of development that was to become and remain the standard in big-band jazz. The section-playing that Henderson employed was based on European principles (eschewing to some extent the het-

113

erophonic sound ideal), but the riffs and improvisations and the character of the rhythmic propulsion were African-American. The process of riffing had long been prominent in ring and ring-derived music, emanating from the recurrent and intermittent repetition of call-and-response figures and motivic interjections. In the Henderson band, the use of these devices was transformed into an organizing concept and, as a trope, underwent constant revision during a performance (and from performance to performance). In other words, the riff became both the object and a means of formal, Signifyin(g) revision. There was much of this troping in the Henderson band, and there was also much musical toasting, for improvisation was a prominent feature of the band. Dicky Wells (1971), one of Henderson's sidemen, says, for example, that "when you hear some of Fletcher's old records, there may be just one jammed chorus, but on the job there'd be a lot more. They called it 'stretching it out'" (37).

Henderson's innovations had far-reaching influence. His 1926 recording of his composition "Stampede" contains riffs and responsorial constructions, a clarinet trio, banjo accompaniment, carefully and effectively arranged section passages, and solos by tenor saxophonist Coleman Hawkins and trumpeters Rex Stewart and Joe Smith. "Wrapping It Up" contains fine and sophisticated, although tempered, ensemble playing of ring tropes: call-and-response constructions, riffs, and muted passages. By the late 1920s, Henderson had expanded his instrumentation to include five brasses, four reeds, and four rhythm instruments while continuing his riff-oriented, section-organized arranging structure. Nearly every active big band began to copy Henderson's successful formula, and by 1932 his work had launched the Swing Era. Henderson, the college-educated, polished, urbane bandleader, became New Negro material, since some of the leadership, most notably Du Bois, had by the mid-1920s begun to recognize the legitimacy of jazz.

While Henderson eschewed the heterogeneous sound ideal as a primary organizing principle, Duke Ellington fully embraced it in an unsurpassed orchestral palette, with not only the instruments themselves providing timbral contrasts, but each of the musicians providing even more such contrast within the confines of his individual instrument. It is well known that Ellington selected his sidemen for stylistic and tonal *difference*. He surely recognized that *Signifyin(g) difference* powerfully enhances the heterogeneous effect. Timbre and rhythm, for Ellington, were inextricably bound, as Olly Wilson (1992a) perceptively notes in presenting an example of the heterogeneous sound ideal:

> When Ellington followed the line "It don't mean a thing if it ain't got that swing" with the line "do-wah, do-wah, do-wah, do-wah, do-wah, do-wah," he illustrated the principle of swing by setting up the implied metrical contrast [that produces swing] and by tying this metrical contrast to a contrast in tim-

bre. The line was not do-ooo, do-ooo, etc.; but do-wáh, do-wáh, which accents the affect of timbral contrast working in conjunction with a cross rhythm.[13] (338)

It was during the Harlem Renaissance that Ellington recorded the works that established him as a composer of first rank—works such as "Creole Love Call," "Black and Tan Fantasy," and "East St. Louis Toodle-oo," of which the last will concern us here. I will examine two of the several versions he recorded—those from 1927 and 1937—both of which appear, side by side, in the *Smithsonian Collection of Classic Jazz* (1973). In the 1927 recording, "East St. Louis Toodle-oo" is structured just as Martin Williams points out in the liner notes (he calls the structure "a song-form section and a secondary theme"): A A B A C C A′ A″ C A. For my taste, it is a rondo-like structure with the opening succession of chords serving simultaneously as a returning theme over which improvisations take place. Viewed in this way, it is reminiscent of the French chaconne, which, we know, frequently appeared *en rondeau*. The intermittent intervening sections, B and C, provide melodic and harmonic relief from the repeating A section. The eight-bar chordal opening by the woodwinds and brass serves as the chaconne progression for the A section, over which the trumpet, baritone saxophone, and clarinet improvise in turn. The trumpet takes A, B, the repeat of the variation on C, and the final A; the baritone sax takes C; the clarinet, A′; the final C section is devoted to a trumpet trio in which the theme of that section is stated for the first time (having been improvised on in its first incarnation).

Several things are notable about this performance. First, it is influenced by New Orleans–style jazz, containing as it does the growls, elisions, and manner of soloing that are characteristic of, or derived from, that style. In the first A section, Bubber Miley's trumpet solo is accompanied, for six of the eight bars, by a countermelody remarkably like those of the New Orleans jazzmen; Fred Guy's banjo plays a steady off-beat accompaniment; Ellington strikes supporting chords in a percussive manner; and Sonny Greer's drums keep time— these last three instruments together functioning just as a New Orleans rhythm section would function. Second, and most notably for my purposes, the chaconne-like progression and the solos are fraught with semantic value: the ostinato seems to make a statement, or proposition, over and over; the soloing instruments are in a "talking" mode, with their improvisations seeming to

---

13. Elsewhere (Floyd 1991, 273), I have defined swing as a quality that manifests itself when sound events Signify on the time line against the flow of its pulse, making the pulse freely lilt; this troping of the time line creates the slight resistances that result in the driving, *swinging*, rhythmic persistence that we find in all African-American music but that is most vividly present in jazz. Swing is not a trope, but an essential quality of the music that *results* from troping of a particular kind. My description is consistent with Wilson's, and it is to this process that I will be referring in future discussions of the phenomenon.

comment on, "answer," "restate," make "by the ways," and confirm what has been "said" and "discussed." This "telling effect" is based, analogously, on black-culture ways of telling, answering, and discussing (except for the "siditty" chaconne-like chord progressions). Additionally, the trumpet trio Signifies on the society band and "symphonic jazz" of Paul Whiteman and other novelty musicians of the period, and the soloists Signify on aspects of New Orleans jazz-band technique. In these ways, this rendition of "East St. Louis Toodle-oo" comments on the state of jazz in 1927, a period during which Ellington and Henderson, most particularly, were making use of a variety of styles.

The 1937 version of "East St. Louis Toddle-oo" (treated here, although it takes us two years beyond the close of the Harlem flowering), features a few of the same players but also several others in an enlarged orchestra. It is a more sophisticated, more elegant rendition, giving proof of the continuing development of the Ellington band and of jazz in general. The structure of this version (A A B A A' A" A) is close to that of 1927, except that the C theme has been dropped. Other than that, the main differences between the two are that the band in the 1937 version is technically more advanced and the arrangement is more elaborate, containing more sophisticated and varied articulations, more inner parts, more part-harmony, many harmonized doo-wahs, and more striking use of the capabilities of the full ensemble. This rendition is slower than the 1927 performance and, the New Orleans influences having disappeared, more appropriate to a New York nightclub than to a jook joint or core-culture dance hall. The intense and "pretty" vibrato of all the instruments in this rendition, contrasted with the almost straight tones and nearly subdued accompaniment of the 1927 version, evinces an increase in confidence and sophistication—even pretension—on the part of Ellington and his musicians and reflects the influence of the musical gains made by the band and the musicians in the intervening years. This performance also demonstrates Ellington's versatility, his ability to incorporate into his style whatever elements might contribute to its character, and his ever-creative artistry. This more elaborate and sophisticated version of "East St. Louis Toodle-oo" doubtless made the New Negroes proud, for the sharp line that divided the intellectuals from the jazz and popular musicians had dissolved by this time (Floyd 1990b, 19).

The Duke Ellington Orchestra was followed in the Cotton Club by Cab Calloway's band. The Calloway band was considered to be one of the best of the big bands during the period 1939 to 1943, in spite of the prowess of those of Hines, Billy Eckstine, Ellington, and Basie. This sixteen-piece, exceptionally talented big band was in demand everywhere; through its radio broadcasts from the Cotton Club, it generated an appreciation for jazz among many segments of American society, ensuring the continuation of the tradition. In his performances, Calloway always made use of African-derived performance practices. The "hi-de-ho" phenomenon, for example, is a classic example of the African-American call-and-response pattern. Aside from having a great instrumental aggregation, Calloway continued the scat-singing tradition introduced by Louis Armstrong in the 1920s. Discussing the African-American basis for this technique and the technique's enhancement of instrumental music, Willis Lawrence James (1955) wrote,

> Somehow, Armstrong and Calloway found the trick of using old folk cry principles to supplement the normal means of singing. . . . Being gifted in voice projection, Calloway invented or adopted a series of nonsense syllables and fitted them into his songs of jazz rhythms. When this was done, people realized the thing as a part of themselves, but they did not know why. They did not realize that they were listening to the cries of their vegetable man, their train caller, their charcoal vendor, their primitive ancestors, heated in the hot crucible of jazz, by the folk genius of Calloway and Armstrong until they ran into a new American alloy. It is possible that neither Calloway nor Armstrong realized what took place. If so, the more remarkable. The response of the orchestra in imitating the cries of Armstrong and Calloway carried the cry into the orchestra itself. The rhythms and inflections have been picked up by the orchestras in general during the last two decades [1935–1955]. This has caused a vital development in dance music. (21)

Armstrong and Calloway made calls and cries contemporary, to be picked up, enhanced, developed, and carried forth by the jazz singers of later years. The Calloway band was an experimental laboratory in which new musical techniques, devices, and procedures were explored; it had a profound impact on the future of jazz and, consequently, American music in general. It was in Calloway's band that Dizzy Gillespie began to develop his own style. The recordings he made with the band in 1940 include performances that reveal elements that would become unmistakable features of Gillespie's mature style—tunes such as "Pickin' the Cabbage," "Boo-Wah, Boo-Wah," and "Bye Bye Blues." Calloway's scat singing also must have had some influence on Gillespie.

All across the land, young black jazz musicians were listening to these bands over the radio, on records, and—the lucky ones—in live performances, inspired by their musicianship and Signifyin(g) prowess. These young aspirants used the performances of the musicians in these bands as measures of their own prowess, "woodshedding" constantly to gain control of their art; making efforts to be heard by top musicians and to become known in local, regional, and national jazz circles; hoping to be "sent for" by Basie, Calloway, Jimmy Lunceford, Chick Webb, or Ellington: "Being sent for was recognition and status. Usually it meant New York with a nationally known outfit" (Smith 1991, 40).

These bands and their leaders helped bridge the split that existed in Harlem between the strivers and the "show people" and contributed substantially to the eradication of the class distinctions that plagued the Renaissance. Eventually, all the elements of black society found a place in Harlem's cultural cauldron, eventually closing ranks against the visiting white voyeurs and exploiters of the neighborhood (Floyd 1990b, 21–23, 25). This exploitation, together with other forces and developments, brought the Harlem flowering of the Renaissance to an end (25). The other forces included (1) the expatriation to Europe of some of the concert-hall musicians, such as Roland Hayes, and Henry Crowder,[14] and many of the entertainers, including Josephine Baker, Noble Sissle, and Ada "Bricktop" Smith; (2) the arrival of radio and moving pictures, which reduced nightclub and concert attendance; (3) the establishment in many cities, by 1929, of "regulations prohibiting jazz from public dance halls" (Carroll and Noble 1988, 321), diluting much of the movement's force and ambiance; and (4) the onset of the Great Depression, which dried up the patronage for the arts and letters. The Harlem flowering of the Renaissance ended in the mid-1930s, as the Chicago flowering was beginning.

Robert Bone (1986) has posited the notion of a Chicago Renaissance that spanned the years 1935 to 1950 and that featured ideals and practices that parallel those of the Harlem movement.[15] Bone's hypothesis is persuasive when one compares the main features of the Harlem flowering with the black cultural activity that took place in Chicago. As the Harlem Renaissance had been made possible by patronage, so the activity of black artists and intellectuals in Chicago was supported by public and private funding, primarily from the Works Progress Administration, as well as from some of the sources that had sponsored Harlem's literary activity of the 1920s (the Julius Rosenwald Fund, the Wanamaker family, the Harmon Foundation, and Casper Holstein). As A'Lelia Walker's Dark Tower had served as the primary gathering place for black intellectuals in Harlem, Horace Cayton's and Estelle Bonds's Chicago

14. Crowder was a pianist who was a "central figure" in Washington, D.C., Chicago, and New York music circles before World War I. He moved to Europe in the 1920s and lived with shipping heiress Nancy Cunard, who dedicated her *Negro Anthology* (1930) to him. He returned to the United States for good in the early 1930s (Crowder 1987). Crowder's *Henry-Music* (1930), a set of six songs published by Cunard's Hours Press in Paris, included mediocre settings of two poems by Cunard and one each by Richard Aldington, Walter Lowenfels, Samuel Beckett, and Harold Action. A notation in *Henry-Music* claims that the songs were recorded on Sonabel, but all sources searched (OCLC, RILN, and the Rigler-Deutsch Index) reveal only one recording showing Crowder's involvement, as either composer or musician: "Honeysuckle Rose," with Crowder taking a piano solo, recorded by Jean Tany's Hot Club on the Belgium label in 1941.

15. This Chicago movement is not to be confused with the "Chicago Literary Renaissance" discussed by Kramer (1966), which during the first four decades of the twentieth century embraced the works of white writers and poets such as Carl Sandburg, Floyd Dell, Theodore Dreiser, Sherwood Anderson, Edward Lee Masters, Vachel Lindsey, and Harriet Munro.

homes served a similar purpose in the Chicago flowering. As the Harlem Renaissance had the white Carl Van Vechten and the black intellectual Alain Locke as liaisons with white supporters of the movement, Chicago's nonblack supporters were encouraged and attracted primarily by Edwin Embree, the white administrator of the Julius Rosenwald Fund. As in Harlem, the Chicago Renaissance was based on the premise that African Americans would "measure up" to the artistic, intellectual, cultural, and economic standards of the white world and eventually become part of a race-free society (Bone, 455–456). The Harlem Renaissance had been driven in part by the racial politics of W. E. B. Du Bois, and the activity in Chicago was stimulated to some extent by the revolutionary politics of Richard Wright, as reflected in his novels *Native Son* (1940) and *Black Boy* (1945).[16] The Harlem Renaissance had been fueled by the African-American folk experience, but sustained by an integrationist outlook; so was the activity in Chicago. The attitudes toward music that prevailed among middle-class blacks in Chicago in the 1930s were identical to those of the Harlem Renaissance intellectuals: some accepted the spiritual as incomparable black folk music, to be used as the foundation for "high art," but rejected the blues and only tolerated jazz, considering the former as socially unredeeming and the latter as decadent; others viewed all vernacular black music as aesthetically valuable, if not socially acceptable. In Chicago, as in Harlem, the music of the rent-party, theater, and cabaret worlds was separate from, yet ironically supportive of, some of the New Negro ideals.

According to Grossman (1989), Chicago in the early years was filled with "aromas of southern cooking . . . ; the sounds of New Orleans jazz and Mississippi blues; [southern] styles of worship; [southern] patterns of speech" (262), all of which fit into "an interactive process" in which these cultural activities and values modified and were modified by new ideas, values, and habits within the context of northern discrimination, economic insecurity, and an urban life-style that was new to recent migrants. This interactive process created among Chicago's African Americans an impulse toward an ardent self-affirmation that found its most public expression in the city's community of musicians, writers, and visual artists. In the music, it was probably manifest as early as the second decade of the twentieth century, when the blues and jazz began to make an impact on Chicago and when, in 1919, the National Association of Negro Musicians was founded there to effect "progress, to discover and foster talent, to mold taste, to promote fellowship, and to advocate racial

---

16. Consider, for example, two passages in *Native Son:* "Goddammit, Look! We live here and they live there. We black and they white. They got things and we ain't. They do things and we can't. It's just like living in jail" (23). "Who knows when some slight shock, disturbing the delicate balance between social order and thirsty aspiration, should send the skyscrapers in our cities toppling" (368).

expression" (Cuney-Hare [1936] 1974, 242).[17] But in spite of significant early activity by such figures as Kemper Harreld, Maude Roberts George, and Estelle Bonds, this great impulse for self-affirmation apparently did not flourish on a large and impressive scale until the 1930s.

On June 15, 1933, the Chicago Symphony Orchestra presented an evening of "Negro Music and Musicians," featuring Roland Hayes in a performance of Coleridge-Taylor's "Onaway, Awake, Beloved" from *Hiawatha's Wedding Feast,* pianist Margaret Bonds in a performance of white composer John Alden Carpenter's *Concertina,* and the premiere of Florence Price's Symphony in E Minor ("Gershwin Plays" 1933; "Noted Tenor" 1933, 21). Because of the unprecedented magnitude of this event, it should be taken as the landmark event for the musical aspect of the Chicago Renaissance, preceding by more than eighteen months the year of commencement fixed by Bone. This concert had been preceded by two major accomplishments by black composers in Chicago: Florence Price's completion of her Symphony in E Minor (1932) and William Dawson's completion of his *Negro Folk Symphony* (1934).

Price's symphony has not been recorded or published, so I will not discuss it here. But another of her achievements can be discussed: the Piano Sonata in E Minor—the first major piano work of the Negro Renaissance. Harmonically and melodically rich and well crafted, this unpublished but now commercially recorded twenty-five-minute work is filled with brief rhythmic motives and accompanying figures, typical African-American rhythms, broad, heavy chords, flowing melodic lines, and ersatz spiritual and dance tunes. The first movement (Andante-allegro) consists of two themes reminiscent of African-American dance tunes, treated here in a much more delicate, lyrical manner, developed, and brought to conclusion in a dramatic close. The second movement (Andante), a rondo, begins with a tune reminiscent of the spiritual. It is based on the following rhythm, which I have already cited as highly characteristic of the genre: ♫♩ . The third movement (Scherzo: allegro), also a rondo, begins with a theme made of rapid scale passages in triplets; this is followed by a broad, sweeping line that contrasts with all the other themes in the work; the third theme is a variant of the primary theme of the second movement. Dance rhythms abound in this section, which brings the movement, and the work as a whole, to a close with rapid scale passages and strong, insistent chords in a brilliant, bravura ending.

---

17. The philosophy and efforts of the NANM carried forward the nationwide black concert activity dating from the mid-nineteenth century, which was exemplified by the Creoles of Color performing in New Orleans's Philharmonic Society Orchestra led by Constantin Duberque and Richard Lambert (1842); by Philadelphia's soprano Elizabeth Taylor Greenfield's concertizing between around 1850 and 1870; by Washington, D.C.'s Colored Opera Company (1872); and by the activity in 1876 of New York's Philharmonic Society.

Dawson began his career in the mid-1920s with the publication of choral arrangements of spirituals, among which were "King Jesus Is A-Listening" (1925) and "I Couldn't Hear Nobody Pray" (1926). Among his other works are numerous arrangements of spirituals, the Sonata in A for violin and piano (1927), the Trio in A for piano, violin, and violoncello (1925), the *Scherzo for Orchestra* (winner of a Wanamaker Prize in 1930), and *A Negro Work Song for Orchestra* (1940), which was commissioned by the Columbia Broadcasting System. In the same year that Price's Symphony in E Minor was premiered, Margaret Bonds, who studied with Price and with Dawson and whose mother's home was one of the two principal gathering places for Chicago Renaissance intellectuals (Walker-Hill 1992a, 11), won a Wanamaker Prize for her song "Sea Ghost." She later set texts by Langston Hughes (for example, "The Negro Speaks of Rivers," 1946) and celebrated the Great Migration in her ballet *The Migration* (1964).

Chicago's vocal artists also actively contributed to the prevailing spirit of renaissance. On December 26, 1937, La Julia Rhea made her operatic debut with the Chicago Civic Opera Company, singing the title role in *Aïda;* in the same production, William Franklin debuted as Amonasro. The Chicago guild of the Pittsburgh-based Negro Opera Company presented *Aïda* in October 1942 and in February 1943. The second performance, before an audience "about equally divided between white and colored opera lovers," won "the highest praise" from critics ("Civic Opera" 1943; "Opera 'Aida'" 1943). Chicago baritone Theodore Charles Stone made his Town Hall debut in 1940 and began to tour regularly as a concert singer. In 1942, soprano Hortense Love, also of Chicago, debuted in New York City's Town Hall; Etta Moten, who had moved to Chicago in 1934, appeared as Bess in the 1942 production of George Gershwin's *Porgy and Bess,* after which she toured extensively in the United States as a concert singer (Southern 1982, 283). These and many other events that took place between 1933 and 1950 give evidence of the abundant concert-music activity of the period.

In the vernacular arena, the Chicago Renaissance years saw significant musical ferment in the development of black gospel music, the rise of urban blues, and important developments in jazz. After vocal blues became acceptable to record companies, so did a pianistic form called boogie-woogie, its first documents appearing in the 1920s and its first widespread urban manifestations taking place in Chicago. Pete Johnson, Roosevelt Sykes, Pine Top Smith, Cow Cow Davenport, Meade Lux Lewis, Jimmy Yancey, and Albert Ammons were masters of the style. In boogie-woogie, cross-rhythms are produced by the right hand playing triple figures against the duple divisions of the left hand's eight-to-the-bar, rumbling ostinato (which really swings when played by a boogie-woogie master). The rolling left hand is the key to the style, providing the propulsive, four-beat jumpy rhythm that gives the music its characteristic

121

pump and flow. The I-IV-V chord progressions—delineated by the heavy, jerky, bass ostinato—support treble filigree, short runs, and sharp chords. By the 1920s, boogie-woogie had become enormously popular on Chicago's rent-party circuit, having originated in the late 1880s or 1890s in the jooks and barrel houses of the South (although it was not called boogie-woogie until the 1920s) and brought to Chicago in the Great Migration.[18]

Developing and existing side by side with ragtime, but used primarily as house-party music in small, intimate venues, boogie-woogie was more rhythm-oriented than ragtime, with its bass ostinato serving as the controlling element for all other, "resultant" musical activity (compare Jones 1959, 1:53, 54) and a Signifyin(g) right hand producing figures that contrasted with and complemented the ostinato. Wendell Logan (1984) has pointed out the rhythmic and functional relationship between the ostinati of boogie-woogie and the African time-line concept, stressing that "much of the music of the black diaspora which is organized around the ostinato principle is dance music" (193). So although African time-line retentions can be found elsewhere in the music of African Americans, the technique as a *functional,* melodic bass-ostinato concept did not enter practice until the advent of boogie-woogie or its progenitors. As the time line functions in African music, so the ostinato functions for boogie-woogie—as a vehicle for other figures and lines. Logan, noticing that this principle has had broad and determinative effects on black music, concludes that it (1) influenced the change in jazz from a two-beat to a four-beat feel and (2) caused the eighth-note subdivisions of the beat to be interpreted as uneven durations, moving from ♫♫ to ♫♫ to ♩♪♩♪ , the last coming to be known as swing eighths. Boogie-woogie was created by blacks in the American South, but spread quickly to the northern urban areas when the Great Migration began. In the recorded performances of Meade Lux Lewis, Jimmy Yancey, and Albert Ammons, the genre can be observed in its formal guise. Lewis's "Honky Tonk Train" (1937), for example, contains all the elements typical of the style: a twelve-bar structure, eight beats to the bar; ostinato bass; improvised, vocally conceived right-hand figures; and a percussive approach. In this performance, as in others, the encounter of the right-hand figurations with the left-hand ostinato produces occasional polyrhythms that, together with the percussive attack and the blues mode, place the style squarely in the African-American musical tradition. In its heyday, boogie-woogie was extremely popular in some segments of the black community; a nationwide craze prevailed in the late 1930s and early 1940s, after which the genre's popularity waned, ending in the early 1950s. The Chicago boogie-woogie pianists were the Windy City's counterparts of the Harlem striders, dominating the city's rent-party circuit.

18. For examples of the style, see *Original Boogie Woogie Piano Giants* (1974).

By the 1920s, a modified form of New Orleans jazz had developed in Chicago, created by the New Orleans musicians who had moved there—most notably King Oliver, Louis Armstrong, and Johnnie Dodds. Our knowledge of early jazz is extrapolated primarily from the body of recordings made by Oliver, Armstrong, and Jelly Roll Morton in Chicago from 1923 to 1929—specifically, the Paramount sides of Oliver's Creole Jazz Band, the Hot Five and Hot Seven recordings of Armstrong, and Jelly Roll Morton's Red Hot Peppers sides.

For my purposes, Morton's contribution can be heard best on his 1926 recording of "Black Bottom Stomp." This performance is governed to a large extent by the Call–Response principle, relying on Signifyin(g) elisions, responses to calls, improvisations (in fact or in style), continuous rhythmic drive, and timbral and pitch distortions that are retentions from the ring. At every point, "Black Bottom Stomp" Signifies on black dance rhythms and makes use of the time-line concept of African music. The latter is the rhythmic foundation for the entire piece, but is kept in the background for the most part and sometimes only implied; it is a continuous rhythm that subdivides Morton's two beats per bar into an underlying rhythm of eight pulses. This continuous, implied, and sometimes sounded pulse serves the function of a time line over which the foreground two-beat metric pattern has been placed, and it serves as the reference pulse for the two-beat and four-beat metric structures and the cross-rhythms and additive rhythms that occur throughout the performance. The clarinet and banjo frequently emphasize this time line with added volume, thereby bringing it into the foreground as a Signifyin(g) trope. Over this time line, improvisation takes place—improvisation that Signifies on (1) the structure of the piece itself, (2) the current Signifyin(g)s of the other players in the group, and (3) the players' own and others' Signifyin(g)s on previous performances. These Significations take place at the same time that the performers are including within their improvisations timbral and melodic derivations from the ring: the trombone's smears (elisions); the elided phrasings of the muted trumpet; tropes that revise, extend, and update call-and-response, calls, cries, hollers, and shouts—all accompanied by figures that Signify on foot-patting and hand-clapping after-beats, cross-rhythms, breaks, stop-time tropes, and occasional four-beat stomp rhythms. The performance is fraught with the referentiality that Gates describes as "semantic value," exemplifying (1) how performers contribute to the success of a performance with musical statements, assertions, allegations, questings, requestings, implications, mockings, and concurrences that result in the "telling effect" that Murray (1973) has described and (2) what black performers mean when they say that they "tell a story" when they improvise.

Morton's art clearly looked back to New Orleans, but that of Oliver and Armstrong looked forward. Oliver had as his model the legendary Buddy Bolden; Armstrong, notwithstanding other influences, took Oliver as his. Comparing Oliver's recorded work with the descriptions of Bolden's art that we encountered in chapter 3, we can assume that Oliver appropriated Bolden's power and manner of improvising and added his own impeccable control and, perhaps, more scale-like passages. Armstrong built on Oliver's foundation and innovations, molding the art of jazz with his own conceptions and, in the process, revolutionizing it and setting standards that would guide all who were to come after him. Although there were few solos in the Oliver band's performances, the two-trumpet team of Oliver and Armstrong was superb, creating breaks, inventing ideas to fill them, and effectively voicing the intervals between their parts within the context of sensitive ensemble playing.

It was in Chicago that Armstrong became the world's most influential jazzman, developing his art and technique to a level that was then unapproachable by other trumpet players. We can get some idea of the artistic influence that Armstrong and other New Orleans players had on the elaboration of jazz, and of the technical level Armstrong had attained by the mid-1920s, from four recorded performances: "Dippermouth Blues" (1923), "Hotter Than That" (1927), "West End Blues" (1928), and "Weather Bird" (1928).

"Dippermouth Blues," an instrumental in the style of the loose melodic heterophony of New Orleans jazz, showcases Oliver's improvisational style and ability. His wa-wa choruses and Johnnie Dodds's clarinet solo are good examples of the improvisation-by-paraphrase technique of early jazz. Apparently, Oliver was the first professional player to mute his instrument, employing bottles, cups, and utensils constructed specifically for distorting the sound of his cornet, a uniquely African-derived practice that surely must have been employed in African-American folk music before Oliver made it common in professional circles.[19] On "Dippermouth," Armstrong was a sideman, but by 1928 he had emerged, with the Hot Fives, as "king." His "Hotter Than That," with Kid Ory on trombone and Dodds on clarinet, is an early example of extended instrumental and vocal improvisation. It is a sixteen-bar blues that makes use of a banjo shuffle-rhythm, elisions, riffs, polyrhythms, and call-and-response figures (the last on the seventh chorus). Ory and Dodds perform at a high level, and Armstrong is dazzlingly superb. His scat singing here is impressive, reminiscent of the way Africans teach rhythm through vocables. "West End Blues," with Fred Washington on trombone, Jimmy Strong on clarinet, and Earl Hines on piano, reveals movement away from the New Orleans ensemble tradition, with Armstrong having developed a virtuosity that showcases

---

19. It is well known that village Africans traditionally have distorted and enhanced the natural sounds of musical instruments (perhaps in search of the heterogeneous sound ideal) by placing membranes over the amplifying tubes of marimbas, adding beads to the outsides of gourds that already contain seeds, adding rattles to the heads of drums, and the like.

his out-of-tempo, cadenza-like introduction and enhances a linear complexity within the ensemble.

Armstrong had brought with him to Chicago, as had so many others during the Great Migration, the elisions, vocables, and other tropes of the blues. But from the Hot Five recordings onward, his unique and effective attacks and releases, his treatment of vibrato and rubato, and his way of phrasing and floating over, behind, and in front of the beat—that is, his *Signifyin(g) on it*—gave his performances a tremendous and unique swing. His movement away from the duple-beat divisions of New Orleans jazz to triple divisions created polyrhythms that added buoyancy and additional swing. His dominating lead cornet shifted away from the communal practices of the New Orleans ensemble to a leader/improviser-dominated practice that is also of Call–Response provenance. In addition, Armstrong began to move away from paraphrase toward the construction of new melodies—Signifyin(g) revisions—which opened the way for the more dramatic improvisations that would follow in succeeding decades. "Weather Bird" is a duet showcasing the impressive individual and collective improvisations of Armstrong and Hines. Armstrong's sureness and authority of tone, attack, and pitch are impressive here, and his effective use of terminal vibrato and subtle use of elision, turns, mordents, and hemiola figures demonstrate the level of his art in the 1920s. Hines's style is based somewhat on ragtime conventions, but it certainly transcends the strictness of that genre, making use of Signifyin(g) octaves in the melodic line and reverting sometimes, however briefly, to a comping style that would be fully developed later. Employing advanced ideas of phrasing, accentuation, and rhythm, the level of imagination in the performance is high, elevated by the artistic stimulation of each player on the other. This solo-and-accompaniment performance of Armstrong and Hines began to move the music clearly away from both New Orleans– and Chicago-style jazz toward developments that would be more fully developed in the 1930s and 1940s.

To jump from the Armstrong–Hines "Weather Bird" collaboration of 1928 to the formation of the Earl Hines band in 1942 may seem a considerable leap, given the rapid change and elaboration of jazz and the difference in style and content between "Weather Bird" and the Hines band of the early 1940s. But since my focus in this book is on revolutionary high points, and not on the step-by-step evolution of the music, the developmental gap I leave between Hines's 1928 "Weather Bird" performance and his 1942 big-band activity is intentional and justified. For my purposes here, Hines is simply a convenient, logical connector of events because of his contribution of the comping piano style, which first appeared in "Weather Bird," and the musical freedom he allowed in his big band to the rise of that genre.

The Earl Hines band of 1942 to 1944, which included Dizzy Gillespie and Charlie Parker, was a hothouse of experimentation, an "incubator of bebop," according to Stanley Dance (1977, 90). Gunther Schuller confirms this by telling of the time, in 1943, when he "heard the great Earl Hines band. They were playing all the flatted fifth chords and all the modern harmonies and substitutions and Dizzy Gillespie runs in the trumpet section work" (quoted in Dance, 290). Cliff Smalls, a member of the band, reports that "Dizzy and Charlie [had solos], but they were not big stars then, although they were playing the way that made them famous" (quoted in Dance, 266). Hines himself reports that Gillespie wrote the famous bebop tunes "Night in Tunisia" and "Salt Peanuts" while he was in the Hines band (quoted in Dance, 90). Neither Gillespie nor Parker could have missed Hines's comping technique, which by that time he had probably developed beyond what he had demonstrated in "Weather Bird." In 1944, Gillespie and Parker left Hines to join Billy Eckstine, another "important pioneer of bebop," whose band included Miles Davis, Tadd Dameron, Dexter Gordon, Art Blakey, Fats Navarro, Gene Ammons, and other bebop notables. Gillespie remembers: "I'll never forget the record date Billy Eckstine had at National after he left Early. He had me write one of the arrangements, for the *Good Jelly Blues*—Jelly, Jelly, you know. Talking about bebop, we were beeeee-boppin' behind him!" (quoted in Dance, 261).[20] We shall explore the implications of this early experimentation in chapter 6.

Throughout the history of African-American music, the genres of the tradition have been created and developed through the synthesizing of their various elements by makers of black music. It was in Chicago that one of the most notable of these syntheses occurred: Thomas A. Dorsey's melding of blues elements with those of the religious hymn to make the gospel blues, spawning both what came to be known as the "Dorsey Song" and the choral gospel-blues style (Harris 1992). Dorsey had been assisted in his rise by the following individuals successively: the Reverend W. M. Nix, one of the singing preachers of the day, whose emotional, inspirational, improvisational singing of the song "I Do, Don't You" at the 1921 National Baptist Convention convinced Dorsey of the viability of blues tropes in the singing of religious music and spurred him to continue in that direction; the evangelistic singer Theodore Fry, who, between 1930 and 1932, teamed with Dorsey to present and promote Dorsey's songs on the church circuit; Sallie Martin, who, beginning in 1932, promoted Dorsey's songs and organized his publishing affairs; and Mahalia Jackson, who, between 1939 and 1944, sang and promoted

---

20. Unfortunately, the Hines band in which Gillespie and Parker played never recorded, but we do have Eckstine's recording of "Jelly, Jelly" (1940).

Dorsey's songs on the church circuit and performed them at conventions. Jackson's voice was one of incomparable range and power, and her sound and delivery were equally distinguished.

Dorsey's relationship with Jackson in the religious realm may have been similar to his earlier relationship with Ma Rainey in the blues arena. For much of Rainey's career, Dorsey served as her pianist, bandleader, and songwriter. Sometime before 1920, he joined the church and began performing there as a pianist; he "backslid" in 1921, after his first gospel publication, "I Do, Don't You," to organize a band for Rainey, and again around 1928, when he wrote the blues hit "Tight Like That" (Southern 1971, 403; Work 1949, 141–142).[21] Having been known variously as Texas Tommy, Smokehouse Charley, Barrelhouse Tom, and Georgia Tom, by 1924 Dorsey had not only become "one of the major blues composers in Chicago," but was acquainted with the hymns of Charles Albert Tindley (Harris 1992, 75, 81) and the performance practices applied to them by performers such as Sister Rosetta Tharpe and Blind Joe Taggart, all of which fully prepared him to achieve what he desired.

Tindley had smoothed the path for the development of African-American gospel music and the later crystallization of its style. He had created space in his songs to accommodate the call-and-response figures and improvisations that, together with flatted thirds and sevenths and other core-culture performance practices, would come to make the style. Tharpe's performance of Tindley's "Beams of Heaven," in which she accompanied her own conservative vocal delivery on the guitar, is a steady, rhythmic rendition of the sixteen-measure song, with accompanying figures that recall blues guitarists of the period. Taggart's 1927 recording of "The Storm Is Passing Over" is a more demonstrative interpretation of a Tindley song. A shouter, Taggart gives a fervent vocal rendition, and his guitar accompaniment is based squarely in ring values: polyrhythms abound, occasioned by Taggart's improvisatory, rhythmically free delivery of the vocal over a steady and repetitive guitar pattern.[22] The ground rhythm in this performance parallels—is almost identical to—those of juré and juba, particularly the former, and it closely approximates the ground rhythms in Mississippi John Hurt's "Big Leg Blues" and Rube Lacy's "Ham Hound Crave," on which I commented in chapter 3. Taggart's vocal delivery here also comes close to the blues singing of some of the Mississippi Moaners. Although I do not know that Dorsey was directly influenced by Tindley,

21. For examples of Dorsey's blues writing and performance, including "Tight Like That," see *Georgia Tom Dorsey: Come On Mama, Do That Dance, 1928–1932.*

22. This rhythmically free delivery is related to Armstrong's way of "floating" above the beat. It would be interesting to know the extent to which this practice was used in black folk music between the turn of the century and 1930. Although its "invention" is sometimes attributed to Armstrong, I wonder if the practice had not already been present, to some extent, in core culture.

it appears that by the late 1920s Dorsey was prepared to exploit the possibilities suggested by Tindley's exemplary structures and to capitalize on certain of the compositional possibilities suggested by performers like Tharpe and Taggart (I would find it hard to believe that Dorsey was not familiar with their work).

Dorsey came to national attention after his song "If You See My Savior, Tell Him That You Saw Me" (1926) was performed by Willie Mae Fisher at the National Baptist Convention in Chicago in 1930 (Harris 1992, 175–179). But it was the publication, in 1932, of "Take My Hand, Precious Lord" that established him as a major figure. "Precious Lord" received a "resounding affirmation" in its premiere performance by Theodore Frye (with Dorsey at the piano) at Ebenezer Baptist Church in 1932. Taken around to other churches by the duo, it apparently received equally rousing welcomes; those receptions led ultimately "to the rise of gospel blues as an established song form in old-line churches" (244). With this slow gospel song, Dorsey expanded on Tindley's practice of leaving gaps and spaces for "ring" play and added innovations of his own. Most of Dorsey's songs are composed of sixteen-measure sections and make use of blues inflections, favoring flatted thirds and sevenths and off-beat melodic accents, and "Precious Lord" is not an exception. The simple but unique melody line, accompanied by harmony that is advanced for the genre, is a gospel singer's delight; and the poetry and setting of the lyrics are superb. Marian Williams's 1973 recording of the piece[23] is a powerful and moving rendition, with blue notes, bent notes, elisions, timbral variations, and moans delivered in a full, rich voice. The supporting piano and organ frequently engage in call-and-response interplay and wordless yea-sayings of prodigious semantic value, bringing them into the foreground at appropriate points. The blues, jazz, and spiritual elements in this performance, including melodic and rhythmic paraphrase, are effectively and inextricably fused in a touching, fervent, and moving presentation. The instrumentalists on the recording—Lloyd Gary on piano, Paul Griffin on organ, Howard Carrol on guitar, and Earl Williams on drums—splendidly support the singer's powerful climaxes, the organist's swells combining with the pianist's repeated motives and single notes to enhance the singer's elevations; and there is splendid Signifyin(g) interplay between the piano and organ—real inter*play*—that complements Williams's effort. In her delivery, Williams intensifies aspects of Dorsey's text with repetitions of syllables and words, with bent notes, and with spoken interjections ("Lord, here's what I *want* you to do for *me*") and intensifies the music by displacing selected notes at the octave and by eliding certain grace notes.

Songs such as Dorsey's and precursors of performances like Williams's provided a new foundation for shout worship in black urban Protestant churches

23. Williams sings "Precious Lord" on *Precious Lord: New Gospel Recordings of the Great Gospel Songs of Thomas A. Dorsey.*

in the 1930s and beyond. Shout worship—which, as we saw in Chapter 3, had continued since slavery in the Pentecostal and Holiness churches of the nation's cities—constituted, in Harris's opinion, modern, urban "bush arbor" (or "brush harbor") worship, a throwback, or continuation, of the disguised and clandestine forest meeting places where slaves held worship and strategy meetings in which they had "a good time, shouting, singing, and praying just like we pleased" (former slave, quoted in Harris 1992, 245). Eventually, Harris tells us,

> this special communal gathering actually crept into the high worship hour itself in Baptist old-line churches, particularly with the deacon's prayer and song service that was held just prior to the high worship hour. But such a literal echo of the "bush arbor" prayer and shout threatened the new old-line aesthetic so much that a church like Pilgrim Baptist had to move it out of the main sanctuary into the basement—perhaps unaware that the cellar was a more authentic setting than the upstairs formal meeting hall by any stretch of the imagination. (248)

Harris (1992) suggests that Dorsey's Pilgrim Baptist Church chorus could be considered a resurrected version of the praying and singing bands of the nineteenth century (which I mentioned in chapter 2), whose practice it had been "to carry on their shouting, clapping, and ring dancing after sermons or as an appendage to the formal worship" (207). The gospel chorus originated in 1928 at Chicago's Metropolitan Community Church, when Magnolia Butler established a group to supplement the music of the Senior Choir; this led to similar choirs at Bethel A.M.E. and Quinn Chapel. But the gospel-*blues* chorus had its debut in that auspicious year 1932, when Dorsey and Frye established the chorus at Ebenezer, engaging the interest and participation of transplanted Southerners who believed in the "bush arbor" aesthetic (187–200). The gospel-blues choruses multiplied and became exceedingly popular. They would play increasingly important roles in black Protestant churches over the succeeding years and decades.

The importance of boogie-woogie, jazz, and gospel music in the Chicago Renaissance is evident from references and allusions to it in some of the literature and other artistic output of the movement. For example, Gwendolyn Brooks's poems "Queen of the Blues" and "of De Witt Williams on his way to Lincoln Cemetery," both included in *A Street in Bronzeville* (1945), treat, in the first instance, the life of a blues singer and, in the second, the nature of black life itself, with a spiritual text at the end: "Swing low swing low sweet chariot. Nothing but a plain black boy." In Richard Wright's *Native Son*, which makes no significant mention of music, Bessie, Bigger's girl, is a character

129

whose "speech and life-style embodies in no simple way the spirit of the *blues*," according to Edward A. Watson (1971, 168). For Watson, "Bessie's blues are an extension of the earthly complaint in the tradition of Ma Rainey and Bessie Smith" (168). In Bessie's speech—her "songs"—he finds "characteristic blues themes which fall naturally under the three divisions of the book" (171). In this way, Wright achieves a subtle wedding of literature and black music—a wedding that expresses the essentials of black life in early-twentieth-century America.

The magazines of the Chicago Renaissance promoted such musical–literary interaction. The short-lived *Negro Story* published Bucklin Moon's short story "Slack's Blues" (1944) and Vernon Loggins's "Neber Said a Mumblin' Word" (1944), a story based on the Negro spiritual of that name. Its final issue presented a column headed "Music," the first of what was to have been a regular feature, promising that "the current interest in the Negro's part in our jazz history started by *Lionel Hampton's Swing Book* will be exploited to the fullest" ("Music" 1946).[24] The early issues of *Abbott's Monthly,* a literary magazine, carried features on and advertisements for musical solo acts and groups such as the Four Harmony Kings and Walter Barnes's Royal Creolians.

Lionel Hampton's Swing Book (Browning 1946),[25] a quintessential product of the period, contained sections devoted to musicians, dancers, singers, arrangers, and blues music. It also included sections such as "Literary Arts and Jazz," which featured poetry; "Fiction on Jazz" by James O. Wilson, Langston Hughes, Onah Spencer, and others; and "Notes on Jazz," "Swing and Listening," and "Swing and the Armed Forces." The book also featured biographies and photographs of the most prominent musical figures of the day, including Hampton himself, Ellington, Count Basie, Lucky Millinder, and Jimmy Lunceford; a column on jazz artists of the future; and a jazz bibliography. Revealing the contemporary values and perceptions of the music and other arts of the day, the book contains much ephemeral information, many obscure photographs, and brief biographical sketches and comments of a large number of black jazz musicians.

Certain figures of the Harlem Renaissance had strong influence on the Chicago activity. In 1940, for example, former Harlem Renaissance writer Arna Bontemps served as cultural director for a planned state-sponsored American Negro Exposition in Chicago. He brought with him Langston Hughes, to write the book for *Jubilee: A Cavalcade of the Negro Theater.* Margaret Bonds and

24. *Negro Story* was published from May 1944 to May 1946. A full run of the magazine is at the Carter G. Woodson Regional Library, Chicago Public Library.

25. I am grateful to Robert Bone for informing me of the existence of this book, whose cover is graced by the name of the great jazz and swing drummer and vibraphonist. He had brought it to my attention long before I ran across the reference in the April–May 1946 issue of *Negro Story*. And I thank Dan Morgenstern of the Jazz Institute of Rutgers University for access to a copy of this rare document.

W. C. Handy assisted Hughes, and Duke Ellington and gospel songwriter Thomas A. Dorsey set to music two sets of lyrics that Hughes wrote especially for the show (unfortunately, it was never produced; see Rampersad 1986, 386).

From all indications, the Chicago Renaissance had less coherence, as a culture-building movement, than did the Harlem movement; it spawned no prevailing black string quartets or symphony orchestras and no black-composed operas, although it did have a branch of a black opera company. But during this period, the vernacular genres grew powerfully in influence and complexity. The blues was extended and elaborated in ways that would allow it to be transformed into rhythm and blues, rock 'n' roll, and, eventually, rock music; Chicago jazz served, in a specific case, as an incubator of bebop; and the Dorsey songs and their progeny extended and elaborated black gospel music, setting the stage for the emergence of modern gospel.

Like the Harlem movement, the Chicago Renaissance was a flowering of Afro-American arts and letters. Unlike the Harlem manifestation, however, in which recognition and theorizing took place simultaneously with its activity, recognition of and theorizing about the Chicago Renaissance is only now beginning. But the Harlem and Chicago flowerings are all of a piece—aspects of a worldwide movement that had its beginnings in the 1890s and continued into the middle of the twentieth century. The Negro Renaissance embraced Washington, D.C., Atlanta, Paris, London, and other large cities around the world—cities that served as bases for the dissemination of the art and ideas of Paul Robeson, W. E. B. Du Bois, Robert Nathaniel Dett, James P. Johnson, Langston Hughes, Duke Ellington, Roland Hayes, Richard Wright, Edmund Jenkins, William Grant Still, Thomas A. Dorsey, Florence Price, Earl Hines, Alain Locke, and all the other important figures of the movement (Floyd 1990b; Green 1990).

The way ragtime, blues, jazz, and gospel musics developed during the Negro Renaissance was in some ways determined by the modernist mind-set and by New Negro philosophy. To what extent this is true I cannot prove—in part because of the absence of written confirmation of such influences, because of the participants' failure to have perceived or articulated such influences, and because the social posturing, dissembling, and denials that typically exist among competing class and caste groups make statements by some participants of the movement somewhat unreliable (many of the intellectuals and entertainers had a stake in denying such influences, since they tended to support their own particular and most pressing causes). As far as the concert music of the period is concerned, it is clear that in Harlem the initial artistic ideas of the Negro Renaissance were best and most fully realized in Dett and Still, and that in Chicago the same ideals were most fully realized in Dawson, Price, and Bonds. The Negro Renaissance's greatest musical contribution to American culture was its exploration, extension, elaboration, and crystallization of the black aesthetic and the example that aesthetic set for the composers who would mature in the 1960s and beyond. There were certain casualties along the way, of course, most notably Will Marion Cook and William L. Dawson, both of whom had ambitions and talent that transcended what they accomplished. Both might have been prodigious composers of concert-hall music had real opportunities existed for them. But the fields of entertainment and education were the loci of whatever opportunities then existed and, in the face of continual resistance on the part of white culture, Cook and Dawson responded to the beckonings and seductions of Broadway and the teaching profession, respectively. Cook found it impossible to pursue a career as a concert violinist or composer of concert-hall music, and no one would or could take up and sustain the specific trail he blazed in writing show music. Dawson's ambitions were thwarted and redirected because of racial discrimination and because of the turn that the social, intellectual, and artistic climates took, as we shall see, in the 1940s and 1950s.

In spite of the casualties, however, there were many successes. The accomplishments of Cook (in spite of being a casualty in the realm of concert-hall music), Joplin, Dett, Henderson, Ellington, and Still, for example, are culturally, socially, and humanistically significant, for in realizing some of the goals of the Negro Renaissance, they vindicated the faith and the guiding and driving forces of the movement. Joplin, Dett, and Still, for example, *explored* the use of ragtime, spirituals, and blues, respectively, as foundations for extended composition; Tindley, James P. Johnson, Armstrong, Hines, Dett, Henderson, Ellington, Parker, Gillespie, and Still *extended* the reach of ring tropes, creating new possibilities and styles variously through the expansion of the heterogeneous sound ideal, more extended troping, and the introduction of new tropes such as riffs, flatted fifths, and extended improvisations; Armstrong, Hines, Tatum, Ellington, Price, and Gillespie *elaborated* the tradition, bringing to it more intricate revisions and articulations through the revision of timbre, rhythm, melody, and harmony; Dorsey *crystallized* the black gospel style by stabilizing the explorations of Tindley and others through his own stylizations of the extensions and elaborations of ring tropes. In the world of concert music, Dett, Still, and Price, in particular, aside from the developmental and crystallizing contributions they made, produced admirable works of concert music: Dett with the oratorios *The Chariot Jubilee* and *The Ordering of Moses*, Still with the *Afro-American Symphony*, and Price with the Symphony in E Minor.

The leaders of the Harlem flowering of the Negro Renaissance had felt certain that African-American composers possessed the musical talents to achieve their goals—indeed, the fact had already been proved in the years before by

Burleigh, Cook, and Joplin. But on the large scale, their goals were to some extent undermined by the imperatives of modernism. First, Renaissance leaders' apostasized the mythological foundations of black music: consciously or unconsciously, they expected ideology to replace myth, which they found incompatible with their modernist methodology (Joplin's *Treemonisha* was symbolic of this rejection). What they did not understand, however, was that their musical goals would not be adequately supported by or realized through the combined and rationalized principles of formalist composition and New Negro ideology. Of course, the formalist skills were necessary, but rather than ideology, the production of successful works of black music required the foundation of *myth,* which resides not in the mind, as does ideology, but in the intuitive images and metaphors of cultural memory and ritual. It is the supportive structure of myth, together with its ritual trappings, that drives cultural memory and its expression; and many of the composers' confusion of ideology with myth (as a result of their rejection of African-American ritual) resulted in a dearth of artistic communication. This dearth was at the root of the composers' failure to produce in quantity the repertoire for which the movement's leaders had hoped, for when the genuine passions of myth are replaced by rationalized ideology, what results is vapid, or insincere, music. (Even *Treemonisha's* libretto was obliged to embrace myth in order to reject it.)

Second, as marginalized petitioners for entry into the larger social order, Renaissance leaders were obliged—or they preferred—to accept the modernist distinction between high culture and low culture, for if privilege was to be given the high, they would eschew the low (and they had within their midst a capable articulator of the "high" in the person of Alain Locke, who had the respect and ears of many of the Renaissance's patrons and publishers). With most of the artists successfully negotiating the realm of the "low" and ignoring the "high," there was bound to be some consternation on the part of the intellectuals; and the entertainers were bound to be aware of this consternation. But some of the movement's younger artists would not accept this distinction as part of the prevailing ideology. As Langston Hughes retorted in response to the admonitions of the leadership,

> Let the blare of Negro jazz bands and the bellowing voice of Bessie Smith singing Blues penetrate the closed ears of the colored near-intellectuals until they listen and perhaps understand. . . . We younger Negro artists who create now intend to express our dark-skinned selves without fear or shame. If white people are pleased we are glad. If they are not, it doesn't matter. We know we are beautiful. And ugly too. The tom-tom cries and the tom-tom laughs. If colored people are pleased we are glad. If they are not, their displeasure doesn't matter either. We build temples for tomorrow, strong as we know how, and we stand on top of the mountain, free within ourselves. (quoted in Lewis 1981, 191)

133

Thus Hughes and many of his peers also subverted the movement by undermining the leadership's attempt to focus on achievement in the realm of high art. The replacement of myth and ritual with ideology was part of the strategy (conscious or unconscious) to merge social, political, and artistic values in a frontal assault on access to the fruits of white society. But the individualistic values inherent in modernism (necessary, admittedly, for the rise of composers) were still foreign to the progeny of a culture in which communalism had been the norm and who were now experiencing various forms of alienation. All of this resulted in a social tension in which those accustomed to the organic unity of rural Afro-America could not or would not adjust entirely to the change and felt abandoned by the urban intellectuals and artists who were driven by the individualistic impulse. Thus two cultural universes existed: one based on the values of the jook, in the form of rent parties, cabarets, and after-hours joints; the other, on those of the concert hall, the art gallery, the conductor's podium, and the composer's studio. Of course, there were those who successfully negotiated this breach, as evidenced by the collaboration of James P. Johnson, Waller, Still, and Handy on the performance of Johnson's *Yamakraw* (*A Negro Rhapsody*)[26] and Cook's and Still's composition of works that included the values of both cultural universes.

The musical goals of the Negro Renaissance were realized, but in ways that were not evident and certainly not planned. The "extended forms" that Renaissance leaders wanted to see produced *were* produced by Duke Ellington, although not as European-derived concert-hall music. But the New Negroes may not have perceived these accomplishments as relevant to their goals, since Ellington's works did not meet their social requirements: Renaissance leaders' use of the term "symphonic" (meaning "orchestra") was motivated by the politics of concert attendance, of "racial elevation," and of the high-minded aspirations of Alain Locke and other intellectuals. One wonders whether in the face of such conflicts the musical outcomes of the Harlem and Chicago flowerings would have been different and more substantive had there been gatherings and discussions between the musicians and the intellectuals similar to those that took place in the Dark Tower among literary artists, Renaissance leaders, society leaders, and publishers. But these conflicts, differences, and paradoxes, significant as they may have been, should not obscure an essential unity that dominated the movement. That unity lay in black nationalism, for even with the movement's integrationist stance, black nationalism was its *real* ideology, and some of its imperatives gave direction to all who would embrace them. The problem was that this unity could not properly drive Renaissance ideals because of the conflict between those values and the mythological values of the core culture. The primary contributions of black nationalism lay in

26. A version of Johnson's *Yamakraw*, for piano alone, can be heard on *The Symphonic Jazz of James P. Johnson (1894–1955)* (1986).

its giving root to the movement, unifying all classes and castes of African Americans in their attempt, thwarted though it may have been, to build a culture.

The paradoxical nature of the movement—the ideologists' repudiation of black folk music in its pristine forms while embracing it in its more elevated ones, the desire to have the blues without Esu, art without myth—characterized it, exceptions notwithstanding. That the modernist rejection of the mythology of the past and the adoption and promotion, in exalted form, of its artistic progeny was a fundamental contradiction apparently never occurred to most of the players in the movement,[27] many of whom had an ambivalent desire to eat their cake and have it, too.

27. Dett apparently realized and accepted the mythological underpinnings of the spiritual, although he did not flaunt or promote them; and Still's success, I believe, to the extent that it was distanced from myth, was a rare triumph of ideology, probably facilitated by its tribute to ritual.

CHAPTER 6

Transitions: Function and Difference in Myth and Ritual

The tree cannot stand up without its roots.
Zairian Proverb

One must be absolutely modern.
Arthur Rimbaud

In the 1940s, certain transitional events began to take place in African-American music—events that would have far-reaching effects and would change the course of black music in subsequent decades. These events took place as follows:

1. In jazz, the rise of bebop, with its creators returning to and embracing elements of African-American myth and ritual, changed the course of the genre.

2. In popular music, the rise of rhythm and blues laid the foundation for rock 'n' roll and soul music and also caused an incursion of black music into white society.

3. In concert-hall music,[1] certain black composers embraced myth, paid homage to ritual, and produced works of high qual-

1. The imprecisions and problems associated with the terms "concert-hall music," "concert music," "classical music," and other such descriptors of the elite, European-derived "cultivated" musical tradition are well known. I have no wish to justify the use of any of these terms (including the choice I have made here) to describe the music of that tradition, or to make allowances

ity and import, signaling the rise of black composers of first rank in American society.

This chapter is devoted to an elucidation of these events, with emphasis on the role of myth and ritual in bringing them about.

According to an African-American toast,

> Deep down in the jungle, way back in the sticks
> The animals had formed a game called pool. The baboon was a slick.
> Now a few stalks shook, and a few leaves fell.
> Up popped the monkey one day, 'bout sharp as hell.
> He had a one-button roll, two-button satch.
> You know, oner them boolhipper coats with a belt in the back.
> The baboon stood with a crazy rim,
> Charcoal gray vine, and a stingy brim,
> Handful of dimes, pocket full of herbs,
> Eldorado Cadillac, parked at the curb.

(Abrahams [1963] 1970, 148)

Modern toasts demand modern music.[2] The experiments of Charlie Parker, Dizzy Gillespie, and others in the big bands of Cab Calloway, Earl Hines, and Billy Eckstine had joined in the early 1940s with the experimentation of other musicians such as Thelonious Monk, and these experiments had moved into and were accelerated by the more intimate milieu of the nightclub. Throughout the 1940s, small-band jazz began to thrive again in clubs on New York's Fifty-second Street, in Harlem, in Greenwich Village, and in such cities as Philadelphia and San Francisco. Having been dormant since 1929, when big bands became vogue, combo jazz had not exercised its innovative force for nearly a decade. But in the midst of the Swing Era, the potentials of combo jazz began to be explored again. The emerging cabarets hosted late-night sessions in which young musicians were able to carry on the older practices of their elders. Many of these fledgling cabarets were primarily after-hours joints, derivatives of the jook—part of what Hazzard-Gordon (1990, x–xi) has labeled "the jook continuum" (as also were honky-tonks and rent parties). These after-hours clubs hosted jazz's experimental movement. In this environment, the young lions of the movement formed their experimental excursions into

---

for their inadequacies. I trust readers will know from the context of the discussion what I mean when I use these terms, just as they will know what I mean by the word "popular," which is equally imprecise.

2. Bebop was and sometimes still is referred to as "modern music" by those among its sup- **137** porters who consider the term "bebop" belittling and denigrating.

a new music. This new music expressed the emotional realities of musicians in the midst of a powerful verisimilitude—swing music—that they felt repeated and encouraged the same suppressions and denials that black musicians had been experiencing since the ascendance of ragtime. Inspired by the possibilities inherent in new harmonic, rhythmic, and timbral resources, and by the "carving" exploits of their predecessors, the young lions of the movement created a music that, in spite of its revolutionary intent and qualities, was based squarely in the tradition of the ring. The blues was its bedrock and propelling force, but in expressing the emerging values of a new age, these experimentalists (1) evolved a new harmonic conception, using extended chord structures that led to unprecedented harmonic and melodic variety; (2) developed an even more highly syncopated, linear rhythmic complexity and a melodic angularity in which the blue note of the fifth degree was established as an important melodic–harmonic device;[3] (3) reestablished the blues as the music's primary organizing and functional principle;[4] (4) returned the percussive sounds of ring culture to their original place of importance; and (5) expanded on the prevailing extension of improvisation from paraphrase to melodic invention by adding to it harmonic elaborations they described as "running changes," the perfection and proper use of which produced prodigious improvisers. In this new music, sixteenth-note and triplet figures carried the rhythmic momentum, substitute chords of the seventh, ninth, eleventh, and thirteenth enriched the harmonic structure, and the tempi were sometimes outlandishly fast. The role of the drums changed from time keeping to phrase making—emphasizing, punctuating, clarifying, facilitating, and assisting in the harmonic, melodic, and textural definition of the music. Hence the music was fraught with semantic value, but it was a semantics unknown to the uninitiated—a new "language" with which they would have to familiarize themselves, one that *Signified* like no other. These innovations constituted the bebop revolution that lasted for approximately a decade and established a style that was the primary jazz dialect from the 1950s through the 1970s.

The bebop cauldron was a hotbed of epic toasts and of the cutting contests in which these toasts thrived. Apropos is Neil Leonard's (1987) recounting of an encounter that Sonny Stitt had with Art Pepper:

> Stitt called for "Cherokee," a demanding number of notoriously difficult chord changes, at the time used to test a player's nerves and skill. He counted it off at breakneck speed and, as [Art] Pepper said, "He was flying. We played the head, the melody, and then he took the first solo. He played, I don't know,

3. The use of the flatted fifth was not new; it had been used by Don Redman in his "Chant of the Weed" (1932). The beboppers were simply reviving and emphasizing it.
4. In addition to the blues, other chord changes used frequently by bop players are those of standards such as "I Got Rhythm," "How High the Moon," and "Indiana."

about forty choruses. He played for about an hour maybe, did everything that could be done on a saxophone, everything you could play, as much as Charlie Parker could have played if he'd been there. Then he stopped. And he looked at me. Gave me one of those looks, 'All right, your turn.' And it's my job; it's my gig. I was strung out. I was hooked. I was drunk. I was having a hassle with my wife, Diane, [who] threatened to kill herself in our hotel room next door. I had marks on my arm. I thought there were narcs in the club, and I all of a sudden realized that it was me. He'd done all those things, and now I had to put up or shut up or get off or forget it or quit or kill myself or do something.

"I forgot everything, and everything came out. I played way over my head. I played completely different than he did. I searched and found my own way and what I said reached the people. I played myself, and I knew I was right and the people loved it, and they felt it. I blew and I blew, and when I finally finished I was shaking all over; my heart was pounding; I was soaked in sweat, and the people were screaming; the people were clapping, and I looked at Sonny, but I just kind of nodded, and he went, 'All right.' And that was it. That's what it's all about." (79–80)

Apocryphal or not, this account covers the gladiatorial aspect of the jazz life and suggests the mythological and coping strategies that continue to inform it, including Signifyin(g), fronting, and core-culture evaluation. It clearly describes a cutting session between two individuals, an event initiated—verbally or not—by Stitt and accepted—willingly or not—by Pepper. Harking back to the game rivalry and rhyming contests of Afro-America (for example, the dozens) and of Africa and to the band battles of early jazz in New Orleans, Chicago, and New York, such contests were the competitive proving ground of jazz manhood and musical achievement. Individual cutting contests had been common among the Harlem striders, where the Big Three went to war frequently with territorial interlopers and visiting "gunslingers."

In this event, Pepper was "hooked" and "drunk," a condition that recalls the African custom of ingesting narcotic or hallucinogenic substances in order to induce or enhance possession and trance (Zahan [1970] 1979, 17), a custom that was continued or revived in the early days of jazz. Pepper "forgot everything," just "blew and . . . blew, . . . shaking all over"—a state reminiscent of the "horses of the gods" being possessed to the extent that they "became" their specific *orisha*, assuming all their particular dance movements and behaviors. This forgetting of oneself is a state that many improvisers strive to attain. Leonard (1987) tells of another event, in which Sonny Criss, in his first opportunity to play with Charlie Parker, was aided by his idol. When Criss, anxiously concentrating "on bop's challenging new technical procedures," found himself stymied, "Parker put him straight" by saying, "Don't think. Quit thinkin'" (73–74). It is a rather common belief among some jazz performers that when they think about what they are doing their performances are in-

139

hibited. Stories about self-induced trances abound. Leonard quotes trombonist Trummy Young as saying, "When I go on the bandstand I don't know nobody's out there. I don't even know you're playing with me. Play good and it will help me. I don't know you're there. I'm just playing" (73). What this means is that, when improvising, jazz musicians rely on the intuitions and instincts of cultural and motor memory, which are most accessible when they transcend conscious, rational thought.[5]

The arbiter of the Pepper–Stitt encounter was "the people." It was they who would decide who cut whom, and they did so in this case by their supportive response to Pepper's Signifyin(g) tropes. This, too, has precedent in the culture, where public appraisal has always been the means of judging narrative and musical contests. Pepper's description of his physical and mental condition during the encounter was a Signifyin(g) one, designed to enhance the telling of his favorable outcome; and he was fronting, probably, when Stitt issued the challenge. What is ironic and informative about this is that Pepper is a white musician who was thriving on African-American cultural memory and tradition.[6] (Perhaps it's Esu, *god of irony*, at it again.) Stitt's Signifyin(g) "All right" also recalls Esu, "the most . . . colorful of the orishas," who in one tale strutted in, "redoubtable, . . . flashed an insolent grin," and "swaggered across the room" (González-Wippler 1985, 29, 31). In Afro-America, the hip musician, the blowing trickster, has learned many lessons, musical and otherwise, from this African god of interpretation. Such were the behaviors of the jazzmen of the 1940s and 1950s, a legacy of African and African-American game rivalry.

In spite of what we might know and understand about the mechanics of improvisation in black music, its full nature is elusive, for its essential musical facilitators are based in cultural memory, where the intuitive resources and instinctive assets of Call–Response reside. These resources and assets include a reservoir of semantic-like expediencies from which these troping devices are recalled—expediencies that reside always in the background, awaiting recall at appropriate times. The technique, the knowledge of structure and theory, and the external ideas that facilitate and support improvisation, then, must be called on to convey, in coherent and effective presentation, what emerges from cultural memory. It is this dialogical effectiveness that jazz musicians strive

5. But those who use the easy route of drugs eventually pay dearly—both musically, because consistent excellence requires that the supporting tools remain well honed and confidently in hand, and personally, because of the serious physical and emotional toll drugs take on users. For some perspective on drug use in the United States, see Carroll and Noble (1988, 246).

6. I mean by "cultural memory" all that I have said about it to this point. But I would like to add here that by "cultural memory" I also mean what Spillers (1991, 48) refers to as "homogeneous memory and experience"—memory and experience that has become intuitive or intuitively interpreted. It is not racially exclusive, for in absorbing the elements, practices, and transformations of a tradition, one also absorbs its cultural memory.

for as they create and re-create, state and revise, in the spontaneous manner known as improvisation; it is this Signifyin(g) revision that is at the heart of the jazz player's art; and it is this Signifyin(g) revision that debunks the notion that jazz is merely a style, not a genre,[7] for in meeting the substantive demands of Signifyin(g) revision, it is not merely the *manner* in which attacks, releases, sustainings, tempi, and other technical-musical requirements are rendered that makes jazz. On the contrary, it is the dialogical *substance,* the content *brought to* and *created in* the experience, that determines a genre. Style is a given. But as with any genre, it is the substance and its structures that make the difference—the *Signifyin(g)* difference—in jazz.

Joe Henderson's description of his approach to improvisation, told to John Murphy (1990), is instructive in this regard:

> I've probably been influenced by non-musical things as much as musical things. I think I was probably influenced by writers, poets—I mean just a full scope in relation to the written word. You know how to use quotation marks. You know how you quote people as a player. You use semicolons, hyphens, paragraphs, parentheses, stuff like this. I'm thinking like this when I'm playing. I'm having a conversation with *somebody.* (15)

This brief allusion to the phrase definers and cadences—the points of rest and summing up so diligently stressed in textbooks on music theory and in books on musical aesthetics and so important to the effecting of semantic value (chapter 10)—extends the semantic analogies of Gates (1988) and Murray (1973) (chapter 4), adding what might be called "punctuation" and "chunks of musical thought" to our concept of semantic value in black music.

Parker's admonition to Criss ("Don't think!") implies the improviser as riding-horse. The beboppers were riding-horses for nameless *orisha:* like the gods, individual soloists had their own favorite rhythms, with drummers playing these rhythms "behind" and "underneath" the players, supporting them and driving them on to greater heights of inspiration and creativity. The similarity of the jazz-improvisation event to the African dance-possession event it too striking and provocative to dismiss, but in the absence of a provable connection, it can only be viewed as the realization of an aspect of ritual and of cultural memory. Perhaps the elaboration of jazz improvisation from melodic paraphrase to running changes may be viewed as a long search for the essentials of spirit possession (although it would not be divine) and represents the closing of a circle: from ring shout to the beginnings of jazz (a derivation and a beginning), from the melodic embellishments of early jazz through the epic jazz tropings of the beboppers (including Coltrane), in which the essentials of the emotional fervor of the ring are appropriated.

---

7. This is from the conventional wisdom, seldom written down. But for a somewhat elaborated expression of the notion, see Adorno ([1967] 1986, 121–123).

141

This merger in jazz improvisation of the mythological and the rational constitutes a crossroads where Africa meets Europe on equal terms, with the rhythmic and intuitive essentials of the ring engaging the melodic, harmonic, and logical essentials of European popular and concert-hall music. It is a crossroads at which intuitive inspiration, represented by Parker's admonishment "Don't think!" meets Joe Henderson's brand of semantic rationality. In this successful event, it is Esu's horse being ridden, for it is always being improvised capriciously, with much virtuosity (Jahn 1961, 63–64).

In 1944, Charlie Parker had a bebop hit with "Now's the Time," a recording that featured himself, Miles Davis on trumpet, Dizzy Gillespie on piano, Curley Russell on bass, and Max Roach on drums. The tune was recorded again at Storyville, on September 22, 1953, featuring Parker, Herb Pomeroy on trumpet, Sir Charles Thompson on piano, Jimmy Woode on bass, and Kenny Clarke on drums. In this later version, the performance opens with a twelve-bar blues, sans head.[8] There follow three solos of three choruses each, featuring Parker, Clarke, and Thompson. These nine choruses are followed by six sets of "fours" played by sax, drums, trumpet, drums, sax, and drums, successively, which lead to two statements of the head to close out the performance. Parker is in good form, and the contributions of Pomeroy and Thompson are particularly notable. On his first chorus, Pomeroy picks up on the last figure of Parker's saxophone solo, modifying it slightly and moving smoothly and logically into his own new motives and melodic inventions, which he develops over his three choruses, until Thompson enters and picks up Pomeroy's closing motive. Ring elements are readily evident in Thompson's solos: on his second chorus, comping left-hand chords, which normally appear directly on beats 1 and 3 (or on the second half of them), are shifted, in the second half of bar 7 and in all of bar 8, to beats 2 and 4. This creates an effective off-beat accompaniment to the melodic excursions of the right hand and sets the harmonic structure one beat behind its normal placement in a very effective rhythmic and harmonic conflict. At bar 9, he is back on the beat, closing out this chorus and moving into his third, where in bars 1 and 3 he approximates blue notes with two-note clusters. In bars 7, 8, and 9 of the third chorus, he introduces cross-rhythms by playing a repeated three-note motive in duple rhythm. Thompson closes his solo by dropping back into the comping mode, under Parker's saxophone. Just before the fours begin, Clarke becomes more assertive, playing an accompanying "fill" that closes Thompson's third chorus and leads into Parker's first set of "four." Clarke alternates fours with Parker and Pomeroy, with Clarke's final four leading into the head. On the repeat of the head, Woode's bass, which has been relegated primarily to pizzicato time

---

8. In the jazz lexicon, the term "head" means the opening tune, or "theme," of a jazz performance.

keeping, switches to an arco passacaglia-like line, doubled in the piano's low register. This makes for a very effective closing of the performance.

Bebop's embracing of the blues and its reestablishing of the primacy of rhythm in jazz revealed its developers' commitments to their heritage and their realization that a successful revolution lay in the power of that heritage. In this thinking and in all the ritual of bebop, its players—modernists all, in a sense—did what the turn-of-the-century and Harlem Renaissance modernists refused or were not able to do: they merged rationality and myth—with musically significant results—and they accomplished this by focusing on the blues and on rhythm. Their use of the blues and percussive rhythm was complemented by their use of European-derived techniques; their dialogical melodic, harmonic, and rhythmic juxtapositions of blues elements and European-derived extended chord structures created this most unusual amalgam called bebop. Bebop reflected—and its practitioners exulted in—not only the pleasure and excitement of musical discovery and achievement, but also the joy and exuberance of myth and ritual.

Another black-music genre was emerging simultaneously with the ascendance of bebop and on the heels of boogie-woogie's popularity: rhythm and blues (R&B). Known in some circles as "the father of rhythm & blues," Louis Jordan, with his Tympani Five, helped spread R&B across America via jukebox and radio. In a kind of shuffle-boogie style that employed both swing and blues elements, Jordan produced a number of early hits, all million-record sellers: "Is You Is or Is You Ain't My Baby" (1944), "Caldonia" (1944 or 1945), "Beware, Brother, Beware" (1946), and "Choo Choo Ch'Boogie" (1946). These were accompanied and followed by a score of others.[9] Jordan described his own contribution when he said, "With my little band, we made the blues jump" (quoted in Shaw 1979, BM-6). Jordan's "Choo Choo Ch'Boogie" is band-based boogie-woogie with a swing beat realized through riff-based melodies and accompanying figures, swing saxophone playing, and a vocal by Jordan. It is a clear example of the adaptation of the piano-conceived boogie figurations to swing conceptions and of how the two styles were fused to make R&B. Nearly all of Jordan's output is boogie-based. Among others participating in these early developments were T-Bone Walker, Charles Brown, Joe Liggins (of Honeydripper fame), Roy Milton, Ruth Brown, Ray Charles, Little Richard, and Sam Cooke. Milton, in turn, influenced Ike Turner, Fats Domino, and others. His contribution to the repertoire and style is well represented on the album *Roy Milton and His Solid Senders: The Grandfather of R&B,* which contains seventeen tracks cut between 1945 and 1951, some of them more heavily

9. Much of Jordan's output can be heard on the album *Let the Good Times Roll.*

based in the blues than is Jordan's music. Jordan and the Tympani Five, Liggins and the Honeydrippers, and Ruth Brown were dominant in the late 1940s and early 1950s, a time when others mentioned here were also highly popular.[10]

In 1949, saxophonist Paul Williams recorded an R&B version of Parker's "Now's the Time" and called it "The Hucklebuck." It became an R&B hit. Based on a boogie-woogie bass, with a swing rhythm and a riff-based bebop melody line, "The Hucklebuck" was a real synthesis of ring-derived devices, procedures, and styles. Recorded on December 15, 1948, it featured Williams on alto (and, apparently, baritone) saxophone, Phil Gilbeaux on trumpet, Miller Sam on tenor sax, Floyd Taylor on piano, Herman Hopkins on bass, and Reetham Mallet on drums. It opens with a four-bar introduction followed by a two-part head: an original tune for its A section, and the "Now's the Time" head for its B section. Williams's "Hucklebuck" is much slower than Parker's "Now's the Time"; it is a typical pumping, mid-tempo, bluesy, R&B dance piece. The four-bar introduction is very much like pure boogie-woogie, although it is taken from Parker's melody. In the A section of the first chorus, which consists of a melody of long, sustained notes harmonized by Williams's group in thirds, the pianist's right hand plays boogie-woogie–inspired figures that Signify on the melody. Then enters Parker's theme, also harmonized in thirds and accompanied by a strong R&B backbeat. The second chorus features in its A section Williams's big-toned baritone saxophone, backed by the horns' swing-derived riffs; the B section features Gilbeaux's trumpet, also backed by riffs. Then comes the head—this time, however, with its B section first, followed by A, at the end of which a voice interjects "Hey! Not now, I'll tell you when." This is followed by B again, which fades for eight bars, closing out the rendition. Throughout the performance, the ♩ ♪ ♪ ♪ ♪ cymbal rhythm, together with the usual accompanying backbeat on the snare drum and the saxophone riffs, reveal the swing side of the piece's origins, while the boogie-woogie bass, the melodic filigree, and the twelve-bar blues structure attest its blues lineage.

While both Parker's and Williams's performances are based in the blues, the moderate tempo of "Now's the Time"; its drummer's steady *ting, ting, ting, ting* on the cymbal, ubiquitous off-beat stabs and filigree on the snare drum and tom-tom, and occasional bass-drum "bombs"; and the soloists' angular melodic lines, motivic development, and melodic–harmonic complexity all contrast sharply with the slow and deliberate tempo, swing cymbal rhythm, simple blues harmonies, and soloists' direct statements of "The Hucklebuck." But both—each in its own way—make significant contributions to the continuing elaboration and extension of African-American music. The semantic value of

10. For a survey of the music of these and other R&B stars, see *Anthology of Rhythm and Blues* (1969–　).

the bebop tune is attested and confirmed by the words to which it has been set in its R&B reincarnation: "Do the Hucklebuck!" Composed to accompany a black dance of the same name, "The Hucklebuck" fits into a tradition in which a long line of black musicians produced dance songs that became popular and musically important (for example, Chris Smith in 1913 with "Ballin' the Jack," Armand Piron in 1922 with "I Wish I Could Shimmy Like My Sister Kate," and James P. Johnson in 1923 with "Charleston"). So popular was "The Hucklebuck" that it was covered almost immediately by Tommy Dorsey, Frank Sinatra, Roy Milton, and Lionel Hampton. An early instance of crossover, it marked the end of R&B as a segregated music (Shaw 1978, 169).

The convergence in "The Hucklebuck" of boogie-woogie, swing, and bebop brings us to another crossroads. In thinking about either "Now's the Time" or "The Hucklebuck," generic distinctions blur: sometimes the jazz piece is blues; sometimes the blues piece is jazz—one is both, both are one. One moment it is Esu; the next, it is the Signifying Monkey. One moment blues interprets swing; the next, swing interprets blues. Bebop interprets R&B, and R&B interprets bebop. The signifier of one moment becomes signified on in the next. These convergences constitute a musical crossroads that brings Esu's contradictory nature to mind. Just as "Now's the Time" is "The Hucklebuck" and jazz is R&B, Esu, as we have seen, is at once male and female, good and evil, benevolent and malevolent. Thought of in this way, the meaning of the collision is enhanced, which demonstrates some of the hermeneutic power of Gates's theory.

Much of the power of Gates's hermeneutic lies in our ability to use the vernacular to read the formal. In recognition of that, I would now like to give attention to black music's formal tradition, for the moment emphasizing and exploring (1) the role of myth and ritual in concert-hall music, (2) how the abandonment of myth in African-American modernism affected black composers in their pursuit of the goals of the Negro Renaissance, and (3) how both myth and ritual affected the future of the concert-hall music of black composers.

There are two main reasons that African Americans did not, during the Negro Renaissance, produce a large number of musically significant concert-hall works. First, emerging from slavery only in the 1860s, significant numbers of African Americans were barred from majority-culture musical institutions and, consequently, were generally prohibited from learning and internalizing the behaviors, myths, and rituals associated with concert-hall practices. Second, many African-American composers ignored or rejected the myths and rituals of their own culture, making impossible the fusing of their traditional myths with the rituals of the concert hall. In order to clarify and elaborate these reasons, I will explore the presence and use of myth and ritual in concert-hall music and the importance to marginalized petitioners of their having access to high culture and to its apprenticeship institutions.

Myths are ostensibly historical but largely fictional narratives designed to explain natural phenomena, to give accounts of events of religious, social, and political import, and to pass on the exploits of deities and heroes of particular cultures. Rituals are formal procedures that elaborate and celebrate myths and customs. Concerts, operas, and recitals are rituals, complete with procedures and codes of conduct that make up the ceremonies that carry and celebrate the myths of high culture. The rituals of the concert hall typically include four elements:

1. They last between one and a half and two and a half hours.
2. They present a more or less standard repertoire that is occasionally spiced with new or esoteric works.
3. They are attended by spectators who sit quietly and attentively, passively (and sometimes gravely) taking in the performances of the programmed works.
4. They are presented by musicians who perform the music with serious and earnest demeanor, expression, and posture and who acknowledge, at the completion of a composition, the audience's applause.

Fundamentally, the ultimate goal of the concert-hall ritual is the perfect performance and intense enjoyment of "great works." Musical presenters repeat this ritual countless times in countless places, decade after decade, replacing selected "standard" works of this tradition with others equally standard, more or less, in the twenty-four to thirty programs that make up each organization's subscription series. The entire process is truly a "rite of winter" (Fleischmann 1988, 15). Frederick Starr (1988) complains that it is a "secular equivalent of the Puritan worship service: long, serious, utterly predictable, and ever so good for your soul," characterized by "puritanical and turgid earnestness, and ritualized performance" (5). It is also "a pluralistic event that provides an outlet for fashion, prestige, civic pride, heightened national consciousness, as well as musical delight" (Mueller 1951, 186). Edward Said (1991) contends that the ritual of the concert hall, nourished by "rituals of learning, traditions of pedagogy, protocols of accreditation, performance, display, and so forth," is a ritual of "social abnormality," an "extreme occasion" of "unseen faculties and powers" of musicians that can be "experienced only under relatively severe and unyielding conditions" (56, 17). This ritual requires appropriate dress (evening dress, black or white bow ties and tails for the musicians) and the "rapt attention of its spectators" (2), with the "distancing effect" of the "staggeringly brilliant effects of the performer" adding to a mix that is socially alienating (3).

The concert-hall ritual is based on and celebrates myths: mythology about concert-hall music, mythic narratives of the distant past, and mythology of recent folk cultures and of various religious and social institutions. The mythology about the concert hall propagandizes the ostensible artistic supremacy of the musical products of European—particularly German and Italian—origin and derivation. This myth was created in nineteenth-century Europe by philosophers such as Schopenhauer and composers such as Richard Wagner (Mueller 1951, 291, 192). It was initially perpetuated and promoted in the United States by conductors such as Carl Bergmann and Theodore Thomas, the latter proclaiming that if some did not like Wagner, "we will play him until they do," and that music was a "powerful character building force" that would "by its uplifting force . . . convey the listener to a higher plane" (quoted in Mueller, 292). This myth perpetuates the notion that only the music of the "standard repertoire" is worth serious attention and that it is to be repeated, concert after concert, season after season, for the moral and spiritual uplift of an educated (and indoctrinated) public.

The second type of mythology essential to the Western concert tradition—that of the narratives of the distant past—infuses and helps drive its creative impulse by providing composers with culturally and spiritually significant subject matter and artistic stimulus. It consists principally of the myths and legends of the Greeks of antiquity and of the western European, Judeo-Christian stories of legend and history. Some works based on myths or legends of the distant past that immediately come to mind are Peri's *Euridice* and Monteverdi's *Orfeo,* Gounod's *Faust* and Berlioz's *The Damnation of Faust,* Debussy's *Pelléas and Melisande,* Wagner's *Der Ring des Nibelungen* and *Tannhäuser,* Schoenberg's *Moses and Aaron,* and Stravinsky's *Oedipus Rex.* The power of such myth in concert-hall music is told by Eero Tarasti in *Myth and Music* (1979):

> If the renaissance of Greek tragedy played a decisive role in the birth of opera, the reconstruction of a Russian wedding ritual in Stravinksy's *Les Noces,* on the other hand, or the creation of the world as interpreted by Sibelius in his *Luonnotar* or Scriabin's *Prometheus Mystery* . . . possess . . . the very idea of mythical communication. . . . Many other "mythical" compositions also reveal the same search for some original form of musical and human expression in general. It is this, perhaps often purely intuitively felt connection, which provides these works with their continuous and indisputable emotional power and effect upon the human mind. (13)

147

The third category of myth—that of more modern folk cultures and of various religious and ceremonial events—includes the liturgical works of Bach and Palestrina, Handel's *Royal Fireworks Music,* Mozart's *Requiem,* Brahms's *Academic Festival Overture,* Stravinksy's *Symphony of Psalms* and *The Rite of Spring,* Liszt's *Hungarian Rhapsodies,* Bartók's *Dance Suite,* Copland's *Fanfare for the Common Man,* Roy Harris's *Folk Song Symphony,* Virgil Thomson's opera *Four Saints in Three Acts,* and many other compositions whose titles may or may not betray their origin or character. Tarasti's work is particularly pertinent here. In *Myth and Music,* he addresses the question of the interrelationship between myth and music, distinguishes a mythical style in music, and identifies how myth is portrayed in works of music. Focusing on "primal mythical communication," he shows how works of music can allude to myths and manifest the mythical through their stylistic features. Tarasti refers to Honegger's mythologization of a train in *Pacific 231* as an example of how myth can subordinate music by depicting the running of a train as a mythical symbol. In Tarasti's view, composers, using musical sign systems, can reconstruct or depict myths or aspects of myths, evoking rituals and other primal social functions and practices and thus causing listeners to experience relationships with the primal mythical realm (1979, 12, 13, 14, 27, 28).

Composers effect the mythical in musical compositions by exploiting "archaic elements" and "quotations" of folk material that function as "strange" elements within the context of their works and by reconstructing the communication context (Tarasti 1979, 52, 53), as Stravinsky does, for example, in *The Rite of Spring.* For Tarasti, the mythical narration consists of "events, situations and conduct [that] are expressed by words, pictures, and tunes" (57). He cites as examples Wagner's leitmotif technique, in which motives represent mythical characters and functions, such as in the operas *Parsifal, Das Rheingold,* and *Götterdämmerung.* He then discusses the case of program music, particularly the symphonic poem, in which narration is completely absent and the music alone carries the reconstructive burden. He cites as examples here Berlioz's *Symphonie fantastique* and other works in which only the program serves as "text" (59).

As a musico-aesthetic stylistic device, the mythical functions as a complex of meanings and symbols that serve to reconstruct primal communication. The components of this network are archaic signifiers (small *s*) such as scales, dance rhythms, timbres, harmonies, and chord progressions. Later, Tarasti (1979) refers to signifiers such as "open parallel fifths, the combining of high- and low-register passages in unison, glittering upper-register woodwinds" (90), "diminished seventh chords . . . associated with the demonic" (112), "rhythmical core motifs" such as the "hero-mythical" opening motive of Beethoven's Fifth Symphony (91), and, in Honegger's *Jeanne d'Arc,* "bleak, dissonant harmonies built on fourths, along with chromaticism, medieval melodies and neoclassical orchestration with dark and glowing yet at the same time archaically clear-cut timbre [that] suggest the medieval world of superstition, persecution and mysticism" (98). Tarasti's discussion makes it clear that many of the compositional practices of European concert-hall music are in large part based on and supported by the myths and the realities of the European-derived world.

At the turn of the century, spurred by the prevailing interest in myth and the practice of symbolism, composers such as Eric Satie, Igor Stravinsky, and Sergei Prokofiev reconstructed mythical communication (Tarasti 1979, 273), essentially creating some of the content and expressions of neoclassicism, which emphasized, variously, mythical allegories, a rejection of traditional notation, and simplicity in the treatment of the musical elements. Neoclassicism began in Europe; its early works included Stravinsky's *Pulcinella* (1919–1920) and Piano Concerto (1924), Maurice Ravel's *Daphnis et Chloé* (1909–1911), Francis Poulenc's *Concerto for Two Pianos* (1932), Arthur Honegger's *Rugby* (1928), Paul Hindemith's *Konzertmusik* (1930), and Sergi Prokofiev's Classical Symphony (1916–1917). Neoclassical works written before 1930 were based on eighteenth- and nineteenth-century formal models, stressed the primacy of some variation on tonality, and strove for formal clarity in which new ideas—including modal tonality, pandiatonicism, polytonality, harmonic parallelism, nonlinear tonal logic, additive and asymmetrical rhythm, and other such devices and constructions—could be implemented. Neoclassicism arrived in the United States simultaneously with the European avant-garde that championed noise, chance operations, experimentation with open forms, and new chromatic, timbral, and rhythmic ideas.

In neoclassicism, myth sometimes functions as a stylistic device, as when folk music is exploited to produce a mythical atmosphere in a composition. In such cases, a particular attitude is adopted toward that music, and this attitude creates "the mythical." This *mythical attitude* is a mental posture that some composers assume in an effort to capture the spiritual or original milieu of the music (Tarasti 1979, 52, 53). Tarasti also distinguishes between *dominant* mythic elements, which serve as the context for such musical works, and *subordinate,* or foreign elements, which therefore are raw material. These works also contain Tarasti's channels of communication—devices, or processes, through which primal mythical communication takes place, as in the use of the drum as a channel for communicating the mythical sense of traditional black Africa or diminished seventh chords for the demonic—and the symbolism associated with them (70, 77). With the decline and disappearance of the symphonic poem and the rise of neoclassicism, music and myth, in some cases—such as in works of Stravinsky, Milhaud, and Honegger—lost their associations with narrative structures and discourses and began to rely on "figurations" and "plays on related meanings" (61).

149

Tarasti's "figurations," "plays on related meanings," and "network of signi-fiers" recall Gates (1988), of course, and require brief comment, for in the context of Gates's theory, these elements are tropes, and in the context of my adaptation of his theory, such signifiers and figures constitute the tropes of Call–Response. In African-American music, Call–Response comprises what might be called by linguists "units of signification," which may be said to Sig-nify in the sense Gates uses in his interpretation of the black literary tradi-tion. In concert-hall music written by some black composers, the two kinds of signifiers—Tarasti's European and European-derived kind and those of Call–Response—combine in a broad and powerful new tradition that begins with Cook, Joplin, Dett, and Still and continues into the present day and that embraces works by black and white composers, the latter including, for ex-ample, George Gershwin's *Porgy and Bess* (1935), Morton Gould's *Spirituals for Orchestra* (1937), and Milton Babbitt's *All Set* (1957).[11]

A key claim of Tarasti (1979), for my purposes, is his statement that "only many different symbolisms and connections between music and the other se-mantic fields of a culture make the mythical emerge in its full cogency in the area of music" (329). This statement supports and vindicates my juxtaposi-tion of Stuckey (1987) and Gates (1988) and provides justification for my em-phasis on myth and ritual in concert-hall music.[12] The truth of Tarasti's claim, I believe, has been proved in this and the preceding chapters, but will be more fully demonstrated in those that follow.

Thus the concert-hall tradition is driven by the assumption that "great mu-sic" exists and that it should be perpetuated for the greater good of high cul-ture; it assumes the existence of a proprietary place of presentation and of the propriety of the behaviors sanctioned for that space and its ceremonies. In much of the music of the elite concert hall, music and myth are combined, and the music reconstructs myth through the use of archaic elements and mu-sical quotations that signify the primitive, the folk, the national, and other mythical styles. Additionally, however, the music of the concert hall is viewed by some as a consumer good, to be produced and sold for the enjoyment and aesthetic nourishment of those who value and can afford it. These values of high culture were embraced by turn-of-the-century black modernists and by the thinkers of the Negro Renaissance. The first published propagation of the

11. Babbitt's *All Set* contains such "superficial aspects" of jazz as "its very instrumentation, its use of the 'rhythm section,' the instrumentally delineated sections which may appear analo-gous to successive instrumental 'choruses,' and even specific thematic or motivic materials" (Bab-bit, quoted in Wuorinen 1974).

12. A casual (or perhaps not so casual) question by Richard Crawford led me down this path. In an early discussion I had with him about my intention to write about Signifyin(g) and the ring shout, he asked, "Does it have anything to do with ritual?" My answer at that time was a tentative "Yes, I think it does." Little did I know, however, that this question would nag me un-til I pursued it this far.

specifically musical aspects of these values appeared in the *Negro Music Journal,* all fifteen issues of which were published in 1902 and 1903. As reported and demonstrated by William E. Terry (1977), the journal's "technical articles, musical criticism, . . . reports on the musical activities of individuals and organizations," and other writings were devoted strictly to "worthy and appropriate music" (146, 147). The journal promoted the propaganda of the "elevating influence" of concert-hall organizations, the preeminence of the musical "masters" of Europe (Bach, Handel, Haydn, Mozart, Beethoven, Schubert, Schumann, Wagner, and the rest), and the preeminence of the whites among "some American song writers," including, for example, Dudley Buck—here misnamed "Bush"— and Mrs. Jessie L. Gaynor (150, 154, 155). The journal praised black singer Theodore Drury's plan to organize a stock company to support the building of an opera house for African Americans, recognized a need for the establishment of "a few large black orchestras," heralded the establishment of the black Washington Conservatory of Music in 1903, and kept its readership informed about major works by black concert-hall composers (156, 158, 160). The journal rejected the popular music of the black heritage; its contributors and its editor, J. Hillary Taylor, contended that popular music is "vulgar" and "degrading," with "low and sensuous purposes" (Alice Louise Parker, quoted in Terry, 149), "an evil music that should be wiped out as other bad and dangerous epidemics have been exterminated" (Taylor, quoted in Terry, 149). In short, the *Negro Music Journal* and its readers completely embraced the mythology of the concert-hall tradition at the expense of African-American popular music.

In contrast to the assumptions of the transplanted European-derived concert-hall tradition, the African-American musical tradition is fueled by African and African-American cultural memory, by Call–Response performance practices, by performances in functional venues (jooks, dance halls, and churches), and by the participation of its spectators in the performance event by way of their responding to "calls" through yea-saying and the materiality of hand clapping, foot patting, and other body movements. The African-American tradition does not recognize a distinction between high and low music, nor does it recognize "great music" or, generally, "master composers." (In black culture, the noncomposer Count Basie is as esteemed as the composer Duke Ellington; the emphasis is on performance, and the *making* of music is valued as highly as the composing of it.) In black culture, works of music are truly transactions between human beings and organized sound, and audience participation is central to their success. It is this tradition that the thinkers of the Negro Renaissance tried to jettison in favor of what they saw as the advantages of high culture. Consequently, the musical assimilation they so desired could not be

151

realized, since the music of the black tradition would not be truly effective without the support of its ritual value base. As Tarasti (1979) notes, "rite realizes myth and that is why they are inseparable" (21). The rejection of African or African-American myth and the devaluation of the ritual context of black music (the ring), I believe, put the black composers of the Harlem Renaissance at a serious disadvantage.[13]

The thinkers and the composers of the period viewed the desired rapprochement between white and black traditions from the standpoint of their limited perceptions and understandings of late-nineteenth- and early-twentieth-century nationalism. They did not realize or understand the importance of myth and ritual to the making of this music. They also did not understand, acknowledge, or see the importance of the facts that the European musical forms—sonatas, symphonies, concertos, and so on—had been enduring over decades, even centuries; that none of these musical genres came from cultures that were fundamentally or largely opposed to them; and that none of the music carried the freight of devaluation based on race or source of origin. This lack of understanding short-circuited the aspirations of the leaders of the Harlem Renaissance.

For the composers of the Harlem flowering to have achieved large-scale success in creating works according to the movement's credo, they would have had to negotiate two myth–ritual systems: (1) a European-derived outlook that was difficult to internalize without formal training or participation in white musical institutions, and (2) the mythic basis of their own culture, which, in the name of progress, they felt obliged to reject. Furthermore, they would have had to solve the problem of fusing the content of the black mythic system with the ritual trappings of mainstream high culture.[14]

William Grant Still began to compose in the 1920s, when both neoclassicism and American musical nationalism were gaining ascendancy in the United States (Salzman 1988, 87–90). The American avant-garde of the period included composers such as Edgard Varèse (*Intègrale*, 1924; *Ionization*, 1931), George Antheil (*Ballet méchanique*, 1925), Henry Cowell (*Some Music*, 1927),

---

13. Among the ideas responsible for this jettisoning of myth and ritual were those promulgated by W. E. B. Du Bois and Booker T. Washington. Du Bois proclaimed that black culture would be saved by its most talented members, its Talented Tenth. This notion fueled ideas such as those that appeared in the *Negro Musical Journal*—ideas that were uncompromising to the extent that those who held them rejected the cultural foundations of their culture. And Washington's rejections of leisure placed so much emphasis on the economic and political implications of productive labor that he and his followers had no time for or interest in myth; it is conceivable that, for this reason, many of those inclined to pursue musical composition did not do so. (Admittedly, unlike the Harlem Renaissance thinkers and the promoters of Washington's worker mentality, I have here the advantage of hindsight and evolved thinking.)

14. Many of the readers of the *Negro Music Journal* certainly had access to high-culture musical establishments, but few were composers of any significance and ability (Still and Dett were two exceptions). Most were performers and music teachers of one sort or another.

Adolph Weiss, and Lee Ornstein. Varèse was one of Still's composition teachers.[15] Still's works under Varèse's tutelage included *From the Land of Dreams* (1924) and *Darker America* (completed in 1926), both of which were written in a highly dissonant style that Still himself, as well as others, described as "ultramodern" (Arvey 1984, 67; Haas 1975, 115). Still quickly deserted this "ultramodern" style, however, and turned to tonal music with a racial theme, composing in 1926 *Levee Land,* a work that led, stylistically, to the *Afro-American Symphony* (1930).

With these works, and in his status as a student of Varèse, Still associated himself with "the young composers' movement" in America, a movement supported by a number of organizations established for the purpose of promoting the composers and the new music of the day (Oja 1992, 148–149). American composers whose works were performed by these organizations include John Alden Carpenter, Charles Tomlinson Griffes, Wallingford Riegger, Charles Wakefield Cadman, Arthur Foote, Ruth Crawford Seeger, Aaron Copland, and Roy Harris. Between 1926 and 1931, eleven of Still's works were performed by four of these organizations—Howard Hanson's American Composers Concerts, George Barrère's Little Symphony, the International Composers Guild, and the Pan American Association of Composers (169).

In turning to "racial" music, Still joined an American school of composers that wedded the classical tradition with American folk and stylized popular music. This movement included Copland, Gershwin, Harris, and Marc Blitzstein, all of whom contributed to the output of a "period of innumerable symphonic 'Hoedowns' and 'Square Dances' as well as of . . . a broad, serious, symphonic style, strongly tonal, . . . based on traditional patterns often rather awkwardly organized to fit the new local color material" (Salzman 1988, 89). This movement, which had begun around the turn of the century, encompassed works such as Copland's Piano Concerto (1927) and orchestral suites *Billy the Kid* (1938) and *Rodeo* (1942) (both made from ballets), Gershwin's *Rhapsody in Blue* (1923) and *An American in Paris* (1928), Harris's *When Johnny Comes Marching Home* (1935) and Third Symphony (1939), and Blitzstein's opera *The Cradle Will Rock* (1937). Earlier works in this tradition included the "Camp Meeting" movement in Charles Ives's Third Symphony (1904), Henry F. Gilbert's *Dance in Place Congo* (1908) and "Shout" in his *Negro Rhapsody* (1912), and John Powell's *Rhapsodie Nègre* (1918?).

Still, then, participated in three different movements of the period, all of which in some way overlapped: the first was the avant-garde; the second, the rise of American musical nationalism; and the third, as we saw in chapter 5, the Harlem Renaissance. After rejecting the avant-garde, Still eventually triumphed in the nationalist and Harlem Renaissance realms with the *Afro-*

15. Still studied with Varèse from 1923 to 1925. He had previously studied under George Whitefield Chadwick, in 1922.

American Symphony, a work that blended African-American and European elements more successfully, in my opinion, than those of any other composer of the period. It was not only the Harlem Renaissance in itself—or by itself—that put Still on the path to the realization of the Renaissance credo, but also his experiences with the neoclassical and American nationalist trends of the larger musical culture. Between 1930 and 1950, Still and other African-American composers produced several meritorious works of concert-hall music. These included William Dawson's *Negro Folk Symphony* (1932), Robert Nathaniel Dett's oratorio *The Ordering of Moses* (1932), Still's *Three Visions* (1936), Florence Price's *Song to the Dark Virgin* (1941), Julia Perry's *Prelude for Piano* (1946), Ulysses Kay's *Concerto for Orchestra* (1948), and Howard Swanson's *Short Symphony* (1948), which won the Music Critics Circle Award, and his piano piece "The Cuckoo" (1949).

Two vocal compositions published in 1949, Still's *Songs of Separation* and Swanson's "The Negro Speaks of Rivers," will help demonstrate the impact that neoclassicism and American nationalism had on black composers of the period. Until Still composed *Songs of Separation,* it had been thirty years since a black composer had published a successful song cycle (Harry T. Burleigh's *Five Songs of Lawrence Hope* [1919] had been the last). In *Songs of Separation,* Still set the verses of five black poets: "Idolatry," by Arna Bontemps; "Poème," by Philippe-Thoby Marcelin; "Parted," by Paul Laurence Dunbar; "If You Should Go," by Countee Cullen; and "A Black Pierrot," by Langston Hughes. In this work, Still instructively and appropriately brings together themes from disparate cultural sources in the kind of fusion of cultures for which he is known. Orin Moe (1980), in a study of the cycle, describes it as "exceptional" and explains that "the linch-pins are the first, third, and fifth songs. They move the drama forward, are strong and complex in imagery, shape the formal structure of the cycle, and project a forceful, rhythmic style. The second and fourth songs are interludes. Both are gentle love lyrics, suffused with sleep and dream imagery and redolent of popular song" (34–35). He concludes that "white 'classical' music, American popular song, French popular song, folk song, jazz and blues are woven into a unified, dramatically vivid style, . . . unified under the predominating technique of black American music" (35–36). But the theme of separation, the subject of Still's cycle, confirms the composer's consciousness of "otherness." *Songs of Separation* gives expression to the separation of lovers, but, given the nature of Still's life, as told by his wife in *In One Lifetime* (Arvey 1984), it can also be read as a cultural metaphor, an image of the quest for entry into the culture at large, particularly in "A Black Pierrot"—a symbol that Signifies on the state of American cultural norms, struggles, and aspirations.

"The Negro Speaks of Rivers" (1942, published in 1949), the first published song of Howard Swanson (1907–1978), is a masterly setting of the Langston Hughes poem:

I've known rivers:
Ancient as the world
And older than the flow
Of human blood in human veins.
My soul has grown deep like the rivers.

I bathed in the Euphrates when dawns were young.
I built my hut near the Congo,
And it lulled me to sleep.
I looked upon the Nile,
And raised the Pyramids above it.
I heard the singing of the Mississippi,
When Abe Lincoln went down to New Orleans.
And I've seen its muddy bosom turn all golden in the sunset.

I've known rivers:
Ancient, dusky rivers:
My soul has grown deep like the rivers.

Suffused with stylized elements of the spiritual, the blues, and jazz, Swanson's setting is replete with additive rhythms and cross-rhythms, black-culture inflections, and passages that approximate improvisation. Figures such as ♫♪♩♪ , ♩．♪ , and ♪♩ , all characteristic of the spiritual, abound in stylized form. What I call the "rivers" motive, the ♪♩♪♩ that seems to push and pull in the manner of men at work moving river vessels or heavy and recalcitrant objects or animals, is used as a kind of ostinato. This constantly repeated motive underlies a proud, stately, recitative-like melody in a very effective setting that contains two kinds of events that place the African-American stamp on this song: chord progressions and voice-leadings typical of jazz and spirituals—notably at the end of the cadenza—and pendular thirds at cadences, such as "human blood in human veins" and "like the rivers." The song also contains tone paintings, such as the flowing, rippling effect in the piano to represent the river; the "open" sound on the first syllable of the world "*sun*-set," with downward movement to the second chord on the second syllable; the restful, quiet feeling of the chord on the word "sleep"; and the descending character of the passage that accompanies the phrase "went down to New Orleans."

This setting of "The Negro Speaks of Rivers" makes it evident that Swanson was not only a product of the Negro Renaissance—a composer who would "elevate" the black folk forms—but also a master composer of *song*, period. Furthermore, while the subject in this case is a Hughes poem that celebrates the black heritage, and while Swanson made use in this setting of the musical currency of his heritage, he was equally adept at setting texts by white po-

155

ets on entirely different subjects, as evinced by his treatment of works by T. S. Eliot, Carl Sandburg, and May Swenson. While Swanson is not ordinarily identified with either the Harlem or the Chicago flowering of the Negro Renaissance movement (the bulk of his output and all his most important works were too late for Harlem, and he did not live in Chicago), his song output certainly belongs among the best in the Negro Renaissance's musical repertoire—and among the best of African-American art-song literature in general. As an inheritor of the legacy of the Negro Renaissance, he confirms its value and its success.[16]

The concert-hall fusions of Still and Swanson are examples of a process that has consistently fueled the elaborations of black music. Yet another fusion of the period is Camille Nickerson's *Five Creole Songs* (1932), in which the language of the Louisiana Creoles of color—a French patois that resulted from the mixture of French and African languages—is placed in a musical setting made up of French, Spanish, and African performance styles.[17] The settings are of putatively original folk songs from French and Spanish colonial Louisiana—the Creole counterpart of the Negro spirituals—placed in a sophisticated musical setting by Nickerson. The dialogics effected by the mix of French and the African languages, plus the French, Spanish, and African musical elements, create marvelous scenes from black Creole life. Nickerson's cycle serves as a celebration of Creole culture—a revisiting of the drumming impulse as a foundation for and a final arbiter in black music. *Five Creole Songs* is a celebration of Dance, Drum, and Song within the context of concert-hall myth and ritual, touting and flaunting Dance through the invitation of "Dansé Conni Conné," Drum through the antics of "Michieu Banjo," and Song through the lyricism of the sultry "Chère, Mo Lemmé Toi" and "Fais Do Do." "Dansé Conni Conné" is a "nursery song" with Latin rhythms, an example of how nurses amuse babies with improvisatory singing (Floyd 1992). "Michieu Banjo" is a lighthearted song with a marked rhythm. It portrays the town dandy, a mulatto who is envied because of his fine clothes and his prowess as a guitar-playing entertainer. "Chère, Mo Lemmé Toi" is a Mardi Gras song, acquired from others by Creoles and translated into their vernacular patois. "Fais Do Do" was used by Creole mothers to frighten their children into obedience, in this case by telling the child that if she does not go to sleep, sleep will come and eat her up. The marked character and repetition of the general rhythm ♫♫ and its variations in "Michieu Banjo" and "Dansé Conni Conné" create mythic effects because of its archaic character.

16. Seven of Swanson's songs—"Joy," "Ghosts in Love," "Night Song," "Still Life," "The Junk Man," "The Valley," and "The Negro Speaks of Rivers"—can be heard on *Seven Songs* (ca. 1950).

17. Four of the songs are available on *The Black Music Repertory Ensemble in Concert* (1992). For a contemporary discussion and description of Creole slave songs, see Cable ([1886] 1969a, 47–68).

In 1946, with *A Short Overture,* Ulysses Kay made a statement about his potential prowess as a composer, signaling the quality of what was to come in future years. Kay's work eschewed the black aesthetic, squarely promoting and celebrating the myth and ritual of European-derived concert-hall music.[18] The work is in sonata form and makes use of neoclassical conventions, sporting a very rhythmic and insistent first theme followed by a second that is flowing and wide-ranging. The development section makes use of both themes, with motives from the second theme used primarily as an accompaniment to the first. Fragments of both themes are tossed from instrument to instrument and from register to register, treated sometimes in augmentation and stretto as the movement moves inexorably toward a recapitulation in which the second theme returns first and the first theme is announced by the restatement of the two sharp chords that open the work. Kay had completely internalized concert-hall musical conventions, his education at the University of Arizona and the Eastman School of Music having prepared him well to succeed. In 1947, *A Short Overture* won the George Gershwin Memorial Award. In the 1950s, Kay would emerge as a major American composer.[19]

These successes in the 1930s and 1940s by Still, Swanson, Price, Nickerson, and Kay did not have significant impacts in wider musical circles, but some of this music—the smaller pieces and the choral works—was kept alive in the 1950s by Harlem Renaissance survivors and their students in black colleges such as Fisk, Hampton, Virginia State, and Howard University, and at the Eastman School of Music.

In closing this chapter, I return briefly to the question of the importance of appropriate apprenticeship to success in the composition of concert-hall music. World War II brought African Americans more opportunities for advancement than did World War I. In 1944, soon after the War Department announced the end of segregation in selected military facilities, the U.S. Navy Music School made preparations to admit its first African Americans and opened its doors to them on January 13, 1945 (Bergman 1969, 504; Floyd 1975, 22). Following the war, the GI Bill made college education more affordable for African-American war veterans. This resulted in not only increased enrollment in black colleges, but also expanded teaching opportunities in black colleges for former GIs trained in the service music schools. The Great Lakes Naval Training Center prepared several musicians who would have an impact on music education in black colleges: bassoonist Huel Perkins, for example,

18. Although he was influenced and inspired by Still early on, Kay's works from the 1940s are more revealing of debts to Howard Hanson, with whom he studied at Eastman, and Hindemith.

19. For details of Kay's career, see Southern (1982, 226–227).

went to Southern University in Baton Rouge; violinist Brenton Banks to Tennessee State College in Nashville; violinist Thomas Bridge to Virginia State College in Petersburg; percussionist Henry Porter Francois to Langston University; trombonist Leonard Bowden to Prairie View A&M College. Great Lakes veteran Ulysses Kay eventually emerged as a composer of note, and cellist Donald White went on to join the Cleveland Symphony Orchestra. Dozens of other service-trained musicians, as well as Negro Renaissance veterans, were appointed to the faculties of black colleges, where they joined the growing number of civilian black graduates of music schools, particularly Oberlin, Juilliard, Eastman, Vandercook, and the Chicago Musical College.[20] One of the primary leaders and intellectuals of the Harlem Renaissance, Charles Johnson, assumed the presidency of Fisk University, and poets James Weldon Johnson and Arna Bontemps and artist Aaron Douglas joined him there as faculty and staff members; Dett had already gone to Hampton Institute. For the first time, there were black college music students and teachers in numbers, establishing the concert-hall apprenticeships, with their tradition of learning and pedagogy, that would eventually produce composers familiar enough with concert-hall myth and ritual to compose on a par with composers of the larger society. These composers would emerge in the 1950s and 1960s and mature in the 1970s and 1980s. In the meantime, these new opportunities brought new expectations that, together with other social and political forces, would result in further rejection of black myth and ritual.

At the same time, however, the rise and crystallization of bebop and R&B and the music of composers such as Still, Swanson, and Margaret Bonds stood as transitional strains that would fuel the further development of the Call–Response imperative. Rhythm and blues, bebop, and the concert-hall music of most black composers have in common the embracing of ring values and their dialogical merging with values from European concert-hall music, a process that would ebb, flow, and become more sophisticated in the coming decades. Bebop, for example—with its fast tempi, asymmetrical rhythms, angular melodies, motivic figures, and complicated harmonies—became a listener's music; those who previously danced, responded to calls, and yea-said became respecting spectators who venerated the creativity of bebop virtuosi. Finger popping became "uncool," replaced by passive and attentive absorption of the music. Ironically, while the performers were engaged in the perpetuation and exploration of black myth and ritual, many of the black spectators became more distanced from it—in their "cool," they were "insiders" who, more and more, looked in from the outside. This state of affairs was merely a continuation of the Negro paradox, a result of

20. In my years as a college undergraduate, nearly all my male music professors at Florida A&M University were army or navy veterans, some of whom had attended the service music schools.

the modernist mind-set that privileged and rewarded individualism over collectivity, rationality over cultural memory, ideology over myth, and European-derived over African ritual values. It was an inevitable result of the cultural and artistic dialogics that continued to fuse the cultures that contribute to and constitute the United States of America.

CHAPTER **7**

Continuity and Discontinuity: The Fifties

When a child has learned to wash his hands properly, he may have dinner with this parents.
Ghanaian proverb

The blues was like that problem child that you may have had in the family. You was a little bit ashamed to let anybody else see him, but you loved him. You just didn't know how other people would take it.
B. B. King

The Negro Renaissance came to a close in the early 1950s in the wake of two developments. The first centered around claims and perceptions that much of the black-oriented cultural and artistic activity of the 1940s had been Communist inspired. Such claims were encouraged and investigated in those years as part of broader investigations of the House Un-American Activities Committee (HUAC); the publication *Red Channels* even listed the names of suspected sympathizers.[1] In this threatening envi-

1. Among those harassed or questioned by the HUAC between 1947 and 1956 were singer-activist Paul Robeson, poet Langston Hughes, baseball player Jackie Robinson, film star Canada Lee, singer and film star Lena Horne, and folk singers Joshua White and Harry Belafonte (Navasky 1980, 186–194). *Red Channels: The Report of Communist Influence in Radio and Television* (1950), a special report of the newsletter *Counterattack: The Newsletter of Facts on Communism*, listed individuals who ostensibly had past or present links with "communist causes." For detailed information about the contents and effects of such listings, see Cogley ([1956] 1971) and Miller ([1952] 1971).

ronment, the newer black artists, their careers endangered by innuendo and slander, distanced themselves from left-wing associations and from black-nationalist activity.

The second development was a "promise of integration." This promise, which took hold at the turn of the decade, manifested itself in a large number of unprecedented events, among which were a decision by the NAACP to launch a full-scale attack on segregation in education, resulting in five segregation cases being argued before the Supreme Court; the ordering of the admission of the first African Americans to the University of Texas, University of Virginia, and Louisiana State University law schools; the beginning of African Americans' service as alternate delegates to the United Nations (Marion Anderson and Zelma George among them); the seating by the American Medical Association of its first black delegate; the awarding of the Pulitzer Prize to Gwendolyn Brooks for her collection of poems *Annie Allen;* and the acceptance of Althea Gibson as a competitor in the National Tennis Championships in Forest Hills, New York. These and other events, all occurring in 1950, were followed in subsequent years by equally momentous ones, including Ralphe Bunche's receiving the Nobel Peace Prize in 1950 and appointment as undersecretary of the United Nations in 1955 and the inclusion in the platforms of the major political parties in 1952 of statements rejecting bigotry and embracing desegregation (Bergman 1969, 523–532). Then came the Supreme Court's decision in *Brown* v. *Board of Education* (1954), which declared unconstitutional existing separate-but-equal educational facilities, and the subsequent Little Rock school-integration troubles, in which whites violently resisted the order until federal troops were mustered by President Eisenhower.

These events and others signaled the imminent death of Jim Crow, and it was thought that the achievement of political and cultural equality would require that African Americans conform to more acceptable artistic standards and behaviors. Langston Hughes was now regarded by some younger blacks as "an outmoded racial chauvinist" and his "harping on blues and jazz . . . an archaic position . . . in the dawn of integration" (Rampersad 1988, 207). Now, black America was inclined to put behind it the "race" dramas, novels, and music of the past and prepare itself for a new day: black artists retreated into a conformative mode that would last until the 1960s.

The desire among musicians for full inclusion in America's musical culture further subordinated the powerful ring impulse, and the suppression of that impulse resulted, I believe, in a spiritual vacuity that, together with continuing oppression and mean-spirited exclusion and insensitivity on the part of some whites, created in African Americans a new despair that they concealed by fronting and allayed through Signifyin(g). Jook musicians donned tuxedos, and composers wrote music that conformed to the tenets of the so-called New Criticism that approved only art that evaded social context. This resulted in a quick decrease in the number of concert-hall compositions that employed **161** ring tropes; by the 1950s, nearly all of the musical output of composers avoided obvious manifestations of the black aesthetic.

The momentum of the Negro Renaissance had been powerful enough, though, to ensure that the composition of such works would not come completely to an end. Margaret Bonds's song cycle *Three Dream Portraits* (1959); for example, while structurally and materially European-derived, is also unequivocally African American in subject matter and treatment. In it, Bonds freely but subtly uses ring-derived procedures to set texts by Langston Hughes. The songs are all strophic in form and laced with word painting and imagery, but they also make occasional use of ostinatos, flatted sevenths, improvisation-like passages, and blues-like progressions. Hughes's text in "Minstrel Man" instructs and chides, but Bonds's music pleads for empathy with the black experience; her jazz-like figures and chords sparsely decorate her otherwise impressionistic textures, and the accompaniment is filled with syncopated and additive rhythmic figures. The lilting "Dream Variation," a reflection of the desire to dance, is also impressionistic in character. Employing word painting and metaphor, the text and its setting identify the blackness of one's skin with the night and with tenderness. The expressive range of "I, Too" is wide, despite the song's brevity; its text reflects variously on discrimination and on ways of coping with it, on the yearning for neighborly coexistence, and on the eradication of prejudice. These settings, powerful aesthetic miniatures, call for the realization of the promise of integration, exemplifying in their amalgamation of text and tune the possibilities inherent in that promise. It is at once an appeal to conscience and a demonstration of readiness.

William Grant Still's output in the 1950s included three compositions that have been recorded on the album *Works by William Grant Still* (1990). "Citadel," with its lush, impressionistic harmonies, reveals the composer as the true romantic he was for nearly all of his career. The setting of Virginia Brasier's text is through-composed and devoid of ring tropes, reflecting Still's commitment to the European-derived tradition. "Song of the Lonely," set to a text by Verna Arvey, is through-composed, impressionistic, and romantic. But *Ennanga*, a three-movement work, is named after an African harp and, in places, recalls the West African *kora;* it features a European harp and a string ensemble. The first movement, making use of pentatonic melodies and African-American harmonic and melodic structures, is rife with pendular and falling thirds and with what Still must have thought were approximations of African rhythms; the second movement emphasizes pendular thirds, particularly at the ends of phrases; and the third movement, sprightly and dance-like and featuring harp glissandi, recalls the third movement of the composer's *Afro-American Symphony.* All three pieces—the two songs and *Ennanga*—are highly expressive, graced with tasteful, intermediary climaxes, and are expressively performed in this recording.

As early as 1944, Ulysses Kay's prize-winning orchestral work *Of New Horizons* had begun to move black concert-hall music away from African-American nationalism into a neoclassicism devoid of ring-derived traits. Kay followed this work with *Short Overture* (1946) and *Three Pieces after Blake* (1952), both of which, with their apparent objectivity, restraint, and formal conformity, established Kay as a composer of merit. In the 1950s, George Walker established himself as a composer with his Piano Sonato No. 2 and his Concerto for Trombone and Orchestra, both completed in 1957. These works, too, eschew the black aesthetic and conform instead to the prevailing musical, intellectual, and social ideologies of the larger culture.

Walker's Sonata No. 2 is based on the oscillating thirds that open the first movement (Adagio non troppo) and recur in various permutations throughout its four movements. The second, marked Presto, is a very brief scherzo with an opening that features jagged intervals and asymmetrical phrasings. The Adagio third movement features heavy, slow-moving chords that contrast with lyrical passages; it ends with repetitions of the melody. The Allegretto is a sonatina-like movement consisting of bravura passages that contrast with singing, legato statements.[2] The Concerto for Trombone and Orchestra features, in its first movement, a kind of rondo that sandwiches two occurrences each of the B and C themes between five appearances of the primary A theme. It opens with the mythic sounds of early- and mid-century neoclassicism, effected by the composer's use of the xylophone and drum in connection with short, sharp chords. Narrow-range melodies with a stepwise, pendular movement contrast with cascading ones—all oppositions that suggests alternately both stasis and movement in a primal-sounding configuration that has the air of European-based ritual. Near the end of the movement, a slow-moving cadenza brings back the B theme, which is followed by a coda-like extension that comments on A. In the second movement (Grave), a single melody is introduced immediately by the bassoon, elaborated by the strings, and passed, in another permutation, to the trombone. Effective timbres enhance and complement the melody in its few other sonic and contrapuntal permutations, and portamento and pizzicato strings provide a complement and contrast to the trombone's presentations. Oboe and flute provide counterpoint to the main melody. The fourth movement (Allegro) recalls Stravinsky: the trombone's statements are supported by sharp chords and additive rhythms, all played staccato and pizzicato.

These works by Walker and Kay are examples of the neoclassical retreat by black composers in 1950s, which represents the understandable and proper desire of African Americans to be included as full participants in America's European-derived musical culture. There was a positive result of this apostasy. As bell hooks (1990) has written in a later and different context,

2. For other works for piano by Walker and other black composers, see Horne (1992).

> Working from a base where difference and otherness are acknowledged as forces that intervene in western theorizing about aesthetics to reformulate and transform the discussion, African-Americans are empowered to break with old ways of seeing reality that suggest that there is only one audience for our work and only one aesthetic measure of its value. Moving away from narrow cultural nationalism, one leaves behind as well racist assumptions that cultural productions by black people can only have "authentic" significance and meaning for a black audience. (110)

Meanwhile, in the field of jazz, similar aspirations prevailed and gave rise in that genre to two streams of development. The "cool school," driven by the formation and development of the Miles Davis band (a nonet consisting of trumpet, trombone, French horn, tuba, tenor saxophone, baritone saxophone, piano, bass, and drums), made its first impact in a broadcast from New York's Royal Roost nightclub on September 4, 1948 (preserved on the recording *Miles Davis and His Orchestra*). The band was developed to put into practice theories that had begun to emerge among a few white and even fewer black jazz musicians in the years after World War II. These theories, with their basis and inspiration in the ballad playing and lyricism of Charlie Parker, Lester Young, and Miles Davis and in the constructions of the concert-hall tradition, led to a music that, compared with bebop, used slower and more moderate tempi, fewer notes, less rhythmic activity, evenly spaced eighth notes, more timbral variety, and European-derived textural conceptions. Cool jazz was a highly structured, highly calculated, low-intensity music; it made use of traditional European structures such as rondo and fugue and was sometimes set in 3/4, 5/4, 7/4, or 9/8 meters, in addition to the regular 4/4 meter typical of previous styles. The emphasis in cool jazz was more on composition and arranging than on melodic improvisation, and this emphasis mirrored Davis's and others' preferences for nuance and understatement. But the movement rejected the blues inflections and other African-derived elements so vital to the black aesthetic. Eschewing the musical values and practices of Call–Response, cool jazz leaned toward things European rather than African, and its music, therefore, was more staid and reflective than that of previous styles. But Davis was playing on the verges, exploring the crossroads where African-American and European myth and ritual meet, "reveling in the merging of contrasting approaches and sounds," and affirming "the wide-ranging variety of African-American perceptions themselves" (Tomlinson 1991, 256). The Harlem Renaissance thinkers would have embraced this kind of realization, I believe. But it was a realization achieved primarily by white musicians, in spite of Davis's ostensible leadership role. Cool experimentation continued from the 1948 nonet recording on through the 1950s, reaching its peak of popularity in 1958 with one of Davis's collaborations with white composer Gil Evans, the album *George Gershwin's Porgy and Bess.*

Beginning in the early 1920s, George Gershwin composed music influenced by and based on black musical devices and traits, including the opera *Blue Monday Blues* (1922), the concerto *Rhapsody in Blue* (1924), and the orchestral tone poem *An American in Paris* (1928). Gershwin had been schooled and indoctrinated in the African-American musical cauldron that was the Harlem Renaissance (Kirkby 1966, 53), and in 1934 he prepared to write the music for a libretto based on DuBose Heyward's novel *Porgy* (1925). In preparation for the task, he supplemented his Harlem-based knowledge and experience with first-hand contact with southern black folk traditions, gained in at least one of his two trips in the early 1930s to Charleston, South Carolina, where the opera is set. The first, in December 1933, was a brief exploratory visit; the second, a stay of three months beginning in June 1934, during which he mined the rich southern core culture by absorbing some of the content and style of the traditional black folk music on which he would base his score (Jablonski 1987, 267, 272). Heyward's libretto (based on his novel and on the 1927 play of the same name, written with his wife, Dorothy) and the lyrics of Ira Gershwin came together with Gershwin's score to form a moving black opera, *Porgy and Bess*.

The Davis–Evans collaboration is a recomposition of thirteen of the opera's tunes, rendered by an orchestra of two flutes, three French horns, two saxophones, four trumpets, four trombones, a tuba, a string bass, and drums. Davis, the only soloist, plays fluegelhorn and trumpet. This collection includes the sweetly tart and pungent "Buzzard's Song," the bittersweet and sentimental "Bess, You Is My Woman Now," the jazzy "Gone," the brief, spiritual-like "Gone, Gone, Gone," the beautiful "Summertime," the searching "Bess, Oh Where's My Bess," and the solicitous and persistent "Prayer," with its copious bent and blue notes, followed by "Fishermen, Strawberry and the Devil Crab," "My Man's Gone Now," "It Ain't Necessarily So," "Here Come de Honey Man," "I Loves You, Porgy," and "There's a Boat That's Leaving Soon for New York." This album is a good example of one aspect of the orchestral jazz of the cool school, but the best thing about it is the power of Gershwin's tune and Davis's revision of "Summertime." Otherwise, it falls flat, the insinuating inflections adding little or nothing to the substance of the pieces.

But cool jazz stimulated even more ambitious activity, including the effort to bring together European-derived classical music and jazz in a unified form known as Third Stream, the second of the two developments I mentioned earlier.[3] Taking the lead were John Lewis and the Modern Jazz Quartet (MJQ), which was made up, initially, of the rhythm section of the great Dizzy Gillespie Big Band of 1946 to 1950: Lewis on piano, Milt Jackson on vibraharp,

3. The term "Third Stream," according to a variety of sources, was coined in 1957 by Gunther Schuller, who was the movement's "most eloquent spokesman" (see, for example, Budds 1978, 72).

Ray Brown on bass, and Kenny Clarke on drums.[4] The Third Stream works of this group, which made its first recording in 1952,[5] combine the instrumental combinations, formal procedures, and musical mannerisms of the so-called First Stream (concert-hall music) with those of the so-called Second Stream (jazz). In 1959, the group presented a "landmark concert of Third Stream music with the Beaux Arts String Quartet [BASQ] at Town Hall in New York" (Southern 1982, 277). A typical number from this recital (recorded on *Third Stream Music*) is Lewis's "Sketch"—a blend of colors, textures, and procedures that judiciously intersperses precomposed passages with improvised ones. Lewis's Bach-based, bop-phrased solo work is presented with MJQ backing, and then is superimposed over the European phrasings of the BASQ. Jackson's swinging, blues-oriented work on vibes is effectively layered over that of the other players in a seamless three-part piece that ends with an ensemble passage played by the two groups. In performing music such as this, in concert attire and in hallowed places, the MJQ sought public endorsement and Establishment respect. DeVeaux (1991) apparently agrees:

> Classical music seemed like an exclusive club that in an egalitarian spirit might be persuaded to integrate. The discreet, gently swinging tonal structures of the Modern Jazz Quartet, performed by black men in tuxedos in concert halls for respectful audiences, provided a comforting image of what membership in this club might look like. (546)

Further, observes Gennari (1991):

> The new Lenox School of jazz at Music Inn in the Berkshires of western Massachusetts . . . as the site of the formation of the Modern Jazz Quartet; the inception of the Schuller-led Third Stream movement; concerts by established artists; . . . lectures and reportage by [Martin] Williams, [Marshall] Stearns, and others . . . seemed to augur a brightening future for jazz in terms of institutional formation and audience development. . . . Contributing to this process of bourgeoisification was the European orientation of the Third Stream, the new fusion of classical music and jazz forged by The Modern Jazz Quartet, Gunther Schuller, and others, as well as the ersatz symphonic effects and melodic romanticism of many "cool" jazz productions. . . . Regardless of how dismissive *some* jazz critics may have been of the Third Stream and cool in the late '50s, however, *all* jazz critics benefited from the larger, economically and culturally more powerful audiences these subgenres secured for jazz. (479)

This may have been so, but the music was problematic for more than the critics. The musicians of the cool and Third Stream schools tended to discard ring values, diluting the powerful expressions of Call–Response. An example of this dilution is the MJQ's ineffective 1957 version of Parker's "Now's the Time," in

4. Brown was replaced by Percy Heath in 1952; Clarke, by Connie Kay in 1955.

166 5. The album, *The Modern Jazz Quartet / The Milt Jackson Quintet*, contains renditions of "All the Things You Are," "La Ronde," "Vendome," and "Rose of the Rio Grande."

which, after a shaky start, the performers get into a cool groove but do not tell much of a story because of their too subtle treatment of the ring tropes they employ. This performance pales beside the Parker original and also beside its R&B derivative. What was bebop is now "smooth jazz," as some call this style, except for Jackson's solo chorus and the last three-fourths of Lewis's. In my view, it is a pastiche of two styles that parodies the original. Two more tunes in the same collection (*The Modern Jazz Quartet Plus*), "The Golden Striker," part of a film score, and "Three Windows," are European-oriented concert-hall music played in the swinging style of jazz, as evidenced by Lewis's composed-sounding accompaniments.[6] Only Jackson's improvisatory skills bring these performances into the realm of ring-based music. For those who were emotionally and ideologically committed to the African-American side of the musical mix, many of the products of the cool/Third Stream trend were viewed either as vapid cultural irrelevances or as musical, social, and cultural threats to "real" black music.

But in spite of the spiritual vacuity of most cool jazz—as evidenced by its paucity of ring traits—its acceptance by the young white and black college students of the 1950s, as a result of the widespread successes of the Modern Jazz Quartet, the Dave Brubeck Quartet, the Australian Jazz Quintet, and other such aggregations, had made jazz more respectable in "proper" (that is, white) social circles. At the same time, the greatness and popularity of black jazz pianists such as Art Tatum and Oscar Peterson, both of whom were favorites of the black intelligentsia, were widely appreciated and applauded, and there began to emerge a rapprochement between the polarized aesthetic factions.

Notwithstanding the directions that were taken by cool/Third Stream musicians and by some African-American composers of concert-hall music, ring-derived procedures remained ascendant in other quarters. In the big-band arena, for example, Count Basie continued to carry the flame. In its early years, the Basie band had specialized in head arrangements. These constructions, similar to and reminiscent of African performance practice, consisted generally of a basic riff (read "time line") against which other riffs and rhythmic–melodic figures would be set. The rhythmic result was usually a percussive and polyrhythmic overlapping of call-and-response patterns. Basie's technique of head-arranging is described by a former sideman:

> Basie would start out and vamp a little, set a tempo, and call out, "That's it!" He'd set a rhythm for the saxes first, and Earl Warren would pick that up and lead the saxes. Then he'd set one for the bones and we'd pick that up. Now it's

---

6. "The Golden Striker" is European-sounding in spite of its being based on the third strain of Jelly Roll Morton's "King Porter Stomp." I think Martin Williams (1983, 180) would have said, if he had been speaking from the Signifin(g) mode, that "The Golden Striker" Signifies on Henderson's arrangement of "King Porter Stomp." **167**

> our rhythm against theirs. The third rhythm would be for the trumpets. (Wells 1971, 55)

Speaking about black bands in general, W. O. Smith (1991) elaborates with a colorful and provocative scenario:

> Can you imagine a situation like this? Somebody starts off with a riff . . . and goes not more than a couple of bars when he is picked up by the rest of the members in his section—we'll say it's the saxophone section—and within the space of two bars or less, the riff is harmonized with each saxophonist instinctively grabbing his part, usually with the correct notes. Then the trumpet section, at the correct instant, plays a counter riff, something like the call and response pattern of the black church. This, too, is instantly harmonized in three or four parts, depending on the number of trumpets. Mind you, everybody has different but effective notes. The trombone section, not to be outdone, then plays a counterpoint to the whole arrangement. From the very beginning, the rhythm section realizes harmonic patterns or chord changes implied by the first riff, and the result is a new addition to the repertoire. Mix all of this with appropriate solos by the most dynamic soloists accompanied by the appropriate section and the appropriate riff. What we usually got was a crowd pleaser. (38–39)

This is "Red Hill Churchyard" troping in a big band, the chicanery of the trickster on stage.[7]

Thoughts of head arrangements recall for me Basie's 1938 recording of "Doggin' Around"—an example of the tremendous swing generated by his hard-driving four-to-the-bar renditions. The performance is filled with accented riffs, growls, and assorted solos. It begins with Basie's ostinato-like boogie treble pattern, which sets the stage for what is to come. Later, Lester Young plays a solo in his characteristically light, graceful, swinging style, phrasing ahead of and behind the beat as he creates new melodies. The successes of the Basie band continued into the 1950s, while Ellington stood at the crossroads, Esu-like, with *A Tone Parallel to Harlem* (1951), a work that, in its formal properties, effectively bridges the myths, rituals, and properties of the concert hall and the Saturday-night function. The piece was the result of a natural progression from Ellington's work of the 1920s, about which he (1973) later wrote,

> Call was very important in that kind of music. Today, the music has grown up and become quite scholastic, but this was *au naturel*, close to the primitive, where people send messages in what they play, calling somebody or making facts and emotions known. Painting a picture, or having a story to go with what you were going to play, was of vital importance in those days. (47)

---

7. Such troping was typical of the riffing, shouting, driving, black big bands of the 1930s, 1940s, and 1950s, the most prominent of which, in addition to Basie's, were those of Chick Webb, Jimmy Lunceford, Cab Calloway, and Duke Ellington.

A Tone Parallel to Harlem is a profound manifestation of Ellington's observations. A good example of his mastery of the large form, this work begins with a muted trombone playing three calls, successively, that "say" Harrr . . . lemmmm! in falling minor thirds, with ensemble responses to each. As village African trumpeters "called" the names of their ensembles (chapter 1), Ellington here uses the trumpets in his band to call the name of the community he loved most. Then he extends and elaborates these opening statements, through paraphrase and development, into an expansive jazz work, a thirteen-minute "suite," as he called it, that expressed aspects of Harlem culture, recapitulating and summarizing much of what had been accomplished in the world of the jazz orchestra up to that time and revealing Ellington's own sophisticated integration of traditional African-American intervallic and call-and-response figures into a large formal structure. Ellington's melodies in this work grow through his expansion and development of the call figure that opens the work, and they move on through later sections that contain, variously, a Latin-like chorus with riffs—what might be called a riff-chorus—and a melody that appears first as a solo, then with one, two, and three countermelodies, and finally with homophonic accompaniment. The piece is, in one sense, a kind of "concerto" for jazz orchestra whose form is built through the juxtaposition of energetic and aesthetically provocative solo and ensemble work with subtle, quiet sections. A hard-hitting coda brings the work to a close.

Throughout this composition, as with much of Ellington's work, one is struck by the way unusually orchestrated passages give birth to equally unusual solo timbres and ideas that, in spite of their singularity, contribute to the continuity of the whole. The orchestrated events are timbral, harmonic, melodic, and stylistic amalgams whose properties are aesthetically inseparable from one another. The absence or modification of any one of the properties of the stylistic, orchestral, or inflexional renderings of a particular amalgam would vitiate the nature and effect of the whole, and any attempt to imitate or approximate a particular amalgam with a mixture of other combinations would prove futile. Ellington's meldings of performers' stylistic and timbral peculiarities with his own harmonic, melodic, and textural resources and ideas result in *true* amalgams, instances of which include combinations such as Quentin Jackson's (or Britt Woodman's) muted trombone, Jimmy Hamilton's clarinet, and Wendell Marshall's bass; Woodman's muted horn and Jackson's open horn; Jackson's or Woodman's muted trombone, Harry Carney's baritone sax, and Marshall's bass; and Woodman's trombone, Hamilton's clarinet, and Paul Gonsalves's tenor saxophone. The individual instruments in each group play lines in counterpoint with one another, and in some passages I find it impossible to identify the instrumentation through listening alone. I think these amalgams are, in part, what Ellington's collaborator Billy Strayhorn was referring to when he coined the term "Ellington effect."[8] Highly sensitive to the special and inimitable "tonal personalities" of his sidemen, Ellington exploited, individually and collectively, their particular and singular sounds. But the key to the power of the Ellington effect lies in its embodied sound, the visceral expressive effect that, in Ellington's amalgams, exudes and evokes, by way of the prodigious semantic value of their sounds, the callers, criers, and "story" tellers of the African and African-American past. Ellington's sidemen, variously, were callers in an unusual and inimitable Call–Response environment.

Another example of how technical mastery, cultural affinity, and individual and collective artistry can combine to produce consummate art is Ellington's performance with Mahalia Jackson of a musical setting of the Twenty-third Psalm, recorded on *Black, Brown and Beige* (1958). Here Jackson, Ellington, and the members of the orchestra employ a number of devices, techniques, and procedures from small-combo and big-band jazz, vocal gospel music, and European orchestral music in an instance of musical cooperation and community. Each performer's unique contribution combines with those of the others to make an effective rendition, with Ellington's piano complementing Jackson's delivery and enhancing the overall sound of a performance of sensitivity and restraint. Jackson is strong, confident, and spiritually profound in a context that reveals her stylistic and musical flexibility and that of Ellington and his band. This thorough and complete reconstruction of the well-known, standard musical conception of the psalm remakes the melody and harmony of its model and, through the use of complementary and provocative countermelody, maintains its inevitable logic. The work can hardly be considered jazz in the most common understanding of the term; it is religious concert-hall music. Here, Ellington, like Davis in his cool-school renderings, is playing on the verges, revealing the versatility and possibilities of his art and that of African-American music in general.

Mahalia Jackson's art originated in her southern home of New Orleans and was honed on the core-culture church circuit with the Thomas Dorsey songs and other music of the black religious tradition. Most of the black churches of the land from which she sprang used the spiritual as the musical basis for worship and continued that tradition into the 1950s. The performances of these congregations—rhythmically and melodically embellished in some cases and freely improvised in others—evolved in rhythmic crescendos that culminated in experiences of matchless religious intensity: "the quality of the singing was distinctive for its shrill, hard, full-throated, strained, raspy, and/or nasal

---

8. The term is meant to describe Ellington's musical attitude, "the contributions of his sidemen," and his approach to orchestration (Rattenbury 1990, 13–32).

tones, with frequent exploitation of falsetto, growling, and moaning" (Southern 1983, 447). Hand clapping, of course, was a constant, and the piano accompaniments of the Primitive Baptist Church, characterized by the embellishment and improvisation of spiritual melodies, graced these vocal and physical expressions. It was this and other music of the black church, with its communal and congregational thrust, that became the focus of the music of the civil rights movement.

Spurred by the bus boycott in Montgomery, Alabama, and its satellite activities in other southern cities in the mid-1950s, and led by the Southern Christian Leadership Conference (SCLC), the civil rights movement was the setting in which the spiritual became effective as unabashed protest music. The failure of white Americans and their local, state, and federal leaders to recognize the social and political wrongs that oppressed African Americans, combined with black citizens' lowered tolerance for traditional means of mediating grievances, resulted in national nonviolent, direct action by organized groups. This new protest movement of civil disobedience was characterized by sit-ins, freedom marches, pray-ins, social and political negotiations, and appeals to white conscience.

As natural and as spontaneous as the use of the spirituals and hymns in this church-based protest activity may have seemed, the foundation for it had been laid, in one sense, by the Wings Over Jordan Choir. From its inception in 1937 to its demise in 1949, this Cleveland-based group was broadcast each Sunday over the CBS radio network, its music and messages going into the homes of hundreds of thousands of African Americans all across the nation. One of the choir's purposes was to "promote goodwill and understanding between the races,"[9] and in serving this function it also served as a forum for individuals such as Adam Clayton Powell, Sr., Langston Hughes, and other outstanding "race" leaders of the period. Traveling across the nation in buses, the Wings Over Jordan Choir refused to perform before segregated audiences. Some of the best work of this highly polished choir of spiritual singers can be heard in the collection *The Wings Over Jordan Choir* (1978). Its incomparable arrangements and harmonizing are evident on "I've Been 'Buked and I've Been Scorned," "Amen," and "Where Shall I Be," the last being one of those spirituals in which the verse is rendered slowly and rubato, sorrow-song style, and the chorus up-tempo, jubilee style. Ring tropes, used sparingly but effectively, are represented in "Swing Low, Sweet Chariot" (the "mi-Lawdy" interjection), "Trampin'" (call-and-response structure), and "Rock-a My Soul" (short, repeated phrases and additive rhythms). Impressive also are the choir's variable humming, its impeccable intonation, its unerring precision, its subtle rendering of blue notes, its vibrato, its marching-bass trope in "Swing Low," its spe-

---

9. As stated by a founding member in a recent television special about the group.

cial effects in "Over My Head (I Hear Music in the Air)" and "Rock-a My Soul," and its "high hoos" in "I Cried and I Cried," a song that became a favorite of black congregations everywhere in the 1950s. The choir's popularity among both blacks and whites, its refusal to accommodate segregation at its concerts, its stature as a radio-network fixture, and its presentation of the spirituals both as culturally viable aesthetic expressions and as songs of freedom, faith, and documentation, set the precedent and the context for southern protest activity among blacks in the 1950s.

Also continuing to develop in the South in the years after Jackson left New Orleans (she moved to Chicago in 1927) were the great vocal quartets, mentioned briefly in chapter 3, which sang spirituals and early gospel songs.[10] Quartets traveled the church circuit and recorded prolifically in the North. The *Birmingham Quartet Anthology* (1980) documents in a modern recording the musical prowess of groups such as the Silver Leaf Quartet, the Kings of Harmony, the Famous Blue Jay Singers, and the Golden Gate Quartet. It reveals the heavy presence of Negro spirituals in the repertoires of these quartets from the late 1920s through the 1940s, with exemplars being "My Soul Is a Witness" (Silver Leaf Quartet, 1928), "Poor Pilgrim of Sorrow" (Kings of Harmony, 1945), and "Bound for Canaan Land" (Famous Blue Jay Singers, 1946). The text of the Dunham Jubilee Singers' "I Dreamed of Judgment Morning" (1930) is performed in typical quartet style, with the emphasis on ensemble blend and balance; but the elisions, blue notes, and occasional falsetto passages are delivered by voices that sometimes rasp and strain in the African-American manner. "Clanka-Lanka," the Famous Blue Jay Singers' 1931 version of "Sleep On, Mother," is also rendered in the style of black core-culture singers, emphasizing the falsetto tenor lead and the riff-like "clanka-lanka" accompaniment. The instrumentally conceived clanka-lanka figuration was duplicated by subsequent groups.[11] "Clanka-lanka" was to have significant influence on later developments, as we shall see.

The quartets of the 1920s and 1930s had emerged out of the fertile musical regions of Jefferson County, Alabama, and the Tidewater of Virginia, as well as from other areas of the South, and were succeeded in the 1940s by more polished and sophisticated quartets such as the Charioteers, the Deep River Boys, and the Golden Gate Quartet.[12] In the 1950s, the great quartets reached their peak, and one of the most popular was the Soul Stirrers, who introduced

---

10. A few female groups existed, but the tradition was almost all male.

11. In the liner notes of the *Birmingham Quartet Anthology,* Seroff lists twelve gospel quartets that used the figure on other songs between 1931 and 1950 and cites as a "modern counterpart" the doo-wop refrain of the street-corner groups of the 1950s.

12. The Golden Gate Quartet can be heard to good effect on *I Hear Music in the Air: A Treasury of Gospel Music.*

the alternating lead to gospel quartet singing (a device that would be taken up by the pop quartets of the 1960s). The lead singers freely negotiated the musical ecology with melismas and bent notes, with Sam Cooke's falsetto cries and yodels leading the group in its church-wrecking exploits. Their artistry can be heard on *The Original Soul Stirrers Featuring Sam Cooke,* in which Cooke and Rebert Harris are featured as leads—Harris on Charles Tindley's "We'll Understand It By and By" (1905) and alternating with Paul Foster and Cooke on "He'll Welcome Me" and "Touch the Hem of His Garment." On "By and By," Harris's tight vibrato and somewhat raspy delivery can be heard to good effect. "Touch the Hem of His Garment" reveals his influence on Cooke (the tight raspiness) as well as Cooke's own independent style and delivery (the superb voice with its occasional openness, the bent notes) and touches of the well-known Cooke yodel.[13] Among other important quartets of the 1950s were the Caravans, the Dixie Hummingbirds, the Five Blind Boys of Mississippi, the Five Blind Boys of Alabama,[14] the Gospelaires, and the Mighty Clouds of Joy.

The Famous Ward Singers debuted in 1934 with Mother Gertrude Ward and daughters Clara and Willa. Later, Marion Williams and Henrietta Waddy were added to the group. Their performance of W. Herbert Brewster's "Surely God Is Able" (1948) had a significant influence on subsequent singing styles, primarily through Marion Williams's well-known elided permutations of shaking bent notes on the "Shure-lay-ay, shure-lay-ay" call-and-response passage near the end of the performance, which *surely* wrecked houses, private and church. But even before Williams's excursions, the Wards' short, repeated phrases, high hoos, heavy use of call-and-response phrases, and ♪|♫♪♪♪♪♪| rhythmic connectors in a Call–Response environment set the stage for Williams's dramatic finish.[15] Solo, duo, and trio performers were also part of the gospel mix of the 1950s, including the Florida-bred and -based duo the Boyer Brothers (James and Horace). Recordings from the 1950s are not available, but their 1966 performance of Lucie Campbell's "He'll Understand" (1950) is a marvelous example of their art.[16] Performed in the typical 12/8 meter of the period, it contains prominent and frequent figurations such as "calling" and "responding" interjections of "Oh yes," "Don't you know," "Oh yes he will," "Unhh hunh," high hoos, held *yeses,* and other core-culture aesthetic commentary that punctuate the performance throughout. These melodic figurations and spoken interjections are complemented occasionally by instrumental figures such as

13. Cooke's gospel-pop versatility can be heard on *The Two Sides of Sam Cooke.* Cooke made his successful transition from gospel to pop stardom with the hit "You Send Me" (1957).

14. The 1980s "edition" of the Five Blind Boys of Alabama can be seen and heard on the videotaped performance of the stage musical *The Gospel at Colonus* (1985).

15. This performance can be heard on *Best of the Famous Ward Singers of Philadelphia, PA.*

16. This song is listed in Jackson (1979) as "He Understands, He'll Say Well Done."

Contrasting with the Ward Singers and the Boyer Brothers, the Wings Over Jordan Choir occupied the other end of gospel's ensemble and stylistic spectrum, specializing almost strictly in spirituals. Essentially, Wings Over Jordan represented the end of a tradition—one that, while continuing to have currency in black colleges across the nation well into the 1960s, graciously gave ground to the small gospel groups and the rising gospel choruses that had been spawned by Dorsey and others. An example of the passing of the torch can be observed by first listening to the Wings Over Jordan Choir's gospel-oriented performance of "When I've Done the Best I Can" and then comparing their performance of Lucy Campbell's "He'll Understand" with that of the Boyer Brothers duo. The restrained, European-oriented "When I've Done the Best I Can" is a nod and a tribute to the emerging style, and the Boyer Brothers' rendition of "He'll Understand" stylistically supersedes its predecessor with youthful vitality and modernized ring devices in the manner of the more contemporary renderings of the gospel soloists and choruses of the period.

But as impressive as were the Boyer Brothers, the Ward Singers, the choruses, and other gospel performers of the 1950s, it was the gospel quartets that would have the widest and most immediate impact on other black-music genres. A syncretizing of several styles, their performances were characterized by precise rhythmic articulation; improvisatory, blues-inflected melismatic and motivic delivery; rhythmic, melodic, and harmonic repetition; emphasis on the primary chords (I, IV, V); call-and-response dialogue involving the singers and their accompanying instruments; and the encouraging, yea-saying vocal interjections of performers and audiences alike. And these quartet performers did not leave it to the jazzmen to continue the tradition of individual and group competition. Through the imaginative use of Call–Response, they cut and carved one another as much as did the jazzmen. Heilbut (1985) quotes an informant as saying that singers such as Joe E. Union of the Flying Clouds, Reverend Latimore out of the Kings of Harmony, and Leroy Barnes of the Evangelist Singers were " 'legends, like Wyatt Earp.' " Like outlaw heroes, quartet singers could take over a town and leave the slain stretched out. Who was the toughest, the deepest, the most spiritual? Who shouted the most people?" (47). So the 1950s was a period in which, together with all the other activity, the quartet leads were "the baddest men on the road."

The gospel quartets greatly influenced the development of the R&B quartets of the 1950s, the relationship going back more than two decades, to the emergence of a secular aspect within the gospel-quartet tradition. The Birmingham Jubilee Singers' 1929 recording of "Eliza" (which contains a variation of the clanka-lanka riff and other vocalized instrumental tropes, some of which sound as if they were collectively improvised) and the Golden Gate Quartet's "My Walking Stick" of 1939 (whose vocalized accompaniment passages approximate the sounds of an instrumental ensemble, complete with riffs, call-and-response figures, and a vocalized "instrumental" chorus) are examples of the secular novelty pieces that some of the gospel quartets recorded. The Jones Boys Sing Band was one of the jive-tradition groups active in the 1930s; its "Pickin' a Rib" (1935), when compared with the secular output of the gospel groups, shows the similarities in style and musical content between the secular-gospel and jive traditions. Recordings such as these spread the techniques of gospel quartet throughout the core culture. And the venerated criteria of "time, harmony, and articulation" (Seroff 1990, 27), so well known in quartet circles for the formal judging of gospel-quartet performances, served unofficially as training precepts for the emerging R&B quartets. This is evident when one compares, for example, the output of the Jones Boys Sing Band with that of the Mills Brothers: the style of the former portends that of the latter. The Ink Spots, on the contrary, sang white-oriented pop material (although nicely but sparingly spiced with black expressive devices), scoring their first hit in 1939 with "If I Didn't Care." Other hits followed until the group reached its peak in the mid-1940s. The Ravens and the Orioles sang "black," the Ravens scoring first with "Ol' Man River" (although certainly not a "traditional" number) in 1947 and the Orioles in 1949 with "It's Too Soon to Know." In imitation of the clanka-lanka and other accompanying devices of gospel-quartet music, the jive and rhythm groups of the later 1940s employed instrumentally derived sounds and figures such as "doo-wop," "ohh-waa," "ko-ko-bop," "oo-bi-dee," and "sh-boom." The wide adoption of such devices in the 1950s effected a continuity between the music of the newer secular quartets and that of the older ones, as well as within and among the new groups themselves. These burgeoning street-corner quartets, called "doo-wop" by some, emerged to crystallize the style; the Dominoes' "Sixty Minute Man" (1951) and the Orioles' "Crying in the Chapel" (1953) were early hits.[17]

17. For a musical survey of this tradition, listen to *History of Rhythm and Blues Vocal Groups*, vol. 5 (1983).

In 1949 *Billboard* magazine introduced the term "Rhythm & Blues" to replace "Race" as a marketing label, but the term did not embrace jazz, traditional blues, and other folk genres, as had the earlier designation.[18] At the time, "Rhythm & Blues" denoted only "an ensemble music, consisting of a vocal unit (solo or group), a rhythm unit (electric guitar and/or string bass, piano, drums), and a supplementary unit (generally the saxophone and sometimes other winds)" (Southern 1983, 499). But it embraced music as disparate as that of the doo-wop quartets, Louis Jordan and His Timpani Five, Roy Milton, Chuck Berry, Little Richard, and the Chicago bluesmen.

The electric guitar had been established in Chicago blues in the late 1940s. Muddy Waters's "Louisiana Blues" was in the vanguard of the heavily amplified Chicago blues style; as Robert Palmer (1981) tells us, this performance "had a power all its own . . . the power of electricity. It was irresistible" (99). After "Muddy 'vented electricity," as they say in Chicago blues circles, Little Walter amplified his harmonica, Sonny Boy Williamson added a rhythm section, and by the late 1940s the Chicago blues style had crystallized in the commercial output of these musicians, as well as that of Elmore James, Jimmy Rogers, and Robert Nighthawk, all of whose work constituted, in the 1950s, "the recorded pinnacle of Chicago blues" (215). The album *Wizards from the Southside* (1984) is somewhat representative of the work of these musicians and helps to demonstrate Palmer's claim. Containing performances by Little Walter, Sonny Boy Williamson, Howlin' Wolf, John Lee Hooker, and Bo Diddley, with such stalwart sidemen as Jimmy Rogers and Robert "Junior" Lockwood on guitar, Willie Dixon on bass, and Otis Spann on piano, it is filled with Saturday-night, core-culture, back-country dance music. The piano, bass, and drums, used as accompanying instruments throughout the album, provide shuffle-blues beats, asymmetrical phrasings, and folk timbres and devices that enhance the singing of the vocalists. Especially effective are Muddy Waters's "Rollin' 'n' Tumblin'" (1950) and "Still a Fool" (1951), both of which feature his signature guitar–vocal unison and various call-and-response phrasings; John Lee Hooker's "Walkin' the Boogie" (1952), on which he is a veritable one-man band; Little Walter's "Mellow Down Easy" (1954), which demonstrates his prowess on the mouth harp; Bo Diddley's "She's Mine, She's Fine" (1955) and "I'm a Man" (1955), both of which feature his Latin-influenced beat and harmonic riffs; and Muddy's "Mannish Boy" (1955), which tropes—or is troped by—Diddley's "I'm a Man."

Howlin' Wolf's "Evil" (1954) is special. It is a twelve-bar blues delivered in his coarse, emotional style. The vocal shadings and timbral changes he effects in his strained, sometimes falsetto delivery are complemented and intensified

18. According to Dannen (1991, 87), the term "rhythm and blues" was coined in 1949 by *Billboard* staff member Jerry Wexler.

by the band's syncopated backbeat, the piano's treble boogie figurations, the instrumentalists' brief, simultaneous improvisations—particularly those of the piano and mouth harp—and Otis Spann's melodic filigree and semantic-laden musical commentary. These musical devices and configurations heighten the meaning and import of a text about the supposed "evils" that take place in a man's home when he is away, admonishing that "you better watch your happy home." The Chicago bluesmen later added feedback and distortion treatments to the musical mix and continued to modify the traditional sounds and timbres of the music.

Also prominent among the R&B stars of the early 1950s was Ruth Brown, whose work resulted in numerous hits. Brown was Louis Jordan's female counterpart in popularity, but her delivery was more deeply rooted in the African-American vocal tradition. Her rendition of "(Mama) He Treats Your Daughter Mean," typical of her style, is an elision- and squeal-laden, riff-based, sixteen-bar blues. Her vocal on "R&B Blues," a slow eight-bar blues with the obligatory one-chorus tenor saxophone solo, is a more "modern" rendering than the blues singing of earlier female blues singers such as Bessie Smith, or of the Chicago bluesmen; it has obviously been informed by the more polished style of the male band singers of the 1940s and 1950s, such as Joe Turner, Billy Eckstine, and Joe Williams.[19] But "Love Me, Baby," a twelve-bar blues, is more typical of her provocatively sensuous, slow-blues delivery; and "Happiness Is a Thing Called Joe," a show-tune, reveals her stylistic versatility. Her delivery on "Happiness" recalls the style of Billie Holiday and, at the same time, looks forward to the delivery of Diana Ross.

In the 1950s, R&B reached the pinnacle of its popularity outside the core culture in the recorded performances of Chuck Berry, Little Richard, Hank Ballard, the Dominoes, the Coasters, the Platters, the Shirelles, and other individuals and groups. But it was now becoming rock 'n' roll. Although Jackie Brenston's "Rocket Eighty-Eight" (1951) is recognized by some commentators as the recording that ushered in the rock 'n' roll style (Reese 1982, 26), Little Richard and Chuck Berry emerged in the mid-1950s as the premier black rock 'n' roll artists. Berry became known variously as "the epitome of rock & roll," "the creator of rock & roll," "the father of rock," "Mr. Rock 'n' Roll," "the greatest rock lyricist this side of Bob Dylan," and "the poet laureate of Teenage Rock" (Reese, 6; Shaw 1979, 35). He became famous with "Maybellene" (1955), "the first-ever record to win Billboard's Triple Crown, entering the pop, country and R&B charts" (Reese, 23–24), and followed it with "Roll Over Beethoven" (1956), "Johnny B. Goode" (1958), "Reelin' and Rockin'" (1958), "Back in the U.S.A." (1959), and a host of other hits. He had been influenced

---

19. Turner's blues singing can be heard on *Careless Love* (1959?); Williams's, on *Big Joe Williams and Sonny Boy Williamson* (1970); and Eckstine's, on *Mr. "B"* and *Together.*

by the music of the Chicago bluesmen and by the shuffle-boogie of Louis Jordan; his acknowledged idols, in addition to Jordan, were Muddy Waters, T-Bone Walker, Bo Diddley, Little Richard, and the ballad singer Nat Cole. The unflagging hop-shuffle, syncopated, and contrasting rhythms and the textural contrasts of Berry's R&B renditions are evident in "Reelin' and Rockin'," "Roll Over Beethoven," and other songs that spoke to the youth of the 1950s about their new-found sexual freedom, their unprecedented access to automobiles, and their rejection of many of the moral and social attitudes taught by their parents and other authority figures. Berry's message was carried by a musical vehicle that was essentially African but was tempered by a pop- and country-oriented delivery. In this way, he elaborated the black tradition and infused it into the youth aspects of the larger culture.

Little Richard is reputedly "twice as important as the Beatles and Stones put together" in the history of rock 'n' roll (Johnny Otis, quoted in White 1984, 218), "the greatest Rock 'n' Roll legend of our time" (Dick Clark, quoted in White, 218), and "the greatest singer of all time" (Kenny Everett, quoted in White, 219). White insists that while "Elvis had sexuality, Chuck Berry his masterly lyrics, and Fats Domino his rich New Orleans R'n'B beat . . . [i]t was Richard's voice, with its sheer naked and joyous energy, which broke through established musical structures and changed the way of life for a whole generation" (77). Little Richard emerged from the core culture, where, as he himself says,

> You'd hear people singing all the time. The women would be outside in the back doing the washing, rubbing away on the rub-boards, and somebody else sweeping the yard, and somebody else would start singing "We-e-ell . . . Nobody knows the trouble I've seen . . ." And gradually other people would pick it up, until the whole of the street would be singing. Or "Sometimes I feel like a motherless child, a long way from home." . . . Everybody singing. I used to go up and down the street, some streets were paved. But our street was dirt, just singing at the top of my voice. There'd be guitar players playing on the street—old Slim, Willie Amos, and my cousin, Buddy Penniman. I remember Bamalama, this feller with one eye, who'd play the washboard with a thimble. He had a bell like the school-teacher's, and he'd sing, "A-bamalam, you shall be free, and in the mornin' you shall be free." (quoted in White, 15)

In and about his hometown, Little Richard says, he "heard all the best artists and bands that were on the touring circuit then, people like Cab Calloway, Hot Lips Page, Cootie Williams, Lucky Millinder, and my favorite singer, Sister Rosetta Tharpe" (quoted in White, 17), all of whom had their own brand of Call–Response. Richard's "Long Tall Sally" (1956), "Tutti Frutti" (1956), and other hits made a big impact on the youth culture of the 1950s. According to White,

Richard opened the door. He brought the races together. When I first went on the road, there were many segregated audiences. With Richard, although they still had the audiences segregated in the building, they were *there* together. And most times, before the end of the night, they would all be mixed together. Up until then, the audiences were either all black or all white, and no one else could come in. (69)

Such racially integrated experiences transferred across racial and cultural lines some of the musical and social values of Call–Response. Bruce Tucker (1989) posits that Berry and Little Richard were "proto-postmodernists" because "their musical, sartorical, and performing styles proposed . . . a counter-discourse" (271, 272). For Tucker, postmodernism deconstructed the cultural authority of modernism[20] and its resistance to things different from those that sprang from the mind-set it had created. Examples of this assault, observes Tucker, are

Chuck Berry's "duck walk," Presley's bumps and grinds, Jerry Lee Lewis's wanton destruction of pianos, Little Richard's bizarre stage theatrics. As part of the counter-discourse of early rock 'n' roll, such practices not only assaulted high culture but also brought sexual display into the public realm, which is finally the same thing, for it is the body . . . that is excluded by the dominant discourse of mid-century modernism. (279)

One aspect of Berry's particular assault can be seen not only in his instruction to Beethoven that he should "roll over" and "tell Tchaikovsky the news" of R&B's threat to their domain, but also in his implied criticism of bebop, cool jazz, and Third Stream music in the song "Rock and Roll Music":

I got no kick against modern jazz
Unless they try to play it too darn fast
And change the beauty of the melody
Until it sounds just like a symphony.

(quoted in Tucker, 279)

The transformation of R&B into a racially integrated music, with blacks and whites claiming it as their own, which had begun in the 1940s with the success of "The Hucklebuck," was accelerated and fully achieved by Berry and Little Richard, who were the prime catalysts in the transformation. Berry, according to Robert Christgau, successfully reclaimed

guitar tricks that country and western innovators had appropriated from black people and adapted to their own uses 25 or 50 years before. By adding blues tone to some fast country runs, and yoking them to a rhythm and blues beat

20. For brief comment on *African-American* modernism, see chapter 4.

179

and some unembarrassed electrification, he created an instrumental style with biracial appeal. Alternating guitar chords augmented the beat while Berry sang in an insouciant tenor that, while recognizably Afro-American in accent, stayed clear of the melisma and blurred overtones of blues singing, both of which enter at carefully premeditated moments. (quoted in Tucker 1989, 281–282)

Meanwhile, Little Richard, "producing classic rock 'n' roll hits at an astonishing clip and finding himself with a huge interracial audience, feared the consequences of becoming a sex symbol for white girls" (285). He therefore took on an ambiguous sexuality and developed a ridiculous stage manner and persona that made him appear to be exotically harmless to parents of white teenagers (286). In other words, he became Esu, male/female, a symbol of androgyny. In this, Little Richard donned a new—and truer, I might add—minstrel mask.[21]

One of the most significant musical events of the 1950s was the emergence of the Miles Davis combos. Following his nonet experience, Davis returned to a sextet format, where his cool but blues-based nuances and understatements were combined with the complex drumming of Art Blakey and the vigorous playing of Sonny Rollins, Jackie McLean, and Lucky Thompson. Other members of his combo were, on occasion and sometimes alternately, bassist Percy Heath, pianist Horace Silver, drummers Kenny Clarke and Philly Joe Jones, and trombonist J. J. Johnson. In 1954 Davis recorded "Blue and Boogie" and, on the reverse side, "Walkin'." This latter tune marked his return to bebop, but it was bop with a harder sound. Making use of the specific talents and inclinations of the musicians at hand, Davis produced music that was different from that of the nonet. These renditions, performed by Davis, Johnson, Sir Charles Thompson, Silver, Heath, and Clarke, signaled a return to the values of the ring, and some of the then-unique sounds in "Walkin'" were to become clichés of what came to be known as "hard bop." It was bop played with a bluesy, funky delivery, with lots of forceful interaction between trumpet and drums, employing elements from gospel and R&B. The style is characterized by off-beat accents, open fourths and fifths in the chords, riffs, Call–Response vocal inflections, simple melodies, and ring-based ostinatos.[22] In the vanguard, as always, Davis had started another trend, and other chief exponents of the style emerged: pianist Horace Silver; Art Blakey's Jazz Messengers; the Julian

21. See my brief mention in chapter 4 of Baker's (1987) discussion of the donning of the minstrel mask by black spokespersons at the dawn of African-American modernism.

22. Logan (1984, 201–205) points out that a large number of hard-bop pieces make use of black-derived ostinato patterns, including Cannonball Adderly's "Sak O' Woe," Bobby Timmons's "This Here" ("Dis Heah"), Benny Golson's "Killer Joe," Horace Silver's "Señor Blues," and Yuseff Lateef's "Brother John."

"Cannonball" Adderley Quintet; pianists Barry Harris and Tommy Flanagan; trumpeters Clifford Brown, Thad Jones, and Art Farmer; alto saxophonists Adderley and Jackie McLean; tenor saxophonists Sonny Rollins and Joe Henderson; trombonists J. J. Johnson and Curtis Fuller; bassists Joe Chambers and Sam Jones; guitarists Kenny Burrell and Wes Montgomery; and drummers Blakey, Max Roach, and Philly Joe Jones. Their effort, conscious or unconscious, to reaffirm the musical values of the ring led them to create a style that used simpler melodies and harmonies than bebop, funkier and more complex rhythms, new formal constructions, and gospel-oriented phrasings, all of which brought to jazz a new vitality.

The Adderley Quintet's "Work Song" and "Mercy, Mercy, Mercy" are heavily gospel oriented and reflect the "church" ambience that results from audience involvement in a live performance marked by responsive interjections, yea-saying, and voluntary and involuntary emotional eruptions—an experience obviously African in style and substance. Here, the music and the audience's responses to it combine in a moment of aesthetic unity in which considerable communication takes place. It is an experience that resides near the middle of an emotional continuum that ranges from an audience's polite listening and acknowledgment of a cool-school performance to the sheer ecstasy of an audience's participation in a sanctified shout.

At a different place on the hard-bop continuum is the work of the Hank Mobley Quartet. This group's *Peckin' Time* (1958)—which features Mobley on tenor saxophone, Wynton Kelly on piano, Paul Chambers on bass, and Charlie Persip on drums—contains two worthy examples on its reverse side: "Stretchin' Out" and "Git-Go Blues" are interesting variations in the head-solos-head format of traditional bebop. In "Stretchin' Out," the trumpet, saxophone, and piano take numerous choruses. In "Git-Go Blues," a twelve-bar blues, the musicians stretch out again, with the funkiest of the solos being the five choruses taken by the bass, which comes in on the twenty-fifth chorus of the performance. These two performances are not as "hard" as the hard bop of, say, Horace Silver or as funky as that of, say, organist Jimmie Smith. But it speaks the hard-bop language in a more refined (not better, just different) manner.

Also falling into the hard-bop category in the 1950s was Thelonious Monk, a stride pianist who had turned to bebop in the 1940s. A recently released Monk compilation, *The Best of Thelonious Monk,* contains first versions of fifteen well-known originals from the late 1940s and early 1950s—tunes such as "Ruby My Dear," "Well You Needn't," "'Round Midnight," "Criss Cross," and "Straight No Chaser." Playing with Monk on this recording are Idrees Sullieman, George Taitt, and Kenny Dorham on trumpet; Danny West, Sahib Shihab, and Lou Donaldson on alto saxophone; Lucky Thompson on tenor saxophone; Gene Ramey, John Simmons, Al McKibbon, and Nelson Boyd on bass;

181

Milt Jackson on vibes; and Art Blakey, Shadow Wilson, and Max Roach on drums. As a performer and composer, Monk, even within the iconoclastic be-bop idiom, is unique. On these recordings can be heard the off-center rhythms and "sour" notes and intervals for which he is known, particularly in "Evidence"; his exploitation of melodic and harmonic dissonance, as in "Mysterioso"; his occasional and unique treatment of note runs, as in "Four in One"; his use of motivic, or riff-based, melodies, as in "Well You Needn't"; his departure from such constructions in favor of long, note-filled lines in "Evidence" and "Skippy"; and his use of the ostinato principle in "Thelonious." In Monk's playing, almost every event is unexpected, either in its placement or in its manifestation; as a composer, he delights in ironic constructions (as does Esu, trickster and god of irony).

The term "hard bop" is a catchall expression for an experimental return to the use of basic ring tropes and for music characterized by the clichés that resulted from that experimentation. Davis started the trend, but as others picked up the mantle, he began to move away from it with his experiments in the early 1960s, which would yield powerful results.

The 1950s came to a close with cool jazz and hard bop vying for prominence, with the end of gospel's golden age, with the New Criticism and neoclassicism continuing to influence the concert-hall activity of black composers, and with R&B and rock 'n' roll in decline in the wake of Little Richard's retirement to the ministry, Chuck Berry's two-and-a-half-year prison sentence on morals charges, and the rise of the vapid and diluted croonings of singers such as Pat Boone and others of his generation of rock 'n' roll stylists. It would take a revolution to reinvigorate the African-American musical tradition and bring the ring tropes again to ascendance. And that revolution was just around the corner.

CHAPTER **8**

The Sixties and After

Hornblowers! Blow in unison!
Bugandan folk saying

**There is something suspicious about music, gentlemen.
I insist that she is, by her nature, equivocal. I shall not
be going too far in saying at once that she is politically
suspect.**
Thomas Mann

The 1960s brought to full flowering the modern
civil rights movement. It was a period of success
and failure, of courage and fear, of discipline and
disorder. It embraced the 1963 March on Washington and saw passed the Civil Rights Act of 1964,
which outlawed discrimination in public accommodations and employment. It was a time that saw
the assassinations of Malcolm X and Martin Luther
King, Jr., the latter's death spurring riots in 125
American cities from April 4 to April 11, 1968 —
ironically coinciding with the signing, on April 11,
of the Civil Rights Act of 1968, which was meant
to end discrimination in the sale and rental of private housing. It was a momentous decade in the
fight for equal rights for all Americans (Bergman
1969, 610–611).

It was during the 1960s that the flight of whites
to the suburbs accelerated and American cities de-

teriorated.[1] This deterioration was highlighted by the urban riots of the 1960s, which the Kerner Commission later studied and determined were the direct result of white racism (*Report* 1968). These upheavals, spurred by disillusionment, neglect, what some African Americans saw as the impotence of the nonviolence movement, and the belief that the melting-pot metaphor was never intended to embrace blacks, brought to the civil rights movement a strident militancy, and "black power" became the watchword.[2] Stokely Carmichael declared, "Let it be known that we don't need threats. This is 1966. It's time out for beautiful words. It's time out for euphemistic statements. And it's time out for singing 'We Shall Overcome.' It's time to get some Black Power" (quoted in Miller 1971, 691). And with the emergence of this quest for black power,

> the old Movement dreams seemed to have exploded into nightmares. Tanks and troops of the U.S. Army and the National Guard were in the streets. Helicopters sent their powerful lights and intimations of death down into the fiery nights. The call for Black Power, the cry of "Burn, baby, burn!" and the image of young Black Panthers with guns in their hands could be heard and seen across the land. Now countless men and women saw blazing visions of a nationwide, armed black liberation struggle. Embracing and embroidering their memories of Malcolm, they fashioned new dreams out of the hard materials of black urban life, faced the cruel centers of white American fear. And the singers—if they sang at all anymore—now declared, "Before I'll be a slave, there'll be a Honky in his grave." (Harding 1981, xv)

African Americans donned new masks—dashikis and Afros—Signifyin(g) turned inward and sometimes ugly, and one of the musics of black protest was a new and angry jazz.

The apparently contradictory stances and actions of the period manifested themselves multifariously, with the philosophies of King and Malcolm X representing contrasting views of the struggle for freedom. These two perspectives, and the activities each spawned, expressed the prevailing philosophical struggles of the black community in a period characterized by an unusual juxtaposition of pessimism and optimism, idealism and pragmatism in a social, political, and cultural cauldron from which would spring, ironically, a new intellectual and artistic energy, a new cultural awakening.[3]

1. Middle-class blacks began to leave also, in the wake of the passage of the Civil Rights Act of 1968, but primarily in search of integration, to acquire the fruits of the American dream, which they felt were finally within reach.

2. In 1966, Stokely Carmichael became head of the Student Non-Violent Coordinating Committee (SNCC), and he and Floyd McKissick, head of the Congress of Racial Equality (CORE), began to promote black power. The NAACP's Roy Wilkins rejected the slogan (Bergman 1969, 596).

3. This new awakening has been described by some scholars as a "Second Renaissance" that had its onset somewhere between 1954 and 1963 (see, for example, Bigsby 1980; Marr 1972; Turner 1987).

This awakening was set into motion on May 1, 1963, when the play *Dutchman,* by LeRoi Jones (Amiri Baraka), opened at the Cherry Lane Theater in New York. The play, considered one of the season's best off-Broadway dramas (Hewes 1964, 405), is about a black man and a white woman in a hypothetical subway incident. The woman propositions the man, Signifies on his color, and then stabs him with a knife. In the process, black rage is, according to David Littlejohn, "channeled equally into [the] two antagonists," their dialogue conveying "the shrill, sharp, absolutely open insult-trading of cool modern neurotics, hiding nothing except everything" (quoted in Draper 1992, 125). This play, with its shocking treatment of the race problem in America, inspired similar works by other black playwrights and led to the inclusion of ultranationalistic content in other black art forms as well.[4] It spurred the creation of a literary and artistic cauldron that included works by visual artists such as the plastic artists of the Chicago group AfriCobra and the New York organization Weusi, by the painter David Driskell and the sculptor Richard Hunt, and by writers such as Nikki Giovanni, Stephen Henderson, Maya Angelou, Eugene Redmond, Leon Forrest, Larry Neal, Ishmael Reed, Don L. Lee, Addison Gayle, Jr., and the Last Poets.[5]

This activity was known collectively as the Black Arts Movement, a nationalistic, Pan-African cultural awakening that was "nurtured by a belief in the positive value of blackness" (Davis and Harris 1985, xii). It signaled a return to myth: it became acceptable, respectable, even expected, for African Americans to seek out, believe in, and display their mythological roots. By the end of the 1960s, "black is beautiful" and "black pride" had become rallying cries, and there prevailed the widespread conviction that ordinary black citizens could master the requirements of leadership, intellectual participation, and artistic creation. In this respect, unlike the Harlem Renaissance's reliance on the "talented tenth" idea, this new awakening was egalitarian.

Jazz was the music of the Black Arts Movement. The literary figures of the 1960s wrote poetry that celebrated it, others theorized about its value, and most became conversant with the prowess and particular skills of the genre's most notable practitioners. Amiri Baraka's *Blues People* (1963), *Black Music*

4. In 1964, LeRoi Jones and other black artists established the Black Arts Repertoire Theater School. Among the plays produced in its first year were Jones's *Experimental Death Unit # One, Black Mass, Jello,* and *Dutchman* (a videotaped performance of which has been released).

5. Works by the Last Poets, whose street verse was central in New York's core culture from 1968 to the mid-1980s, can be read in El Hadi and Nuriddin's *The Last Poets: Vibes from the Scribes* (1985), and some of it can be heard on the record album *The Last Poets* (ca. 1970). Especially meaningful in this discussion are Jalal Nuriddin's poems "Jazzoetry" and "Bird's Word."

(1967), and *The Music* (1987), A. B. Spellman's *Four Lives in the Bebop Business* (1970), and Albert Murray's *Stomping the Blues* (1976) are examples of writings about jazz and the blues by prominent literary figures; Addison Gayle's *The Black Aesthetic* (1971) includes ideological essays such as Jimmy Stewart's "Introduction to Black Aesthetics in Music," LeRoi Jones's "The Changing Same (R&B and New Black Music)," Ron Welburn's "Black Aesthetic Imperative," and Leslie Rout's "Reflections on the Evolution of Post-War Jazz."

The leading jazz figures of the 1960s were Miles Davis and John Coltrane. Davis had begun by reshaping jazz standards in new and different ways, redefining the role of the rhythm section, and introducing abrupt changes of tempo, and even silences, in his performances. In his album *Miles Smiles* (1966), especially on "Circle" and "Footprints," he began floating over the rhythm section. Later, rather than floating on top of the section or playing on the beats, he and his sidemen began to cut into the rhythmic flow, becoming part of its texture and leaving spaces for the excursions of the drummer.

By the late 1960s and early 1970s, as Carr (1982) assesses, the old theme–solos–theme structure of postwar jazz had been discarded, and Davis "had reworked the traditional New Orleans jazz idea of collective improvisation behind a leading solo/melody voice" (178). In this, Davis's approach to texture and structure came to have more in common with early jazz than with the bebop tradition, from which he had emerged. Furthermore, his more fully integrated, evolving style began to bring about a more primeval ensemble sound, which, in its emotional character, recalls African ensemble music, the shout, and, in less evident ways, New Orleans jazz. The drums no longer merely "play time," but complement, color, and texture the lines and the instrumental combinations. The causal, predetermined harmonic framework of traditional jazz was replaced by a more static harmonic environment in which pedal points establish key centers, and modal scales, together with this relative harmonic stasis, give improvisers more melodic and structural freedom. Hence, phrase lengths became more irregular, chord changes more unorthodox, and the range of expression greater and more appropriate to the new struggles and fulfillments of the 1960s. The whole musical environment was repetitive, hypnotic, funky, and exciting, insinuating the entire black musical tradition, including its African manifestations. During this period, rock elements first appeared in Davis's work. On *E.S.P.* (1965), for example, in a piece titled "Eighty One," one hears rock rhythms and an ostinato, a device that was common to R&B, that had been used frequently in hard bop, and that now had a growing currency in jazz. The ostinatos employed by jazz musicians of the 1960s and beyond contained a high level of rhythmic and melodic interest that sometimes completely displaced conventional notions of melody.[6]

Both Davis and Coltrane experimented early on with group performances in which modal scales served as the basis for melodic invention and in which chord progressions no longer prevailed as the controlling factor. As Davis (1989) explains:

> Modal music is seven notes off each scale, off each note. It's a scale off each note. . . . The composer-arranger George Russell used to say that in modal music C is where F should be. He says that the whole piano starts at F. What I had learned about the modal form is that when you play this way, go in this direction, you can go on forever. You don't have to worry about changes and shit like that. You can do more with the musical line. The challenge here, when you work in the modal way, is to see how inventive you can become melodically. It's not like when you base stuff on chords, and you know at the end of thirty-two bars that the chords have run out and there is nothing to do but repeat what you've done with variations. I was moving away from that and into more melodic ways of doing things. And in the modal way I saw all kinds of possibilities.[7] (225)

In a statement remarkably like this one, but with significant additions, Davis explains his approach to modal improvisation and its advantages:

> When you go this way . . . you can go on forever. . . . It becomes a challenge to see how melodically inventive you are. . . . Movement in jazz is . . . away from the conventional string of chords, and a return to emphasis on melodic rather than harmonic variation. There [are] fewer chords but infinite possibilities as to what to do with them. (quoted in Chambers 1983, 280)

So for Davis and his sidemen, the playing of "changes" became passé, and their "time–no changes" approach to improvisation was accompanied by an emphasis on melodic invention, paraphrase, and thematic development that represented, essentially, a return to the improvisational concerns of early jazz. This emphasis also recalls the music making of African drum ensembles in which the master drummer sets patterns that are repeated and elaborated in interrelated and interlocking patterns.

6. Coltrane's "Tunji" (1962) and "Naima" (1959) and McCoy Tyner's "You Stepped Out of a Dream" (1976) use the technique, as does Weather Report's "Gibraltar" (1976) and numerous other works of the period (Logan 1984, 206–209). An earlier example of Davis's use of an ostinato, together with a high degree of harmonic stasis, can be found in his 1959 recording of "Concierto de Aranjuez."

7. Davis had been influenced by the possibilities of Russell's (1959) theoretical work. But, inspired by the African legacy, Davis had seen these possibilities even before Russell explained them to him: "[I] went to this performance by the Ballet Africaine and it just fucked me up what they was doing, the steps and all them flying leaps and shit. And when I first heard them play the finger piano that night and sing this song with this other guy dancing, man, that was some powerful stuff" (Davis, 225).

In Davis's musical environment, the drummer, the bass player, and the piano player were allowed a great deal of freedom from their traditional time keeping and "comping" responsibilities, and they played more equal roles in performance.[8] Pianists were at this time avid users of quartal harmony, and the ensemble roles of the drums and piano became more "melodic" in concept. Polyrhythms abounded, and the music's textural density and dynamic range were increased and enriched through the increase in tonal colors and collective improvisation. Among Davis's albums on which these innovations can be heard are *Miles Smiles* (1966), *In a Silent Way* (1969), and *Bitches Brew* (ca. 1970). It was on this last album that Davis expanded his rhythm section into an ersatz African "drum" ensemble—ten musicians on drums, electric pianos, electric guitar, electric bass, acoustic bass, and various small percussion instruments—playing polyrhythms, cross-rhythms, ostinatos, and jazz and funk figures that recall the elements and excitement of the ring shout. In all of this music, chord progressions became less important, harmonies became more or less static, and there was an increase in the use of ostinatos, polyrhythms, and collective improvisation, and of stabs, smears, and other devices of distortion. It takes only a little reflection, then, to relate this trend to African performance practices in which repetitive patterns, harmonic stasis, little melodic development, a high degree of rhythmic interest, and collective improvisation define the style: the performances of the Miles Davis bands of the late 1960s and early 1970s recall West African ritual music making and evoke West African myth through the collectivity of their renderings. So what, on the one hand, is musical evolution—progress toward development and complexity—is, on the other, a return to primeval musical roots and a continuation of ancient practices.

John Coltrane, following his album *Giant Steps* (1959), produced *A Love Supreme* (1964), *Ascension* (1965), and at least twenty other albums, all of which utilized some of the innovations of the Davis band, in which Coltrane had been a sideman. In addition, however, Coltrane's music was filled with

---

8. Davis's liberation of the drummer appears to have been a natural extension of earlier experiments. For example, in the 1950s Max Roach and Art Blakey had traveled in Africa to study drumming and returned to make fresh and important infusions into jazz music. Blakey's recordings *Holiday for Skins* (1979)—the title of which perhaps Signifies on David Rose's sappy *Holiday for Strings* (I'm grateful to Richard Crawford for this insight and reference)—and *The African Beat: Art Blakey and the Afro-drum Ensemble* (1962) are examples of the results of his interest. Roach, who had already raised jazz drumming to a new level of musical maturity with his playing of lines, phrases, and comping patterns, contributed *We Insist: Freedom Now Suite* (1960). In the 1960s, Nigerian drummer Olatunji began playing with jazz musicians such as John Coltrane, Clark Terry, and Randy Weston, whose album *Uhuru Africa* provided commentary on the African struggle for liberation. The innovations found in these recordings became important sources of information, ideas, inspiration, and technique for jazz drummers and surely led to some of the developments that were carried out later by Elvin Jones, Lenny White, Tony Williams, Billy Cobham, and avant-garde drummers Sonny Murray, Andrew Cyrille, Milford Graves, and Beaver Harris.

the imagery of Africa and of the African-American church, with ring imagery reflected, Weinstein (1992) believes, in *Ascension:*

> The thirty-eight minute *Ascension* doesn't so much "progress" to a clear dramatic resolution as much as complete a circle. This sense of music completing a cycle speaks to the circle image in many traditional African religions. While the Christian symbol of the cross graphically illustrates the intersection of worldly time and eternity, the circle suggests that through experiencing the rhythmic cycles of worldly life consciously and repeatedly, we spin ourselves into a sense of the divinely eternal. (68)

But this cyclical form is also symbolic of the ring—the source of the tropings used to make the music. So *Ascension,* representing transcendence, the upward impulse, itself Signified on the spirituality of the ring. Whether or not the performing musicians understood or even perceived these connections, they are there for us to imagine. Ultimately, I believe, such connections and meanings reside in the cultural memory—the "collective unconscious"—from which they can be retrieved with the slightest stimulation from ring tropes.

Coltrane's concern with the Africa theme is evident in his eighteen Africa-theme recordings listed by Weinstein (1992, 63), who recognized that Coltrane's output in the 1960s was essentially rooted in Africa and the East, as evidenced in titles such as "Liberia," "Dahomey Dance," "Africa," and "Tunji"—the last for Nigerian musician Olatunji.

As I noted in chapters 2 and 3, the employment of pentatonic scales as a basis for melodic development was a feature of African and African-American folk music, and the practice was used extensively in R&B. Coltrane used it frequently, and Sonny Rollins made the device common in his improvisations.[9] Related to this use of pentatonicism is a limited return to the African-American spiritual as a source of inspiration, celebration, and memorialization. Coltrane's album *"Live" at the Village Vanguard* (1961) contains "Spiritual" and his "Song of the Underground Railroad," which celebrates and memorializes the courage of escaping slaves and "conductors" in their flights to freedom.[10] "Alabama" was composed by Coltrane in memory of the 1963 Birmingham, Alabama, church bombing in which white racists murdered four black children. Archie Shepp's album *Goin' Home* (1977) is a collection of spirituals that includes, among others, "Steal Away to Jesus" and "Go Down Moses." Albert Ayler's *Spiritual Unity* (1964) appropriately contains procedures that are reminiscent of the gospel sound, expressing African-American evangelistic fervor.

9. See, for example, "Poinciana" on *Graz 1963 Concert: Max Roach Quintet and Sonny Rollins Trio* (1966).

10. "Spiritual" and "Song of the Underground Railroad" can also be heard on *Afro Blue Impressions* (1977) and *African Brass* (1974), respectively.

In his last years, Coltrane added a new dimension to his emotional arsenal. Whether it was due to his own intentions or to the perceptions of others, he is remembered by some as one of the angry jazzmen. Miles Davis (1989) said that

> Trane's music and what he was playing during the last two or three years of his life represented, for many blacks, the fire and passion and rage and anger and rebellion and love that they felt, especially among the young black intellectuals and revolutionaries of that time. He was expressing through music what H. Rap Brown and Stokely Carmichael and the Black Panthers and Huey Newton were saying with their words, what the Last Poets and Amiri Baraka were saying in poetry. He was their torchbearer in jazz, now ahead of me. He played what they felt inside and were expressing through riots—"burn, baby, burn"—that were taking place everywhere in this country during the 1960s. It was all about revolution for a lot of young black people—Afro hairdos, dashikis, black power, fists raised in the air. Coltrane was their symbol, their pride— their beautiful, black revolutionary pride. I had been it a few years back, now he was it, and that was cool with me. (285–286)

Coltrane's art has been referred to by some of his followers as "mysterious"; by others, as "spiritual." It has a mysterious aura because it is not easily accessible—less so, in fact, than many of Coltrane's followers will admit. It has a spiritual aura because of its modal melodic structures. It is both mysterious and spiritual because of its contemplative tone and character. In short, it is both mythic and ritualistic, containing Tarasti's "channels," Esu's improvisational skills, and the Signifying Monkey's figurative adeptness. The "spiritual" aspect is a function of cultural memory—memory of the importance and function of myth and ritual in African-American community—the term "spiritual" being used here as a symbol for African mythology and religion. For those who view Coltrane's art as spiritual, he is a priest, a *jazz* priest whose spirituality and priestliness are emphasized and legitimized by his creative acumen.[11] Coltrane, says Amiri Baraka (1967, iii), is "the heaviest spirit."

Ascension is an "energy" piece that approaches free jazz, with the eleven players utilizing modal scales for their improvisations, which alternate or overlap in loosely organized, collectively improvised ensemble sections and individual solos. This emphasis on cooperation and community was reflected also in other social, musical, and political arenas.[12] For many young musicians, jazz cooperatives began to replace the disappearing jam sessions as vehicles

---

11. Armstrong, Parker, Davis, and Eric Dolphy also fit into this category of priest, for "great improvisors are like priests: they thinking only of their god" (Stephane Grappelli, quoted in Leonard 1987, 74), and, I believe, they *thought* of themselves as priests.

12. Although Coltrane was participating in jam sessions as late as 1960, for both him and Davis, gladiatorial exploits had become passé.

of initiation and apprenticeship, and jazz was becoming a concert-hall music to a degree that it had never been before.[13]

In 1962 in Chicago, Muhal Richard Abrams launched the Experimental Band, in which musicians performed on the conventional jazz instruments as well as on a variety of "little instruments" that brought forth numerous and unusual timbres and textures to accompany the traditional horns, strings, and percussion or that sounded as sections and choirs important in themselves. Out of this band evolved the Association for the Advancement of Creative Musicians (AACM), whose aesthetic and ideological agenda, according to Ronald M. Radano (1992), was to revitalize "the African-American musical sensibility through the oppositional language of modernism" and supply "the basis for a grand signifying riff on mainstream valuations" (80). The AACM was formed in the spirit of the new nationalism and Pan-African brotherhood that prevailed in the 1960s:

> An Africa-inspired cultural nationalism became the official party line of the AACM. . . . Creative Music was a dialect of the mother tongue, a creation with African origins that had been spiritually preserved in the slave culture of the United States. Evoking images of the musician-seer of tribal Africa, many AACM musicians spoke in priestly terms of black music's spiritualism, which, they believed, revealed a kinship with the ancient mythmakers, the original cultural guardians of black people. (87)

For the AACMers, "spiritualism celebrated African notions of community and ritual" and was viewed as a metaphor "for a brand of collectively improvised music that exceeded the constraints of harmony" (90). In their thinking, the traditional harmony of European-derived music was a stifling "metaphor for white cultural dominance and oppression. . . . In rhythm and melody, on the other hand, the musicians identified formal attributes that stressed the communal, multilinear orientation of West African styles from antebellum spirituals to blues, jazz, and funk" (90). Thus the music of the AACM, built around the values of individuality within collectively, was "an improvised art that, through incessant rehearsal, could mimic the designs of complex orchestrations" (83).

13. Although jazz had been presented in concert and quasi-concert formats as early as the first decade of the twentieth century and in the 1940s by bebop musicians (DeVeaux 1991), it was not until the 1950s that the "jazzman-as-entertainer" concept was challenged. It was Davis who refused to tell jokes, smile at his audiences, or announce the titles of the tunes to be played or the names of his sidemen, implying that (1) the music should speak for itself and (2) the jazz artist had no responsibility to his audience beyond that of communicating through his artistic medium. In this way, ironically, he sought and demanded respect for his art and his person. By the 1970s, Davis's behavior and demeanor had become an accepted part of his approach to music making.

From this collective musical and political association grew several performing organizations that played to audiences in little theaters, churches, coffee houses, colleges and universities, and other welcoming venues throughout Chicago. The most famous of the groups to grow out of the AACM was the Art Ensemble of Chicago (AECO), made up of Roscoe Mitchell on flute, clarinet, and saxophone; Lester Bowie on trumpet, piccolo trumpet, and fluegelhorn; Joseph Jarman on saxophones; Malachi Favors (Maghoustus) on double bass and Fender bass; and Famoudou Don Moye on drums. The group can be heard and seen to good effect on *The Art Ensemble of Chicago: Live at the Jazz Showcase,* a video recording of a 1981 nonstop set in which the group is at its finest. With a backdrop sign announcing "Great Black Music: Ancient to the Future"; with a stage full of percussion instruments, African and otherwise, together with saxophones, clarinets, flutes, trumpets, and fluegelhorn, a string bass, and a Fender bass; and with three of the group's five members in real or imitation African garb and painted faces, the ensemble gives AECO treatment to genres such as bebop, New Orleans jazz, and North African melodies, as well as rhythms and impressions from and of R&B/rock and other forms and styles. The expressions run the gamut from soft and subtle to loud and frenzied, from abstract to teleological, from simple to complex, from easy to virtuosic, from loving to angry, from beeps to blasts, whistles to gunshots, whispers to horns.

This fifty-minute set begins with "We-Bop," a stylized Signification on bebop. But varied and discreetly spaced cymbal, bell, whistle, and gong sounds quickly move the stylization out of the realm of bebop (although the bass player and drummer remain rather true to the style). There is no repeat of the head, and a transition featuring hand percussion moves the performance into "Promenade: On the Côte Bamako," which is signaled by the trumpet and carried thereafter primarily by drums and other percussion instruments. "Bedouin Village" is signaled by a change in drumming patterns and style, followed by the entry of the soprano saxophone imitating a North African oboe. The saxophonist's florid melodic explorations—ornaments and all—float over the complex drumming of the other musicians. "New York Is Full of Lonely People" opens with the bass playing a pizzicato melody accompanied by the drummer's playing of the brushes on a variety of cymbals and drums in the style of the swing music of the 1930s and 1940s. Hand percussion and trumpet then emerge with a contrasting elaboration of the bass's opening theme, joined by the tenor sax in countermelodic and unison excursions that contrast sharply, in tempo and in mood, with what has been introduced before. Then the alto saxophone enters, playing over an immense and unusual variety of snapping, tinkling, popping, honking, tooting, and whistling sounds that Signify, in increasing complexity and profusion, on the confused and confusing real-life street sounds of New York. Mitchell's furious soprano saxophone runs add to the confusion, and as the intensity decreases and the section comes to its close, his piccolo and clarinet make low-keyed statements. Although I am not sure where this section of the performance ends, specifically, and the "New Orleans" segment begins, it seems that the trumpet and tenor saxophone signal the opening of the latter when they begin to improvise collectively on the spiritual- and hymn-like melodies that introduce the AECO's stylization of a New Orleans brass band on parade, complete with street noises and the band's up-tempo return. "Funky AECO," a postmodern Signifyin(g) on R&B/rock, with the Fender bass playing a short ostinato under the pentatonic melodic figures of the tenor saxophone and against the straight-eighth beat divisions and back-beat of the drums, leads to the group's sign-off, "Theme (Odwalla)," which, bebop-like, ends the set to appreciative and sustained applause. The range of timbres in the AECO's performance is immense, with its array of drums, horns, bells, rattles, and scrapers complementing the variety of winds, brass, and percussion. The group's expressive range is also wide, with whispers contrasting with bombast and legatos with staccatos in startling effectiveness.

The AACM introduced to jazz recording, for the first time, a series of unaccompanied extended solos on instruments other than the piano, recalling lone African soloists on fiddles, harps, lutes, lyres, zithers, and flutes and reestablishing solo performances in the African-American musical tradition.[14] Such unaccompanied improvisations can be heard on albums by two AECO personnel, *Congliptious* (1968), by Malachi Favors (Maghoustus), and *Solo Saxophone Concerts,* by Roscoe Mitchell, as well as on Anthony Braxton's *For Alto* (1969). The last is presented in Braxton's typical highly mannered saxophone style, with his abrupt shifts from powerful and loud to delicate and soft, from harsh to deft lyricism, and back again; his signature rhythm ♩ ♪♩ ; his exploitation of the extreme upper register; his use of overtones, severe octave jumps, split tones, bent notes, and subtones; his abrupt phrasings; and his use of many notes played at extreme speeds. Even Braxton's ballads *move*, with much use of filigree and florid connecting material, as on "To Composer John Cage," which is also an excellent example of his control of all registers (and his movement between them) and his adroitness with trills. The bebop-like "To Artist Murray De Pillars" is an example of his affinity for and transformation of the blues.

The AACM members also explored polytonality, chromaticism, and serialism for what those might offer their mix. The title cut of Mitchell's album *Nonaah* (1977), with its arresting, wide-ranging, angular melody, is a study in building tension through insistent and almost exact repetition with an eventual, although gradual, increase in timbral, pitch, and rhythmic variety. "Erika" is a powerful and virtuosic solo improvisation in which Mitchell explores upward beyond the customary range of the alto saxophone. Then comes a brief and explosive solo version of "Nonaah." "Off Five Dark Six" is a duet by

---

14. The first jazz wind instrumentalist to be recorded unaccompanied was Coleman Hawkins. Listen to his "Picasso" (1948). **193**

Mitchell and Braxton—the latter on sopranino sax—a pointillistic piece that bows to the African-American tradition only in certain of its timbral qualities. The last side of the two-album set ends with a quartet of alto saxophones playing a version of the title cut, which begins with the same insistent repetition as did the solo version, this time in polyphony and creating a kind of "stabilized tension" that grips the listener. Saxophonists Joseph Jarman, Wallace McMillan, Henry Threadgill, and Mitchell are remarkably accurate and consistent as they repeat for four minutes the angular, polyphonic idea that opens the piece. Then there is a slight break—silence—preceding a slow and lyrical second section that builds tension again and resolves it beautifully on a conventional, and much needed, major chord. The third section is a brief "disjointed" episode that moves to a "quick" section that recalls the opening round, bringing the piece to a close with a collectively improvised flourish reminiscent of New Orleans jazz. This album demonstrates Mitchell's rather pointillistic style, his penchant for using lots of space to isolate pitches or groups of pitches, his ability to be either economical or generous with notes, his unusual and effective ballad style (on "Ballad"), his ability to juxtapose conflicting rhythms, his proclivity for distorting the normal tone quality of the saxophone, and his inclination toward virtuosity.

Another AACM product, Air, was formed in Chicago in 1971 and included Henry Threadgill on woodwinds, Fred Hopkins on bass, and Steve McCall on drums. This was a sophisticated free-jazz trio with a highly sophisticated repertoire and style of playing that communicated effectively with a wide and varied audience. Their album *Air Time* (1978) contains five superb cuts on which the members of the trio interact as one, exploiting the colors of their instruments, with Threadgill adding even more variety as he switches to other saxophones, flutes, and—his own invention—the hubkaphone, a collection of varipitched hubcaps, gongs, and bells, suspended on a frame. On *Air Time,* the group's exploitation of timbre and their simultaneous improvisations are their main ties to traditional African-American music, although their range extends to ragtime, jazz, and blues.[15]

The harmonies, melodies, conventions, and devices of centuries of African-American music inform and permeate the otherwise abstract music of these Midwesterners and of others not mentioned here. Litweiler (1984) quotes Threadgill as saying,

> I began thinking about the personalities in the group and how they played. I kind of got into writing for people rather than just writing music. So often, you hear this one instrument out front, and these other two instruments are some kind of accompaniment. Well, I'm really trying to get away from that. So I'm writing music from the concept as if I were a drummer. Sometimes I go

15. See also the album *Air Lore* (1979).

from the bass, but right now I'm involved in writing for the drums. . . . It changes the whole frame of reference in terms of what accompaniment is all about, you know. It kind of kills accompaniment and puts everything on an equal footing, and that's what I'm after. (194)

Such thinking about music is essentially African, although screened through a postmodern filter, and it recalls Ellington, who wrote for the "tonal personalities" of his sidemen (chapter 7); it also recalls the membranophone, idiophone, chordophone, and aerophone ensembles of black Africa and the legendary New Orleans ensembles.

Much of the free-jazz activity of the 1970s took place in the loft studios of New York City—apartment venues that were set up as alternatives to commercial establishments. Studio Rivbea, Ali's Alley, Soundscape, and others, which served as alternatives to the unproductive and inhospitable nightclub scene, were havens of free jazz. A number of the players who performed in them had moved to New York from the Midwest, the West Coast, and the East Coast and had banded together in cooperatives that spawned new voices and new music. The music of some of the members of these cooperatives can be heard on the five-disk set *Wildflowers: The New York Jazz Loft Sessions* (1982), which includes performances led by Maurice McIntyre (Kalaparusha), Ken McIntyre, Sunny Murray, Sam Rivers, and others, and groups such as Air. Among the cooperatives of the period in other cities were Union of God's Musicians and Artists Ascension Orchestra (UGMAA) of Los Angeles, Creative Arts Collective of Detroit, and Creative Music Improvisors Forum of New Haven, Connecticut.

The efforts of Davis, Coltrane, and the AECO and other products of the AACM represent but individual examples of the contributions made by jazz figures and groups of the 1960s, 1970s, and 1980s to the continuation of Call–Response. These musicians and many others brought melodic drumming to jazz. They modified the roles of, and in some cases even replaced, functional harmony as a basis for improvisation. They introduced to jazz the use of quartal harmony, polytonality, atonality, and pantonality; the abandonment of the head and the employment of free group improvisation; the fusion of jazz with other musics; the advent of individual, free improvisation; an expanding sound vocabulary that included harmonics and false tones; and "plucking, stroking, and hammering the strings of a piano . . . singing, grunting, and screaming through wind instruments . . . the simultaneous playing and singing through wind instruments . . . rattling sticks inside the piano . . . and singing into the drumhead to make it vibrate" (Budds 1978, 26).

Sometimes when "new" sounds emerge in jazz they are perceived as foreign to the black-music tradition and, consequently, are unacceptable to many critics, mostly white, who reside on the margins of the culture. For example, John

195

Coltrane's sound was strongly criticized as being inferior, but was applauded and appreciated by listeners from within the culture (perhaps because they noted its ring value, something primevally relevant and aesthetically appropriate). Although Coltrane's sound was different from the sounds of jazzmen who had preceded him, Manu Dibango (quoted in Thomas 1975, 202) perceives that it was strongly reminiscent of the sounds of African oboists of North Cameroon. Ornette Coleman's sound, even more than Coltrane's, was criticized by some jazz critics. Coleman's sound is also mythic in character.[16] But new sounds and devices revitalize and mythicize the music, contributing mightily to the continuation of ring values in jazz and in world music. The star improvisers and composers of jazz music have served as the divinities of jazz ritual, versions of Esu, god and trickster: King Oliver, Louis Armstrong, Jelly Roll Morton, Coleman Hawkins, Duke Ellington, Charlie Parker, Dizzy Gillespie, Miles Davis, John Coltrane, Ornette Coleman, and all the other great ones—each having inspired his own myths, legends, and tales (see, for example, Leonard 1987, 118–135). "Bird lives" is a slogan reminiscent of the living dead of African mythology. As put by Charles Mingus, "Bird is not dead; he's hiding out somewhere, and he'll be back with some new shit that will scare everybody to death" (quoted in Leonard, 128). African cultural memory lives on in the descendants of the ancestors and continues to inform the music and effect its continuity.

In the 1960s, gospel music became entertainment. Individuals and groups such as James Cleveland, Andraé Crouch and the Disciples, and the Edwin Hawkins Singers began to perform in theaters, auditoriums, and stadiums, bringing new sounds from the core culture into the cultural arenas of mainstream America.[17] Gospel choirs were organized in colleges and universities across the land, and longtime gospel stars began to receive wider exposure. The musical styles of these artists, while reflecting the affirmations of the new age, were also continuous with the tradition.[18] But both the sounds and the venues of 1960s gospel were wide-ranging. The instruments of R&B had become part of gospel's accompanying ensembles; church and community gospel choirs and choruses

16. See, for example, Coleman's *The Shape of Jazz to Come* (1959) and *Free Jazz* (1960).

17. Although these performers deserve credit for finishing the church as the exclusive domain of gospel music, the trend had begun as early as the 1950s, as evidenced by the increasing extra-religious popularity of Mahalia Jackson, Sister Rosetta Tharpe, and Clara Ward, and by the CBS radio network's *Mahalia Jackson Show* (Schwerin 1992, 64–70, 84–85).

18. They could be traced back through Mahalia Jackson, Thomas A. Dorsey, and Charles A. Tindley, through the turn-of-the-century quartets and the early musical expressions of the Primitive Baptist and Pentecostal Holiness churches, through the spirituals and shouts of the slave community, to the music of village African peoples.

had begun to perform with symphony orchestras (although only on "special occasions"); performers had begun to feel comfortable on the concert stage and with the mass media; the material and stylistic borrowings from jazz and R&B were even more common in gospel than they had been before; and the down-home, gut-bucket fervor of earlier gospel had been overlaid and even replaced by the slick veneer of Motown-like productions. But the characteristic vocal sound of the gospel voice remained the same: the gospel delivery, with its typical embellishments and subtle rhythmic treatments, was retained and even enhanced, as were its yea-saying and call-and-response patterns and phrasings. In other words, the more refined contemporary black gospel music retained the characteristics of its predecessors, and its performance still depended on a performer–audience call-and-response rapport unlike that of any other musical experience. In addition, the role of the gospel singer as a caller, as a "'leader' of a service, not the only participant" (Boyer 1979, 8), continued, even in the crossover forms of the genre—the "message" songs that bridge the gap between gospel and soul (Boyer, 10), such as "Oh Happy Day" (1969) by the Edwin Hawkins Singers and "Respect Yourself" (1972) by the Staples Singers. Such message songs were the nucleus of the repertoire of contemporary gospel in the 1960s.

The Reverend James Cleveland was the prime catalyst in the modernization of the gospel sound. A product of Thomas A. Dorsey's chorus and Roberta Martin's pianistic style, with additional influences from jazz and blues, Cleveland had a compositional and performance style that was lilting, funky, and intensely driving. Combining his funky delivery with the disciplined approach of the emerging "young people's choirs" in Baptist churches, Cleveland, by the late to mid-1960s, had become gospel's leading figure. His choral sound and style are evident on the album *James Cleveland and the Southern California Community Choir* (1976),[19] a collection of impressive ensemble and solo renditions of traditional and contemporary gospel songs, all done in Cleveland's innovative style. The youthful tonal qualities and voicings, organ colorations, R&B rhythms and harmonies, unique call-and-response phrasings, and jazz inflections of this choir opened the way for the choirs, small groups, and singers that would follow.

Cleveland's protégés and successors include Jessye Dixon, Edwin Hawkins, Shirley Caesar, Andraé Crouch, and gospel/soul singer Aretha Franklin, all of whom extended and elaborated Cleveland's concepts and those of the tradition at large through the 1970s and into the 1980s. In 1983, the Word label released the compilation album *The Record Makers*. The songs on this album, taken from a variety of other Word gospel albums,

19. See also *James Cleveland: With Angelic Choir.*

clearly illustrate the direction being taken by several modern gospel artists in the 1970s and early 1980s. On "The Lord Will Make a Way," Al Green's effective and emotional falsetto, accompanied by a rhythm section and light strings, is restrained, with light-gospel hollers and yea-sayings sparingly employed. The Mighty Clouds of Joy sing "Everybody Ought to Praise His Name," making spare use of moans and guttural sounds within a true and effective gospel style. "I Don't Wanna Stay Here," by the Don Degrate Delegation, with accompaniment provided by organ, piano, and drums, employs call-and-response phrasings, efficacious yea-sayings, authoritative interactions between soloists and group, jazz and blues figurations and harmonies, and effective tension–repose devices; it is rhythmically playful, musically expressive, and solidly grounded in Call–Response. Edwin Hawkins's responsorial "Oh Happy Day" has a tune built over a persistent R&B-derived figuration that is emphasized by a backbeat and a bass ostinato; the soloist sings with a hoarse, husky, breathy delivery, and the rendition is fraught with call-and-response phrasings that build to a climax and then gradually fade out. The performance is slick, subdued, controlled, and rhythmically fresh, apparently directed toward both the gospel and the crossover youth market. Falsetto, tension-building through control of loudness and textural variation, control of attacks and releases, and rhythmic improvisation mark it as a contemporary performance. The Reverend Milton Brunson's eclectic "It's Gonna Rain" makes use of polyphony, hand clapping, call-and-response phrasings, falsetto-scat vocals, and a jazz/R&B-based rhythmic accompaniment. Exploiting both ensemble precision and improvisation-like passages, it looks back to traditional gospel styles but is essentially contemporary. Bobby Jones and New Life perform "Martin," in tribute to Dr. Martin Luther King, Jr., using parts of the live recording of King's "I Have a Dream" speech. Although presented in gospel-ballad style, "Martin" is not a gospel song per se, since its textual concerns go beyond the confines of the church or of liturgical, deity-oriented, salvational, textual considerations. "Come & Go with Me," sung by Shirley Caesar with Bernard Sterling, is jazz based and makes use of call-and-response phrasings, a walking bass line, tight group harmonies, and gospel timbres, and features a purely gospel delivery by Caesar; but the performance is faded out before it reaches the typical gospel climax. The New York Community Choir's "Get in a Hurry," a solo-based piece requiring ensemble precision, makes use of a fast shuffle beat, repetitions of phrases and rhythmic figures, a tambourine accompaniment, and the preacher-like talking-over-the-music technique commonly employed by gospel singers. The vocal delivery and harmonizing on the Williams Brothers' "Don't Doubt the Lord" are in the style of traditional gospel quartet music, but this performance is contemporary in its slick accompaniment, particularly in the musical figures played by the string section.[20]

In the 1980s, a gospel version of Sophocles' drama *Oedipus Rex* was produced as *The Gospel at Colonus,* a powerful dramatic work that combines features of late Greek drama, such as protagonist and chorus, with gospel preaching and the singing of soloists, quartets, and other groups. This remarkable integration of acting, speaking, and singing in Call–Response delivery is a stunning reinterpretation that summarizes the gospel tradition while revealing and expressing the universality of human experience. In the 1985 version of the production (which is available on video), two gospel quartets are featured: the Five Blind Boys of Alabama and J. J. Farley and the Original Soul Stirrers. Their presence, their acting, and their renditions of "Stop! Do Not Go On," "A Voice Foretold," "Never Drive You Away," and "Eternal Sleep" suggest the symbolism of both the original Greek myth and African-American ritual.

The gospel song tradition is summed up in the publication *Songs of Zion* (1981), a collection prepared for use by the United Methodist Church. Besides containing traditional songs and original compositions by Clara Ward, James Hendrix, Thomas A. Dorsey, Alex Bradford, Charles A. Tindley, Lucie Campbell, James Cleveland, Edwin Hawkins, Roland Carter, and others, the collection gives "keys to musical interpretation, performance, [and] meaningful worship," ensuring the continuation of the tradition through a didactic treatise for use by church leaders and congregations. Irene Jackson's *Lift Every Voice and Sing: A Collection of Afro-American Spirituals and Other Songs* (1981) is also a compilation of spirituals, hymns, and gospel songs, in this case reflecting the tradition of black Episcopalians, although it is not didactic. *The New National Baptist Hymnal* (1982) is the Baptist version of the contemporary black hymnal. For Roman Catholics, *Lead Me, Guide Me: The African-American Catholic Hymnal* (1987), contains more than four hundred songs and includes "some of the finest hymnody in the African American tradition, both Catholic and ecumenical."[21] An earlier collection that served as a source of songs for black worship is *Gospel Pearls* (1921), also in-

---

20. Among the other gospel soloists prominent in the 1960s were Albertina Walker, Inez Andrews, and Delores Washington, all of whom are featured on *The Best of The Caravans* (1977). Video performances by numerous soloists and groups can be seen and heard in the Harold Washington Library Center of the Chicago Public Library. The center's Jubilee Showcase Collection consists of thirty-four videocassettes that contain a hundred television shows, hosted by Sid Ordower, produced between 1963 and 1984 on WLS-TV, Chicago's ABC network station. Among the performers featured in these shows are Jessye Dixon, the Staple Singers, James Cleveland, the Reverend Milton Brunson and the Thompson Community Singers, Shirley Caesar, Dorothy Love Coates and the Original Gospel Harmonettes, Roberta Martin, Andraé Crouch, the Edwin Hawkins Singers, the Soul Stirrers, Robert Anderson, and the Mighty Clouds of Joy. Copies of fifty of these shows are also held by the Library and Archives of the Center for Black Music Research of Columbia College, in Chicago.

21. News release, Communications Department, Catholic Diocese of Cleveland, 1985.

tended for black congregations but containing mostly songs from outside the specifically black tradition.[22] This publishing activity reveals how gospel figures continue to contribute to and influence African-American musical continuity within and without the genre and how they continue to contribute to the documentation of African-American cultural achievement and history.

It was the music of these songbooks, together with the congregational singing of their contents by notable and not so notable spiritual and gospel singers, that served as inspirational music for the civil rights activity of the 1960s, marking these efforts, in the words of two observers and participants, as "the greatest singing movement this country has experienced" (Carawan and Carawan 1990, 1). The Student Non-Violent Coordinating Committee (SNCC) and the Southern Christian Leadership Conference (SCLC) entered the fray, and "in 1961 the Freedom Riders swept through the South" (3), organized and led by CORE volunteers and singing spirituals, hymns, and labor songs. Common-meter and long-meter hymns had been the staples of the movement of the 1950s, and in the 1960s they were joined by "gospel songs that protest boldly and celebrate eventual victory" (1). All of the music of the early civil rights movement was based in a congregational singing in which "the singers share a communal moan that enriches the depth of struggle and pain and rises in peaks of celebration—joy—and, sometimes, shouting" (Reagon 1990, 6).[23] In 1964, the SNCC Freedom Singers organized a "Sing for Freedom," sponsored by the Highlander Folk Schools, SNCC, and the SCLC. The music of this workshop, like that of the entire movement, consisted primarily of songs derived from the black religious community—revised tunes and texts repeated in the communal, Signifyin(g) manner of the black tradition (Carawan and Carawan, 3).

So in the 1960s, gospel music was involved in cross-fertilizations that embraced the music of the core-culture church, the entertainment arena, and the

22. Two additional hymnbooks used by African Americans in earlier years, are *Pentecostal Hymns, No. 2: A Winnowed Collection* (1895) and *Full Gospel Songs* (1923). For a history and analysis of black hymnody, see Spencer (1992).

23. The gospel community was linked directly, even inextricably, with the civil rights movement. The admirers and associates of Martin Luther King, Jr. included gospel singers Alex Bradford, Dorothy Love Coates, Marion Williams, and, especially, Mahalia Jackson. At the request of King, Jackson sang the spiritual "I Been 'Buked and I Been Scorned" at the Lincoln Memorial on the occasion of the 1963 March on Washington. Six years earlier, she had sung the same spiritual at the Prayer Pilgrimage for Freedom in the same location. In the late 1960s, she was a business partner of future NAACP leader Benjamin Hooks (Schwerin 1992, 168). At King's funeral, Jackson sang Dorsey's "Precious Lord, Take My Hand," reputed to be King's favorite song. According to Heilbut (1985, 70), it was Jackson, a "loyal friend and supporter," who brought King to Chicago in 1966, "when all the [local] preachers were too scared" (Jackson, quoted in Heilbut, 72). Lewis (1970, 314), says it was the Coordinated Council of Community Organizations (CCCO), made up of six local civil rights groups, that invited King to Chicago. For another comment on the resistance of some of Chicago's ministers to King's presence in Chicago and Jackson's facilitation of his visit, see Schwerin (1992, 150–151).

fight for social and political equality, thereby beginning to insinuate itself into the larger society.

In chapter 7, I mentioned the indebtedness of rock 'n' roll to R&B.[24] In the transition, black and white rockers borrowed and absorbed some of the musical practices and performance traits that had been derived from the ring, including charcteristic riffs, boogie-woogie ostinatos, vocal lines that are internally heterogeneous, adherence to the time-line principle, timbre-distortion practices, the improvisation and *materiality* of the music making (including performance practices such as Presley's pelvic gyrations), and the general dramatic tendency of the music. The degree of timbral distortion in the rock music that emerged in the 1960s, particularly the sonic innovations of heavy metal, is one of the primary elements that mark it as different from R&B. But even this was based in the sonic values of the ring. Jimi Hendrix, known as the rock movement's "Heavy Metallurgist par excellence" (Shaw 1982, 169), had a musical conception and sound rooted in the black core culture, most particularly in the Delta blues tradition and in the music making of Chuck Berry and Little Richard. The early bluesmen, laying bottlenecks and knives to the strings of their guitars, had laid the foundation for the brass-muting jazzmen, and both set the stage for Hendrix, who used fuzz faces and other commercial devices, as well as a number of custom-made implements (Menn 1978). Such distortions can be heard in, for example, "Are You Experienced?" and "Voodoo Chile," both available in the posthumous compilation *The Essential Jimi Hendrix* (1978–1979). Hendrix had been especially influenced by Little Richard, and their affinity can be heard as he plays with Richard on the albums *Little Richard Is Back* (1964) and *Friends from the Beginning—Little Richard and Jimi Hendrix* (1972). Another influence and teacher was Albert King, who,

> like Hendrix, was a left-handed player who used a right-handed guitar upside down. He passed on to the eager young musician his own trademark—a sound that slurred up and then dropped down, like a saxophone sound. He taught him fingerings using the thumb and frettings on the guitar to bend the strings horizontally instead of vertically. (White 1984, 128)

Hendrix's apprenticeship in R&B bands such as those of Little Richard, Curtis Knight, and the Isley Brothers, and his exposure to Ike Turner, Albert King, and other R&B stylists, contributed to the development of his own style and

24. Following the transformation of R&B into rock 'n' roll—a metamorphosis effected, mainly, by Chuck Berry, Little Richard, and Elvis Presley—the Rolling Stones ("Carol," "Come On," "Around and Around," "Johnny B. Goode") and the Beatles ("Roll Over Beethoven," "Too Much Monkey Business") borrowed heavily from Berry (Reese 1982, 58–59).

to his use of ring tropes. But eventually, heavy metal became his overall conceptual framework, a sound that, in spite of its current association with white-oriented rock, goes back to Howlin Wolf's recordings in the early 1950s:

> Wolf first recorded for Phillips toward the end of 1950, and in January 1951 Chess released a single, "Moaning at Midnight," with "How Many More Years" on the flip. The music was astonishing, and Phillips never did a better job of capturing a mood. "Midnight" began with Wolf alone, moaning in his unearthly moan. Willie Johnson's overamplified guitar and Willie Steel's drums came crashing in together and then Wolf switched to harp, getting a massive, brutish sound and pushing the rhythm hard. "How Many More Years" featured Willie Johnson more prominently, and his thunderous power chords were surely the most *electric* guitar sound that had been heard on records. Wolf's rasping voice sounded strong enough to shear steel; this music was heavy metal, years before the term was coined. (Palmer 1981, 234)

Aspiring rockers of the 1960s and 1970s would identify Wolf as their inspiration and model. Although the music they created was based in cultural and social values different from those of R&B, its essential sound is certainly traceable to Wolf, both directly and through Hendrix, who had also been influenced by Chuck Berry, Muddy Waters, T-Bone Walker, Louis Jordan, Bo Diddley, Little Richard, and others. In fact, the fuzz, distortions, wah-wahs, and bent notes of rock guitarists entered rock not only through Hendrix, but also by way of white imitators of Wolf, Muddy Waters, and the other Chicago bluesmen.

On *Band of Gypsies* (1970), which is thoroughly rock, Hendrix's debt to Call–Response is clear. In it, B. B. King–style guitar lines and elements of Muddy Waters's style (signature riff figures) and Wes Montgomery's mannered approach (octaves and other double stops)[25] are fused with the rock idiom. Listen especially to "Machine Gun" and "Power of Soul." Echoes of Little Richard, albeit faint, can be heard on the "Changes" vocal. One of Hendrix's most gripping performances was also one of the most Signifyin(g) events in American-music history: his 1969 performance at Woodstock of "The Star Spangled Banner." The consecutive descending thirds that open the introduction, followed by Hendrix's unaccompanied "talking" guitar passage, immediately identify this performance as ring based. As the performance progresses, Hendrix inserts "calls" at "the rocket's red glare" and "comments" appropriately at "the bombs bursting in air" and other "telling" points. Here, Hendrix is a musical teller of the narrative, using his instrument in a manner similar to that of the African callers discussed in chapter 1 and the "tone painters" of

25. Listen, for example, to King's "Caldonia" and "I Got Some Outside Help" on *B. B. King "Now Appearing" at Ole Miss* (1980) and Wes Montgomery's "Polka Dots and Moonbeams" and "In Your Own Sweet Way" on *The Incredible Jazz Guitar of Wes Montgomery* (1960).

the European classical tradition. Hendrix's sound here comes out of the tradition of Howlin' Wolf's "Moanin' at Midnight" and "How Many More Years," and his distortions from the practices and proclivities of numerous ancient and modern African and African-American music makers.

As far as rhythm is concerned, Hendrix's music is primeval. David Henderson (1983) tells of an African conga drummer's reaction to Hendrix's performance style:

> Rocki's father was a voodoo priest and the chief drummer of a village in Ghana, West Africa. Rocki's real name was Kwasi Dzidzornu. One of the first things Rocki asked Jimi was where he got that voodoo rhythm from. When Jimi demurred, Rocki went on to explain in his halting English that many of the signature rhythms Jimi played on guitar were very often the same rhythms that his father played in voodoo ceremonies. The way Jimi danced to the rhythms of his playing reminded Rocki of the ceremonial dances to the rhythms his father played to Oxun, the god of thunder, and lightning. The ceremony is called voodoshi. (250–251)

As the basis of Hendrix's music is mythic and ritualistic, it is also related to soul music, which also relies on the primeval, mythic, ritualistic expressions of the black church, which in turn, of course, have some of their roots in the same tradition from which voodoshi derives.

The term "soul" was first used as a musical label in the mid-1950s, when jazz musicians of the hard-bop/funk persuasion employed it to explain and publicize their conscious and deliberate return to their sonic roots. The label was quickly appropriated by the record industry and became associated with black popular music of R&B derivation. But the term "soul" had been used in reference to gospel music for years before becoming current in R&B. In a 1958 interview, Mahalia Jackson related:

> What some people call the "blues singing feeling" is expressed by the Church of God in Christ. Songs like "The Lord Followed Me" became so emotional . . . [they] almost led to panic. But the blues was here before they called it blues. This kind of song came after spirituals. The old folk prayed to God because they were in an oppressed condition. While in slavery they got a different kind of blues. Take these later songs like "Summertime"[;] it's the same as "Sometimes I Feel Like a Motherless Child" . . . which had the blue note in it. The basic thing is *soul* feeling. The same in blues as in spirituals. And also with gospel music. It is soul music. (quoted in Ricks 1977, 139 [my emphasis])

The actual style that would come to be called soul had its beginnings in the 1950s, when Ray Charles exploited the gospel sound to create fusions of black religious and R&B music.[26] By 1954, Charles had recorded the then contro-versial "I Gotta Woman" (based on the gospel song "My Jesus Is All the World to Me") and in 1959 he released the equally "blasphemous" "What'd I Say," using moans, screams, sexual innuendo, and churchy piano in both perfor-mances. "What'd I Say" alternates and combines gospel-style call-and-response fervor with the erotic expressionism of R&B. The introduction in "Hallelujah" (1956) is gospel/jazz, followed by a superb blend of gospel, blues, jazz, and R&B. "Drown in My Own Tears" (1959) is almost pure gospel in its sound, especially in the nature and use of its ornaments, bent notes, cries, and piano figurations, particularly the $\frac{12}{8}$ ♫ | ♪ ♪ ♫ ♪ ♪ ♪ ♪ ♪ figure; but the text is secular, which may have made the song seem, in its heyday, internally incongruous and even sacrilegious.

It was not until the 1960s that the sound of soul became a worldwide so-cial and commercial phenomenon, set off in 1967 by Aretha Franklin's "I Never Loved a Man" and "A Natural Woman." But examples abounded before that auspicious year, including "I Found Love" (1962) by the Falcons, "Shout and Shimmy" (1962) by James Brown, and "Soul Dance Number Three" (1967) by Wilson Pickett. Sam Cooke, James Brown, and Otis Redding were the pri-mary male soul singers of the early to mid-1960s. The late 1960s saw such soul hits as "Soul Man" (1967) and "Soul Limbo" (1968) by Sam and Dave, "Say It Loud: I'm Black and I'm Proud" (1968) by James Brown, and Isaac Hayes's *Hot Buttered Soul* (1969). Franklin had taken Clara Ward of gospel's Ward Singers as her primary influence,[27] although she had also taken cues from Mahalia Jackson, Marion Williams, James Cleveland, and other gospel singers. Some of these influences are revealed in "I Never Loved a Man," in which obviously secular lyrics are set gospel-style over a repetitive rhythmic pattern surrounded by occasional gospel-piano figures and sparse figures from the horns and guitar.

In the meantime, there had emerged in 1961 the Motown sound—pop-soul—featuring Diana Ross and the Supremes, Gladys Knight and the Pips, Smokey Robinson and the Miracles, the Imperials, Marvin Gaye, Stevie Won-der, and others. Employing "tambourines, hand clapping, continuous loop melodies, and call-and-response voicing" (Shaw 1979, BM-10) as well as a "busy bass,"[28] Motown turned out an impressive and unprecedented array of R&B hits. The initial intent at Motown was to make music that was palatable to white audiences, to create, as Robinson attests, "music with a funky beat and great stories that would be crossover, that would *not* be blues. And that's

26. The word "soul" appeared in a few song titles in the 1950s, including Charles's "A Bit of Soul" (1955).

27. The art of Clara Ward can be heard on *Clara Ward Singers: Lord Touch Me*.

28. The creation of the busy-bass sound has been attributed to Jamie Jamerson, who "came out of Washboard Willie and the Super Studs of Rhythm" (Ritz 1985, 72).

what we did" (quoted in Hirshey 1984, 133). A string of hits from 1964—the Supremes' "Where Did Our Love Go?" "I Hear a Symphony," and "Baby Love" and Mary Wells's "My Guy"—exemplify the Motown philosophy, which stressed the sublimation of ring tropes in favor of appeal to a broad audience.[29] But they did not go too far astray: the subtle call-and-response phrasings, rhythmic repetition, multimetric patterns, and backbeat continued the tradition. Indeed, while seducing white listeners with elements that would appeal to them, Motown sought to educate its listeners to some of the attractions and values of ring music: the insistent repetition of the continuous loop melodies and their accompanying backbeat served not only as African-American expressive-seduction devices, but also as educational tools. As Isaac Hayes observed,

> Now it was the standard joke with blacks, that whites could not, cannot clap on a backbeat. You know—ain't got the rhythm? What Motown did was very smart. They beat the kids over the head with it. That wasn't soulful to us down at Stax, but baby it sold. (quoted in Hirshey, 184)

And nothing was left to chance. Motown producers controlled all aspects of production, with the restrictions on the blues and gospel elements growing more and more rigid year by year. Eventually, the only obvious nods to the tradition were the backbeat and the tambourine. In the 1970s, however, the Motown sound was invigorated by Stevie Wonder, before his departure from the label, with his "Living in the City" (1973) and other more black-infused releases; in the early 1980s, Michael Jackson extended that revitalization.

Meanwhile, other black-owned and black-oriented labels emerged as soul labels. First, Philadelphia International Records (PIR) joined Motown as a major black label, releasing a string of hits by Jerry Butler, the O'Jays, Melvin and the Blue Notes, Billy Paul, Teddy Pendergrass, and others who were adept at exploiting and adding to the synthesis of R&B, gospel, and blues that is soul. The slick productions of Motown and PIR contrasted sharply with the southern soul of Stax, a white-owned, black-oriented operation in Memphis, among whose artists were Rufus Thomas, Carla Thomas, Otis Redding, Booker T. and the MG's, Sam and Dave, Isaac Hayes, and a number of other down-home musicians. Influenced by the slowly evolving sound of soul that was maintaining and reaffirming ring traits, these Stax groups and individuals were performing black pop, pop-gospel, and pop-soul music.

The persistence of black musical traits and of the music itself proves the durability of Call–Response. It is the driving power of black music's mythic roots—its master trope of Call–Response and its specific cultural memory ("the

---

29. It appears that Motown had been influenced by the pseudo-operatic schlock-rock of late-1950s teen idols such as Pat Boone, Fabian, and Frankie Avalon. To the degree that that influence prevailed, African-American musical traits were diminished.

memory is in the music," said Bechet)—that makes *all* black music so productively and enduringly vital.

In the European and European-derived concert world, the musical expressionism that arose before 1920 with Arnold Schoenberg and was perpetuated by Alban Berg and Anton Webern had become more widespread following World War II[30] and the method and potentials of Schoenberg's twelve-tone serial technique more widely taught in colleges and universities. By the 1950s, elements of serial technique, and conceptions derived from it, were being used by an even wider variety of European composers, including Ernst Krenek, Rolf Liebermann, Karlheinz Stockhausen, Luigi Dallapiccola, Luigi Nono, Luciano Berio, and Pierre Boulez, and by United States–based composers such as Roger Sessions, Milton Babbitt, and Leon Kirchner, among others. Mid-century influences from Europe came from such composers as Stockhausen (*Klavierstücke XI* and *Zeitmasse,* both 1956, and *Zyklus,* 1957), Pierre Boulez (*Le Marteau sans maître,* 1955), and Luigi Nono (*Il canto sospeso,* 1956). In the meantime, aleatoric and indeterminate procedures had been developed in the United States by John Cage, whose use of chance methods such as the throwing of dice and the use of the Chinese *I Ching* were becoming influential. In addition, Earle Brown, Morton Feldman, and Christian Wolff had formed a New York school of aleatory music that would have wide influence (Salzman 1988, 161). Examples of the aleatoric works of the 1950s and early 1960s are Feldman's *Projections* (1951), Cage's *Music of Changes* and *Imaginary Landscape No. 5* (1952), Wolff's *For Piano I* (1952), and Brown's *Available Forms I* (1961) and *Available Forms II* (1962). The electronic-music experiments initiated in Europe at the Cologne Electronic Studio in the early 1950s spread immediately to the United States, where in 1952, Otto Luening and Vladimir Ussachevsky established the Columbia University electronic studio, using "live-recorded sound in conjunction with tape techniques" (149). In the same decade, minimalist ("System") composition emerged, with composers making use of subtly shifting tonal and rhythmic figures in a search for new means of varying and constructing repetitive musical configurations. Minimal, or systematic, music is based on repeated patterns achieved through the gradual, incremental growth of repeated material. It is music in which harmonic stasis, rhythmic and pitch repetition, and progressive, integer-based large-scale structures define the style. The origins of minimalism can be found in various Eastern musics, particularly that of black Africa (Steve Reich studied African drumming at the Institute of African Studies, University of Ghana), and in some of

---

30. See, for example, Berg's *Lyric Suite* (1926) for string quartet and *Wozzeck* (1914–1923) and Webern's *Five Pieces for Orchestra,* Op. 10 (1912) and Symphony, Op. 21 (1928).

the music of Eric Satie and John Cage. By the 1960s, several African-American composers were creating successful serial, aleatoric, and electronic works, and by the 1980s, minimalist works began to appear in the black-music repertoire.

The diversity of style and media in the concert-hall music of African-American composers of the 1960s is wide-ranging and includes works for concert band, such as William Grant Still's *Folk Suite for Band* (1964), Hale Smith's *Somersault* (1964) and *Expansions* (1967), and Ulysses Kay's *Forever Free* (1962);[31] electronic and electronically assisted works, such as Olly Wilson's *Cetus* (1968) and *Sometimes* (1976); aleatoric works, such as Wendell Logan's *Proportions for Nine Instruments and Conductor* (1968); serial pieces, such as Smith's *Contours, for Orchestra* (1962); freely atonal but closely notated works, such as T. J. Anderson's *Squares: An Essay for Orchestra* (1965); chamber works laced with jazz and gospel elements, such as Anderson's *Variations on a Theme by M. B. Tolson* (1969) and David Baker's *Through This Vale of Tears* (1986); and other experimental pieces such as Talib Rasul Hakim's *Sound Gone* (1967).

Ulysses Kay continued in the style that had brought him success in the 1940s and 1950s. *Fantasy Variations* (1963), a highly contrapuntal, tonally free, chromatically oriented, motive-laden work of variable-length sections, is squarely and exclusively in the European-derived tradition. It is characterized by a frequently repeated four-note motive, subtly changing meters, and a brilliant, richly textured orchestration that exploits the expressive effects of antiphonal structures, whole-tone melodies, quartal harmonies, tone clusters, and polychords. The perceptual focus of the work is on the opening motive and its subsequent pitch and rhythmic permutations in polyphony, inversion, retrograde, and other treatments that appear in florid solo and duet imitations and in various ensemble configurations. In presenting these permutations, all the instruments get to "say," or "say something about," the "subject" of the work. This composition is a true set of "fantasy variations," but, perceptually at least, it is "developmental," seeming to form itself from the inside out, rather than having been formed or forming itself in sections. The piece ends with a full thematic statement that seems to realize the implications and potentiality of the opening motive, including many of the musical meanings inherent in the "comments" made on it throughout its quarter-hour duration. The work is a mighty orchestral oration that ends in a grand, lyrical, summarizing conclusion.

In the concert works of other black composers of the 1960s, we see a confluence of styles, techniques, expressive devices, and traits borrowed from African-American genres as well as from European concert-hall music. Hale Smith's rhythmic and chordal conceptions and outright borrowings of ragtime

---

31. For a list of other works for band by black composers, see Everett (1978).

and jazz elements are almost an unconscious part of his thinking, since jazz, he says, has been "integrally a part of my maturation process."[32] In Smith's work, influences from the Ellington and Basie bands show through in his syncopated, multimetric constructions and "delayed approach to the beat," and in some of his chord voicings. His *Contours, for Orchestra* is a serial work inspired in part by Afro-Cuban and Brazilian dance music. Although solidly in the European concert tradition, *Contours* communicates universally, its expressive potential especially enhanced by elements that have their basis in Call–Response. The changes in meter and the phrasings in the score reflect the additive rhythms typical of ring-derived music. The opening measures of the quick-moving first section are particularly rich in rhythmic constructions, in riff-like, punctuation-style trumpet figures, in jazz-voiced chords in some of the violin passages, in an ostinato-like quality in the solo piano and trombone lines, and in jazz-like phrasings for the brief flute and trumpet solos. These elements are effectively integrated into a conception that is clearly *not* jazz, since the work is developed along the lines of European practice. This first section is brought to a close with a return of fragments of the opening ideas.

The slow lyricism of the second section of *Contours* contrasts with the more vigorous first section, but the composer's jazz-derived rhythmic approach still prevails, particularly his practice of "tying short notes into longer ones" (Smith 1984). The writing for trombones and trumpets is obviously jazz-influenced, as are the final chordal constructions. *Contours* is a twelve-tone composition, but the melodic, harmonic, and rhythmic constructions are always related to a clear beat structure. With *Contours*, Smith subtly and unobtrusively brings Call–Response into the realm of the concert hall, contributing to a cross-cultural continuity that is, and has been for decades, changing the character of American and world music.

T. J. Anderson's *Variations on a Theme by M. B. Tolson* consists of settings of six selected text fragments. A cantata for soprano and chamber ensemble, the work is scored for alto saxophone, trumpet, trombone, violin, cello, and piano and is an exemplary fusion of European, twelve-tone-derived pointillistic techniques with African-American performance practices. The six text selections are taken from Tolson's *Harlem Gallery, Book 1: The Curator* and *Libretto for the Republic of Liberia*, three from each book, and are set in four musical sections in a kind of musical mosaic.[33] The first section of the piece is more European-oriented than the later ones, although it does make use of some at-

---

32. This and subsequent quotes are from a telephone conversation I had with Smith in 1984.

33. Tolson's books *Rendezvous with America* (1944), *Libretto for the Republic of Liberia* (1953), and *Harlem Gallery, Book 1: The Curator* (1965) identify him as a rather esoteric and difficult poet who, nonetheless, speaks ironically, intensely, sometimes agonizingly, and most effectively of race relations in America and the world.

tacks, phrasings, and fall-offs in the African-American manner. The second section consists of three successive, unaccompanied recitative treatments of Tolson's poems. The third section is more lyrical than those before it and contains more ring-derived elements: instrumental and vocal smears, bent notes, lip trills, a suggestion of "ghosting" as the word "peace" is whispered, and other subtropes of the ring. The coda-like fourth section is introduced by a collectively improvised passage and a trumpet–sax unison passage that recalls bebop heads. The texts are delivered as written, in vernacular pronunciation. Funky jazz smears, jazz-sax vibrato, jazz-chord voicings, blues and jazz phrasings, improvised or improvisation-like passages, jazz-like accompaniment figures, flutter tonguing, and fall-offs infuse the work. At the statement and repetition of the phrase "Come back, baby, come back" on pendular thirds, the jazz and blues character of the piece increases, with subtropes of the ring being exploited increasingly; one chordal figure Signifies on Arthur Cunningham's "Lullabye for a Jazz Baby"; and an ersatz blues progression brings the piece to a close.[34]

Alvin Singleton's *Shadows* is minimalist, and we see here again an affinity between black music and the avant-garde—the kinship between the hypnotic repetitiveness of African-derived music and the hypnotic repetitiveness of minimalism. Using four to six pitches, the piece develops slowly. Louder and softer events alternate, some including pitches of long duration that oscillate in judiciously shifted, timbred, spaced, and placed configurations. Throughout the development of the piece, repetitive rhythms and timbres, and successive, simultaneous, and overlapping seconds and thirds abound. The result is excitingly hypnotic, gradually building until, at thirteen minutes and fifty seconds into the work, the musical ecology takes on the character of a jazz orchestra, replete with stylized off-beat trumpet riffs over a reverse hemiola ostinato that continues for four minutes over trombone "splaats" in a stylized, Call–Response dance section. Then the percussion enters and brings this work to a rousing dialogical climax. Singleton's minimalist, riffing repetitions here represent a sounding of African and African-American myth through a stylized mimetic of the ritual practice of the black jazz orchestra.

Olly Wilson's *Of Visions of Truth* (1990) is a song cycle for baritone, tenor, and soprano voices. Written in the composer's own heterogeneous sound language, the work is also a true amalgam—a wonderful and effective marriage of the languages of African-American music and European-derived expressionism. The work's four movements are separated by interludes that provide contrast with and emotional relief between the main statements. "I've Been 'Buked," the work's first movement, is a repetition and revision of the Negro

---

34. For a list of works by Kay, Smith, and Anderson, compiled in the mid-1970s, see Baker, Belt, and Hudson (1978, 7–13).

spiritual "I've Been 'Buked and I've Been Scorned," a setting of text and tune in a Signifyin(g) revision that pays tribute to all the past singers of the song. The first section of the movement, featuring the baritone, treats tune and text in a halting, repetitive, motivic manner, the composer commenting on the old spiritual from the perspective of his own position in African-American history. The entry of the tenor, slow and languid, connects the first section to the second, a shorter, lyrical, smooth, sinuous trio that features all three singers. Slow developing, with repetitions, fragmentation, and elaborations of textual elements and units, the work tropes the black folk tradition through stylized calls, cries, and literal statements of short portions of text and tune. "Lullaby," a very slow and tender song, Signifies on the old songs that have lulled numerous black babies to sleep across the land. The text, written by the composer to celebrate "Mama's little brown baby," is set to a melody that makes use of ring-derived pendular and flatted thirds throughout. The bebop-like "IKEF" is set to a text by Henry Dumas and based on the melody of "Shortenin' Bread." "If We Must Die," with a text from Harlem Renaissance writer Claude McKay's poem of the same name, features tenor and baritone in a celebration of the slaves' call to arms against attacks by those who would keep them enslaved and oppressed. The movement ends with a rousing contrapuntal treatment of male voices singing,

> If we must die
> Like men,
> We'll face the murderous cowardly pack;
> Pressed to the wall
> Dying, but fighting back.[35]

In this contrapuntal exchange, pendular thirds are prominent in voices and in instruments, and the baritone simulates an African time line against which the tenor "plays styles." The main strength of this ring-troped concert work lies in its mythic character, exemplified in the calls and cries of the baritone; in the archaic and faraway quality of the second movement's lullaby; in its legendary and ritualistic qualities (for example, the play-party narrative of "Shortnin'," heightened by the use of the bebop idiom); in the metaphoric, evolutionary dope-smoking rituals of "IKEF"; and in the primal rhythms of the last section of the final movement.

The use of ring tropes by African-American composers may be either obvious or subtle, but the tropes are present in some form or fashion in the works of most African-American composers, albeit sometimes disguised by method and technique or even unintentionally employed. Recall Smith's statement

---

35. For the full text of the poem, see McKay (1953, 36).

about how his experience with jazz and ragtime music affects or contributes to his style: that his rhythmic and chordal conceptions and outright borrowings of ragtime and jazz elements are so much a part of his thinking that they have been "integrally a part of my maturation process," that his jazz-derived practice of "tying short notes into longer ones" is now essentially part of his being as a composer. Recall that Smith's *Contours* is based on serial procedures and Anderson's *Variations* on nonserial expressionist techniques, but that they both spring from the black aesthetic as well as from European-derived compositional practices.[36] Only Esu—Janus-faced god of irony, trickster and god of divination, interpreter of the culture—could guide such a balancing act, and only his cousin, the Signifying Monkey, could ensure its success.

---

36. For lists of works for the concert hall by black composers, see Baker, Belt, and Hudson (1978), de Lerma (1984), Horne (1990, 1991, 1992), Tischler (1981), and Walker-Hill (1992b).

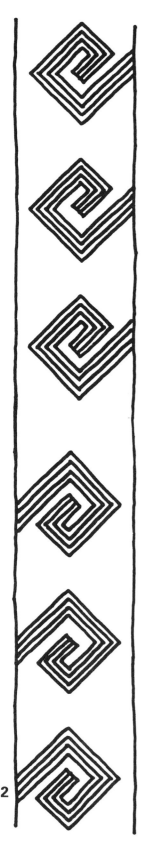

CHAPTER **9**

Troping the Blues:
From Spirituals
to the Concert Hall

**The calves follow their mothers. The young plant grows
up near the parent stem. The young antelope leaps where
its mother leaped.**
Zulu proverb

**By tropological revision, I mean the manner in which a
specific trope is repeated, with differences between two
or more texts.**
Henry Louis Gates, Jr.

In one of the two relatively extensive statements
on music in *The Signifying Monkey*, Gates (1988)
claims:

> There are so many examples of Signifyin(g) in jazz
> that one could write a formal history of its devel-
> opment on this basis alone. One early example is
> relatively familiar: Jelly Roll Morton's 1938 record-
> ing entitled "Maple Leaf Rag (A Transformation)"
> Signifies upon Scott Joplin's signature composi-
> tion, "Maple Leaf Rag," recorded in 1916. Whereas
> Joplin played its contrasting themes and their
> repetitions in the form of AABBACCDD, Morton
> "embellishes the piece two-handedly, with a
> swinging introduction (borrowed from the ending
> to A), followed by ABACCD (a hint of tango here)
> D (a real New Orleans 'stomp' variation)," as
> Martin Williams observes. Morton's piano imitates
> "a trumpet–clarinet right hand and a trombone-
> rhythm left hand." Morton's composition does

not "surpass" or "destroy" Joplin's; it completely *extends* and tropes figures present in the original. Morton's Signification is a gesture of admiration and respect. . . .

Improvisation, of course, so fundamental to the very idea of jazz, is "nothing more" than repetition and revision. In this sort of revision, again where meaning is fixed, it is the realignment of the signifier that is the signal trait of expressive genius. . . . It is this principle of repetition and difference, this practice of intertextuality, which has been so crucial to the black vernacular forms of Signifyin(g), jazz—and even its antecedents, the blues, the spirituals, and ragtime—and which is the source of my trope for black intertextuality in the Afro-American formal literary tradition. (63, 64)

Because I want to demonstrate the applicability of this concept to black music, over time and across genres, I will begin my exploration with a brief look at intertexuality in spiritual and blues texts.

One of the best known spirituals is "Swing Low, Sweet Chariot":

> Swing low, sweet chariot,
>   Coming for to carry me home;
> Swing low, sweet chariot,
>   Coming for to carry me home.
>
> If you get there before I do,
>   Coming for to carry me home;
> Tell all my friends I'm a-coming too,
>   Coming for to carry me home.

The chariot "trope" has been repeated and revised many times under many titles.[1] In these songs, the chariot variously will "swing low" to pick up and carry the slaves home, to ride the singers up "over Jordan." It brings peace, rest, and release from the secular world. It is "good news" that "the chariot's coming" to allow the slaves to "trabble on" to heaven. The chariot of the songs is sometimes one in which "King Jesus" rides, being pulled by "four white horses side by side." It rides across the sky and "stops," which means "good news" for the righteous. At other times, the chariot, rather than flying, "rolls along," pulled this time by "twelve white horses," and it

---

1. My survey of seventeen printed anthologies of spirituals published between 1867 and 1933, all of which appear in the Cleveland Public Library's *Index to Negro Spirituals* (1991), revealed eleven spirituals with the word "chariot" in their titles and an additional twenty-three whose texts include the word (Appendix).

has only one or two wheels that run either "by faith" or "by the grace of God."[2]

In the spirituals, such intertextual repetitions and revisions were taking place even as the songs were being made and as they developed during and after slavery—for example, four horses become twelve, the chariot rolls rather than flies—and these tropings continued through the heyday of the sorrow songs and jubilees.

Eventually, a different chariot appeared on the American cultural landscape. Unlike the chariot of the spirituals, this new chariot was sometimes anthropomorphized: as in Peetie Wheatstraw's "C and A Blues," it would, with its steam whistle, "holler back at you":[3]

> Well now let me tell you people : what the C and A will do for you
>   now
> Well now it will take your little woman : then will holler back at you
> Mmm hate to hear : C and A whistle blow
> Mama now it blows so lonesome baby : honey because I want to go
> Mmm few more days : few more nights alone
> Baby then I'm going to pack my suitcase : honey now I will be gone
> Well now when a woman takes the blues : she will hang her head and
>   cry
> Well now when a man takes the blues : please now he will catch him
>   a train and ride
> Mmm going to write me a letter : mama going to mail it in the air
> Well well well going to send it up the country : mama now to see if
>   my little girl there
>
> (Taft 1983, 293)

From the end of the Civil War to the year 1873, thirty thousand miles of railway track were laid in the United States to carry trains from east to west and north to south. Bluesmen were immediately fascinated by the trains that rode this track, and they wrote songs about them.[4] The trains in these songs have names, whistles that blow, and engines that break down; some are slow,

---

2. See, for example, "Swing Low, Sweet Chariot," "Gwineter Ride Up in De Chariot Soon-a in De Mornin'," "Great Day," "Up on De Mountain," "De Band O' Gideon," "'Zekiel Saw De Wheel" (Johnson and Johnson [1925, 1926] 1981); "Good News, de Chariot's Comin'" (Dett 1927); "Oh Wasn't Dat a Wide Riber" (Armstrong and Ludlow [1875] 1971); "He's the Lily of the Valley" (Dett 1927; Pike [1875] 1971); "March On" (Pike [1875] 1971); "Tell It" (Hallowell [1907] 1976).

3. Cirlot, in *A Dictionary of Symbols* (1971), points out that the railroad train is "a corruption of the essential symbol of the chariot" (359).

4. My survey of Taft's *Blues Lyric Poetry* (1983) turned up 30 titles containing the word "train" or "trains" and 220 songs in which the word is included in the text.

and some are fast; they run on lines that cross, and as they cross they travel "up the way," "out west," and "down south"; they take away lovers, sometimes in boxcars, and may never bring them back.[5] The railroad train represented independence of movement for newly freed slaves, a certain amount of autonomy and liberation, and it allowed rapid escape from threatening conditions. Wheatstraw evokes the symbols both of escape and of perceived male–female differences and relationships when he sings, " . . . when a woman takes the blues : she will hang her head and cry . . . when a man takes the blues : please now he will catch him a train and ride."

The trope of the railroad train[6] has also been repeated in strictly instrumental form. In 1927 DeFord Bailey, a harmonica player with the Grand Ole Opry, recorded his impressions of the Dixie Flyer and the Pan American, two trains he had been able to observe in his youth at Newsoms Station, just west of Nashville.[7] Discussing his harmonica imitations of the trains, Bailey says:

> I worked on my train for years, getting that train down right. I caught that train down just like I wanted in a matter of time. I got the engine part. Then I had to make the whistle.
>
> It was about, I expect, seventeen years to get that whistle. It takes time to get this stuff I'm talking about, original. You don't get no original stuff like this in a day or two. It takes years to get it down piece by piece. I got that whistle so it would have a double tone to it, a music tone.
>
> And when cattle was on the track and all that kind of thing, how to make a scary or distressed blow. Then I knowed how to make a harp sound like it was going over a trestle or a deep curve. Like when you in the mountains and going through a tunnel. I could blow like that; and like when you going through a tunnel, you might meet someone, like a person.
>
> I done all that kind of stuff when I was a boy; I'd listen to everything. (quoted in Morton 1991, 78)

The recording of Bailey's "Pan American Blues" indicates that he studied and practiced well. In it, the whistle, the movement of the wheels, the escaping

5. These images can be found, for example, in the following blues lyrics (all in Taft 1983): Jelly Roll Anderson, "I. C. Blues" (6); Lottie Beaman, "Goin' Away Blues" (17–18); Ed Bell, "Frisco Whistle Blues" (19); Lonnie Clark, "Broke Down Engine" (61); Sam Collins, "Yellow Dog Blues" (64); Walter Davis, "L and N Blues" (71); Papa Charlie Jackson, "Up the Way Bound" (119); Blind Lemon Jefferson, "Sunshine Special" (130); Maggie Jones, "Box Car Blues" (156); Eurreal "Little Brother" Montgomery, "Out West Blues" (202–203); Clara Smith, "Down South Blues," "Freight Train Blues" (239–242); Hanna Sylvester, "Down South Blues" (263–264).

6. The musical significance of the railroad train as it is related to the blues has been treated, in one way or another, by several writers. See, for example, Murray's discussion of trains and "railroad onomatopoeia" in *Stomping the Blues* (1976, 124–126); Oliver's treatment in the chapter "Railroad for My Pillow," in *Blues Fell This Morning* (1961); and Palmer's analysis, in the chapter "Heart Like Railroad Steel," in *Deep Blues* (1981). A broader treatment is in Cohen's *Long Steel Rail* (1981).

7. On Bailey, see Jones ([1980] 1990) and Morton (1991).

steam, and the train's increasing speed are effectively, even startlingly, imitated. While metaphorically dispensing steam and blowing the whistle, Bailey gives the astonishing impression that he is simultaneously keeping the wheel-mimicking rhythm going, so true and exact is his sense of rhythm and tempo. There is no melody line in this piece, but double stops abound, not only in Bailey's imitation of the train's wheels, but also in those whistles to which Bailey refers. In "Dixie Flyer Blues," Bailey begins with the clackety-clack of the wheels, adding a whistle (more elaborate than that of the Pan American version) that is almost a blues tune, but certainly a holler, with all its semantic implications. In fact, the semantic value of Bailey's whistle is palpable, with falling and oscillating thirds carrying the load, and the wheels and steam of the train approaching the listener by way of Bailey's crescendos, making this a "talking" as well as a traveling train.

Also included in the train-instrumental genre is Meade Lux Lewis's "Honky Tonk Train" (1937), a twelve-bar blues for piano in which a boogie-woogie ostinato represents the moving train's wheels and treble figurations its variety of whistles. The changes in rhythmic, tonal, and melodic activity throughout the rendition suggest different tempi, various whistles, changes in speed, and even different sets of wheels. Lewis's rhythmic placement is uncanny and superb.

These two chariots—the horse-drawn heavenly chariot and its steam-driven, land-borne, rail-riding descendant—have been celebrated in African-American myth and legend for more than a century. In African-American lore, both the chariot of the spirituals and the train of the blues are metaphors for freedom. As tropes, they have undergone repetition and revision in numerous musical works. The spiritual itself is a major trope that has been repeated and revised countless times in many musical works, including, for example, Robert Nathaniel Dett's large choral works *The Chariot Jubilee* (1921), in which he makes use of "Swing Low, Sweet Chariot," "Ride Up in the Chariot," and "Father Abraham," and *The Ordering of Moses* (1932), in which he tropes "Go Down Moses" and "He Is King of Kings" (Ryder 1990, 65). Trains have been troped in numerous blues songs, in jazz (for example, Duke Ellington's "Take the A Train"), and in many other works and performances of music.

I shall now trace, through several manifestations, two subtropes—one of the spiritual and one of the railroad train. The first is what I am calling here the "Sometimes" trope, which had its genesis in the spiritual "Sometimes I Feel Like a Motherless Child." The second is the trope of the *riding* train, which should be distinguished from the freights (unless they've been "hopped") and those that are simply *observed* by songsters such as Bailey.

> Sometimes I feel like a motherless child,
> Sometimes I feel like a motherless child,
> Sometimes I feel like a motherless child,

A long ways from home, a long ways from home;
True believer! A long ways from home.

Sometimes I feel like I'm almost gone,
Sometimes I feel like I'm almost gone,
Sometimes I feel like I'm almost gone,
Way up in de heab'nly lan', Way up in de heab'nly lan',
True believer! Way up in the heab'nly lan'.

Sometimes I feel like a motherless child
Sometimes I feel like a motherless child,
Sometimes I feel like a motherless child,
A long ways from home.

(Johnson and Johnson [1925, 1926] 1981, 2:30–33)

In the African-American musical tradition, intragenre and cross-genre troping is widespread, with lines and phrases of songs being borrowed and used
as needs and desires arise. Such troping, as momentary as it sometimes is, is
nevertheless frequent. An example of this minor troping is the use in blues
songs of a phrase from "Sometimes I Feel Like a Motherless Child." In "Big
Chief Blues" (1927), for example, blues musician Furry Lewis tropes such a
phrase in a song that refers to an imagined or a real Indian chief:

I'm going away baby : take me seven long months to ride
January, February : March April May June July
I was three years old : when my poor mother died
If you mistreat me : mistreat a motherless child.

(Taft 1983, 168)

Lewis uses the phrase "motherless child" in line 4 to convey the same sense
of despondency, loneliness, and mistreatment that is conveyed by the spiritual
from which it is borrowed.

In "Panama Limited" (1930), Washington "Bukka" White brings a slightly
larger portion of the original text into the blues:

I ain't got nobody : take me to see this train
Mmm : mmm
Fare you well : if I don't see you no more
Mmm : Lord Lord Lord Lord
I'm a motherless child : I'm a long ways from home
Mmm : mmm
This train I ride : it don't burn no coal
Mmm : mmm.

(Taft 1983, 300)

White trades more heavily on the emotional ambiance of the "motherless child" line than does Lewis, intensifying it with "Mmm : Lord Lord Lord Lord," which takes up an entire line of text. Here, the hum is used as an intensifier for "Lord," and, together with the repeats of "Lord," the line intensifies the emotional atmosphere of a larger portion of the song. In the final lines of text, the word "it" is also used as an intensifier, "it" being a repetition, in its pronoun form, of "this train."

The first extended troping of the *tune* of "Sometimes I Feel Like a Motherless Child" was George Gershwin's repetition of it in *Porgy and Bess* (1935) as "Summertime."[8] In the first phrase, Gershwin tropes (1) the spiritual's intervallic structure, which is made up of minor and major thirds and major seconds, (2) the spiritual's rhythm, by replacing the rhythm of the first three beats of the tune with his own on-the-beat rhythm in augmentation, (3) the tune's melodic and rhythmic structures, and (4) the spiritual's beat and intervallic structure. It is also evident that the phrase endings of both tunes are characterized by descending motion and that both melodies are constructed of repeated rhythmic patterns, but those of "Summertime" are stretched over four measures while those of "Sometimes I Feel Like a Motherless Child" occur over two. Rhythmically, in other words, "Summertime" is a kind of augmentation of the "Sometimes I Feel Like a Motherless Child" melody. And within this context, the spiritual rhythms ♪♪ ♪♪ ♪ of "Sometimes I Feel Like a Motherless Child" are replaced in "Summertime" by the jazz-related figurations ♪ ♩ ♪♩♪♩. Harmonically, the two tunes follow basically the same harmonic scheme (Floyd 1993, 39–42).

The text of "Summertime" is completely new, thereby transforming the original lament into a kind of summertime pacifier:

> Summertime an' the living is easy
> Fish are jumpin', an' the cotton is high.
> Oh yo' daddy's rich, and yo' ma is good lookin',
> So hush, little baby, don' yo' cry.
>
> (Gershwin, Hayward, and Gershwin 1935)

To demonstrate an extension of this troping, I would like to return to the Miles Davis–Gil Evans 1958 collaboration *George Gershwin's Porgy and Bess*

---

8. Another early use of "Sometimes I Feel Like a Motherless Child" as a trope occurs in a Henry Creamer and Turner Layton song. One of Duke Ellington's 1933 recordings of their "Dear Old Southland" has one of Ellington's trumpeters introducing the "Sometimes" theme as the song's middle section, following the opening-theme statement of the "Deep River" tune. It can be heard on *The Indispensable Duke Ellington*, vol. 2 (1933). I thank Ellington scholar Mark Tucker for calling my attention to Ellington's recordings of this composition. The Ellington recording is a Signifyin(g) revision of the 1930 Louis Armstrong hit "Dear Old Southland." Thanks to Richard Wang for supplying this information.

(chapter 8). This version of "Summertime" is an extended solo by Davis, the orchestra backing him with sonorous and effectively orchestrated riffs. His muted horn, excellent and inimitable note choices, rhythmic placement, and lovely paraphrasing of the Gershwin melody contribute effectively to a superb remaking of this classic. Of course, no text at all is present in this performance; Davis improvises slightly over an orchestra consisting of four trumpets, four trombones, two saxophones, three French horns, two flutes, tuba, double bass, and drums. This version of Gershwin's revision—itself a revision of the "Sometimes" spiritual—begins with Davis presenting the melody, in moderate tempo, over a composed riff-ostinato accompaniment made up of the pattern that begins on beat 2 of the second complete measure of the Gershwin melody

thereby Signifyin(g) again on the rhythm that was displaced in Gershwin's revision. Following his initial statement of the melody, Davis improvises on each chorus. By way of this rendition, Davis and Evans have changed the emotional ambiance of the traditional tune from that of a sorrow song, through Gershwin's hot-weather lament, to a mid-tempo jazz ballad.

Another revision of "Sometimes I Feel Like a Motherless Child" appears in the sixth movement of David Baker's *Through This Vale of Tears* (1986), a song cycle for tenor, string quartet, and piano. This work is a memorial to Martin Luther King, Jr., and a commentary on his assassination. The texts in the cycle are taken from the Twenty-second Psalm, from the spiritual "Sometimes I Feel Like a Motherless Child," and from poetry by Mari Evans, Solomon Edwards, and Charles Hines. "Sometimes I Feel Like a Motherless Child" begins with the tenor softly humming the tune, as a traditional caller or crier might do. Abruptly and more loudly, he interjects the call "Ohhh, my bru-u-therrr!" after which the string quartet enters with dissonant chords, followed by the piano, which accompanies the tenor's tune with chords and melodic filigree. The text is exactly that of the traditional spiritual, and the tune, presented in its entirety, varies only slightly, in one or two places. The slow-moving tune is then accompanied variously by block chords, slightly dissonant, and by sinewy progressions and countermelodies in the strings and piano. The movement's mythic quality is enhanced by the unaccompanied humming that introduces it, and the original quality of this spiritual is maligned not at all by the modern dissonances and the elliptical and asymmetrical pitch movement. In this piece, the tenor repeats text and tune and the instruments revise it in a moment of Signifyin(g) revisitation.

Olly Wilson's *Sometimes* (1976) is a poignant and powerful Signification on the original spiritual. This work for tenor and tape (17 minutes, 20 seconds in length) was written especially for tenor William Brown. It was the composer's intention to re-create the "profound expressions of human hopelessness and desolation that characterize the traditional spiritual, but also simultaneously on another level, . . . [to react to] the desolation that transcends hopelessness" (Wilson 1992a). Textually, the work begins with Brown's prerecorded voice whispering "motherless child, motherless child," with the tape in echo. This gives way to tape timbres exclusively until the live voice enters at 2 minutes, 35 seconds and presents, fragmented, the words "Sometimes I feel . . ." At 4 minutes, 40 seconds the first climax is reached, and five seconds later Brown sings, "True believer . . . like a motherless child . . . a long way from home." Later, the following words and phrases are stated, repeated, and rhythmically revised: "will be . . . long . . . will . . . be . . . times . . . feel . . . like a . . . will . . . -a . . . 'lie-e-ever . . . some . . . time . . . tiii-iimes! . . . truuuu," and so on, leading into more words that are fragmented between live voice and tape. Following an unaccompanied cadenza, in which Brown fragments as much of the text as been previously presented, the taped sounds begin again, with the fragmentation continuing and imitation between voice and tape building through repetition, rhythmic revision, and increases in density. The tenor signals the work's closing section by humming, then whistling, part of the tune. Taped sounds close out the work, repeating "long . . . way, long way . . ."

Throughout *Sometimes,* text and tune are severely fragmented, stretched, and placed in ever new and interesting juxtapositions on tape and also between tape and live tenor voice. Text intensifiers are introduced and repeated, and heterogeneous sound events occur in the taped sounds, within the vocal line, and between voice and tape. Oscillating thirds, reminiscent of the black folk cry, pervade the piece and, together with the tenor's faraway humming and whistling, give it a mythic flavor. Tongue trills, elisions, high hoos, breath expulsions, and sibilant sounds, all interjected between or articulated over provocative tape sounds, add to the mythic quality of this work of Call–Response. In this work, Brown is a caller, and also a crier, both "live" and on tape.

From its origin as a sorrow song, through tropings of it that range from brief textual borrowings, such as in the blues songs of Furry Lewis and Bukka White, to the extended melodic and motivic reworkings of tune and text in Gershwin's "Summertime" and Wilson's *Sometimes,* the spiritual "Sometimes I Feel Like a Motherless Child" has served as the source of a wide variety of musical expressions. Yet it is only one example of the possibilities inherent in the products and processes of Call–Response.

The power of these products and processes is equally potent within and among other genres, as will be revealed in my tracing of the second of our two subtropes, the trope of the riding train.

In "Box Car Blues" (1924), Maggie Jones sings:

> Every time : I see a railroad track
> Feel like riding : feel like going back
> Catch a train : that's headed for the South
> Going back south : to get smacked in the mouth
> Got a man : way down old Texas way
> Going to meet him : ain't got time to stay
> Got the box car blues : feel like a tramp
> Going to be down : in a Texas camp
> Told the engineer : to drive them down
> Broke and hungry : tired of tramping around
> Boxcar Boxcar : don't you carry two
> Ride me rode me : soothe my boxcar blues.

(Taft 1983, 156)

Jones here gives commentary both on the hundreds of thousands of miles of track that were laid to carry people and things and on the relationship of her love life to the trains that traveled the rails. Her subtle yet highly effective use of double entendre and other sexual suggestions is ingenious, as in lines 7, 9, and 12. The melody line of "Box Car Blues" is made up almost exclusively of falling and oscillating thirds that float over and are sometimes intersected by the boogie-type figurations of the piano; the typically short phrases are invariably answered and commented on by the trombone with statements of prodigious semantic value.

Jones's song is but an example of blues songs that Signify on riding trains. Recall, for example, Wheatstraw's "C and A Blues" and White's "Panama Limited." Both of these, in addition to title and text, treat the riding train musically. Wheatstraw's wide-ranging melody makes use of falling fifths and contains frequent train-whistling high hoos, and the piano accompaniment makes use of train-whistling repeated treble notes as well as filigreed responses to calls. White begins his rendition with a vamping, wheel-running, unflagging rhythm in the guitar and banjo, over which he lays, alternately, vocal patter and singing. The singing passages, in addition to expressing textual content, serve simultaneously and ingeniously as imitations of train whistles. The guitar, too, has its whistling imitations, made by ringing elided and graced notes.

The black poets of music became even more ambitious as their resources increased. Duke Ellington had a fascination for trains, perhaps because he spent so much time on them, traveling between one-night stands. Among his recorded "train" pieces are "Choo-Choo," "Daybreak Express," and "Happy-Go-Lucky Local," of which the last will concern us here. Featured in "Happy-Go-Lucky Local" (1946) are varieties of whistle imitations, chugging rhythms,

221

and evocations of hissing steam, all of which together give a powerful impression of a riding train. The piece begins with a signal whistle that in its dissonance suggests more the modern diesel than Bailey's steam engine; the steady bass and trombone riffs take the role of Bailey's clackety-clacking wheels in the "Dixie Flyer Blues." Then follows what I will call the "Night Train" riff (since it was later made into a popular R&B song of the same name by tenor saxophonist and bandleader Jimmy Forrest),

which is accompanied by train-whistling woodwinds. Metaphorical air-horns and whistles, "blown" by various members of the orchestra, continue as the piece progresses. In spite of the Ellington band's constant continent-traversing rail travel over the years, this train, Ellington tells us, is a local "with an upright engine that was never on schedule, and never made stops at any place you ever heard about." It is a "grunting, groaning, and jerking" train whose fireman "played tunes on the whistle" (Ellington 1973, 184). In their imaginative renderings, the musicians describe their own perceptions of aspects of this local transport, including the hypnotic, rocking, rolling rhythms of its wheels and the piercing intensity of its whistles, bells, and horns. Somehow, the listener is lured into imagining the conductor walking the aisles, taking tickets, and talking with passengers. The music seduces one to picture stops along the way, with the activities and discussions of passengers and conductors continuing through it all. This music tells the story of the "Happy-Go-Lucky Local," how the musicians feel about it, and all that it encounters along its way. And the double meanings of the blues are "in the notes" of a twelve-bar structure in which Ellington's local says much more than Bailey's interstate steamers, for Ellington was much more conversant with trains and all their meanings and functions than was Bailey, who apparently was primarily an observer. In its journey, the double meanings contained in the various sound gestures of the piece unfold, as in trumpeter Cootie Williams's high whistles that say "Ohh yeahhh" and "yeahh!" as he makes the sexual metaphor.[9] The "Happy-Go-Lucky Local" is a Signifyin(g) symbol, filled with the metaphors of local travel. Ellington and his sidemen employ semantic metaphor to suggest what a rider might experience in a local commuter train and to symbolize the train as a metaphor for sex, as does Bukka White when he sings, "This

9. Recall that Ellington (1973) regarded his music as "*au naturel*, close to the primitive, where people send messages in what they play, calling somebody or making facts and emotions known. Painting a picture, or having a story to go with what you were going to play, was of vital importance in those days" (47). Although "Happy-Go-Lucky Local" was recorded in the 1940s, this outlook is evident in the entire output of Ellington and his sidemen.

train I ride : it don't burn no coal." Black music frequently makes use of sexual metaphor, since it is so closely related to dance, which is related to the primal procreative impulse.

In Wendell Logan's *Runagate Runagate* (1989), a setting of a collage poem by Robert Hayden,[10] Harriet Tubman is Esu revisited, a trickster figure who is at once benevolent and malevolent, loyal and duplicitous, one who places the second terms of these oppositions at the service of the first: malevolence and duplicity undermine slave holders for the purpose of the benevolent liberation of Tubman's fellow blacks. Following a brief and vigorous introduction, Logan begins his musical description with musical commentary on the text of the spiritual "Many Thousands Go" and then treats the escape of a runagate through the swamps of the South, bound for freedom as he journeys "from can't to can." At the point in the score where the author's protagonist notices "many thousands crossing over," Logan Signifies on the movement of the riding train and its whistle with the following troping configuration: the straight eighth-note figure ♫♫♪ ♫♫♪ represents the chugging of the engine, and the ♪. ♪. figure the blowing of the whistle (Example 2). The train increases its speed, then slows, stops.

Later, the runagate encounters Tubman, who seductively invites him,

> Come-ride, my-train
> Come-ride, my-train
> Come-ride, my-y train.

The singer's presentation of "Oh that train, ghost story train through swamp and savanna, movering over the trestles," and so forth, is accompanied by a train-like rhythm on the muffled drum, over which the cello states an ostinato in virtual canon, at the octave, with the tenor. Then Tubman again invites the runagate to "Come ride-a my train / Come ride-a my train," this time using the post-intensifier "-a" to enhance her bid. Finally, the runagate's insistence that he "mean[s] to be free" is accompanied by the rhythms that attended the train's first appearance (Example 2); this rhythm gains in intensity as it is increasingly elaborated on by the violin and the piano. A section marked "Majestic" features another virtual canon on "Oh that train." The work ends with a "called" "Mean to be free."

With numerous fall-offs, with falling, rising, and pendular thirds at melodic cadence points, with an appropriate musical treatment of the spiritual text "before I'll be a slave, I'll be buried in my grave," with Tubman's "wanted" status

---

10. A runaway slave was known colloquially as a "runagate." Hayden's poem "Runagate, Runagate" is anthologized in his *Angle of Ascent* (1975). Logan's musical setting of the work, as discussed here, has been recorded on the audiotape *The Black Music Repertory Ensemble in Concert* (1992).

EXAMPLE 2. Wendell Logan, *Runagate Runagate*, excerpt.

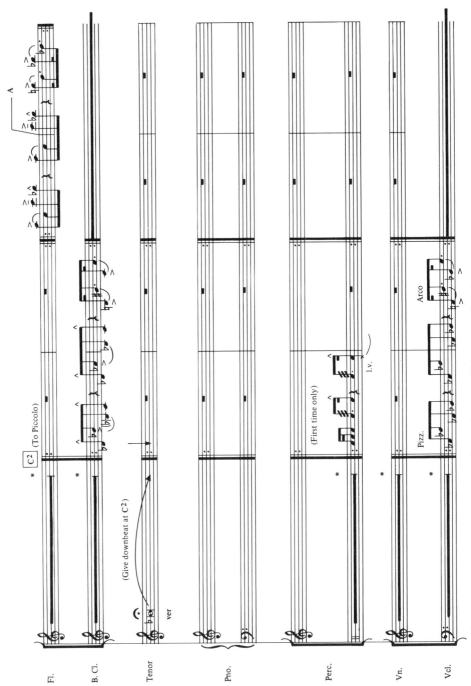

* All players stop wherever they are and begin C² at singer's downbeat (if there is no conductor).

announced in the manner of a call, and with various Signifyin(g) textual events set in the manner of the black street crier, Logan effectively "paints" Hayden's text in the manner of European-derived practice. The singer's rendition of Tubman's invitation to the runagate to "come ride my train," recited in pairs of rising minor thirds in the African-American manner and marked "Soulful" in the score, is seductive. Logan's Signifyin(g) on the "riding" train metaphor of the Underground Railroad has been set up for him in Hayden's poetic rendering of the narrative of the escaping slave—the runagate—and by "conductor" Harriet Tubman's invitation for the runagate to come ride her train. Logan's work portrays a collision of two sets of conflicting rituals: that of the auction block and the hanging tree, on the one hand, and, on the other, that of the steal-away and the escape to freedom. Tubman is a symbolic mediator who, Esu-like, brings the latter set to ascendance.

These tropes of the riding train and of the chariot are fraught with metaphor and symbol. Logan, for example, uses the drum—symbol of "primordial sound, and . . . vehicle for the word, for tradition, and for magic" (Cirlot 1971, 89)—as a mythic communication channel, referring listeners to a long-ago cultural milieu in which ancient traditions were made and perpetuated and in which early political and social struggles were waged. All the performances and works discussed here reflect the emotional and visceral power of music that results from performers' and composers' adaptation of their musical resources, techniques, and materials to the fictive stuff of myth and legend.

Throughout the history of black music in the United States, it has been through the repetition and revision of texts, through the interplay of black language and black music in a long chain of Signifyin(g) tropes, that African-American peasants became and continue to be poets in a land that initially denied them the right to be called artists of any stripe. But poets they have become, as makers of the spirituals and the blues, as creators of R&B and rock 'n' roll, and as composers of works for the concert hall. It is clear from the nature of their texts and their tunes that the makers of this music—the repeaters and revisers of the musical derivatives of the ring—have privileged and honored the spirit of Esu as, for example, that spirit is personified in the redoubtable Harriet Tubman, who bid many thousands to come ride her train.

CHAPTER **10**

The Object of Call–Response:
The Signifyin(g) Symbol

Watch the chameleon: it treads ever so carefully, and it can make itself hard to see.
South African proverb

Criticism is the endeavour to find, to know, to love, to recommend, not only the best, but all the good, that has been known and thought and written in the world.
George Saintsbury

A critic advises
not to write on controversial subjects
like freedom or murder,
but to treat universal themes
and timeless symbols
like the white unicorn.

A white unicorn?
Dudley Randall

Human existence comprises the interaction of individuals and groups with one another and with their environment—individuals associating, cooperating, and differing, interacting with nature, building and gathering, and celebrating human and supernatural events. It is men, women, and children at leisure, at play, and at work—striving, achieving, thinking, longing, desiring, and creating. In these activities, we experience the ebb and flow of life in complex manifestations of tension and repose, such as imbalance and adjustment, opposition and accommodation, aspiration and hope, failure and achievement. As an artistic analogue of the human struggle–fulfillment pattern, music transforms these experiences into symbolic form.[1] Reflecting the struggle–fulfillment model, music communicates values associated with the remembrances, anticipations, and interpretations of ordinary living. These expressions, in turn, can take on the qualities of the comic, the sublime, the grotesque, the poetic—all realized in the musical symbol, which gives delight and evokes wonder and awe.

Our responses to music are based on our reactions to the artistic embodiments of struggle and fulfillment. Art organizes and idealizes life, which, in reality, is often unharmonious and capricious. While evidence of organized energies abounds in day-to-day existence, the energies of art are "cumulating and conserving": they idealize experiences whole, complete, in order to effect the ideal balance of relations that constitutes the work of art. In musical works and performances, control is exercised over contrived events, relationships, refinements, and idealizations.[2]

African-American musics, from the folk cries, calls, and hollers of slave life to the concert-hall works of Call–Response, are such expressions— struggle–fulfillment in microcosm. For black Americans, the interactions of human living have been manifest most particularly in slaves working, suffering, planning, and making, and in freemen and -women exploring, creating, protesting, and undergoing innumerable acts of adjustment. Transplanted Africans, in spite of their trials in a new and hostile land, took the musical fruits of their legacy and merged them with European vernacular forms, spiritualizing their burden, forging a music peculiarly their own, and triggering a process and an aesthetic that would continue to the present and beyond. Through the energizing and renewing magic of myth and ritual, there emerged from the volatile cauldron of Call–Response a music charged with meanings centuries old—meanings to which the initiated, the knowledgeable, and the culturally sensitive responded in heightened communication.

African-American music has always mirrored a wide range of struggles and fulfillments: the slaves' reflections on the remembered splendor of the African heritage; the sufferings of African Americans in the more than two hundred years of American slavery; the hope engendered by the possibilities of the Underground Railroad and the freedom rhetoric of black abolitionists; the vicissitudes and short-lived possibilities of Reconstruction; the strivings and accomplishments of black artists, scholars, athletes, and soldiers; and the coping

---

1. The framework for this discussion is my interpretation of Dewey's ([1934] 1963) aesthetics, as presented in Floyd (1978).

2. For Dewey ([1934] 1963, 35–40), the term "work," as he applies it to art objects, implies actual work done by the listener in perceiving the constructs of the art object: the object itself becomes a *work* only when the listener has actively engaged in its perception. The relationship is a dialogical one in which object and spectator merge in what Dewey calls "*an* experience."

experiences of contemporary black city dwellers and suburbanites. All these experiences reflect the gropings, failings, and inhibitions, the successes and pleasures, regressings and advancings of the black experience.

Just as African-American life is varied and complex, so is its musical corpus, which reflects, in both the variety of its genres and the range of its use and expression the wide sweep of actions and experiences of black people in the United States. Moreover, because the fund of musical materials of a given culture contains constructions and devices peculiar to that culture, and because this fund of materials reflects the religious, social, and artistic values of that culture, the practices and character of the music of one culture will differ in significant ways from those of another. Thus early African-American music is easily differentiated from European and European-derived music by the distinguishing continuity that links all its genres in a distinctive world of sound.

In their explorations, affirmations, and celebrations, black musicians have been concerned primarily with the improvisation of new "texts" or with portions and elements of old texts—in the latter case embellishing existing melodies with elisions, neutral thirds, blue notes, mordents, shakes, smears, call-and-response figures, and other gestures and processes of Call–Response. Collectively, the process is truly communal and cooperative, as is evident in Ornette Coleman's *Free Jazz* (1960) and other works of the contemporary jazz movement, as players react to and "play off of" one another's melodic and rhythmic creations and elaborations. African-American improvisatory experience is qualitatively different from the fabricating process of prior composition and from the conductor-led precision of European and European-derived orchestral playing. So the proper understanding and experiencing of improvised music requires that it be understood as a process in which "'good' tunes, 'good' arrangements, and so on, are only materials on which a good *performance* can be built, and a good performance is one in which performers and listeners can together explore, affirm and celebrate their culture" (Small 1987, 416). Improvisation seldom yields a distilled and carefully honed product since the process is a kind of "thinking aloud." But improvising musicians gladly take the risks that come with spontaneity as they strive for previously unrealized musical and technical heights. They accept the failures that come inevitably as a part of the process. In improvised music, high ensemble precision may be sacrificed for individuality within the aggregate, with performers and listeners alike tacitly agreeing that imprecision (in attack, pitch, and even ensemble) sometimes has its own value.

The improvisations of mature jazz players are inextricably bound up with their distinctive and inimitable sounds, with their particular note choices, with their special ways of phrasing, and with their musical "signatures." As Berendt (1982) has observed, "What was once created by improvising is linked to the man who created it. It cannot be separated from him, notated, and given to a second or third musician to play. If this happens, it loses its character, and nothing remains but the naked formula of notes" (123). For this reason, the nature and authority of the semantic value of Call–Response are keys to the interpretation of improvised black music. In its unfolding, music progresses by way of "unconventionalized, unverbalized freedom of thought," based on a "wealth of wordless knowledge" (Langer 1979, 243, 244) that resides in the imagination of composer and performer. In other words, the musical symbol "speaks" through an auditory, symbolic semantic, through the "telling effect" of wordless rhetoric that, in Albert Murray's (1973, 86) lexicon, "asserts, alleges, quests, requests, and implies," mocks, groans, concurs, and signifies misgivings and suspicions, evoking these and all the other insinuating qualities of Signifyin(g).

When attending to music, listeners consciously or unconsciously perceive its tension–repose relationships—the rhythmic, tonal, textural, harmonic, and timbral consonances and dissonances, figures and events, individually and in combination, that constitute the musical work or performance. Aesthetic communication takes place when resonant contact is made between listeners' social, cultural, and psychological histories, on the one hand, and, on the other, the struggle–fulfillment configurations idealized in the music. As I have noted before, the most complete musico-aesthetic experience requires that listeners possess the knowledge, perceptual skills, emotional histories, and cultural perspectives appropriate to the various genres. In this regard, Dewey ([1934] 1963), in discussing the importance of "motor preparation" for critics, pointed out that by directing perception "along channels prepared in advance," they will be in a position appropriately to interact with particular works, for "to know what to look for and how to [hear] it is an affair of readiness on the part of the motor equipment" (97, 98). This "motor equipment" must resonate with knowledge about the culture and, in the case of African-American music, with the processes of Call–Response. Those who do not possess this readiness will fail as critics. When attending to a blues song, for example, listeners who hear the bent notes, blue notes, coarse vocal delivery, moans, and grunts of the genre as shameful relics of the American past obviously will not respond positively to the music. Similarly, listeners who hear the comparatively suave, sophisticated, and disciplined expressions of a Ulysses Kay or George Walker orchestral or piano work as "dry," "scientific," or "unemotional" do not appreciate the aesthetic values of European-derived musical expression. Such dissonance and distance in culture and status inhibit—indeed, prohibit—aesthetic resonance.

In black music, the motor equipment of which Dewey wrote is triggered by the tropes of Call–Response. Usually appreciated for their own sake, these

229

tropes are only the tip of the proverbial iceberg. Beneath the surface on which they play is the realm of the unconscious, where the cultural memory functions and from which comes the internalized and remembered cultural perspective that gives deeper meaning to works and performances of music.[3] Put another way, the execution of Call–Response tropes opens the symbolic field, where reside the long-standing, sublimated conflicts, taboos, and myths of personal and group emotional experience and our relationships to them. On this level—the symbolic field—reside the musical instincts and intuitions that drive the creative impulse, and it is from this level that we interpret the appropriateness and effectiveness of the works and performances of Call–Response. The recall of these cultural meanings—the subliminal,[4] inarticulate, and implicit perceptions and relationships that interact with and illuminate the cognitive musical events in works and performances of music—is triggered by the tropings of Call–Response.

This symbolic realm is also the source of Nommo, that singular emotional tone that defines black cultural behavior. Nommo embraces what Johnson and Chernoff (1991, 56) call "musical sensibility" and what Richards (1980, 3) refers to as "ethos." Paul Carter Harrison (1972) provides a striking example of the operation of this Nommo force, quoting from Lonnie Elder's *Ceremonies in Dark Old Men*:

> The chain gang they put us on was a chain gang and a half. . . . I would do it like this! I would hit the rock and the hammer would bounce—bounce so hard it would take my hand up in the air with it—but I'd grab it with my left hand and bring it down like this: Hunh! (Carried away by the rhythm of his story, he starts twisting his body to the swing of it.) It would get so good to me, I'd say hunh! Yeah! Hunh! I'd say OoooooooooOweeeee! I'm wide open now. (Swinging and twisting.) Yeah, baby, I say Hunh! Sooner or later that rock would crack. (42)

Harrison refers to this description as containing "Nommo-inspired gesture and sound that gives validity to the event" (42). The event, if the description of it is true, is certainly culturally authentic; and if, on the contrary, the story is a

3. From the perspective of the Signifyin(g) symbol, the felt relationships between the cognitive object and the symbolic content of the cultural memory confirm that this "deep meaning" exists. I give wide berth to the concept of meaning as, for example, "something that is signified; sense" (*American Heritage Electronic Dictionary* 1989). Those of us who accept the possibility that meaning can exist on the noncognitive level—or *between* the cognitive and noncognitive levels, as I believe this definition recognizes—can feel comfortable with the view that such deep meaning exists. From the viewpoint of this discussion, the concept of deep meaning may be dismissed only if the concept of cultural memory is rejected.

4. See also and compare Kivy's discussion of "subliminal knowing" in *Osmin's Rage* (1988), where he defines it as "the kind of awareness that the musical baptism of simple immersion in a culture produces" and posits it as "a necessary condition for musical appreciation in any musical culture whatever" (179). Kivy's "subliminal knowing" recalls Sidney Bechet's elaboration of Omar's song, the singing of the cultural memory that informs all African-American music.

put-on, it is a marvelous example of *Signifyin(g)*. Nommo becomes conscious as *spirit,* what Harrison calls "the spirit of black consciousness"; and this spirit is religious—religious, that is, in the way Africans experience religion: un-compartmentalized, all-pervasive. And this is why the blues singers, in their secular spirituality, sing "Lawdy Lord" and call on "God" as they trope the vagaries and vicissitudes, commonalities and potentials, of life. For the blues musician in performance, God is but a metaphor—a symbol of the generosity, sustenance, abundance, privations, insufficiencies, caprice, and authority of nature. Thus completing the cycle of cultural creativity, the musical ritual stimulates African and African-American cultural memory and keeps listeners in close touch with the sources and forces of black musical prowess. The music that results from all of this is also a metaphor, a symbol of the African and African-American ritual that made possible its creation. In this symbolic field reside Esu, the critic's muse, and the Signifying Monkey, master of discourse; and here resides also the enchantment of the circle, which signifies rebirth, the renewal cycle.

In the cultural memory of African Americans, *life* is cyclic, as is time, as is their music—and all these elements symbolize the ring and contradict linear progression.[5] The figures and events of African-American music making connect the individual and the group to the realm of the cultural memory, to the realm of spirit and myth. And it is myth that privileges the figures and metaphors that validate the blues musicians' music making and their place in the culture. It's all a circle. In another context, in which he details Ernst Cassirer's description of myth, C. H. Knoblauch (1992), citing comments from several of Cassirer's writings, says:

> Myth is an account of life, though one unbounded by the conventions of discursive logic; it is an enactment of the human condition, of the ways in which human beings are situated in the world. The account is dramatic rather than theoretical, grounded in unselfconscious belief rather than skepticism, and formed from perceptions that are always "impregnated with . . . emotional qualities." What is depicted is "a world of actions, of forces, of conflicting powers," in which objects are always "benignant or malignant, friendly or inimical, familiar or uncanny, alluring and fascinating or repellent and threatening." In myth, dreams and desires become projected as reality. . . . The mythic imagination focuses on the "sensible present," the immediate, palpable experience of nature. (224)

5. Consider, for example, the tension between the forward movement of a New Orleans brass band and the circling motions of the individual and small groups of its second line. Consider also a musical performance such as the Supremes' "Where Did Our Love Go," in which a cyclic, eight-measure harmonic pattern underlies a melody that turns on itself, also every eight measures, over and over again. (Only the requisite R&B tenor saxophone solo provides melodic contrast in this performance.)

This mythic imagination is invoked by the bluesman, by the singer of spirituals, and by the gospel diva in their Signifyin(g) revisions.

Aesthetic deliberation about African-American music requires a perceptual and conceptual shift from the idea of music as an object to music as an event, from music as written—as a frozen, sonic ideal—to music as making, or, as Christopher Small (1987, 69) puts it, from music to *musicking*. Such a shift, in turn, mandates recognition of the viability and validity of the community from which the music springs. Although in European-derived concert-hall culture the song and its maker are the most revered, in African-American musical culture it is the singer—the one who not only sings but also modifies the song. This valuing of perpetual creation is reflected in the heavy emphasis on embellishment and improvisation in African-American–music making, particularly in the blues, jazz, and gospel genres. Risk taking in performance is common, and it, too, is highly valued. Such adventure is sometimes individual, as in the case of the lone blues singer with acoustic guitar or of the jazz player, reaching for pitches that lie outside the instrument's normal range and striving to create and perfect new figurations, runs, and gestures. Sometimes the adventure is communal, as in solo–congregation gospel music or the collective improvisations of New Orleans or free-jazz players, the performers accompanying their Call–Response tropings with physical gestures that define and support their musical eloquence. In the nineteenth century, the immediate experiencing and use of calls, cries, and hollers, game and social songs, spirituals and dance music were the chief sources of their value. That is, the functional efficacy of the music, whether in work, play, or ritual, was of primary concern. But the primary functional efficacy of African-American music should not obscure its essential terminal (aesthetic) value, for in its elaboration, it has also acquired a contemplative value that has increased as the music's instrumental worth has receded, as with jazz, whose value as dance music was superseded in the 1940s by that of R&B.

Essentially and most fundamentally, the African-American musical experience is largely self-criticizing and self-validating.[6] As such experiences unfold, for example, listeners show approval, disapproval, or puzzlement with vocal and physical responses to, and interaction with, events as they occur. African Americans serve critical notice on inferior music making either by withholding their participation or, as in New York's tough Apollo Theater in the 1940s

---

6. I distinguish operationally between "African-American music" and "black music." *African-American music* emanates directly from the black experience in America, descended from the calls, cries, hollers, spirituals, ragtime, and blues of the slavery and post-slavery periods; it includes jazz, R&B, black gospel, and all the forms to which these genres have given birth. *Black music,* on the contrary, is any music composed or performed by people of African descent, including African-American music, African music, and European and European-derived concert-hall music by black composers. I do not claim that these classifications are satisfactory for everyone, only that they work for my purposes in making the distinctions basic to this discussion.

and 1950s, by addressing their criticism directly to the performers on stage. The culturally attuned are aware when the notes and the rhythms do not fit the context and when the idiomatic orientation is wrong; they know when an act is a Signifyin(g) one, when it is effective, and when it is not. Positive responses range from the more or less vigorous comments and declamations of "Oh yeah," "Cook," "Preach," "Uhn-huhn," and other such exhortings, to the approving nods, shakes of the head, finger snappings, shoulder hitchings, and hip switchings of a knowledgeable and sensitive audience, thus validating the cultural and aesthetic value of Signifyin(g) acts. Their absence generally represents the withholding of approval, revealing "confusion, annoyance, boredom, and . . . indifference" (Murray 1973, 87).

The key to the effective criticism of black music lies in our understanding of its tropings and in our recognition that such tropings are themselves critical acts—expressions of approval and disapproval, validation and invalidation, of past and present tropings and events. In improvised music, such troping is akin to editing, in which the restructuring, shortening, lengthening, and deleting of ideas play an important role; and it is also akin, in its semantic value, to speaking, in which the inflection defines the signification. In the improvising act, such Signifyin(g) revision can make a poor piece a better one (as Louis Armstrong's tropings did for a few banal Tin Pan Alley and Broadway show tunes). Good critics of black music come to grips with the Signifyin(g) act, which, for me at least, is the ultimate artistic manifestation of the human play instinct, a magnificent substantiation of the *playing of* instruments and voices, *playing with* musical ideas, feelings, and emotions, and *playing on* the content of the cultural memory. "Play" is the essence of Call–Response.

This holds true for concert-hall music by African-Americans, some post-1945 jazz, and most of contemporary jazz, all of which have as their purpose the generation or evocation of a musical experience.[7] Set apart from the essential requirements of ordinary living, this music is usually experienced for its own sake, requiring that listeners, in order fully to appreciate its fruits, ob-

7. Because both concert-hall music and jazz have terminal value, some aficionados and musicians refer to jazz as "America's classical music" (see, for example, Gleason 1975, xviii; Scarupa 1986, 35; Taylor 1983, 3, 8, 25). The assignment of this label to jazz is somewhat ironic, since the treatment of jazz by most "classical" musicians has, for the most part, been either hostile or misguided—the latter being more detrimental to our understanding of it than the former. The hostility, in its most harsh display, has taken the form of denigration and exclusion and, in its milder manifestation, has meant the relegation of the genre to the margins of society and of the academy. The misguidedness has also taken two basic forms. In one, jazz performances emphasize the means of presentation (technique) rather than the ideas presented and the way they are mediated (substance). In the other, perceptions of jazz likewise value technique over substance, missing the essential musical and aesthetic point. What is lacking in the first instance is authentic expression, and, in the second, authentic perception. In both instances, the response is inappropriate to the struggle–fulfillment patterns that are the foundation of the music. In the first case, there is no trigger for the cultural memory; in the second, the response, lacking cultural memory, is misplaced.

serve and inquire into the refinements, intensifications, and artificial renderings of struggle–fulfillment. This music should be judged on the extent to
which its materials and their configurations reflect these patterns and values
of ordinary living—on how well, in other words, musical performances and
works function *strictly* as symbols.

For the critic as educator, responsible for mediating between the musical
experience and its potential audience, criticism is an act of discovering, distinguishing, and explaining cultural and musical value in works of music by
identifying the elements that captivate attention and deepen perception—those
elements to which knowers within and without the culture commonly or potentially, consciously or unconsciously, respond. The task of the critic as educator is to explain how well (or, indeed, whether) composers and performers succeed in this capturing and mediating process—that is, to explain
and judge the drama of the progression, juxtaposition, and significance/
Significance of musical events and ideas.

The New Criticism of the 1940s and 1950s isolated the work of art in a formal context that precluded cultural considerations (except those related to the
New Criticism's emphasis on formal complexity). It considered social and ideological concerns and philosophical opinions (other than its own) to be irrelevant to aesthetic evaluation. This attitude is still current in some quarters.
But if by effective music criticism we mean discourse about our understanding of works and performances of music, approaches based on such inquiry
will not accomplish that goal, for in its isolation, the doctrine misses the point
of, and denies its followers the fruits of, the social and aesthetic resonance of
musical and cultural metaphor. The valid and effective criticism of black music must take into account all aspects of the music, including their metaphoric
and culturally specific properties. In this regard, Barbara Herrnstein Smith's
(1990) idea of "pre-evaluation" is useful. Speaking about the evaluation of literary works, she stresses the importance of *classification,* the noticing of events
that, she says, are "very significant in shaping our experiences of their value,
often foregrounding certain of their possible effects" (182). In such pre-
evaluation as applied to music, apparently, listeners can recognize the tacit assumptions on which works and performances are based and mold their criteria accordingly: "Our interpretations . . . and our experience . . . [of a work's]
value are to some extent mutually dependent" (185).

Smith's formulation recalls Dewey's "motor preparation," which for African-
American music is the functional manifestation of the funded musical meanings and cultural values that inform and underlie works and performances.
Sound musical judgments depend on such preparation, for in Dewey's ([1934]
1963) words, "the question of the relation that exists between direct sensuous matter [musical relations, or musical figures and events] and that which
is incorporated with it because of prior experiences [read "accumulated funded

meanings" or "cultural memory"] goes to the heart of the expression of an object [musical composition, or performance]" (99). In other words, for the evaluation of black music, critics must prepare themselves to experience and appreciate the relations that exist between their fund of emotional meanings and the configurations in the music, which suggests also that they must be familiar with the broad range of genres and performance styles and their associated myths and rituals. For black music, among the properties to be noticed during pre-evaluation are (1) the structure of the music's presentation; (2) the presence or absence of Call–Response tropings, either singly or as mascon structures;[8] and (3) the way the perceptions in points 1 and 2 relate to each other (as Baraka [1991] says, "form and content are expressions of one another" [105]).

This task of evaluating black music is not a small one. In executing it, the critic must be able to recognize, relate to, and explain qualities and properties as disparate as the dynamic sensuousness of gospel tropings, the adroitly rendered off-center rhythms of a bebop figuration, the sublime solitude of a wordless blues song, and the complementary oppositions of African- and European-derived musical processes and events. This last quality, or property, has important implications, because music making in developed and developing societies is dialogical. And the good critic will not confuse genuine, dialogical music making with the musical dilutions that pass for it. The former preserves the expressive values of both terms of a fusion; the latter dilutes or suppresses the expressive properties of one term in favor of those of the other. In my opinion, examples of genuine fusion are William Grant Still's *Afro-American Symphony,* T. J. Anderson's *Variations on a Theme by M. B. Tolson,* Olly Wilson's *Of Visions and Truth,* Morton Gould's *Spirituals for Orchestra,* George Gershwin's *Porgy and Bess,* and Milton Babbitt's *All Set* (1957).[9] Among the dilutions are Stravinsky's *Ragtime for Eleven Instruments* and Copland's "Dance" from *Music for the Theater* (Reisser 1982, 280–286). With regard to performance and perception, Peter Rabinowitz (1991) refers to "attributive screens," which, for example, "encourage listeners to hear the music as refined, rather than as earthy and sensual" (170). In referring to the dilutions of Scott Joplin's music that emerged during the ragtime revival of the 1970s, he contends that "these attributive screens place Joplin in the context

8. Henderson (1973, 44) defines "mascon structures" as "a massive concentration of Black experiential energy" that "powerfully affects the meaning" of black art; he points out that *saturation* of works with mascon structures determines the "*depth* and *quality*" that a given work may evoke. For music, I interpret this "massive concentration of experiential energy" as a confluence of Call–Response tropes. In this interpretation, saturation is related to Signifyin(g)—the former a presence, the latter a process. Both are driven by Nommo, which also can saturate the Signifyin(g) symbol.

9. Appropriately, Babbit's *All Set* and Anderson's *Variations on a Theme by M. B. Tolson* are on the same recording, making comparison convenient.

235

of refined concert music rather than brash entertainment, music for listening rather than for background or dancing."[10] In other words, musical and cultural value has been *assigned,* and this assigned value has replaced the initial, context-based value on which rests the expressive properties of the original. Good critics will be aware of such experiential transformations and will comment on them appropriately.

Half-way through the first draft of this book, I encountered Lawrence Kramer's *Music as Cultural Practice, 1800–1900* (1990), which relates literary theory to European musical products of the nineteenth century and seeks parallels between music and poetic texts. Kramer speaks of empowering the interpretive process by opening "hermeneutic windows" through which musical interpretation can view in the music what he calls, variously, "textual inclusions," "citational inclusions," and "structural tropes" (structured structures). Remarkably Gates-like, Kramer's hermeneutic relies on tropes and troping, and his concept of "other-voicedness" is similar to Gates's "double-voiced." Kramer's focus is on musical processes such as "expressive doubling"—"a form of repetition in which alternative versions of the same pattern define a cardinal difference in perspective"—and "reversal"—"a series of dynamic oppositions that lead to reversals of meaning or value" (73; compare Gates 1984: "tropological revision" and "Signifyin(g) revision").

Mark Evan Bonds's (1991) study of musical form contributes yet another perspective from the European-derived side of the equation and focuses on the musical work as orational metaphor, as "wordless rhetoric." This rhetorical concept requires attention to the *manner* in which things happen; it focuses on the musical ideas and internal unity of a work of music and on "the process by which individual units [are] concatenated into a whole" (93). The emphasis here is on themes, ideas, and events as subjects of musical discourse. Since neither Gates's theory nor my interpretation of it addresses large-scale musical form, the oratorical metaphor seems to be a perfect large-scale concept on which we might thread our ideas about musical figures and tropes. Gates's figures and tropes also point to the musical work as performance or oration, as rhetorical, symbolic object; and the orational metaphor can provide a formal context that can bring large-scale structural meaning to the small-scale structures of Call–Response and contribute a context for the larger and broader "telling effects" of black music. Remember also Joe Henderson's comment: "You use semicolons, hyphens, paragraphs, parentheses, stuff like this. I'm thinking like this when I'm playing. I'm having a conversation with *somebody*" (quoted in Murphy 1990, 15).

10. Although late in life Joplin tended to present ragtime as concert music, it is a mistake to represent all of his music as refined in this manner.

I would like to propose an additional orational metaphor: the "rhetorical turn." Literati speak of "turns of phrase" and contemporary linguists speak of "linguistic turns," both of which serve rhetorical functions in the verbal arts (Nelson, Megill, and McCloskey 1987; Rorty 1967). To my way of thinking, such turns are Signifyin(g) figures.

Peter Kivy, in "The Corded Shell" (1989), develops a theory of expression, a cognitive formulation in which expressiveness takes two forms:

1. On the *contour* model, listeners "perceive some similarity between the features of the music and the features of human behavior that characteristically accompany human emotions as their expressions" (149).

2. On the *convention* model, listeners make the traditional associations between specific musical qualities of a work with the extramusical ideas they typically represent.

Included among what Kivy calls "human expressors" are "speech, utterance, gesture, bodily movement, and so on" (58), and since we hear music as analogous to these—in other words, as emotional icons resembling vocal, gestural, and postural expressions—"we must hear an aural pattern as a vehicle of such [an] expression . . . before we can hear its expressiveness" (59).

The references to utterance, gesture, and bodily movement recall several points of convergence among the ideas of Kivy, Gates, and the others I have cited. For example, it seems that the relationship Kivy recognizes between gesture and bodily movement, on the one hand, and expressiveness, on the other, is closely related to Gates's (1988, 59) insistence on the *materiality* of the signifier. Another of Kivy's works, his enlightening *Sound and Semblance: Reflections on Musical Representation* (1984), treats musical pictures and musical representations. *Pictures* are readily recognizable without verbal aids and have an "unaided recognizability" (24). By way of explanation, Kivy points to Arthur Honegger's *Pacific 231,* the cuckoo in Beethoven's Sixth Symphony, and Alexander Mosolov's *The Iron Foundry,* each of which presents, in sound, pictures of what it purports to depict. *Representations* are those illustrations that, unlike pictures, require verbal aids, being unrecognizable without them (22), such as, I assume, battles, storms, and love scenes. Kivy also treats in this work *cross-modal associations,* which occur when musical sounds are described with "non-musical non-sound" words, such as "'bright,' 'sour,' 'soft, [and] sharp'"; adjectives such as "sad, cheerful, melancholy, [and] tender"; and "structural adjectives" that allow us to speak of "long, or sustained notes, jagged rhythms, parallel motion, imitation, one line following another, rising and falling figures, harmony, and so on" (62–63). Cross-modal associations, migrating across perceptual boundaries, effect semantic change, "metaphoric transfer" (63), **237** since they are being used literally in one perceptual mode and figuratively in another; for example, we say that lines "move" and refer to instrumental lines as "voices," potentially adding to the representational matrix "the element of pun" (83).

In Kivy's *Music Alone* (1990), his premise is that "there is pure, nonreferential music and a pure musical experience of it," that "music alone is about nothing at all" (194). Although he limits his premise to the music of the western European musical tradition, he invites readers to determine their own limits in applying the concept. An important feature of *Music Alone* is Kivy's contention that describing a piece of music with "music-theoretical" terms does not and will not thoroughly describe all its "musically significant features"; thus it is essential that we talk about music with terms that describe emotive and other phenomenological properties.

For the cognitivist Kivy, a work of music alone is a quasi-syntactical structure that can be understood in strictly musical terms. It carries no extramusical content and requires no extramusical reference to be experienced or understood. But it *does* have emotional significance, in that it contains properties that are *expressive of* emotions. Rejecting John Dewey's ([1934] 1963) so-called conflict theory of emotion and Leonard Meyer's (1954) elaboration of it, Kivy (1990) denies music "meaning" because it has no actual semantics, for "syntax without semantics must defeat linguistic interpretation" (9). In other words, we cannot say what music means; and to say that it means itself is nonsensical.

In preceding chapters, I have occasionally referred to works of music as Signifyin(g) symbols. The symbol, a subclass of sign, carries indirect, analogical meaning. Thus that which is represented and the object of that representation are related *only because* the listener determines that the relationship exists (Parmentier 1985, 30). Symbolism, therefore, is the result of an "analogy between the visible and the invisible world," a "revelation of the inscrutable" (Cirlot 1971, xx, xxx). Symbolic relationships, then, are determined by listeners on the basis of analogies perceived between musical compositions or events and whatever metaphysical or other images or ideas they determine those events to represent (Lee 1985, 103).

The symbolic nature of music has been noted and discussed by several scholars, including Suzanne Langer, Gordon Epperson, and, in the context mentioned earlier, Dewey. Of these, I am partial to Dewey's ([1934] 1963) conception, which is evident in the following statements:

> Music complicates and intensifies the process of genial reciprocating antagonisms, suspense and reinforcement, where the various "voices" at once oppose and answer one another. (156)

> Music, for example, gives us the very essence of the dropping down and the exalted rising, the surging and retreating, the acceleration and retardation, the

EXAMPLE 3. **Leslie Adams, "For You There Is No Song," mm. 8–11.**

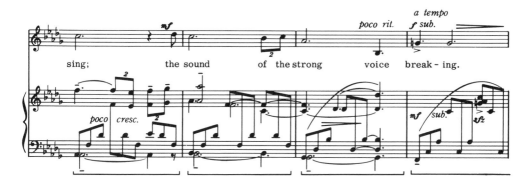

tightening and loosening, the sudden thrusts and the gradual insinuation of things. (208)

[Music] expresses stir, agitation, movement, the particulars and contingencies of existences. (236)[11]

However the symbol is described, in joining together the physical and meta-physical worlds, it "*adds* a new value to an object or an act, without thereby violating its immediate or 'historical' validity" (Cirlot 1971, xiv). Such relationships—reminiscent and impressionistic—are events we intuitively interpret; hence they are related to the cultural memory. They reflect, to borrow Sidney Bechet's term, the "memory behind the music." For symbolism represents, as does the cultural memory, the nonreferential ideas and relationships that members of a culture seem to "know," that feel unequivocally "true."

The use in black music of the representational and symbolic qualities and issues that I have been discussing can be illustrated by noticing their manifestations in the songs and the chamber and orchestral works of African-American composers.[12]

Leslie Adams's "For You There Is No Song" is expressive of soft despair and melancholy bordering on grief. The composer's use of tone painting (what Kivy calls "metaphoric transfer") does not detract from the beauty of his setting; in fact, the setting is enhanced, with the G-natural in measure 11 "breaking" the key center as well as the "strong voice" (Example 3) and at the same

11. If the term "expresses" were changed to "is expressive of," I think Kivy would agree with this formulation, as long as it is *people* doing the stirring. Otherwise, in Kivy's formulation, music would *represent* these qualities.

12. All the following songs are in Patterson (1977) and on the recording *Art Songs by Black American Composers* (1981).

239

EXAMPLE 4. **Leslie Adams, "For You There Is No Song," mm. 24–31.**

time giving contour to the otherwise key-centered melodic line that carries the Edna St. Vincent Millay text. The falling triplets and staggered eighth notes in measures 25 and 26 and measure 30, respectively, signify the dropping of "tears on the page" (Example 4).

John W. Work's "Dancing in the Sun" is a strong setting of a text by Howard Weedun. It has a clear, crisp melody, dance-like accompaniment, and occasional tone painting—the last evinced, for instance, in the "running" metaphor in measure 22, the "whirl" metaphor in measures 25 and 26, and the dance metaphor in measures 27 and 28 as well as 37 and 38 (Example 5). Work's setting of Myrtle Vorst Sheppard's "Soliloquy" also flirts with metaphoric transfer, as the melody climbs to a high G in measures 10 and 11 to signify a mountain's height and "turns" on the staggered triplet in measure 22 to signal a bend in the river as well as a new musical direction, as the harmony modulates from D minor back to the original key of A minor and the opening melody (Example 6).

George Walker's "A Red, Red Rose," a setting of the Robert Burns poem, makes heavy use of major and minor seconds and perfect and augmented

EXAMPLE 5. **John W. Work, "Dancing in the Sun," mm. 21–39.**

EXAMPLE 5. (*continued*)

mat-ter what falls to the rest of the world no mat-ter what's done or un - done

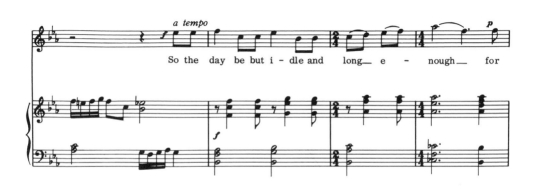

a tempo

So the day be but i - dle and long e - nough for

danc - ing in the sun

For danc - ing in the

242

EXAMPLE 6. **John W. Work, "Soliloquy," mm. 9–23.**

EXAMPLE 6. (*continued*)

fourths. The second section of this dissonant, highly ornamented, three-part song introduces in measure 17 an "other voice," as flatted thirds, fifths, and sevenths are employed (some enharmonically) in a C tonal area (Example 7). This other voice is a blues voice, a dialect voice, one that slightly dislocates itself from what has preceded it and from what quickly follows.

Robert Owens's bittersweet, through-composed setting of Langston Hughes's "Faithful One" (Example 8), with its insistent rhythm and gradual overall rise in pitch, symbolizes progression and gradual elevation and complements a text that denotes action and thought with phrases such as "I go," "She'll let me in," "I'll wander," "comin' back," etc., all underpinned with unflagging, additive rhythm.

EXAMPLE 7. **George Walker, "A Red, Red Rose," mm. 11–17.**

EXAMPLE 8. **Robert Owens, "Faithful One," mm. 1–19.**

EXAMPLE 9. **Hale Smith, "Velvet Shoes," mm. 16–22.**

Hale Smith's setting of Elinor Wiley's "Velvet Shoes," also through-composed, is soft and tranquil even with its comparatively dissonant language. Almost every phrase begins off the beat and includes a prominent use of a falling trichord consisting of a small interval followed by a larger one, as in measure 17 (Example 9).[13] This is vintage Smith, as his commonly used trichord is expressively doubled throughout the song, with each variation of the motive providing a different perspective of it.

Noel DaCosta's *Two Songs for Julie-Ju,* settings of poems by George Houston Bass, is a fount of metaphor and other-voicedness, particularly the second song, which is truly a mulatto text from the standpoint of both the lyric and the music. The first twelve measures of this song contain no ring tropes, but in measure 13 flatted sixths are introduced and, later, thirds, connoting the black voice (Example 10). This black voice continues, in the form of flatted sevenths in measures 18 and 21, moving on to bebop figures, except for a brief return of the "other" voice in measures 36 to 39. The black bebop voice goes on to close the piece (Example 11).

13. This trichord appears in most of Smith's works and recurs in various permutations. Its use is most evident and most powerful in *Innerflections,* but it first appears in his song cycle *The Valley Wind,* from which "Velvet Shoes" is taken. It can also be heard in *Contours, Ritual and Incantations,* and other works.

EXAMPLE 10. **Noel DaCosta, *Two Songs for Julie-Ju,* mm. 13–21.**

Charles Brown's "A Song Without Words" (Example 12) is nonreferential and symbolic; it manifests, without a text, a strong "telling effect." A powerful approximation of human utterance, gesture, and posture, it is Signifyin(g) on the delivery of blues singer Blind Willie Johnson and is an analogue to the human feeling represented in black folk life. The consistently descending phrases, the prevalent pendular thirds, the "worried" notes in the melody, and the required "moaning" delivery all tag this song as a Signifyin(g) symbol. "A Song Without Words" is an interesting formulation, for it is truly a vehicle of Evan Bonds's (1991) intransitive signification, a highly rhetorical cognitive device that portrays the signifier as also the signified; it is a musical oration fraught with African-American semantic value. The accompaniment to the

EXAMPLE 11. **Noel DaCosta,** *Two Songs for Julie-Ju,* **mm. 26–40.**

EXAMPLE 12. **Charles Brown, "A Song Without Words."**

EXAMPLE 13. **Howard Swanson, " A Death Song," mm. 1–10.**

melody is almost, in itself, an "other," European-derived voice, but the un-questionable dominance of the blues melody is overpowering.

"A Death Song," Howard Swanson's setting of the poem by Paul Laurence Dunbar, is the most "black" song in this group, dominated in text and tune by dialect voicings (Baker 1984, 91). Swanson's special and inimitable rhythmic sense has ensured a successful setting of the text in a remarkable marriage of textual and musical interests. Melodically, the flatted thirds and sevenths in the melody are expressive of melancholy and grief (on Kivy's [1989] contour model); the shape of the melody tropes turn-of-the-century black secular song, particularly the blues, as the composed elisions trope the genre (Example 13, mm. 6 and 10). And the structure is also that of a blues, with two-measure statements by the voice followed by two-measure answers by the piano, the two "voices" calling and responding as in a traditional blues song.

All these songs, as analogues to feeling, are symbols; but only some are obviously *Signifyin(g)* symbols, works of Call–Response (for example, Charles Brown, Howard Swanson). In others, the black voice enters only as an *other* voice (for example, George Walker), and still others contain black elements only through the composers' compositional *tendencies* (for example, Hale Smith).[14]

As far as larger forms of black music are concerned, Kramer's (1990) and Bonds's (1991) studies are of particular interest here, because most of the large-scale works discussed in these pages are truly musical orations— generative works that progress without recourse to rules, with figurative sounds serving as the basis for the metaphors through which listeners are expected to follow the thread of the argument.[15] Compositions cited earlier by Ulysses Kay (*Fantasy Variations*), Olly Wilson (*Of Visions and Truth*), Wendell Logan (*Runagate Runagate*), Duke Ellington (*A Tone Parallel to Harlem*), and T. J. Anderson (*Variations on a Theme by M. B. Tolson*), for example, are all orational and generative, and rely on utterance, gesture, and posture to achieve their persuasive proofs, points of reference, predictions, and form. In addition and more specifically, for example, in *Fantasy Variations,* Kay focuses on a rather extreme form of Kramer's expressive doubling, in which the repeated idea reveals more and more of itself as the work unfolds and presents itself fully only at the very end. Wilson, in *Visions,* uses expressive doubling to good effect in each of his five movements. Logan's *Runagate* is an allegory in which Harriet Tubman symbolizes the moral and religious high ground of a drama that involves escaping slaves, their masters, and potential catchers. *A Tone Parallel to Harlem,* Ellington's extended work, reveals his and his sidemen's prowess at expressive doubling and citational inclusion as well as their ability to "paint" "pictures," for *Harlem* is more than a mere picture, fraught as it is also with embedded "representations." Anderson's expressionist *Variations* is fraught with citational inclusions, expressive doublings, pictures, representations, and symbolism.

William Grant Still's *Afro-American Symphony* is significantly unique, as it combines elements of orational rhetoric and conformational structure through the composer's embedding of an original twelve-bar blues in a sonata-allegro format[16] (Kramer's textual inclusion) and employing the blues theme as a

---

14. Among the songs on *Art Songs by Black American Composers* that are not discussed here are William Grant Still's "Grief" and Florence Price's "Soliloquy," two marvelous, highly recommended songs.

15. By combining the ideas of Kramer and Bonds, I do not mean to imply that they would agree with each other's formulations, only that their separate ideas are compatible with my discussion.

16. Such embedding is a tradition in African-American music. Recall that W. C. Handy used the device in his "St. Louis Blues," although this work is obviously not sonata-form. And even before Handy made use of the practice, James Chapman and Leroy Smith embedded a twelve-bar blues in their ragtime piece "One o' Them Things" (1904) (Jasen and Tichenor 1978, 70–71).

EXAMPLE 14. **William Grant Still, *Afro-American Symphony*, "Blues Theme,"** mm. 6–17.

proposition to prove (Example 14). The *Afro-American Symphony,* therefore, is a structured structure (Kramer), concatenated (Bonds), making "correct" the black presence within the larger sonata-allegro structure. The work's four movements are concatenated structures, but the whole is a grand "wordless oration" (Bonds) in which an "ordered succession of thoughts" is presented, moving, delighting, and persuading the listener (Bonds 1991, 53).

These few examples demonstrate, I believe, the compatibility of the theoretical formulations of other scholars with those discussed in previous chapters. Although the ideas of all these scholars differ from one another in sometimes fundamental ways,[17] they also contain many points of agreement and convergence—between, for example, Kramer's expressive doubling and Gates's Signifyin(g) revision; Kramer's "other-voicedness" and Gates's "mulatto texts"; Bonds's "intransitive signification," in which the signifier is the same as the signified, and Gates's Signifyin(g), in which the normal emphasis is switched from the signified to the signifier; Kivy's emphasis on the objectivity of human expression and my emphasis on cultural memory; Kivy's (1990) recognition of bodily human expressors and "behavioral and linguistic routines" (176) and Gates's stressing of the materiality of the signifier; and the symbolic function of Kivy's expressive object and my own insistence on the validity of a Signifyin(g) symbol.

These theories and analytical techniques offer much to the evaluation of black music. But they lack three things that the Call–Response approach provides: (1) a culture-specific means of pre-evaluating works in order to determine which elements are most appropriate to guide perception and interpretation, (2) an explanation of the deep meaning of works and performances of black music, and (3) a means of interpreting relationships between and among

17. Compare Kivy (1984, 29–35) and Tarasti (1979, 27), especially their divergent discussions of Honegger's *Pacific 231.*

musical relations—the music's Signifyin(g) figures—in order to account, the-
oretically, for the call-and-response commentary that takes place between performers and audiences in the black-music experience. These deficiencies confirm my conclusions, already drawn in "Ring Shout!" (Floyd 1991), that a
more culture-specific approach to black music is indispensable to inquiry into
black music, that the use of the black vernacular to examine the formal, à la
Gates, is a productive and revealing approach to musical analysis and interpretation, and that such an approach will reveal black music as a much more
complex and richly textured art than has been made clear by more traditional,
less appropriate modes of inquiry.

As my explorations in "Ring Shout!" and some of the scholarship of Kramer,
Bonds, Kivy, and others have shown, contemporary theories designed for the
analysis of European-derived music are more hospitable to African-American
music than are older European-derived approaches to analysis. Perhaps the efficacy of these new approaches will be even more convincing when they are
applied more thoroughly and in conjunction with the African-American–based
approach developed in these pages.

Robert Nathaniel Dett's *The Chariot Jubilee,* a cantata for chorus, organ, and
vocal soloist—and another manifestation of the "chariot" trope I discussed in
chapter 9—includes, both textually and "citationally" (Kramer), the Negro
spirituals "Swing Low, Sweet Chariot" and "Ride Up in the Chariot." The work
begins with a musical statement of the "coming for to carry me home" phrase
played by the organ, followed by a new and more original statement by the
solo tenor. This is answered, in call-and-response format, by women's voices.
The work unfolds in two sections that correspond to the already stated order
of the spiritual tunes. The first section is in slow and medium tempi, mostly
in chorale style; the second section is faster, more sprightly and fugal, round-
ing off with a wonderful, expressively doubled "Swing Low" theme that is expanded into a comparatively lengthy coda. In the second section, expressive
doubling abounds, and the frequent modulations and key changes give some
events alternating "lifting" and "settling" qualities; metaphoric *posture,* rather
than gesture, is prominent. With these two themes, the work carries a two-
part argument, each theme expressing its distinctive point of view. In the second part, the second tune, "Ride Up in the Chariot," seems persuasive, but
"Swing Low" rallies to surpass it, troping the "chariot" theme and bringing it
around to its point of view. Employing chorale and fugal techniques, the whole
is a mighty, Signifyin(g) revision of the two spirituals in a passionate musical
oration that ends with a stunning troping of the basic character of Handel's
"Hallelujah Chorus." There is mythic quality in this work, but not as much
as one might have expected, given its use of spirituals. It does, however, represent a successful and effective blending of African-American and European-
derived properties: the melodies and the melodic figurations are obviously

255

African-American; the compositional treatment and harmonic complexity, European-derived. The contrasts of lyricism with drama, plaintive yearning with joy, simplicity with complexity, emotional and textural density with spiritual and tonal gravity, and rhetorical turnings with determined linear progressions effectively organize the available sonic energies into a musical oration of hope, quest, and realization, a grand work of Call–Response.

Hale Smith's *Innerflexions* (1991) presents, near its beginning, the composer's signature trichord arrayed in a brilliant, shimmering orchestration. The work unfolds with occasional permutations of the main idea, which consists of the Smith trichord plus an additional note (Example 15). With lyric delicacy, its logic develops cleanly in expressively doubled permutations, which are embraced, as well as penetrated, by splashes of timbral brilliance that caress and support the permutations with smooth, sharp, jagged, and hard-edged articulations. Phrases and events rhetorically turn back on themselves and move in new directions; the listener may easily follow the thread of the musical argument. The work's main idea is woven in and among timbres that contrast and oppose, rather than blend. The dynamic energy increases and decreases in synchronization with the main idea as the latter becomes more or less "argumentative" and forceful. What Smith describes as his "delayed approach" to the beat (Example 16, which also features the trichord), his jazz-voiced chords and phrasings (Example 17), and his clear beat structure all exist in a musical context that is more European-oriented than African-American. *Innerflexions* has an intense spiritual gravity that is stately, somber, and breathtakingly majestic. The main climax comes at approximately seven minutes into the work in a powerful display of brass over a static, "turning" figure in the high strings. The ending of the piece begins with a passage that repeats the work's opening figure (Example 18). Amid a tension realized by both prepared and unprepared dissonances within a basically homophonic texture, there is a lean muscularity that gives mythical grandeur and aesthetic authority to a work in which there are no musical pictures, no musical representations; the piece just delights, persuades, and moves the listener with an ordered succession of utterances, gestures, and postures formed through judicious contrasts of and shifts in delicacy and power, relaxation and vigor, in the organization of sonic energies that constitute this superb musical oration. The Smith trichord triumphs.

Since 1983, T. J. Anderson has been experimenting with a new approach to composition—what he refers to as an "orbiting" procedure in which each performer in an ensemble plays his or her part independently of the others. In these works, each part is notated, but since the various instrumental parts are not vertically related, no score has been produced. The musical relationships in such works are horizontal, with figures and events recurring as the players

EXAMPLE 15. **Hale Smith,** *Innerflexions,* **mm. 44–47.**

EXAMPLE 16. **Hale Smith,** *Innerflexions,* **mm. 139–144.**

EXAMPLE 17. **Hale Smith,** *Innerflexions,* **mm. 164–168.**

EXAMPLE 18. **Hale Smith,** *Innerflexions,* **mm. 1–6.**

EXAMPLE 19. **T. J. Anderson, *Intermezzi*, mm. II, mm. 1–4.**

"orbit" fabricated points, passing one another in their coming and going.[18] In this process, the musicians in a trio, for example, may perform (1) as "a trio with instruments in the same room but as far away [from one another] as possible," (2) "as a solo composition for every instrument," or (3) as a combination of procedures 1 and 2 (Anderson 1983). Anderson's *Intermezzi* (1983) for clarinet, alto saxophone, and piano is the earliest example of his new procedure.[19] In this work, each part has its own tempo, level of loudness, and pitch area, and each player is instructed to ignore and not be influenced by the playing of the others. Although *Intermezzi* introduces Anderson's new "orbiting" process, wide, angular, dissonant melodic lines and nonteleological progressions still mark his work as pointillistic; his use of smears, cadenzas, trills, forearm clusters, and other devices continues to reflect the style of his earlier work.

Crafted in six sections, each of which is designed to last approximately one minute, *Intermezzi* begins with the three instruments entering successively. Within a slow and languorous musical ecology, a lyrical saxophone is predominant, with a caressing clarinet and a commenting piano—alternately hard-edged and gentle—inserting figures supportive of the saxophone. Section 2 is written for saxophone and piano. It begins with a motive in the piano (Example 19) that has been foreshadowed in the saxophone's line a few seconds before, against which the saxophone soars with almost raffish arpeggios and scale-like passages. Section 3 is carried by the saxophone and clarinet, featuring first the saxophone alone. The clarinet enters, seeming off-center melodically, opposes the saxophone, and gradually takes center stage with swagger and jocularity. The two instruments seem to play off each other in a cascading, loose polyphony. In section 4, the clarinet and piano carry the burden,

18. Pianist Billy Taylor (1992), states that "Anderson likens [the experience of listening to his orbiting pieces] to an observer walking through a crowded room that is resonating with independent conversations; the listener focuses on each conversation separately, but can also recognize a harmony resulting from the interplay of the individual parts."

19. Other of Anderson's works based on this principle are *Thomas Jefferson's Orbiting Minstrels and Contraband* (1984), *What Time Is It* (1986), *Ivesiana* (1988), *Echoes* (1991), and *Whatever Happened to the Big Bands* (1992).

the clarinet ascendant, with comments from the piano that seem deliberately designed to support it. In section 5, all three instruments play again, beginning softly, subdued. This section progresses gradually but quickly into an exuberant, grand, quasi-collective improvisation. With its driving, penetrating, disjointed figures reminiscent of riffs, stabs, and ring-based improvisation, this section of the piece resonates spiritually with jazz. In section 6, all three instruments play restful figures that move on to repeated-figure passages in the piano, whose note progressions suggest Baroque-period piano style. The saxophone and the clarinet play their figures in slower rhythms designed to accompany the piano's faster-moving figures.

The whole is nonimitative, contains no call-and-response figures, is polyphonic and polymetric, and is expressionist in style, with felt elements of aleatory and chance music. Although estimated by the composer to last six minutes, the recorded performance of the work is nearly eight minutes long, with the sections beginning approximately at 1 second; 1 minute, 12 seconds; 2 minutes, 16 seconds; 3 minutes, 40 seconds; 4 minutes, 52 seconds; and 6 minutes, 18 seconds into the performance. This more lengthy rendition is due to some of the sections being performed at slower tempos than those suggested by the composer and "tacit" times greater than the one minute indicated by the composer. But because of their musicianship, the three performers, remarkably, end the piece at approximately the same time. In this work, there are no obvious manifestations of the tropes of Call–Response, but, as Singleton's work—for example, *Shadows* (chapter 8)—represents the affinity between African-American music making and minimalism, Anderson's work demonstrates the similarities and affinities between expressionist and African-American musics—off-beat phrase endings and angular melodic construction. Anderson's work is made up of three simultaneous orations, to use Bonds's metaphor, in which the three can become one in a successful aesthetic experience—one could say the perception becomes *an* experience, in Dewey's terms. Utterance, gesture, and moving lines are all there in a work of music alone, in a complex, rhetorical symbolic object.

From these three brief descriptions, it is obvious that contemporary analytical theories from the European-derived tradition have something to offer black-music inquiry, that they are easily combined with ring-based theory for analytical purposes. The more African-derived the piece, the more the Signifyin(g) approach will be relied on; the more European-derived, the more traditional analytical strategies will suffice. In addition, these descriptions of the works of Dett, Smith, and Anderson confirm that black concert-hall music comprises a range of expression within the broader continuum of black music, embracing objects (improvised performances are what I call *transient* objects, since they "pass through" various manifestations of themselves) that range across the continuum.

This concern for the continuum recalls Wilson's formulation. In examining products and derivatives of the ring, he observed that six tendencies prevail in all African-American music:

1. The approach to the organization of rhythm is based on the principle of rhythmic and implied metrical contrast. There is a tendency to create musical structures in which rhythmic clash or disagreement of accents is the ideal; cross-rhythm and metrical ambiguity are the accepted and expected norm.

2. There is a tendency to approach singing or the playing of any instrument in a percussive manner, in which qualitative stress accents are frequently used.

3. There is a tendency to create musical forms in which antiphonal or call-and-response musical structures abound. These antiphonal structures frequently exist simultaneously on a number of different architectonic levels.

4. There is a tendency to create a high density of musical events within a relatively short musical time frame, or to fill up all the musical space.

5. There is a common approach to music making in which a kaleidoscopic range of dramatically contrasting qualities of sound (timbre) in both vocal and instrumental music is sought after. This explains the common use of a broad continuum of vocal sounds from speech to song. I refer to this tendency as "the heterogeneous sound tendency."

6. There is a tendency to incorporate physical body motion as an integral part of the music-making process (Wilson 1983, 3).

While my own listing of African-American musical traits identifies many elements and characteristics of shout and shout-derived music, Wilson in this formulation describes integrated and integrating *tendencies* and *predilections* of African and African-American music making. These fit neatly and complementarily with Call–Response tropings, because they tacitly group the characteristics of the ring into six convenient and compact categories that are revealed even in Wilson's own compositions. *Sinfonia* (1992) is characteristic of Wilson's work: the slow but urgent and inevitable building of climaxes, the powerful licks whose timbres contrast sharply with the surrounding sonic ecology, and the static formulations whose various levels occasionally shift and move, alternately and in stages, toward multiple climaxes. *Sinfonia* is a European-derived work, but thoroughly informed and pervaded by Wilson's

African- and African-American–derived tendencies as they embrace the tropes of Call–Response.

The first of *Sinfonia*'s three movements is a stunning declamation in which the composer's percussive virtuosity is immediately evident, with various drums, a xylophone, suspended cymbals, a harp, and sharp attacks from the violins, muted trumpet, and trombones creating a sound mosaic of percussive tension. The texture is shot through with imitative structures that are clearly African-derived and call-and-response figurations that are punctuated by trombone licks, smears, and splaats (examples of Wilson's "qualitative stress accents"). The timbres, motives, and other events and constructions contrast in dramatic fashion, manifesting the composer's heterogeneous sound ideal. Wilson (1992c) says that this movement unfolds in several successive "waves," each of which begins with a new idea, but, even so, the two-note motive that opens the movement sets the work's sonic character, which is pervaded by intervals of the second and the seventh. Rhythmically, the movement is characterized by cross-rhythms and metrical ambiguities consistent with African and African-American music (and also with the avant-garde).

The wonderfully expressive "Elegy," the work's second movement, is a wordless oration expressive of the composer's grief over the death of his father and that of conductor Calvin Simmons. It begins with a bass drone, over which are played long, shifting notes by the violins that bring the introductory material to a close. The movement's opening melody—long and flowing, with widely spaced intervals—is presented in the violins; the second theme, not nearly so prominent (or effective) as the first, is more closely configured.[20] After complete statements of the second theme by the violins, there is a short period of musical agitation and a short, calm transition to a brief restatement of the first theme to bring the movement to its close.

"Allegro," the vigorous third movement, which the composer calls a "stylized dance," is based on two alternating ideas. The first is a melody of widely spaced intervals, played by the violins; the second, a multimetric rhythmic figure reminiscent of that of Stravinsky (although its "melodic rhythms" are truly riffs and licks from the black tradition, springing from the cultural memory). The vertical and horizontal intervals that constitute the figure consist of major and minor thirds, and trombone licks punctuate the oscillating construction. The movement's two ideas alternate until, in a final section, the dance turns bluesy, jazzy, with folk-like melodic and rhythmic material, replete with stylized riffs.

This entire European-derived, black-oriented work is indeed a mulatto text, speaking in both voices with equal aplomb; therefore, it can be read mean-

---

20. The second theme, according to Wilson, is a reinterpretation of a work he composed for, and which was premiered by, Simmons.

ingfully from either end of the perceptual continuum. The basic timbral and rhythmic constructions that appear in this work are repeated throughout Wilson's oeuvre. Almost all of Wilson's output, including *Akwan, Sometimes,* and *Of Visions and Truth,* all different one from the other, yet unmistakably Wilson, reflects these particular traits and his six tendencies.

Wilson's six tendencies are characteristic of much music by black composers, particularly some of the works of Anderson, Logan, Baker, and Smith, but they are reflected perhaps even more clearly in jazz compositions, such as those of Edward Wilkerson, Jr. In 1991, Wilkerson's group, 8 Bold Souls, recorded an album of the same name, featuring Wilkerson on alto and tenor saxophones, clarinet, and alto clarinet; Mwata Bowden on tenor and baritone saxophones and clarinet; Robert Griffin, Jr., on trumpet and fluegelhorn; Isaiah Jackson, Jr., on trombone and ram's horn; Naomi Millender on cello; Richard Brown, Jr., on double bass; Aaron Dodd on tuba; and Dushee Mosely on drums and other percussion. The album's opening cut, "The Hunt," begins slowly, with an ostinato introducing the theme. The piece is bop-based and riff-laced and extends through Coltrane-like mini-sheets played by Wilkerson on tenor and Braxton-like riffs and gestures played by Bowden on baritone. "The Hunt" is jazz composition at its best, based as it is on Wilkerson's and the other musicians' strengths in creating and developing strong, imaginative rhythmic patterns and constructing unusual and effective polyrhythmic configurations that inspire and support improvisations that are interesting in their own right. The polyphony of "The Hunt" is set in a multimetric framework, which results in rhythmic complexity surpassing that of the cool school's European-derived polyphony, the 5/4 and 7/4 meters of Dave Brubeck, and similar attempts to achieve complexity by other compositionally oriented jazz musicians. And the free-form soloing of the musicians over these multimetric, polyphonic configurations adds one more dimension of complexity to the mix. Another tune, "Shining Waters," begins slowly, the first section featuring chords that progress upward chromatically; single pitches, too, seem inexorably to move in half steps. In the middle of the second of three sections, the musicians repeat the trope of the riding train, with repeated notes in the lower strings and percussion illustrating the train's movement and with Bowden's clarinet blowing the whistle and tooting the horn in approaching and departing announcements. The third section features a cello solo by Millender, followed by Dodd's tuba, which brings back the riding-train trope, this time with the trumpet, clarinet, and saxophones screaming the train's whistle and horn. In "Dervish," theme after theme is presented, all supported by countermelodies, walking lines in the bass, and riffing figures from the other musicians. All these underpin and cajole Wilkerson's lengthy tenor and Jackson's trombone solos. Almost everything in the first half of the piece seems to trope the riding train, especially the drummer's figurations and the riff, played by the low strings, that support

FIGURE 2. Black-music continuum.

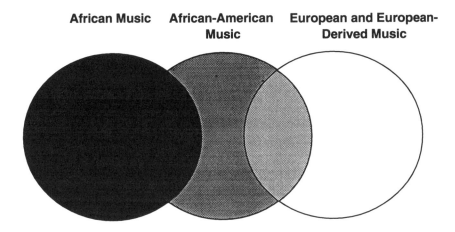

Wilkerson's introductory solo and whistle-blowing sounds. The opening of "Chapel Hill" is certainly metrically ambiguous, with its engaging meter changes. But the initial focus of this piece is on the ostinato played by bass, tuba, and cello under Jackson's extended, humorous solo and on Brown's Signifyin(g), with his bass, on the ostinato's pitch structure, rhythm, and gesture. Other themes appear, slow and lyrical, moderate, or fast and vigorous, with Dodd's funky solo bringing the movement to its end. "Through the Drapes" has a single melodic line that appears in various rhythmic and timbral permutations and melodic variations. After the appearance of an initial contemplative and reflective orchestrated section, loose and sparsely configured, restrained and thinly textured improvisations begin, featuring cello, trombone, and percussion. Soon, another orchestrated section begins, presented in entirely different articulations. It reintroduces the opening theme, intact, to close the piece. The vigorous, big-band–oriented "Favorite Son" opens with the drummer's introduction, followed by a solo on the double bass. A unison theme, à la bebop, follows the two solos and leads to Wilkerson's scorching alto and Jackson's torrid trombone soaring over complex rhythmic configurations that carry the listener, in turn, to improvisatory closing statements by Wilkerson. Throughout *8 Bold Souls,* cross-rhythms and polyrhythms, percussive attacks, call-and-response figures, and metrical ambiguity abound, and the broad continuums of timbre and gesture are consistent with Wilson's heterogeneous sound tendency. In fact, Wilkerson's work reflects in a most substantial and effective way all six of the tendencies identified by Wilson.

These descriptions suggest that black music comprises a continuum that can be illustrated as in Figure 2. This tripartite model visualizes (1) the separate musical experiences of African, African-American, and European-derived

265

cultures and (2) the dialogical potentials within that continuum. Smith's *In-nerflections* occupies a point in the circle on the right side of the model, Dett's *The Chariot Jubilee* resides in the center circle (both are dialogical: one comparatively bold, the other subtle), Anderson's *Intermezzi* and Wilson's *Sinfonia* stand in the oval between the center and right-hand circles, and Wilkerson's *8 Bold Souls* falls in the oval joining the center and left-hand circles.

In some cases, the critic will have the task of determining whether a work or performance of music is truly dialogical or simply a dilution. True dialogism requires that the composer, the performer, and the listener modulate effectively between black vernacular and European-derived voices in a way that keeps the cultural integrity of both intact and viable in a fused product.

This chapter has outlined a theory of interpretation and applied it to works of music. I believe the theory I have evolved illuminates these works, which in turn have illuminated and illustrated the theory. Most of the works discussed in this chapter are, to some extent, works of Call–Response, Signifyin(g) symbols, even those with few ring tropes; they are, more or less, based on or refer to the essentials of Dance, Drum, and Song. Effecting or undergoing various degrees of Signifyin(g) revision, these dialogical musical orations are fraught with semantic value, "telling effect." Some, such as Dett's *The Chariot Jubilee,* make use of intertexuality; others, such as Wilkerson's "The Hunt," trope the riding train. Springing from African myth and ritual in whole or in part, most of these works, or aspects of them, are informed by the cultural memory of that tradition. They are cultural transactions that express the struggle–fulfillment pattern common to human existence in general as well as that particular to the African-American experience. The validity and effectiveness of critics' evaluations of works and performances of African-American music depend on their familiarity with the metaphoric values of Call–Response. Performances and works of Armstrong, Ellington, and Gillespie, and even of Still, Swanson, Bonds, Anderson, Smith, Davis, Wilson, and Logan, convey and mirror the sound qualities, gestures, and nuances of casual and ritualized black oratory and dance. Any valid and effective criticism of them will reflect, directly or indirectly, critics' understandings and appreciations of these essential elements. As critics explore the realm of Call–Response, they will recognize the use and effectiveness (or ineffectiveness) of its Signifyin(g) figures. They will discover and elucidate what makes a piece of African-American music "work" as an effective organization of energies—as a *work* of Call–Response.

CHAPTER **11**

Implications
and Conclusions

We cannot love that which we do not know.
Guinean proverb

In necessary things, unity; in disputed things, liberty; in all things, charity.

In tracing African-American music making from its roots in traditional Africa to its manifestations in the United States, I have focused on the roles of myth, ritual, and the tropes of Call–Response in the continuation of its character. From the African ring, through the ring shout of slave culture, the funeral-parade practices of the early New Orleans jazzmen, and Esu's revisiting of the bluesmen in the 1920s and the beboppers in the 1940s, to the free jazz of the 1960s and the concert-hall works of the 1980s and 1990s, the imperatives of myth and ritual have been evident.

On this journey, we have seen that just as "American civilization grew by getting people out on the verges" and as "a special American creativity [was] found not *within* the enclaves but on the borders between them" (Boorstin 1989, xxiv), so African creativity in America was also found on the verges—and, I might add, also at the crossroads—of African and American musical cultures. In the first three centuries of the African presence in North America, the interactions among calls, cries, hollers, and work songs produced spirituals, blues, ragtime, and jazz; and the play on the verges of those genres later produced gospel, R&B, and new forms of jazz. Early on, this play at the verges and crossroads, based in and triggered by Call–Response, was guided by the essentials of African and African-derived myth and ritual.

Turn-of-the-century African-American modernism was one of a number of cultural developments that gave birth to the New Negro movement of the 1920s, a cultural event that sought to transform certain black social liabilities into cultural and political assets and to change strategies of African-American progress from reactive to proactive. In doing so, the movement catered to white expectations and standards and sought the understanding and goodwill of the larger culture. The Harlem flowering of the movement embraced influences and activities as diverse as Harlem's party culture, Marcus Garvey's Back to Africa movement, James Weldon Johnson's literary world, performances of the Harlem Symphony Orchestra and the Negro String Quartet, Ellington's "jungle" sounds at the Kentucky and Cotton clubs, and Willie "The Lion" Smith's rent-party scene. As the Harlem Renaissance faded, this Negro Renaissance continued in Chicago in a spirit approximating that of Harlem. In the Chicago flowering, there existed Meade Lux Lewis's boogie-woogie rent-party scene, Earl Hines's jazz scene, the gospel cauldron of Thomas A. Dorsey, Richard Wright's literary world, opera for blacks at the Civic Opera House, and performances by the Chicago Symphony and other orchestras of music by composers such as Florence Price and William L. Dawson. In all of this, there was again play on the verges, particularly those bordering the cultures of the African-American musical experience and of the European-derived concert hall.

But turn-of-the-century modernism also helped obscure the memory of black myth and ritual, a loss occasioned by black commentators' wish to conform to the expectations of high culture. Lovinggood (1921), Locke ([1936] 1968), Cuney-Hare ([1936] 1974), and Layne (1942) were interested in "elevating the race" and proving the readiness of African Americans for social equality and racial integration. It is not surprising, then, that none of these writers explored the power of myth in African-American musical life, and none mentions ritual. Committed to the proposition that documented and documentable facts are the only grist for the scholarly mill, the authors of such works necessarily eschewed spiritual and other subjective considerations. In general, matters pertaining to African and African-American myth and ritual have been ignored, tacitly rejected, and even denigrated by some scholars and musicians—in conversation but never in print—as "mystical" and "unprovable," and the pursuit of such ideas has been viewed as "unscholarly" and "methodologically unsound."[1] These attitudes have persisted chiefly because, until recently, no models of scholarship existed that would help illuminate myth and ritual as elements fundamental to black musical expressiveness.

The 1950s saw a new apostasy, albeit brief, in which the New Criticism, the promise of racial integration, and the intimidation tactics of the House Un-American Activities Committee influenced the cultural and artistic beliefs and practices of the black middle class. In the wake of these events, black composers turned away from Call–Response toward compositional styles that were more racially neutral.

Following this brief, second renunciation, *new* "New Negroes" emerged in the 1960s, their militant stance driven and shaped well into the 1970s by the failure of previous efforts to achieve equality in a culture they had helped to build. But unlike the black artists of the 1920s, these artists directed their work toward the core culture; their revolutionary art and politics contrasted sharply with the romantic art and politics of their forebears. Experimentation was ascendant, musical prowess widespread, and concert-hall music by black composers received wider attention. Clearly Esu's crossroads multiplied in the period of this second renaissance, with individual branches of some of these roads crossing still others. At the central crossroads was the Association for the Advancement of Creative Musicians, embracing it all (its motto is "Great Black Music: Ancient to the Future"), modifying present constructions, laying foundations for further development with a spectacular display of musical ecumenicalism forged by its African-derived, Pan-African aesthetic, and revealing its capacity to embrace, or at least pay respectful tribute to, the musical values and systems of several of the world's cultures. Meanwhile, other areas of African-American music were also revitalized, spurred by more popular and commercial interests. The 1980s represented a plateau of sorts, in spite of the new works and activities that mark this period.

Throughout this book, I have tried to stress the importance of performance in the making of African-American music. In the concert-hall tradition, nowhere has this importance been so evident as in the performances of Camille Nickerson's *Five Creole Songs,* Olly Wilson's *Of Visions and Truth,* and Wendell Logan's *Runagate Runagate.*[2] In these performances, the three singers (Bonita Hyman, William Brown, and Donnie Ray Albert) are inspirational purveyors and inciters of Call–Response, priests and priestess of black myth and ritual. The two men, in particular, are "callers"—slaves calling across fields, black street vendors in New Orleans, leaders of song in the forest bush harbors,

---

1. I have heard such statements made by musical academics for nearly all of my academic career, and so have most other college and university professors. An example of the attitude of which I speak is Adorno's ([1967] 1983, 122–123) statements about jazz.
2. All three can be heard on *The Black Music Repertory Ensemble in Concert* (1992).

preachers-as-callers in Pentecostal and mainline Protestant churches, conductors on the Underground Railroad calling prospective riders to ride their trains. These three sang Omar's song, and all African Americans sang it with them, for Omar's song is a subliminal song, heard by all African Americans who possess the memory. We each have our own ancestral subliminal songs, nearly identical but different enough to reflect the differences in our upbringings and informed perspectives.

As the writing of this book was coming to a close, I began to have the feeling that something was missing. Somehow, some concept or idea of underlying and fundamental importance was neither discussed nor discovered; either I was not equipped to unearth this something or it could not be cognitively perceived or elaborated. I began to wonder if that "something" might not reside in or lie below Esu's oppositions, if those oppositions might hold the key to whatever it was I was lacking. I now have the feeling that what is missing is that to which all art aspires: aesthetic truth. Perhaps that truth does reside in Esu's contradictions, at the musical crossroads of "Now's the Time/ Hucklebuck," for example, where ambiguity disguises distinction, where one is both and both are one. Perhaps the truth lies in the Art Pepper–Sonny Stitt collision, that carving encounter where white became black. Or perhaps it lies in Signifyin(g) itself, where meaning is reversed and white texts are black.

Writing this book has been in some ways a mystical experience, one in which epistemological, ontological, and metaphysical distinctions have blurred again and again, where on occasion myth was reality and reality myth—as at the crossroads of cultural memory and cognitive perception, of spiritual sensibility and objective truth, of musical composition and "musicking." Finally, there is the intercultural crossroads of black and white in the United States, without which the music and music making discussed in this book would never have existed and the understanding of which is crucial to constructive social, political, and intellectual discourse.

We are beginning to know and accept the two-way influences of black and white in the making of American culture. John Edward Philips, for example, in his brief article "White Africanisms" (1991), contends that "as much African culture survives now among whites as among blacks in the United States" (25). He goes on to explore the survival of African retentions among white Americans—what he calls "the white American heritage" of African culture (27). Philips begins by restating the five areas in which African culture has survived in white America, originally posited by Herskovitz (1947): (1) music, particularly popular music, jazz, and country music; (2) dialect speech, as it shaped the speech of white Southerners; (3) southern etiquette, of which the spirit is African (although the forms are European); (4) southern cuisine, as it contributed to the seasoning of food; and (5) religious behavior in the form of the group excitation and trances resulting from African and African-derived rhythms and the black preaching style. (Is it surprising, then, that African-American cultural memory could drive and support Pepper in his encounter with Stitt?) Philips then surveys other writings and claims related to the subject. He expands Herskovitz's contribution and calls for an end to segregated studies in the interest of our complete understanding of American society.

Some of the music and ideas I have discussed should debunk several of the wrongheaded notions about black music that have long prevailed in American society. For example, those who use my conceptual framework to interpret the music will find that the works of Ulysses Kay, Hale Smith, and George Walker put the lie to the conventional wisdom that African Americans cannot produce viable art without communicating the fact of their race, and that Olly Wilson's work demolishes the equally conventional notion that race-based art is limited and therefore unimportant. The works by Wilson, T. J. Anderson, and Wendell Logan discussed here, which tie these composers to the Negro Renaissance, show that, rather than compromising aesthetic quality, the combined symbolic force of truly dialogical work can equal, or even surpass, that of either of the single traditions. The implications of Gates's concept of Signifyin(g) revision can be extended by Wilson's view of the fusion process as development. For Wilson (1990), "in order for an influence from one musical tradition to significantly affect the development of another musical tradition, it must modify that second tradition's view of itself at a conceptual level. It must propagate a significantly altered ordering of itself—a new paradigm" (30). I believe that some of Wilson's, Logan's, and Anderson's works do just that: by making use of the myths and the mythic constructions of African-American culture and by treating African-derived myth and ritual within the context of European-derived myth and ritual, they deconstruct and reconstruct the European-derived concert-hall tradition through the embedding and troping processes of Signifyin(g). These embedding and troping processes support both hegemonic and marginal ideology and practice. And this deconstruction/reconstruction makes it necessary for the troped tradition to view itself, partly at least, from the standpoint of the troping tradition.

The entire discussion in this book shows, I believe, that the "blues aesthetic," touted by some black musicians and writers as the foundation of all the black artistic experience, is only one point on a broader black aesthetic continuum. It also shows that there is room on that continuum for those who might be called Call–Response composers, for the "happen-to-be" composers (those who think they write exclusively from the European-derived tradition

271

but just happen to be black),[3] and for those who are sometimes one and sometimes the other and sometimes in between. They all contribute to American and world musical culture.

The works of Nickerson, Still, Swanson, Price, Walker, and Smith discussed in this book perpetuate what Gates (1984) calls the "trope of dualism" (176), a primary trope of racial integration, which produces what Gates (1988) calls "mulatto texts"—texts, that is, "with complex double, or two-toned literary heritages" (152). Although my emphasis on the vernacular focuses on the works that make use of ring tropes and values, I do not apologize for this. Black-composed works in the European tradition, if they are of high quality, have already been given attention and acceptance, as demonstrated by the respect given the works of Kay. But I hasten to put to rest any assumption that my privileging of these works is based on race. In the context of my position, I value Gershwin's music as much as Still's, Pepper's performance as much as Stitt's. But I must give attention to what has been overlooked in the past, perhaps *because* of race. Perhaps my privileging of ring tropes and values here will swing the pendulum of attention just far enough so that proper attention can be given to the entire tradition of American music without regard to racial concerns. For, ultimately, it is not a question of placing one over the other, but is really, as Gates (1991) contends,

> a question of perspective, a question of emphasis. Just as we can and must cite a black text within the larger American tradition, we can and must cite a black text within its own tradition, a tradition not defined by a pseudoscience of racial biology, or a mystically shared essence called blackness, but by the repetition and revision of shared themes, topoi, and tropes, a process that binds the signal texts of the black tradition into a canon just as surely as separate links bind together into a chain. It is no more, or less, essentialist to make this claim than it is to claim the existence of French, English, German, Russian, or American literature—as long as we proceed inductively, from the texts to the theory. (35)

The list of good works by all African-American composers put together is small, naturally, compared with the number produced by European and white American composers of any period. These black composers came from a people who had lived in slavery only sixty years before Dett's *The Chariot Jubilee* was composed, in 1921; whose progress had been thwarted by the imperatives of white supremacy, by gender discrimination, and by economic and social discrimination; whose access to formal musical training had been limited by exclusion from cultural institutions; and many of whose most talented members had been drawn into entertainment and educational fields. Given these

---

3. For an elaboration of this attitude, although in relation to Latinos, see Shorris (1992, 381–405).

circumstances, it is amazing that Joplin could have achieved what he did with *Treemonisha* in 1911, and more amazing that Dett could write *The Chariot Jubilee* ten years later. In the arena of entertainment music, black success was enormous, of course, but for two important reasons. First, there long had been in place an apprenticeship system for ragtime, blues, and jazz artists—a system based on African nurturing principles and honed in slavery and in the postslavery entertainment world. In this system, with talent and perseverance, African Americans had opportunities to excel in a milieu in which vernacular musicians had always been acceptable to and supported by important portions of the larger society (although in ways that were primarily exploitive). Second, the market for popular entertainment in the United States was much larger than that for concert music, and the promoters of popular music, therefore, needed more marketable products.

The zeal for jazz among some musicologists and musicologically oriented scholars and critics, who feel that they have to justify black music to the larger scholarly community, has been both fortunate and unfortunate for African-American music.[4] It is fortunate that through their intense responsiveness to the music, they have helped pave the way for the eventual acceptance of the genre in the academy. These critics' need to have their writings published in mainline scholarly journals and books led them to shape their writings on jazz into academically acceptable form. The mannerisms, limitations, and traditions of academic form and substance help give the impression that the music is merely a species of European-derived music, causing both these critics and their listeners to miss the point of the music's real and essential aesthetic power. Explanations that result from their analyses are usually limited and aesthetically uninformative, for they presume cultural and artistic goals different from those of the tradition from which jazz springs. If the purpose of analysis is to explain and illuminate the aesthetic power of the music, the exclusive application of positivistic analysis to works and performances of black music is not only inadequate, but also a miscarriage of analytical purpose; such analysis reveals nothing about most of the culturally expressive features of the music.

In this book, I have tried to discover a hermeneutic that is African-American in character and in method. My journey in this search has been a kind of historical reconstruction and interpretation rooted in the past of the very aesthetic that I have sought to discover; it has been a search to recapture and describe the special flavor of culturally important musical developments of that past through the interpretation of the cultural residue they left behind. At the same time, I have tried to recognize and give proper attention to the

---

4. It is unnecessary to cite specific works by these scholars, since most of the analytical studies on jazz can serve as examples.

European-derived roots of black music in order to nurture an intellectual musical vision that is dialogically integrating. Most of the concert-hall music that I have discussed is powerful precisely because of its reliance on myth and ritual. Even the works that eschew Call–Response have as a foundation European-derived myth and ritual. But some concert-hall music by black composers suffers from the same malady that affects much contemporary music by white composers: it lacks mythopoeic power; it has no symbolic force.

I have left some important considerations unaddressed, and intentionally so. Some scholars, for example, would perhaps deem it indispensable to distinguish elements of continuity from those of discontinuity within the black musical experience. But that kind of scholarship does not seem necessary for my purposes here or for the purposes of those to whom this book is most directly addressed. I have omitted many important black musicians and their works. One composition that I did not discuss, for example, although it has been twice commercially recorded and published in score, is Howard Swanson's *Short Symphony* (1948). This omission deserves comment. I did not discuss this work because of the poor quality of the recorded performances. Both recordings fail to satisfy me because I believe that the conductors failed to interpret the work properly. In the mid-1970s, I listened many times to these performances, and my musical instinct told me that the *performances* were problematic, not necessarily the work. The score told me that the work had something to say from the perspective of the black experience. Because I believed this to be the case, I programmed the piece for the Festival of Black American Music, held in Carbondale, Illinois, in 1976, to be performed by the Southern Illinois Symphony Orchestra, under the direction of Robert Bergt. Bergt understood that the work's most important aspect is rhythm, and he interpreted the score as a suite of funky dances. The result was an interpretation that surpasses those of the two commercial recordings, in spirit if not in technique and musicality.[5] (Hale Smith, one of Swanson's closest friends, told me later that Swanson's music is "stone, stomp-down music" and that it should be played as such.) This experience underscored the importance of physicality—dance, the body, what I interpret as *materiality*—in the interpretation and performance of certain works of concert music by black composers. And this experience has in some small measure driven the writing of this book.

Another omission from this discussion is the music of Ornette Coleman, the dean of the free-jazz movement and progenitor of much that happened in free jazz in the 1960s. Bringing to jazz a new freedom and cultural orientation, Coleman effectively expressed through his music the social, cultural, and political concerns of the decade. In doing so, he opened doors, broke down barriers, and musically debunked traditional notions and uses of tone, pitch, and process. (As Martin Williams [1973] perceptively stated, "Ornette plays

5. The recording was taped and is available in the Library and Archives of the Center for Black Music Research, Columbia College, Chicago.

field hollers.") Coleman's contributions will be discussed in the sequel to this book, in which my discussion of jazz will begin with his work. Other important composers whose accomplishments are missing from this volume are some of the concert-hall composers whose works appear in Willis Patterson's collection *Anthology of Art Songs by Black American Composers* (1977), composers whose works are included in CBS Records' Black Composers Series (for example, Adolphus Hailstork and Talib Rasul Hakim) and individuals such as Julian Work and Arthur Cunningham. Finally, works entirely choral (or with piano accompaniment) will be treated in the sequel, as relations between the African-American choral tradition and South African a cappella singing will be explored.

The focus in this book has been on the black music of North America; the black traditional and concert-hall music and music making of Africa, Europe, the Caribbean, and Latin America have not been treated. Other omissions include much contemporary black popular music—including reggae, hip hop, and zydeco—and opera from any period. The nature, magnitude, and implications of these genres require that they be treated within a different context, so all of this music will be discussed in a subsequent volume on the black diaspora.

I have tried to avoid the trap of the high–low distinction, giving, to the extent I felt was possible, equal attention to the genres discussed. When lapses have occurred, it has only been because I felt it necessary to follow the direction and momentum of my narrative. Whatever the cause, any slights to genres were unintended, for it is my strong belief that musical values are not inherent in the music itself, but are made by *people* in their relationships with the music. Moreover, I think I have shown that in African-American music the collisions of genres and the play of musicians on the verges have created fusions that, for the black-music specialist, make subspecialties dissolve with inquiry and become useful only for purposes of value-free classification.

Notwithstanding protests to the contrary, there has been a well-known and indisputable musicological tendency, uninformed and culturally irresponsible, to treat black-music genres as aberrant while privileging the symbolic value of white unicorns. I hope that what I have had to say in these pages has shown that it is both self-depriving and destructive of human values to fail to recognize the universal character of the images of African-American myth and ritual, to misunderstand, denigrate, or ignore their renderings, and to ignore their contributions to the human condition.

I have tried to debunk the kind of thinking that denies high-culture value to African-American concert-hall music and seeks to deny blacks the fact of the capacity to excel in the high-culture arena.[6] We have seen that Hale Smith is unique in his use of serial technique to produce highly charged, expressive

---

6. While such views are no longer frequently voiced in polite society, they do exist as sediment.

works accessible to broad audiences (for example, *Contours* and *Innerflexions*) and that Olly Wilson's *Sometimes* is a marvelous use of electronic-music techniques as a frame for African-American troping procedures; it is a work that communicates strongly from both the African-American and European-derived traditions. T. J. Anderson, Alvin Singleton, and Olly Wilson have potentially broken new ground—Anderson with his new orbiting procedure (*Intermezzi*), Singleton by bringing System procedures into black concert-hall music (*Shadows, After Fallen Crumbs,* and *A Yellow Rose Petal*), and Wilson in his complete integration of European-derived and African-derived expressions in a dialogical process that privileges African-derived myth, ritual, and cultural memory. And I think I have made clear my belief that no one race has a corner on cultural memory or on particular musical abilities and practices, recognizing the importance of avoiding the traps of both the European-derived indoctrination goal and the "soul patrol" (Blake 1992, 17). The thinking that sets such traps is not only sloppy and irrelevant, but silly. I am reminded here of Hale Smith's response to my comment that the sparse visual imagery of the score of his *Innerflexions* did not reflect the powerful sound of the music. The eloquent Smith, in referring to the influences on his orchestrational prowess, resorted to the vernacular and said, in part, "My teacher Marcell Dick, Duke, Benny Carter, Mozart—all them cats are part of it."

With regard to the tropes of Call–Response, provocative questions arise: Can these tropes be applied also to inquiry into the other black cultural disciplines? If Sterling Stuckey is correct in his suggestion that all black cultural expression emanated from the ring, then the answer must be yes. African-American poetry, for example, like music, has its off-beat accents; its call-and-response phrasings; its riffs, licks, cries, and hollers; its multimetric configurations. And, like music, African-American poetry is driven by the myths, rituals, and tropes of the culture. What of dance, theater, and the visual arts? To what extent is it possible to formulate common modes of inquiry for all African-American cultural studies, modes that make possible true interdisciplinary inquiry while also ensuring proper and appropriate respect for the traditional boundaries and particularities of the various disciplines? The search for such a common scholarship might also integrate the study of African-American music and culture with Latin American/Caribbean and European studies along the lines of the parallax idea, set forth by Gary Tomlinson (1991) as a concept of knowing

> in which all vantage points yield a real knowledge, partial and different from that offered by any other vantage point, but in which no point yields insight more privileged than that gained from any other. It represents, in other words, a knowing in which none of our vantage points grants us a claim to any more singular status than that of being an other among others. It suggests that our knowledge is fundamentally indirect, not a knowledge of things in themselves but a knowledge of the negotiations by which we make things what they are.

Parallax also configures the most effective means to gain knowledge in a de-centered cosmos: the deepest knowledge will result from the dialogue that involves the largest number of differing vantage points. Knowledge is a product of differing displacements of reality perceived from different viewpoints rather than a singular, authoritative perception. (240)

For me, parallax recalls Mikhail Bakhtin, in whose architectonics the subject is the interlocative or dialogic self. Holquist and Liapunov (1990) explain it best:

The interlocative self [is one that can] change places with another—that *must*, in fact, change places to see where it is. A logical implication of the fact that I can see things you cannot, and you can see things that I cannot, is that our excess of seeing is defined by a lack of seeing: my excess is your lack, and vice versa. If we wish to overcome this lack, we try to see what there is *together.* We must share each other's excess in order to overcome our mutual lack. (xxvi)

In this book, I have leaned toward Bakhtin's ideal more than Tomlinson's but both are worth striving for.

But there is rhythm here. Its own special substance:
I hear Billie sing, no good man, and dig Prez, wearing the zoot
suit of life, the pork-pie hat tilted at the correct angle.
Through the Harlem smoke of beer and whiskey, I understand the
mystery of the signifying monkey,
. . . I reach for the totality of being.

Larry Neal, "Malcolm X—An Autobiography"

Appendix

Spirituals in Which the Word "Chariot" Appears in the Title[1]

Danville Chariot
Going the Ride Up in the Chariot
Good News the Chariot's Coming
Swing Low, Chariot
Swing Low, Sweet Chariot (1)
Swing Low, Sweet Chariot (2)
Roll de Ol' Chariot Along
Roll de Ole Chariot Along
Going Home in the Chariot
Gwineter Ride Up in De Chariot Soon-a in de Mornin'
Good Old Chariot

Anthologies Surveyed

Allen, William Francis, Charles Pickard Ware, and Lucy McKim Garrison, eds. 1867. *Slave songs of the United States.* New York: Simpson.

Armstrong, M. F., and Helen M. Ludlow. [1874] 1971. *Hampton and its students.* Freeport, N.Y.: Books for Libraries Press.

Dett, R. Nathaniel, ed. 1927. *Religious folk-songs of the Negro: As sung at Hampton Institute.* Hampton, Va.: Hampton Institute Press.

Hallowell, Emily, comp. and ed. [1907] 1976. *Plantation songs.* New York: AMS Press.

Johnson, J. Rosamond, ed. and arr. 1937. *Rolling along in song.* New York: Viking Press.

Johnson, James Weldon, and J. Rosamond Johnson, eds. [1925, 1926] 1981. *The books of American Negro spirituals.* New York: Viking Press.

Kennedy, R. Emmett, [comp.]. 1925. *Mellows: A chronicle of unknown singers.* New York: Boni.

---

1. Although two of the titles listed are identical and two others nearly identical, in each case I have listed both because the texts of each pair are different.

Krehbiel, Henry Edward. [1914] 1962. *Afro-American folksongs: A study in racial and national music*. New York: Unger.

Landeck, Beatrice, [ed. and comp.]. 1961. *Echoes of Africa in folk songs of the Americas*. New York: Van Rees Press.

Marsh, J. B. T. 1880. *The story of the Jubilee Singers; with their songs*. Boston: Houghton, Osgood.

National jubilee melodies. 22nd ed. 1900. Nashville: National Baptist Publishing Board.

Odum, Howard, and Guy B. Johnson. [1925] 1968. *The Negro and his songs: A study of typical Negro songs in the South*. Westport, Conn.: Negro Universities Press.

Parrish, Lydia. [1942] 1992. *Slave songs of the Georgia Sea Islands*. Athens: University of Georgia Press.

Pike, Gustavus D. 1873. *The Jubilee Singers and their campaign for twenty thousand dollars*. Boston: Lee and Shepard.

———. [1875] 1974. *The singing campaign for ten thousand pounds*. Rev. ed. New York: American Missionary Association.

Work, John W., ed. 1940. *American Negro songs and spirituals*. New York: Bonanza Books.

Work, John Wesley, ed. 1915. *Folk song of the American Negro*. Nashville: Fisk University Press.

Printed Works Cited

Abbott, Lynn. 1992. "Play that barber shop chord": A case for the African-American origin of barbershop harmony. *American Music* 10, no. 3:289–325.

Abrahams, Roger. [1963] 1970. *Deep down in the jungle: Negro narrative folklore from the streets of Philadelphia*. Hawthorne, N.Y.: Aldine.

———. 1983. *African folktales: Traditional stories of the black world*. New York: Pantheon Books.

Adams, E. C. L. 1928. *Nigger to nigger*. New York: Scribner.

Adorno, Theodor. [1967] 1983. Perennial fashion—Jazz. In *Prisms*. Trans. Samuel and Sherry Weber. Cambridge, Mass.: MIT Press.

Allen, William Francis, Charles Pickard Ware, and Lucy McKim Garrison, eds. 1867. *Slave songs of the United States*. New York: Simpson.

Amoaku, William Komla. 1975. Symbolism in traditional institutions and music of the Ewe of Ghana. Ph.D. diss., University of Pittsburgh. Ann Arbor: University Microfilms.

Anderson, T. J. 1983. Notes. *Intermezzi*. Berlin: Bote & Bock.

Armstrong, M. F., and Helen M. Ludlow. [1874] 1971. *Hampton and its students*. Freeport, N.Y.: Books for Libraries Press.

Arvey, Verna. 1984. *In one lifetime*. Fayetteville: University of Arkansas Press.

B. 1880. Inside southern cabins. Part 2—Georgia. *Harper's Weekly* November 20:749–750.

Badger, R. Reid. 1989. James Reese Europe and the prehistory of jazz. *American Music* 7, no. 1:48–67.

Baker, David N., Lida M. Belt, and Herman C. Hudson, eds. 1978. *The black composer speaks*. Metuchen, N.J.: Scarecrow Press.

Baker, Houston. 1984. *Blues, ideology, and Afro-American literature: A vernacular theory*. Chicago: University of Chicago Press.

———. 1987. *Modernism and the Harlem Renaissance*. Chicago: University of Chicago Press.

Ballanta-Taylor, Nicholas. 1925. *Saint Helena Island spirituals*. New York: Schirmer.

Ballou, Leonard R. 1967. *Handbook of early American Negro musicians*. Elizabeth City, N.C.: Ballou.

Baraka, Amiri [LeRoi Jones]. 1967. *Black music*. New York: Morrow.

———. [1963] 1988. *Blues people: Negro music in white America*. Westport, Conn.: Greenwood Press.

————. 1991. The "blues aesthetic" and the "black aesthetic": Aesthetics as the continuing political history of a culture. *Black Music Research Journal* 11, no. 2:101–110.

Barlow, William. 1989. *Looking up at down: The emergence of blues culture*. Philadelphia: Temple University Press.

Barr, Lillie E. 1883. Negro sayings and superstitions. *Independent* September 27.

Bebey, Francis. [1969] 1975. *African music: A people's art*. Westport, Conn.: Greenwood Press.

Bechet, Sidney. 1960. *Treat it gentle*. New York: Hill & Wang.

Berendt, Joachim. 1982. *The jazz book: Ragtime to fusion and beyond*. Westport, Conn.: Hill.

Bergman, Peter. 1969. *The chronological history of the Negro in America*. New York: Harper & Row.

Berlin, Edward A. 1980. *Ragtime: A musical and cultural history*. Berkeley: University of California Press.

Berry, Jason. 1988. African cultural memory in New Orleans music. *Black Music Research Journal* 8, no. 1:3–12.

Bigsby, C. W. E. 1980. *The second black renaissance: Essays in black literature*. Westport, Conn.: Greenwood Press.

Blackstone, Orin. [1945–1948] 1978. *Index to jazz: Jazz recordings, 1917–1944*. Westport, Conn.: Greenwood Press.

Blake, John. 1992. Running afoul of the soul patrol. *Chicago Tribune* [North Sports Final edition] April 6.

Blassingame, John W. 1973. *Black New Orleans: 1860–1880*. Chicago: University of Chicago Press.

Bodichon, Barbara Leigh Smith. [1857–1858] 1972. *An American diary*. Edited from the manuscript by Joseph W. Reed, Jr. London: Routledge & Kegan Paul.

Bonds, Mark Evan. 1991. *Wordless rhetoric: Musical form and the metaphor of the oration*. Cambridge, Mass.: Harvard University Press.

Bone, Robert. 1986. Richard Wright and the Chicago Renaissance. *Callaloo* 9, no. 3:446–468.

Bontemps, Arna, and Langston Hughes, eds. 1958. *The book of Negro folklore*. New York: Dodd, Mead.

Boorstin, Daniel J. 1989. *Hidden history: Exploring our secret past*. New York: Vintage Books.

Bowdich, T. Edward. [1819] 1966. *Mission from Cape Coast Castle to Ashantee*. London: Cass.

Boyer, Horace Clarence. 1979. Contemporary gospel music—Part 1: Sacred or secular. *Black Perspective in Music* 7, no. 1:5–58.

————. 1985–1988. There's a bright sky somewhere: Black American gospel singers. *Views on Black American Music* 3:12–18.

Brown, Scott E. 1986. *James P. Johnson: A case of mistaken identity*. Metuchen, N.J.: Scarecrow Press and the Institute of Jazz Studies, Rutgers University.

Browning, Alice C. 1946. *Lionel Hampton's swing book*. Chicago: Negro Story Press.

Buckman, Peter. 1978. *Let's dance: Social, ballroom, and folk dancing*. New York: Paddington Press.

Budds, Michael J. 1978. *Jazz in the sixties: The expansion of musical resources and techniques*. Iowa City: University of Iowa Press.

Burleigh, Harry T. [1917] 1969. *Album of Negro spirituals*. Melville, N.Y.: Belwin Mills.

Burlin, Natalie Curtis. 1918. *Negro folk songs*. New York: Schirmer.

———. 1919. Negro music at birth. *Musical Quarterly* 5, no. 1:86–89.

Cable, George Washington. [1886] 1969a. Creole slave songs. In *The social implications of early Negro music in the United States*. Ed. Bernard Katz. New York: Arno Press and The New York Times.

———. [1886] 1969b. The dance in Place Congo. In *The social implications of early Negro music in the United States*. Ed. Bernard Katz. New York: Arno Press and The New York Times.

Cage, John. 1961. *Silence: Lectures and writings*. Cambridge, Mass.: MIT Press.

Campbell, Joseph. 1986. *The inner reaches of outer space: Metaphor as myth and as religion*. New York: Harper & Row.

———. 1988. *The power of myth*. New York: Doubleday.

———. [1969] 1990. *The flight of the wild gander: Explorations in the mythological dimension*. New York: Harper Perennial.

Carawan, Guy, and Candie Carawan. 1990. "Freedom in the air": An overview of the songs of the civil rights movement. *Black Music Research Bulletin* 12, no. 1:1–4.

Carr, Ian. 1982. *Miles Davis: A biography*. New York: Morrow.

Carroll, Peter N., and David Noble. 1988. *The free and the unfree: A new history of the United States*. Rev. ed. New York: Penguin Books.

Chambers, Jack. 1983. *Milestones I: The music and times of Miles Davis to 1960*. Toronto: University of Toronto Press.

Charters, A. R. Danberg. 1961. Negro folk elements in classic ragtime. *Ethnomusicology* 5:174–183.

Christensen, Abigail M. Holmes. 1894. Spirituals and "shouts" of southern Negroes. *Journal of American Folklore* 7:154–155.

Cirlot, J. E. 1971. *A dictionary of symbols*. 2nd ed. New York: Dorset Press.

Civic Opera lauds "Aida" cast. 1943. *Chicago Tribune* February 20.

Clarke, Mary Olmsted. 1890. Song games of Negro children in Virginia. *Journal of American Folklore* 3:288–290.

Cleveland Public Library. 1991. *Index to Negro spirituals*. CBMR Monograph No. 3. Chicago: Columbia College Center for Black Music Research.

Cogley, John. [1956] 1971. Report on blacklisting. In *Blacklisting: Two key documents*. New York: Arno Press and The New York Times.

Cohen, Norm. 1981. *Long steel rail: The railroad in American folksong*. Urbana: University of Illinois Press.

Coolen, Michael. 1991. Senegambian influences of Afro-American musical culture. *Black Music Research Journal* 11, no. 1:1–18.

Cooper, Grosvenor, and Leonard B. Meyer. 1960. *The rhythmic structure of music*. Chicago: University of Chicago Press.

Copland, Aaron. 1967. *Music and imagination*. Cambridge, Mass.: Harvard University Press.

Courlander, Harold. 1963. *Negro folk music, U.S.A.* New York: Columbia University Press.

Croome, William H. 1851. *City cries; or, A peep at scenes in town by an observer.* Philadelphia: George S. Appleton.

Crowder, Henry, with Hugo Speck. 1987. *As wonderful as all that: Henry Crowder's memoirs of his affair with Nancy Cunard, 1928–1935.* Navarro, Calif.: Wild Trees Press.

Cuney-Hare, Maud. [1936] 1974. *Negro musicians and their music.* New York: Da Capo Press.

Dance, Stanley. 1977. *The world of Earl Hines.* New York: Da Capo Press.

Dannen, Fredric. 1991. *Hit men: Power brokers' and fast money inside the music business.* New York: Vintage Books.

Davidson, Basil. 1969. *The African genius: An introduction to African cultural and social history.* Boston: Little, Brown.

Davis, Miles, with Quincy Troupe. 1989. *Miles: The autobiography.* New York: Simon and Schuster.

Davis, Ronald. 1980. *A history of music in American life.* Vol. 2, *The gilded years, 1865–1920.* Huntington, N.Y.: Kreiger.

Davis, Thadious M., and Trudier Harris. 1985. *Afro-American writers after 1955: Dramatists and prose writers.* Detroit: Gayle Research.

Dennison, Sam. 1982. *Scandalize my name.* New York: Garland.

Dett, R. Nathaniel, ed. 1927. *Religious folk-songs of the Negro: As sung at Hampton Institute.* Hampton, Va.: Hampton Institute Press.

DeVeaux, Scott. 1989. The emergence of the jazz concert, 1935–1945. *American Music* 7, no. 1:6–29.

———. 1991. Constructing the jazz tradition: Jazz historiography. *Black American Literature Forum* 25, no. 3:525–560.

Dewey, John. [1934] 1963. *Art as experience.* New York: Putnam.

DjeDje, Jacqueline Cogdell. 1989. Gospel music in the Los Angeles black community. *Black Music Research Journal* 9, no. 1:35–81.

Draper, James P., ed. 1992. *Black literature criticism: Excerpts from criticism of the most significant works of black authors over the past 200 years.* Detroit: Gale Research.

Du Bois, W. E. B. [1902] 1967. *The souls of black folk: Essays and sketches.* Diamond Jubilee ed. Nashville: Fisk University Press.

Ekwueme, Lazarus E. N. 1974. African-music retentions in the New World. *Black Perspective in Music* 2, no. 2:128–144.

El Hadi, Suliaman, and Jalal Nuriddin, eds. 1985. *The last poets: Vibes from the scribes.* London: Pluto Press.

Ellington, Duke. 1973. *Music is my mistress.* New York: Da Capo Press.

Ellison, Jno W., ed. 1916. *Ellison's Clef Club book for New York, Chicago and Boston colored musicians: A standard Clef Club diary and daily reminder for members and patrons.* New York: Ellison.

Epperson, Gordon. 1967. *The musical symbol: A study of the philosophic theory of music.* Ames: Iowa State University Press.

Epstein, Dena J. 1977. *Sinful tunes and spirituals: Black folk music to the Civil War.* Urbana: University of Illinois Press.

Esedebe, P. Olisanwuche. 1982. *Pan-Africanism: The idea and movement, 1776–1963.* Washington, D.C.: Howard University Press.

Everett, Thomas. 1978. Concert band music by black-American composers. *Black Perspective in Music* 6, no. 1:143–151.

Finck, Julia Neeley. 1898. Mammy's song: Negro melody. *Music* 13:604–605.

Fleischmann, Ernest. 1988. The orchestra is dead. *Musical America* January 4:14–16, 27. Microfilm.

Floyd, Samuel A. 1975. The Great Lakes experience: 1942–1945. *Black Perspective in Music* 3, no. 1:17–24.

———. 1978. The musical work of art. *Music Journal* 36, no. 4:12–18.

———, ed. 1990a. *Black music in the Harlem Renaissance.* Westport, Conn.: Greenwood Press.

———. 1990b. Music in the Harlem Renaissance: An overview. In *Black music in the Harlem Renaissance.* Ed. Samuel A. Floyd, Jr. Westport, Conn.: Greenwood Press.

———. 1991. Ring shout! Black music, black literary theory, and black historical studies. *Black Music Research Journal* 11, no. 2:267–289.

———. 1992. Liner notes. *The black music repertory ensemble in concert.* Center for Black Music Research CBMR002-C2.

———. 1993. Troping the blues: From spirituals to the concert hall. *Black Music Research Journal* 13, no. 1:31–51.

Floyd, Samuel A., Jr., and Marsha J. Reisser. 1980. Social dance music of black composers in the nineteenth century and the emergence of classic ragtime. *Black Perspective in Music* 8, no. 2:161–193.

———. 1984. The sources and resources of classic ragtime music. *Black Music Research Journal* 4:22–59.

———. 1987. *Black music biography: An annotated bibliography.* White Plains, N.Y.: Kraus International.

Frazer, Sir James George. 1922. *The golden bough.* New York: Macmillan.

Full gospel songs. 1923. Chicago: Thoro Harris.

Gates, Henry Louis, Jr. 1984. The blackness of blackness: A critique of the sign and the Signifying Monkey. In *Studies in black American literature.* Ed. Joe Weixlmann and Chester J. Fontenot. Greenville, Fla.: Penkevill.

———. 1988. *The Signifying Monkey: A theory of African-American literary criticism.* New York: Oxford University Press.

———. 1991. The master's pieces: On canon formation and the Afro-American tradition. In *The bounds of race: Perspectives on hegemony and resistance.* Ed. Dominick LaCapra. Ithaca, N.Y.: Cornell University Press.

Gayle, Addison, Jr., ed. 1971. *The black aesthetic.* Garden City, N.Y.: Doubleday.

Gennari, John. 1991. Jazz criticism: Its development and ideology. *Black American Literature Forum* 25, no. 3:449–523.

Gershwin, George, DuBose Hayward, and Ira Gershwin. 1935. Vocal score. *Porgy and Bess.* New York: Gershwin.

Gershwin plays with orchestra. 1933. *Chicago Tribune* June 11.

Gilman, Caroline Howard. 1834. The country visit, chapter x, singing hymns. *Rose Bud, or Youth's Gazette* August 9:199.

Gleason, Ralph. 1975. *Celebrating the Duke and Louis, Bessie, Bird, Carman, Miles, Dizzy and other heroes.* Boston: Little, Brown.

Godwyn, Morgan. 1680. *The Negro's and Indian's advocate, suing for their admission into the church*. London: n.p.

Gold, Robert S. 1964. *A jazz lexicon*. New York: Knopf.

Gonzáles-Wippler, Migene. 1985. *Tales of the orishas*. New York: Original Publications.

Gospel pearls. 1921. Nashville: Sunday School Publishing Board, for National Baptist Convention, USA.

Goss, Linda, and Marian E. Barnes, eds. 1989. *Talk that talk: An anthology of African-American storytelling*. New York: Touchstone.

Green, Jeffrey. 1990. The Negro Renaissance in England. In *Black music in the Harlem Renaissance*. Ed. Samuel A. Floyd, Jr. Westport, Conn.: Greenwood Press.

Gridley, Mark. 1983. *Jazz styles*. Englewood Cliffs, N.J.: Prentice-Hall.

Grossman, James R. 1989. *Land of hope: Chicago, black southerners, and the Great Migration*. Chicago: University of Chicago Press.

Guralnick, Peter. 1982. *The listener's guide to the blues*. New York: Facts on File.

Gurney, Edmund. [1880] 1966. *The power of sound*. New York: Basic Books.

Haas, Robert B., ed. 1975. *William Grant Still and the fusion of cultures in American music*. Los Angeles: Black Sparrow Press.

Hall, Baynard F. 1852. *Frank Freeman's barber shop: A tale*. Louisville: Lost Cause Press. Microcard.

Hallowell, Emily, comp. and ed. [1907] 1976. *Plantation songs*. New York: AMS Press.

Hamilton, Virginia. 1974. *Paul Robeson: The life and times of a free black man*. New York: Harper & Row.

Handy, W. C. 1941. *Father of the blues*. New York: Macmillan.

Hanslick, Eduard. [1854] 1957. *The beautiful in music*. New York: Liberal Arts Press.

Harding, Vincent. 1981. *There is a river: The black struggle for freedom in America*. New York: Harcourt Brace Jovanovich.

Harris, Joel Chandler. [1881] 1982. *Uncle Remus, his songs and his sayings*. New York: Penguin Books.

Harris, Michael W. 1992. *The rise of gospel blues: The music of Thomas Andrew Dorsey in the urban church*. New York: Oxford University Press.

Harrison, Paul Carter. 1972. *The drama of Nommo: Black theater in the African continuum*. New York: Grove Press.

Hayden, Robert. 1975. *Angle of ascent: New and selected poems*. New York: Liveright.

Hazzard-Gordon, Katrina. 1990. *Jookin': The rise of social dance in African-American culture*. Philadelphia: Temple University Press.

Heilbut, Tony. 1985. *The gospel sound: Good news and bad times*. 3rd ed. New York: Limelight.

Henderson, David. 1983. *'Scuse me while I kiss the sky: The life of Jimi Hendrix*. New York: Bantam Books.

Henderson, Stephen. 1973. *Understanding the new black poetry: Black speech and black music as poetic references*. New York: Morrow.

Hentz, Caroline Lee Whiting. [1854] 1970. *The planter's northern bride*. Vol. 1. Chapel Hill: University of North Carolina Press.

Herskovits, Melville J. 1947. Problem, method, and theory in Afro-American studies. *Afroamerica* 1, no. 1–2:5–24.

Hewes, Henry, ed. 1964. *The best plays of 1963–1964.* New York: Dodd, Mead.

Hirshey, Gerri. 1984. *Nowhere to run: The story of soul music.* New York: Times Books.

Hobsbawn, Eric. 1983. Mass-producing traditions: Europe, 1870–1914. In *The invention of tradition.* Ed. Eric Hobsbawn and Terence Rangwer. Cambridge: Cambridge University Press.

Holcombe, William Henry. 1861. Sketches of plantation life. *Knickerbocker* June:619–633.

Holquist, Michael, and Vadim Liapunov. 1990. Preface. *Art and answerability: Early philosophical essay.* By M. M. Bakhtin. Austin: University of Texas Press.

hooks, bell. 1990. *Yearning: Race, gender, and cultural politics.* Boston: South End Press.

Hornbostel, E. M. von. 1926. American Negro songs. *International Review of Missions* 15:748–753.

Horne, Aaron. 1990. *Woodwind music of black composers.* New York: Greenwood Press.

———. 1991. *String music of black composers.* New York: Greenwood Press.

———. 1992. *Keyboard music of black composers.* New York: Greenwood Press.

Huet, Michel. 1978. *The dance, art, and ritual of Africa.* New York: Pantheon Books.

Huggins, Nathan Irvin. 1971. *Harlem Renaissance.* New York: Oxford University Press.

Hughes, Rupert, 1899. A eulogy of ragtime. *Musical Record* April 1:157–159.

Jablonski, Edward. 1987. *Gershwin.* Garden City, N.Y.: Doubleday.

Jackson, George Pullen. 1933. *White spirituals of the southern uplands.* Chapel Hill: University of North Carolina Press.

———. 1943. *White and Negro spirituals.* New York: Augustin.

Jackson, Irene V., comp. 1979. *Afro-American religious music: A bibliography and a catalog of gospel music.* Westport, Conn.: Greenwood Press.

———, ed. 1981. *Lift every voice and sing: A collection of Afro-American spirituals and other songs.* New York: Church Hymnal Corporation.

Jahn, Jahnheiz. 1961. *Muntu: An outline of the new African culture.* New York: Grove Press.

James, Willis Lawrence. 1955. The romance of the Negro folk cry in America. *Phylon* 16, no. 1 (first quarter):15–30.

Jasen, David A., and Trebor J. Tichenor. 1978. *Rags and ragtime: A history.* New York: Seabury Press.

Johnson, Hafiz Shabazz Farel, and John Miller Chernoff. 1991. Basic Conga drum rhythms in African-American musical styles. *Black Music Research Journal* 11, no. 1:55–75.

Johnson, James Weldon, ed. 1922. *The book of American Negro poetry, chosen and edited with an essay on the Negro's creative genius.* New York: Harcourt, Brace.

———. [1930] 1977. *Black Manhattan.* New York: Atheneum.

———. [1912] 1989. *The autobiography of an ex-coloured man.* New York: Random House.

Johnson, James Weldon, and James Rosamond Johnson. [1925] 1981. *The book of Negro spirituals.* New York: Da Capo Press.

———. [1926] 1981. *The second book of Negro spirituals.* New York: Da Capo Press.

Jones, A. M. 1959. *Studies in African music.* 2 vols. Oxford: Oxford University Press.

Jones, Jessica Janice. [1980] 1990. DeFord Bailey. *Black Music Research Journal* 10, no. 1:29–31.

Jones, LeRoi. *See* Baraka, Amiri.

Joplin, Scott. [1911] 1972. Vocal score. *Treemonisha*. Chicago: Dramatic.

Juba at Vauxhall. 1848. *Illustrated London News* August 5:77–78.

Kebede, Ashenafi. 1982. *Roots of black music*. Englewood Cliffs, N.J.: Prentice-Hall.

Keck, George R., and Sherrill V. Martin, eds. 1988. *Feel the spirit: Studies in nineteenth-century Afro-American music*. Westport, Conn.: Greenwood Press.

Keil, Charles. 1979. *Tiv song: The sociology of art in a classless society*. Chicago: University of Chicago Press.

Kirkeby, Ed. 1966. *Ain't misbehavin'*. New York: Dodd, Mead.

Kivy, Peter. 1984. *Sound and semblance: Reflections on musical representation*. Princeton, N.J.: Princeton University Press.

———. 1988. *Osmin's rage: Philosophical reflections on opera, drama, and text*. Princeton, N.J.: Princeton University Press.

———. [1980] 1989. The corded shell: Reflections on musical expression. In *Sound sentiment: An essay on the musical emotions, including the complete text of "The corded shell."* Philadelphia: Temple University Press.

———. 1990. *Music alone: Philosophical reflections on the purely musical experience*. Ithaca, N.Y.: Cornell University Press.

Knappert, Jan. 1989. *The A to Z of African proverbs*. London: Karnak House.

Knoblauch, C. H. 1992. Ernst Cassirer and the philosophy of symbolic forms. In *The philosophy of discourse: The rhetorical turn in twentieth century thought*. Vol. 2. Ed. Chip Sills and George H. Jensen. Portsmouth, N.H.: Boynton/Cook.

Kramer, Dale. 1966. *Chicago Renaissance: The literary life in the Midwest, 1900–1930*. New York: Appleton-Century.

Kramer, Lawrence. 1990. *Music as cultural practice, 1800–1900*. Berkeley: University of California Press.

L. E. B. 1879. Life in Charleston. *Independent* September 18.

Labov, William, Paul Cohen, Clarence Robbins, and John Lewis. [1968] 1981. Toasts. In *Mother wit from the laughing barrel: Readings in the interpretation of Afro-American folklore*. Ed. Alan Dundes. New York: Garland.

Landry, Bart. 1987. *The new black middle class*. Berkeley: University of California Press.

Langer, Suzanne K. 1979. *Philosophy in a new key: A study in the symbolism of reason, rite, and art*. 3rd ed. Cambridge, Mass.: Harvard University Press.

Layne, Maude Wanzer. 1942. *The Negro's contribution to music*. Charleston, W.Va.: Mathews.

Lead me, guide me: The African American Catholic hymnal. 1987. Chicago: G. I. A. Publications.

Lee, Benjamin. 1985. Peirce, Frege, Saussure, and Whorf: The semiotic mediation of ontology. In *Semiotic mediation: Sociological and psychological perspectives*. Ed. Elizabeth Mertz and Richard Parmentier. New York: Academic Press.

Leonard, Neil. 1987. *Jazz: Myth and religion*. New York: Oxford University Press.

Lerma, Dominique-René de. 1984. A concordance of scores and recordings of music by black composers. *Black Music Research Journal* 4:60–140.

Levine, Lawrence W. 1977. *Black culture and black consciousness: Afro-American folk thought from slavery to freedom*. New York: Oxford University Press.

Lewis, David Levering. 1970. *King: A critical biography.* New York: Praeger.

⸻. 1981. *When Harlem was in vogue.* New York: Knopf.

Lieb, Sandra. 1981. *Mother of the blues.* Amherst: University of Massachusetts Press.

Litweiler, John. 1984. *The freedom principle: Jazz after 1958.* New York: Morrow.

Locke, Alain. [1936] 1968. *The Negro and his music.* New York: Kennikat Press.

Logan, Wendell. 1984. The ostinato idea in black improvised music. *Black Perspective in Music* 12, no. 2:193–215.

Loggins, Vernon. 1944. Neber said a mumblin' word. *Negro Story* 1, no. 6:67–72.

Lomax, Alan. 1970. The homogeneity of African–Afro-American musical style. In *Afro-American anthropology: Contemporary perspectives.* Ed. Norman E. Whitten, Jr., and John F. Szwed. New York: Free Press.

⸻. 1975. Africanisms in New World music. In *The Haitian potential.* Ed. Vera Rubin and Richard P. Schaedel. New York: Teachers College Press.

⸻. 1977. Liner notes. *Georgia Sea Island songs.* New World NW 278.

Lornell, Kip. 1988. *"Happy in the service of the Lord": Afro-American gospel quartets in Memphis.* Urbana: University of Illinois Press.

Lotz, Rainer E. 1990. The black troubadours: Black entertainers in Europe, 1896–1915. *Black Music Research Journal* 10, no. 2:253–273.

Lovell, John. 1972. *Black song: The forge and the flame.* New York: Macmillan.

Lovinggood, Penman. [1921] 1978. *Famous modern Negro musicians.* 2nd ed. New York: Da Capo Press.

Lyons, Len. 1980. *The 101 best jazz albums: A history of jazz on records.* New York: Morrow.

Marquis, Donald M. 1978. *Buddy Bolden: First man of jazz.* Baton Rouge: Louisiana State University Press.

Marr, W., II. 1972. A second renaissance? *Crisis* 79:198–203.

Martin, Tony. 1983. *The Pan-African connection: From slavery to Garvey and beyond.* Dover, Mass.: Majority Press.

Mbiti, John S. [1969] 1990. *African religions and philosophy.* Portsmouth, N.H: Heinemann.

McKay, Claude. 1953. *Selected poems of Claude McKay.* New York: Harcourt, Brace.

McKee, Margaret, and Fred Chisenhall. 1981. *Beale black and blue: Life and music on America's Main Street.* Baton Rouge: Louisiana State University Press.

Menn, Donn. 1978. Liner notes. *The essential Jimi Hendrix.* Reprise 2RS 2245.

Meyer, Leonard B. 1954. *Emotion and meaning in music.* Chicago: University of Chicago Press.

⸻. 1967. *Music, the arts, and ideas.* Chicago: University of Chicago Press.

Miller, Merle. [1952] 1971. The judges and the judged. In *Blacklisting: Two key documents.* New York: Arno Press and The New York Times.

Miller, Ruth. 1971. *Blackamerican literature: 1960–present.* Beverly Hills, Calif.: Glencoe Press.

Mitchell-Kernan, Claudia. [1979] 1981. Signifying. In *Mother wit from the laughing barrel: Readings in the interpretation of Afro-American folklore.* Ed. Alan Dundes. New York: Garland.

Moe, Orin. 1980. William Grant Still: *Songs of separation. Black Music Research Journal* 1:18–36.

Moon, Bucklin. 1944. Slack's blues. *Negro Story* 1, no. 4:3–8.

Morton, David C., with Charles K. Wolfe. 1991. *DeFord Bailey: A black star in early country music*. Knoxville: University of Tennessee Press.

Mueller, John H. 1951. *The American symphony orchestra: A social history of musical taste*. Bloomington: Indiana University Press.

Murphy, John. 1990. Jazz improvisation: The joy of influence. *Black Perspective in Music* 18:7–19.

Murray, Albert. 1973. *The hero and the blues*. Columbia: University of Missouri Press.

———. 1976. *Stomping the blues*. New York: Doubleday.

Music. 1946. *Negro Story* 2, no. 3:57–58.

Navaksy, Victor S. 1980. *Naming names*. New York: Penguin Books.

Negro folk songs. [1895] 1976. *Black Perspective in Music* 4, no. 2:145–151.

Nelson, John S., Allan Megill, and Donald N. McCloskey. 1987. *The rhetoric of the human sciences: Language and argument in scholarship and public affairs*. Madison: University of Wisconsin Press.

The new national Baptist hymnal. 1982. Nashville: National Baptist Publishing Board.

Nketia, J. H. Kwabena. 1963. *Drumming in Akan communities*. New York: Nelson.

———. 1974. *The music of Africa*. New York: Norton.

Northrup, Solomon. [1853] 1970. *Twelve years a slave: Narrative of Solomon Northrup, a citizen of New York, kidnapped in Washington City in 1841 and rescued in 1853 from a cotton plantation near the Red River of Louisiana*. Westport, Conn.: Greenwood Press.

Noted tenor and Miss Margaret Bonds star with symphony. 1933. *Chicago Defender* June 17.

Odum, Howard W. 1911. Folk-song and folk poetry as found in the secular songs of the southern Negroes. *Journal of American Folklore* 24 (July–September):255–294; (October–December):351–396.

Oja, Carol J. 1992. "New Music" and the "New Negro": Antecedents for William Grant Still's *Afro-American Symphony*. *Black Music Research Journal* 12, no. 2:145–169.

Oliver, Paul. 1961. *Blues fell this morning: The meaning of the blues*. New York: Horizon Press.

———. 1970. *Savannah syncopators: African retentions in the blues*. New York: Stein & Day.

———. 1984. *Songsters and saints: Vocal traditions on race records*. New York: Cambridge University Press.

Ondaatje, Michael. 1979. *Coming through slaughter*. New York: Avon Books.

O'Neall, John Belton. [1848] 1970. *The Negro law of South Carolina. Collected and digested by John Belton O'Neall*. Chicago: Libra Resources. Microfiche.

Opera "Aida" ready for curtain call. 1943. *Chicago Defender* February 20.

Origin of ragtime. 1901. *Metronome* 3:7–8.

Paine, Lewis W. 1851. *Six years in a Georgia prison: Narrative of Lewis W. Paine, who suffered imprisonment six years in Georgia, for the crime of aiding the escape of a fellowman from that state after he had fled from slavery*. New York: Author.

Palmer, Robert. 1981. *Deep blues*. New York: Viking Press.

Parmentier, Richard J. 1985. Sign's place in *Medias Res:* Peirce's concept of semiotic mediation. In *Semiotic mediation: Sociological and psychological perspectives.* Ed. Elizabeth Mertz and Richard Parmentier. New York: Academic Press.

Patterson, Willis, comp. 1977. *Anthology of art songs by black American composers.* New York: Edward B. Marks Music.

Pentecostal hymns, no. 2: A winnowed collection. 1895. Chicago: Hope.

Philips, John Edward. 1991. The African heritage of white America. In *Africanisms in American culture.* Ed. Joseph E. Holloway. Bloomington: Indiana University Press.

Pike, Gustavus D. [1875] 1974. *The singing campaign for ten thousand pounds.* Rev. ed. New York: American Missionary Association.

Puckett, N. N. 1926. *Folk beliefs of the southern Negro.* Chapel Hill: University of North Carolina Press.

Rabinowitz, Peter J. 1991. Whiting the wrongs of history: The resurrection of Scott Joplin. *Black Music Research Journal* 11, no. 2:157–177.

Raboteau, Albert J. 1978. *Slave religion: The "invisible institution" in the antebellum South.* New York: Oxford University Press.

Radano, Ronald. 1992. Jazzin' the classics: The AACM's challenge to mainstream aesthetics. *Black Music Research Journal* 12, no. 1:79–95.

Rampersad, Arnold. 1986. *The life of Langston Hughes.* Vol. 1, *1902–1941: I, too, sing America.* New York: Oxford University Press.

———. 1988. *The life of Langston Hughes.* Vol. 2, *1941–1967: I dream a world.* New York: Oxford University Press.

Randall, Dudley, ed. [1971] 1988. *The black poets.* New York: Bantam Books.

Rattenbury, Ken. 1990. *Duke Ellington: Jazz composer.* New Haven, Conn.: Yale University Press.

Reagon, Bernice. 1990. The lined hymn as a song of freedom. *Black Music Research Bulletin* 12, no. 1:4–7.

Red channels: The report of communist influence in radio and television. 1950. New York: American Business Consultants.

Reese, Krista. 1982. *Chuck Berry: Mr. Rock 'n' Roll.* London: Proteus Books.

Reisser, Marsha J. 1982. Compositional techniques and Afro-American musical traits in selected published works by Howard Swanson. Ph.D. diss., University of Wisconsin. Ann Arbor: University Microfilms.

Report of the National Advisory Commission on Civil Disorders. 1968. New York Times ed. New York: Dutton.

Rice, Edward Leroy. 1911. *Monarchs of minstrelsy.* New York: Kenny.

Richards, Donna Marimba. 1980. *Let the circle be unbroken: The implications African spirituality in the diaspora.* N.p.: Author.

Ricks, George Robinson. 1977. *Some aspects of the religious music of the United States Negro: An ethnomusicological study with special emphasis on the gospel tradition.* New York: Arno Press.

Ritz, David. 1985. *Divided soul: The life of Marvin Gaye.* New York: McGraw-Hill.

Robeson, Eslanda Goode. 1930. *Paul Robeson, Negro.* New York: Harper Brothers.

Rorty, Richard, ed. 1967. *The linguistic turn: Recent essays in philosophical method.* Chicago: University of Chicago Press.

Rosenfeld, Paul. 1929. *An hour with American music*. Philadelphia: Lippincott.

Russell, George. 1959. *The Lydian chromatic concept of tonal organization for improvisation*. New York: Concept.

Ryder, Georgia. 1990. Harlem Renaissance ideals in the music of R. Nathaniel Dett. In *Black music in the Harlem Renaissance*. Ed. Samuel A. Floyd, Jr. Westport, Conn.: Greenwood Press.

Sackheim, Eric. 1975. *The blues line: A collection of blues lyrics from Leadbelly to Muddy Waters*. New York: Schirmer Books.

Said, Edward W. 1991. *Musical elaborations*. New York: Columbia University Press.

Salzman, Eric. 1988. *Twentieth-century music: An introduction*. 2nd ed. Englewood Cliffs, N.J.: Prentice-Hall.

Scarupa, Harriet Jackson. 1986. Setting Malcolm to music. *American Visions* September–October: 31–37.

Schwerin, Jules. 1992. *Got to tell it: Mahalia Jackson, queen of gospel*. New York: Oxford University Press.

Scott Joplin. 1907. *AMAJ* [*American Music and Art Journal*] December 13:5.

Seroff, Doug. 1980. Liner notes. *Birmingham Quartet anthology*. Clanka Lanka CL 144,001/002.

———. 1990. Old-time black gospel quartet contests. *Black Music Research Journal* 10, no. 1:27–28.

Shaw, Arnold. 1978. *Honkers and shouters: The golden years of rhythm and blues*. New York: Collier Books.

———. 1979. The panorama of black music. *Billboard* June:BM4–6, BM10, BM39.

———. 1982. *Dictionary of American pop/rock*. New York: Schirmer Books.

Shorris, Earl. 1992. *Latinos: A biography of the people*. New York: Norton.

Small, Christopher. 1987. *Music of the common tongue: Survival and celebration in Afro-American music*. New York: Riverrun Press.

Smith, Barbara Herrnstein. 1990. Vale/valuation. In *Critical terms for literary study*. Ed. Frank Lentricchia and Thomas McLaughlin. Chicago: University of Chicago Press.

Smith, Hale. 1984. Telephone conversation with the author, September 31.

Smith, N. Clark. 1925. Music score. *Negro Folk Suite*. Chicago: Healy.

Smith, W. O. 1991. *Sideman: The long gig of W. O. Smith*. Nashville: Rutledge Hill Press.

Songs of Zion. 1981. Nashville: Abingdon, for United Methodist Church.

Southern, Eileen. 1971. *The music of black Americans*. New York: Norton.

———. 1973. Afro-American musical materials. *Black Perspective in Music* 1, no. 1:24–32.

———. 1982. *Biographical dictionary of Afro-American and African music*. Westport, Conn.: Greenwood Press.

———. 1983. *The music of black Americans*. 2nd ed. New York: Norton.

Southern, Eileen, and Josephine Wright, comps. 1990. *African-American traditions in song, sermon, tale, and dance, 1600s–1920: An annotated bibliography of literature, collections, and artworks*. Westport, Conn.: Greenwood Press.

Spellman, A. B. 1970. *Four lives in the bebop business*. New York: Schocken Books.

Spencer, Jon Michael. 1987a. The heavenly anthem: Holy Ghost singing in the primal Pentecostal revival (1906–1909). *Journal of Black Sacred Music* 1, no. 1:1–33.

————. 1987b. *Sacred symphony: The chanted sermon of the black preacher.* Westport, Conn.: Greenwood Press.

————. 1992. *Black hymnody: A hymnological history of the African-American church.* Knoxville: University of Tennessee Press.

Spenny, Susan Dix. 1921. Riddles and ring-games from Raleigh. *Journal of American Folklore* 34:110–115.

Spillers, Hortense. 1991. Moving on down the line: Variations on the African-American sermon. In *The bounds of race: Perspectives on hegemony and resistance.* Ed. Dominick LaCapra. Ithaca, N.Y.: Cornell University Press.

Starr, Frederick. 1988. Why I applaud between movements. Speech delivered at the annual meeting of the American Symphony Orchestra League. Chicago, June 16.

————. 1995. *Bamboula! The life and times of Louis Moreau Gottschalk.* New York: Oxford University Press.

Still, William Grant. 1975. A composer's viewpoint. In *William Grant Still and the fusion of cultures in American music.* Ed. Robert B. Haas. Los Angeles: Black Sparrow Press.

Stoddard, Tom. 1971. *Pops Foster: The autobiography of a New Orleans jazzman.* Berkeley: University of California Press.

Stuckey, Sterling. 1987. *Slave culture: Nationalist theory and the foundations of black America.* New York: Oxford University Press.

Taft, Michael. 1983. *Blues lyric poetry: An anthology and a concordance.* Vol. 1. New York: Garland.

Tarasti, Eero. 1979. *Myth and music: A semiotic approach to the aesthetics of myth in music, especially that of Wagner, Sibelius, and Stravinsky.* New York: Mouton.

Tate, Gayle T. 1988. Black nationalism: An angle of vision. *Western Journal of Black Studies* 12:40–48.

Taylor, Billy. 1983. *Jazz piano.* Dubuque, Iowa: Brown.

————. 1992. Liner notes. *Videmus: Works by T. J. Anderson, David Baker, Donal Fox, Olly Wilson.* New World 80423-2.

Terry, William E. 1977. *The Negro Music Journal:* An appraisal. *Black Perspective in Music* 5, no. 2:146–160.

Thomas, J. C. 1975. *Chasin' the Trane: The music and mystique of John Coltrane.* Garden City, N.Y.: Doubleday.

Thompson, Robert Farris. 1983. *Flash of the spirit.* New York: Vintage Books.

————. 1989. The song that named the land. In *Black art—ancestral legacy: The African impulse in African-American art.* Dallas: Dallas Museum of Art.

Tischler, Alice. 1981. *Fifteen black American composers: A bibliography of their works.* Detroit: Information Coordinators.

Tolson, M. B. 1944. *Rendezvous with America.* New York: Dodd, Mead.

————. 1953. *Libretto for the Republic of Liberia.* New York: Twayne.

————. 1965. *Harlem gallery. Book I: The curator.* New York: Twayne.

Tomlinson, Gary. 1991. Cultural dialogics and jazz: A white historian signifies. *Black Music Research Journal* 11, no. 2:229–265.

Tonsor, John. 1892. Negro music. *Music* 3:119–122.

Tortolano, William. 1977. *Samuel Coleridge-Taylor: Anglo-black composer. 1875–1912.* Metuchen, N.J.: Scarecrow Press.

293

Trotter, James Monroe. 1878. *Music and some highly musical people*. Boston: Lee and Shepard.

Tucker, Bruce. 1989. "Tell Tchaikovsky the news": Postmodernism, popular culture, and the emergence of rock 'n' roll. *Black Music Research Journal* 9, no. 2:271–278.

Turner, Arlin. 1956. *George W. Cable: A biography*. Durham, N.C.: Duke University Press.

Turner, Darwin. 1987. Retrospective of a renaissance. *Black Scholar* 18:2–10.

Walker, Sheila S. 1972. *Ceremonial spirit possession in Africa and Afro-America: Forms, meanings, and functional significance for individual and social groups*. Leiden: Brill.

Walker-Hill, Helen. 1992a. Black women composers in Chicago: Then and now. *Black Music Research Journal* 12, no. 1:1–23.

———. 1992b. *Piano music by black women composers: A catalog of solo and ensemble works*. Westport, Conn.: Greenwood Press.

Waller, Maurice, and Anthony Calabrese. 1977. *Fats Waller*. New York: Schirmer Books.

Waterman, Richard. 1948. "Hot" rhythm in Negro music. *Journal of the American Musicological Society* 1:24–37.

———. 1952. African influence on American Negro music. In *Acculturation in the Americas*. Ed. Sol Tax. New York: Cooper Square.

Watson, Edward A. 1971. Bessie's blues. In *Richard Wright: Impressions and perspectives*. Ed. David Ray and Robert M. Farnsworth. Ann Arbor: University of Michigan Press.

Watson, John F. 1881. *Annals of Philadelphia, and Pennsylvania, in the olden time*. Vol. 2. Philadelphia: Stoddart.

Weinstein, Norman C. 1992. *A night in Tunisia: Imaginings of Africa in jazz*. Metuchen, N.J.: Scarecrow Press.

Wells, Dicky. 1971. *The night people: Reminiscences of a jazzman*. Boston: Crescendo.

Wentworth, Harold, and Stuart Berg Flexner, comps. and eds. 1975. *Dictionary of American slang*. 2nd ed. New York: Crowell.

White, Charles. 1984. *The life and times of Little Richard: The quasar of rock*. New York: Harmony Books.

Williams, Martin. 1973. Liner notes. *Smithsonian collection of classic jazz*. Smithsonian Institution/Columbia Special Products P6 11891.

———. 1983. *The jazz tradition*. New and rev. ed. New York: Oxford University Press.

Wilson, Olly. 1973. The black American composer. *Black Perspective in Music* 1, no. 2:33–36.

———. 1983. Black music as an art form. *Black Music Research Journal* 3:1–22.

———. 1990. The influence of jazz on the history and development of concert music. In *New perspectives in jazz*. Ed. David N. Baker. Washington, D.C.: Smithsonian Institution Press.

———. 1992a. The heterogeneous sound ideal in African-American music. In *New perspectives on music: Essays in honor of Eileen Southern*. Ed. Josephine Wright, with Samuel A. Floyd, Jr. Warren, Mich.: Harmonie Park Press.

———. 1992b. Liner notes. *Videmus: Works by T. J. Anderson, David Baker, Donal Fox, Olly Wilson*. New World 80423-2.

———. 1992c. Music score. *Sinfonia*. Newton Centre, Mass.: Gunmar Music.

Wolfe, Charles K., ed. 1991. *Thomas W. Talley's Negro folk rhymes*. Enlarged ed. Knoxville: University of Tennessee Press.

Work, John W. 1949. Changing patterns in Negro folk songs. *Journal of American Folklore* 62:136–144.

Wright, Richard. [1940] 1987. *Native Son.* New York: Quality Paperback.

———. [1945] 1987. *Black Boy.* New York: Quality Paperback.

Wuorinen, Charles. 1974. Liner notes. *Spectrum: New American Music.* Vol. 5. Nonesuch H-71303.

Zahan, Dominique. [1970] 1979. *The religion, spirituality, and thought of traditional Africa.* Chicago: University of Chicago Press.

Zwigoff, Terry. 1987. Forgotten American music: Black string bands and their rare recordings. *Strings* (Winter):16–18.

Sound Recordings Cited

Adderley, Cannonball. Mercy, mercy, mercy. Work song. *The Best of Cannonball Adderley*. Capitol SKA 02939.

Afro-American music: A demonstration recording. Comp. Willis Lawrence James. Asch AA702 ([1970] 1978).

Air. *Air lore*. Arista AN-30143 (1979).

———. *Air time*. Nessa N-12 (1978).

Anderson, T. J. Intermezzi. *Videmus: Works by T. J. Anderson, David Baker, Donal Fox, Olly Wilson*. New World 80423-2 (1992).

———. Variations on a theme by M. B. Tolson. *Spectrum: New American music*. Vol. 5. Contemporary Chamber Ensemble. Nonesuch H-71303 (1968).

Anthology of rhythm and blues. Columbia CS 9802 (1969–).

Armstrong, Louis. Dippermouth blues. Epic LN160003 (1923). Swaggie ST1257. Reissued on *Smithsonian collection of classic jazz*. Smithsonian Institution/Columbia Special Products P6 11891 (1973).

———. Hotter than that. Columbia CL851 (1927). Reissued on *Smithsonian collection of classic jazz*. Smithsonian Institution/Columbia Special Products P6 11891 (1973).

———. Weather bird. Columbia CL853 (1928). Reissued on *Smithsonian collection of classic jazz*. Smithsonian Institution/Columbia Special Products P6 11891 (1973).

———. West end blues. Columbia G304161 (1928). Reissued on *Smithsonian collection of classic jazz*. Smithsonian Institution/Columbia Special Products P6 11891 (1973).

Art songs by black American composers. University of Michigan SM-0015 (1981).

Ayler, Albert. *Spiritual unity*. ESP-Disk 1002 (1964).

Babbitt, Milton. All set. *Spectrum: New American music*. Vol. 5. Nonesuch H-71303 (1968).

Bailey, DeFord. Dixie Flyer blues. Pan American blues. *Harmonica showcase*. Matchbox MSE 218 (1984).

Baker, David. Through this vale of tears. *Videmus: Works by T. J. Anderson, David Baker, Donal Fox, Olly Wilson*. New World 80423-2 (1992).

Basie, Count. Doggin' around. *Smithsonian collection of classic jazz*. Smithsonian Institution/Columbia Special Products P6 11891 (1973).

———. Signifyin'. *Kansas City shout*. Pablo PACD 2310-859-2 (1987).

Birmingham quartet anthology. Clanka Lanka CL 144,001/002 (1980).

Blakey, Art. *The African beat: Art Blakey and the Afro-drum Ensemble.* Blue Note BLP 4097 (1962).

———. *Holiday for skins.* Blue Note BLP 4004/5 (1979).

Bonds, Margaret. Three dream portraits. *Art songs by black American composers.* Claritha Buggs, with piano. University of Michigan SM-0015 (1981).

Booker T. and the MGs. *Booker T. and the MGs.* Atlantic 8202.

Boone, John W. ("Blind"). Camp meeting no. 1. QRS 400034. Piano roll.

———. Rag medly no. 2. QRS 200142. Piano roll.

Boyer Brothers. *The famous Boyer Brothers: Take your troubles to Jesus.* Savoy MG 14143 (1966).

Braxton, Anthony. *For alto.* Delmark DS 420/421 (1969).

Brenston, Jackie. Rocket eighty-eight. Chess 1458 (1951).

Brown, James. *James Brown: Unbeatable sixteen hits.* King 919.

Brown, Ruth. Happiness is a thing called Joe. Atlantic A-292-10 SP.

———. Love me, baby. Atlantic A-290-10 SP.

———. (Mama) He treats your daughter mean. Atlantic A-960-10 SP.

———. R&B blues. Atlantic A-515-10 SP.

Burke, Solomon. *Best.* Atlantic 8109.

Burnett, J. C. Downfall of Nebuchadnezzar. I've even heard of thee. Merrit 2203 (1926).

Caesar, Shirley. *Love calling your name.* Myrrh MSB-6721 (1983).

Calloway, Cab. Pickin' the cabbage. *Jammin' for the jackpot: Big bands and territory bands of the 30s.* New World NW 217 (1977).

Campbell, James. *Blind James Campbell and his Nashville street band.* Arhoolie 1015 (1968).

The Caravans. *The best of the Caravans.* Savoy DBL 7013 (1977).

Charles, Ray. A bit of soul. Atlantic 45-2094 (1958).

———. Drown in my own tears. Atlantic 1085 (1959).

———. Hallelujah. Atlantic 1096 (1956).

———. I gotta woman. ABC 45-10649 (1965).

———. *Modern sounds in country and western.* Vols. 1 and 2. ABC 410, 435 (1962, 1963).

———. What'd I say. Atlantic 2031 (1959).

Cherry, Don. *Complete communion.* Blue Note 84226 (ca. 1960).

Cleveland, James. *James Cleveland: With angelic choir.* Savoy 14067, 14131, 14752.

———. *James Cleveland and the Southern California Community Choir.* Savoy MG 14245 (1976).

Coleman, Ornett. *Free jazz.* Atlantic 1364 (1960).

———. *The shape of jazz to come.* Atlantic 1317 (1959).

Coleridge-Taylor, Samuel. African suite. Danse nègre. Onaway, awake, beloved. London Symphony Orchestra. The black composers series. Columbia M-32782.

Coltrane, John. *African brass.* Vol. 20. Impulse AS-9273 (1974).

———. *Afro blue impressions.* Pablo Live 2620101 (1977).

———. Alabama. *Live at Birdland.* Impulse AS-50 (1963).

———. *Ascension.* Impulse 95 (1965).

———. *Giant steps.* Atlantic SD 1311 (1959).

———. *"Live" at the Village Vanguard.* Impulse A-10 (1961).

————. *A love supreme.* Impulse AS-77 (1964).

————. Naima. *Giant steps.* Atlantic SD 1311 (1959).

————. Tunji. *The John Coltrane Quartet.* Impulse AS-21 (1962).

Cook, Will Marion. Overture to *In Dahomey. The Black Music Repertory Ensemble in Concert.* Center for Black Music Research CBMR002-C1 (1992).

————. Three Negro songs. *Black music: The written tradition.* Donnie Ray Albert, bass baritone; Black Music Repertory Ensemble. Center for Black Music Research CBMR 001 (1990).

Cooke, Sam. *The two sides of Sam Cooke.* Specialty SPS 2119.

————. You send me. KEEN 4013 (1957). Reissued as RCA 447-0566 (1957).

Cunningham, Arthur. Harlem suite: Lullabye for a jazz baby. *The black composer in America.* Oakland Symphony Orchestra. Desto DC-7107 (ca. 1971).

Davis, Miles. *Bitches brew.* Columbia GQ 30997 (ca. 1970).

————. Blue and boogie. *Greatest hits.* Walkin' Prestige PREP 1358 (1954). Reissued as *Greatest Hits.* Columbia CS 9808.

————. Concierto de Aranjuez. *Sketches of Spain.* Arranged and conducted by Gil Evans. Columbia CS 8271.

————. *E.S.P.* Columbia CS 9150 (1965).

————. *George Gershwin's Porgy and Bess.* Orchestra under the direction of Gil Evans. Columbia CK 40647 (1987).

————. *In a silent way.* Columbia PC-9875 (1969).

————. *Miles Davis and his orchestra.* Ozone 2 (1948).

————. *Miles smiles.* Columbia CS 9401 (1966).

Dawson, William Levi. *Negro folk symphony.* American Symphony Orchestra. Decca Gold Label DL 71077 (1963).

Dett, R. Nathaniel. The chariot jubilee. *Music of early black composers.* Morgan State University Choir. Audio House AHS-30F75 (1975).

————. *The ordering of Moses.* Mobile Symphony Orchestra; Talladega University Choir. Silver Crest TAL-428686-S (1968).

Dixon, Jessye. *It's all right now.* Light LS-5719 (1977).

————. *Jesus, I love calling your name.* Myrrh MSB-6721 (1983).

Dorsey, Thomas A. *Georgia Tom Dorsey: Come on mama, do that dance, 1928–1932.* Yazoo L 1041.

————. *Precious Lord: New gospel recordings of the great gospel songs of Thomas A. Dorsey.* Columbia KG 32151.

Dranes, Arizona. *Songsters and saints: Vocal traditions on race records.* Vol. 2. Matchbook MSEX 2003/4 (1984).

Eckstine, Billy. Jelly, Jelly. Bluebird B-11065 (1940).

————. *Mr. "B".* Ember EMB 3338.

————. *Together.* Spotlight 100.

Ellington, Duke. Dear old Southland. *The indispensable Duke Ellington.* Vol. 2. RCA France PM43697 (1933).

————. Dicty glide. Victor 49767 (1929).

————. East St. Louis toodle-oo. *Smithsonian collection of classic jazz.* Smithsonian Institution/Columbia Special Products P6 11891 (1973).

————. Happy-go-lucky local. *Ellington 55*. Capitol W-251 ([1954]).

————. *A tone parallel to Harlem*. Columbia ML4639 (1951).

Ellington, Duke, and Mahalia Jackson. Twenty-third Psalm. *Black, brown and beige*. Duke Ellington and His Orchestra. CBS S 63 363 (1958).

Europe, James Reese. Castle house rag. Castle walk. Clarinet marmalade. Memphis blues. *Steppin' on the gas: Rags to jazz (1913–1927)*. Europe's Society Orchestra. New World NW269 (1977).

The Falcons. I found love. Lu Pine 1003 (1962).

Favors, Malachi. *Congliptious*. Nessa 2 (1968).

Franklin, Aretha. *Aretha's greatest hits*. Atlantic SD 8295 (1971).

————. I never loved a man (the way I loved you). Atlantic 2386 (1967).

Georgia Sea Island songs. New World NW 278 (1977).

Gershwin, George. *Porgy and Bess*. Houston Grand Opera. RCA ARL-3-2109 (1976).

Gillespie, Dizzy. Pickin' the cabbage. *Jammin' for the jackpot*. New World NW 217.

Hawkins, Coleman. Picasso. Verve 2304537 (1948).

Hawkins, Edwin. Oh happy day. Pavillion 20001 (1969).

Hayes, Isaac. *Hot buttered soul*. Enterprise ENS 1001 (ca. 1970).

Henderson, Fletcher. Dichty blues. Vocalion 14654 (1923).

————. Stampede. *Smithsonian collection of classic jazz*. Smithsonian Institution/Columbia Special Products P6 11891 (1973).

————. Wrapping it up. *Smithsonian collection of classic jazz*. Smithsonian Institution/Columbia Special Products P6 11891 (1973).

Hendrix, Jimi. *Band of gypsies*. Capitol STAO 472 (1970).

————. *The essential Jimi Hendrix*. 2 vols. Reprise 2RS 2245 (1978, 1979).

————. *Friends from the beginning: Little Richard and Jimi Hendrix*. ALA LP-1972 (1972).

History of rhythm and blues vocal groups. Atlantic Cat 790132-1 (1983).

Howlin' Wolf. Moaning at midnight. How many more years (1951). Reissued on *The Chess box*. Chess/MCA CHD 3-9332 (1991).

Hurt, Mississippi John. Big leg blues. *Mississippi moaners*. Yazoo L1009.

I hear music in the air: A treasury of gospel music. BMG Music 2099-2R.

Johnson, James P. Yamakraw. *The symphonic jazz of James P. Johnson (1894–1955)*. William Albright, piano. Digital MMD 60066A (1986).

Johnson, James Weldon, and J. Rosamond Johnson. Lift every voice and sing. *Works by William Grant Still*. Videmus. New World 80399-2 (1990).

Jones, Maggie. Box car blues. Columbia 14047-D (1924).

The Jones Boys Sing Band. Pickin' a rib. *The human orchestra*. Clanka Lanka 144,003 (1985).

Joplin, Scott. Maple leaf rag. *Smithsonian collection of classic jazz*. Smithsonian Institution/Columbia Special Products P6 11891 (1973).

————. Original rags. *Jazz*. Vol. 2. Folkways FJ2811 (1953).

Jordan, Louis. *Let the good times roll*. Decca 8551.

Kay, Ulysses. Concerto for orchestra. *American concertos*. Orchestra Sinfónica del Teatro La Fenice. Sarabande VC-81047 (1953).

————. Concerto for orchestra. *The black composer in America*. Oakland Youth Orchestra. Desto DC-7107 (ca. 1977).

————. *Fantasy variations.* Oslo Philharmonic Orchestra. Composers Recordings CRI SD209.

————. *Serenade for orchestra.* Louisville Symphony Orchestra. Louisville Orchestra LOU 545-8 (ca. 1954).

————. A short overture. *The black composer in America.* Oakland Youth Orchestra. Desto DC-7107 (ca. 1977).

————. *Sinfonia.* Oslo Philharmonic Orchestra. Composers Recordings CRI 139 (1950).

King, B. B. *B. B. King "Now Appearing" at Ole Miss.* MCA D2-8106 (1980).

Lacy, Rubin. Ham hound crave. *Mississippi moaners.* Yazoo L1009.

The Last Poets. Douglas Z 30811 (ca. 1970s). [Distributed by PIP Records]

Ledbetter, Huddie ("Leadbelly"). *Leadbelly: Last sessions.* Folkways FA 2941/42 (1962).

————. *Leadbelly: Shout on.* Folkways FTS 31030.

————. Skip to my Lou. Asch SC-79. Disc 5071.

Lewis, Furry. Big chief blues. Yazoo L-1002 (1927).

Lewis, Meade Lux. Honky tonk train. *Smithsonian collection of classic jazz.* Smithsonian Institution/Columbia Special Products P6 11891 (1973).

Little Richard. *Friends from the beginning: Little Richard and Jimi Hendrix.* ALA LP-1972 (1972).

————. *Little Richard is back.* Vee Jay LP-1107 (1964).

Logan, Wendell. Runagate runagate. *The Black Music Repertory Ensemble in concert.* Center for Black Music Research CBMR002-C2 (1992).

Master drummers of Dagbon. Rounder 5016 (1984).

Memphis Jug Band. *Memphis Jug Band.* Vi-21278 Rt RL-322 (1928).

Milton, Roy. *Roy Milton and his Solid Senders: The grandfather of R&B.* Juke Box Lil BL 35647.

Mitchell, Roscoe. *Nonaah.* Nessa n-9/10 (1977).

————. *Solo saxophone concerts.* Sackville 2006.

Mobley, Hank. *Peckin' time.* Hank Mobley Quartet. Blue Note BLP 1574 (1957). Cassette.

Modern Jazz Quartet. *The Modern Jazz Quartet / The Milt Jackson Quintet.* Prestige LP 7059 (1952).

————. *The Modern Jazz Quartet plus.* Verve 833 290-4 (1957).

————. *Third stream music: The Modern Jazz Quartet and guests: The Jimmy Giuffre Three and the Beaux Arts String Quartet.* Atlantic SD 1345 (1959).

Monk, Thelonius. *The best of Thelonius Monk: The Blue Note years.* Blue Note B4 95636.

Montgomery, Wes. *The incredible jazz guitar of Wes Montgomery.* RLP-9320 (1960).

Morton, Jelly Roll. Black bottom stomp. *Smithsonian collection of classic jazz.* Smithsonian Institution/Columbia Special Products P6 11891 (1973).

Murray, David. *Ming.* Black Saint BSR 0045 (1980).

Nickerson, Camille. Five Creole songs. *The Black Music Repertory Ensemble in concert.* Bonita Hyman, mezzo-soprano. Center for Black Music Research CBMR002-C1 (1992).

Original boogie woogie piano greats. Columbia KC 32708 (1974).

Parker, Charlie. Now's the time. Blue Note 85108 (1953). Reissued on *Charlie Parker: The complete Savoy studio sessions.* Savoy S5J 5500 (1978).

Patton, Charley. Devil sent the rain blues. Paramount 13040 (1929). Reissued on *Charley Patton, 1929–1934: The remaining titles.* Wolf WES CD103 (ca. 1980).

Pendergrass, Teddy. Turn out the lights. Philadelphia International ZS8 3773 (1979).

Picket, Wilson. Soul dance number three. Atlantic 45-2412 (1967).

Price, Florence. Sonata in E minor. *Black diamonds: Althea Waites plays music by African-American composers.* Cambria CD-1097 (1993).

———. Song to the dark virgin. *Music at the church of St. Katherine of Alexandria.* Leroy O. Dorsey, bass; Clyde Parker, piano. Lois J. Wright Memorial Concert Series. Vol. 1. KM-1702 (1981).

Rainey, Ma. *Ma Rainey.* Milestone M-47021 (1974).

The record makers. Word MSB-6756 (1983).

Redman, Don. Chant of the weed. Columbia 2675-D (1932). Reissued on Columbia C3L 33.

Roach, Max. *We insist: Freedom now suite* (1960). Reissued on Columbia JC 36390 (1980).

Roberts, Luckey. Nothin'. *Harlem piano solos.* Good Time Jazz M-12035 (1958).

———. Pork and beans. U.S. Music 66186. Piano roll.

Rollins, Sonny. Pent up house. Sonny Rollins Plus Four. *Smithsonian collection of classic jazz.* Smithsonian Institution/Columbia Special Products P6 11891 (1973).

———. Poinciana. *Graz 1963 concert: Max Roach Quintet and Sonny Rollins Trio* (1966). Reissued on Jazz Connoisseur JC 108 (1978).

Roots of the blues. New World NW 252 (1977).

Sam and Dave. Soul man. Stax 231 (1967).

Shepp, Archie. *Goin' home.* With Horace Parlan. Steeplechase SCS-1079 (1977).

Singleton, Alvin. After fallen crumbs. Shadows. A yellow rose petal. *Alvin Singleton.* Atlanta Symphony Orchestra. Meet the Composer Orchestra Residency Series. Elektra/Asylum/Nonesuch 79231-2 (1989).

Smith, Bessie. *The world's greatest blues singer.* Columbia GP33 (1970).

Smith, Hale. *Contours, for orchestra.* Louisville Symphony Orchestra. First Edition LOU-632 (1962).

———. In memoriam Beryl Rubenstein. *The Cleveland composers fortnightly musical club presents . . . Kulas Choir and Chamber Orchestra.* Composers Recordings CRI SD-182 (1959).

———. *Innerflexions.* Slovenic Symphony Orchestra. Composers Recordings CRI CD 590 (1991).

———. The valley wind. *Art songs by black American composers.* Hilda Harris, mezzo-soprano. University of Michigan SM-0015 (1981).

Smith, N. Clark. Negro folk suite. *Black music: The written tradition.* Black Music Repertory Ensemble. Center for Black Music Research CBMR 001 (1990).

Smith, Willie ("The Lion"). Tea for two. *The legend of Willie (The Lion) Smith.* Grand Award LP 33-368 (1958).

Smith, Willie Mae. *Mother Willie Mae Ford Smith: "I am bound for Canaan Land."* Sacred 6015 (ca. 1950).

Smithsonian collection of classic jazz. Smithsonian Institution/Columbia Special Products P6 11891 (1973).

Songs and instrumental music of Tanganyika. Music of Africa. Comp. Hugh Tracy. Decca LF 1084.

Songsters and saints: Vocal traditions on race records. Vols. 1 and 2. Matchbook MSEX 2001/2, 2003/4 (1984).

Soul Stirrers. *The original Soul Stirrers featuring Sam Cooke.* Specialty SP2106.

Spectrum: New American music. Vol. 5. Nonesuch H-71303 (1968).

Staple's Singers. Respect yourself. *WattStax: The living word.* Stax STS-2-3010 (1972).

Still, William Grant. *Afro-American symphony.* London Symphony Orchestra. The black composers series. Columbia M-32782.

————. *Afro-American Symphony.* New NRLP-105 (1974).

————. Songs of separation. *The Black Music Repertory Ensemble in concert.* Hilda Harris, mezzo-soprano. Center for Black Music Research CBMR002-C1 (1992).

————. Songs of separation. *The black composer in America.* Claudine Carlson, mezzo-soprano. Oakland Symphony Orchestra. Desto DC-7107 (ca. 1971).

————. Songs of separation. *Music of William Grant Still.* Orion ORS-7278.

————. Three visions. *Natalie Hinderas, pianist, plays music by black composers.* Desto DC-7102-3 (ca. 1970).

————. *Works by William Grant Still.* Videmus. New World 80399-2 (1990).

The Supremes. *Greatest hits.* Motown 5663 (1967).

————. Where did our love go. *Where did our love go.* Motown 621 (1964).

Swanson, Howard. The cuckoo. *Black American piano music.* Felipe Hall, piano. Da Camera Magna SM-93144 (1975).

————. A death song. The Negro speaks of rivers. *Art songs by black American composers.* Willis Patterson, bass. University of Michigan SM-0015 (1981).

————. The Negro speaks of rivers. *Seven songs.* Helen Thigpen, soprano; David Allen, piano. American Recording Society ARS-10 (ca. 1950).

————. *Short symphony.* American Recording Society Orchestra. Dean Dixon, conductor. American Recording Society ARS-7 (ca. 1952).

————. *Short symphony.* Vienna State Opera Orchestra. Composers Recordings CRI-SD 254 (1969).

Tatum, Art. *The best of Art Tatum.* Pablo 2310-887 (1983).

Threadgill, Henry. *When was that.* About Time 1004 (1982).

Tindley, Charles Albert. Beams of heaven. Sister Rosetta Tharpe, vocal and guitar. Decca 3254.

————. The storm is passing over. Blind Joe Taggart, vocal and guitar. Vocalion 1123. Mellotone M12544. 78 rpm.

Turner, Joe. *Careless love.* Savoy MG 14016 (ca. 1959).

Tyner, McCoy. You stepped out of a dream. *Fly with the wind.* Milestone M-9067 (1976).

Walker, George. Concerto for trombone and orchestra. Denis Wick, trombone; London Symphony Orchestra. The black composers series. Columbia M-32783 (1974).

————. Lyric for strings. London Symphony Orchestra. The black composers series. Columbia M-33433 (1975).

————. Piano concerto. Natalie Hinderas, piano; London Symphony Orchestra. The black composers series. Columbia M-34556 (1974).

Waller, Fats. Carolina shout. *One never knows, do one?* Fats Waller and His Rhythm. RCA Victor LPM-1503.

Ward, Clara. *Clara Ward Singers: Lord touch me.* Savoy MG14006.

Ward Singers. *Best of the Famous Ward Singers of Philadelphia, PA.* Savoy SC 7015. Cassette.

Waters, Muddy. Louisiana blues. Chess 1441, LP1427. Reissued on *The Chess box.* Chess/MCA CHD 3-80002 (1989).

Weather Report. Gibraltar. *Black market.* Columbia PC 34099 (1976).

Wells, Mary. *Greatest hits.* Motown MS 616 (1963).

Weston, Randy. *Uhuru Africa.* Vogue DRY 21006/France (1960).

Wheatstraw, Peetie. C and A blues. Vocalion 1672, 04592.

White, Washington ("Bukka"). The Panama limited. Yazoo L-1026 (1930).

Wildflowers: The New York jazz loft sessions. Douglas NBLP 7045 (1982).

Wilkerson, Edward, Jr. *8 bold souls.* Open Minds SOM 2409-2 (1991).

Williams, Joe. *Big Joe Williams and Sonny Boy Williamson.* Blue Classics BC21 (ca. 1970).

Williams, Paul. The hucklebuck. Reissued on Savoy 45-683 (1949).

Wilson, Olly. Akwan. London Symphony Orchestra. The black composers series. Columbia M-33434 (1964).

———. Cetus. *Electronic music.* Vol. 4. Turnabout TV 34301 (1968).

———. Of visions and truth: A song cycle. *The Black Music Repertory Ensemble in concert.* Center for Black Music Research CBMR002-C2 (1992).

———. Sinfonia. *Olly Wilson: "Sinfonia"; John Harbison: "Symphony No. 1."* Boston Symphony Orchestra. New World 80331-2 (1992).

———. Sometimes. *Videmus: Works by T. J. Anderson, David Baker, Donal Fox, Olly Wilson.* New World 80423-2 (1992).

Wings Over Jordan Choir. *The Wings Over Jordan Choir: Original greatest hits.* Gusto K5-5021X (1978).

Wizards from the Southside. Chess CH 9102 (1984).

Wonder, Stevie. Living for the City. Tamla 54242 (1973).

Films and Videotapes Cited

The Art Ensemble of Chicago: Live from the Jazz Showcase. 1982. University of Illinois, Chicago.

Dutchman. By LeRoi Jones. 1992. Dir. Anthony Harvey. Prod. Gene Persson. African American Perspectives: A Library on Video. Resolution/California Video, San Francisco.

Georgia Sea Island Singers. 1963. Prod. Beth Lomax Hawes. University of California Extension Media Center, Berkeley.

"Georgia shouters." 1928–1929. Film footage made by Lydia Parrish and/or Melville Herskovits. Sound component not located. Human Studies Film Archive, Smithsonian Institution, Washington, D.C.

The Gospel at Colonus. [1985] 1987. Music by Bob Telson. Lyrics by Lee Breuer and Bob Telson. Warner Reprise Video; Films for the Humanities.

"100 television programs featuring America's greatest gospel artists." Jubilee showcase collection. Recorded between January 10, 1963, and January 8, 1984. Harold Washington Library Center, Chicago Public Library.

Roots of resistance: A story of the underground railroad. 1990. With the MacIntosh Singers. PBS Video.

To live as free men. 1940. Motion Picture Division, Library of Congress, Washington, D.C.

Zydeco: Creole music and culture in Louisiana. 1984. Prod. Nicholas Spitzer. Flower Films.

Index

References to musical examples are given in boldface.

Index

African songs (*cont.*)
  of, to African calls, 32. *See also* Dance,
    Drum, and Song
African speech, 32–33, 62
African worldview, 32n.4
Afro-American Symphony (William Grant Still),
  109–110, 162, 153–154, 253–254, **254**
Air (band), 194, 195
Akan, 22
Album of Negro Spirituals (Harry T. Burleigh), 107
Alcindor, John, 101
Aleatoric music, 206
Allen, Richard (hymn publisher), 59
Amen Corner, 45
American Syncopated Orchestra, 104–105
Anansi, trickster tales of, 25
Ancestors, veneration of, 17. *See also* Living-
  dead; Spirits
Anderson, T. J. (composer), 271, 276; compo-
  sitional style of, 256, 260; *Intermezzi*,
  260–261, **260**, 266, 276; *Variations on a
  Theme by M. B. Tolson*, 208–209, 210, 253
Animal tricksters. *See* Br'er Rabbit; Tricksters
Apprenticeship, importance to composers of
  black concert-hall music, 157
Armstrong, Louis, 123–125
Art Ensemble of Chicago, 192–193
Ashanti, gods of, 16
Àshe (life force), 20
Association for the Advancement of Creative
  Musicians, 191, 269
Azusa Street Revival, 63

Bailey, DeFord (harmonica player), 215, 222
Baker, David (composer), 219
Bands. *See* Big bands; Black bands; New
  Orleans–style jazz
Baptist Church, and shouts, 110
Baraka, Amiri: *Dutchman*, 185
Barbershop-quartet singing, 64
Basie, Count, 167–168
Basotho, funeral chant of, 18
Beaux Arts String Quartet, 166
Bebop: form used in hard bop, 181; as per-
  formed by Miles Davis, 180; primacy of
  rhythm in, 143; and ring tradition, 138;
  rise of, 136. *See also* Hard bop
Beethoven, Ludwig van, 237
Berry, Chuck, 177–180, 182, 201
Big-band jazz. *See* Jazz
Big bands: Count Basie, 167; Earl Hines,
  125–126; experimentation of, 137; in
  Harlem Renaissance, 116
"Big Chief Blues" (Furry Lewis), 217
"Big Leg Blues" (Mississippi John Hurt), 80
Birmingham Jubilee Singers, 175
Bispham, David (arts patron), 106. *See also*
  Negro Renaissance
Black Arts Movement, 185
Black bands, 82. *See also* Big bands; New
  Orleans–style jazz

"Black Bottom Stomp," 123
Black Cajuns, 43
Black Christians, attitude of, toward shouts, 38
Black class divisions, 89, 98
Black concert-hall music, 145; decrease in use
  of ring trope in, 161; early composers of,
  136–137; and myth, 147, 149, 150; 1960s
  black composers of, 207; place of, in con-
  tinuum of black music, 261; religious, 170;
  signifiers in, 150; use of folk music in, 153
Black dances, 72. *See also* Dance, Drum, and
  Song
Black elitism, 89, 98. *See also* Harlem Renaissance
Black folk culture, song and poetry in, 49. *See
  also* African culture; African music; African
  religion
Black gospel style, 63, 64. *See also* Gospel;
  Gospel blues
Black music: affinity of, with avant-garde music, 209; African performance practices in,
  51; continuity of, 9; continuum of, 265; as
  cultural memory, 9; European-derived roots
  of, 274; formal tradition in, 107, 145; histories of, 103; metaphors in, 223, 231;
  quartet singing in, 64; religious music first
  published, 58; representation and symbolism in, 239–254. *See also* African music;
  African-American music; Black concert-hall
  music
Black music criticism: analytical theories of,
  261, 266; lack of aesthetic for, 5; requirements for, 234, 235; and Signifyin(g) act,
  233
Black nationalism, 103, 134–135. *See also*
  Pan-Africanism
"Black Pierrot, A" (poem, Langston Hughes),
  154
Black power, 184
Blakey, Art, 188n.8
Bland, James (composer), 60
Blues, 73–78; bluesmen, Chicago, 177–178:
  fascination of, with trains, 214; instrumen-
  tal techniques in, 80; as propelling force for
  bebop, 138; and religion, 231; urban, in
  Chicago Renaissance, 121, 122; vocal style
  of, 77–78, 80. *See also* African-American
  music; Jazz
Bolden, Charles "Buddy" (trumpeter), 79, 84
Bonds, Margaret (composer), 121, 162
Bontemps, Arna (writer), 130, 158
Boogie-woogie: in Chicago Renaissance, 121,
  122; elements of, in rhythm and blues, 143
"Box Car Blues," 221
Boyer Brothers, 173
Brady, William (composer), 59
Braxton, Anthony (saxophonist), 193–194
Br'er Rabbit, 48; as model for Bugs Bunny, 48;
  Signifyin(g) of, 95. *See also* Tricksters
"Br'er Rabbit and Br'er Lion" (story), 48
"Bright Star Shining in Glory," 43

309

Index

DaCosta, Noel (composer), 247, **248**
Dance, Drum, and Song, 6; communal context of, 33; components of, 33, 96; and continuity of African-American music, 50; as element of African-American cultural unity, 57; as expression of African worldview 23; in *Five Creole Songs*, 156; indispensability of, to ring, 7; influenced by jook houses, 66; during nineteenth century, 60, 61; reflected in parades, 83; in religion, 19, 43, 64; and ritual, 20, 26; and spirituals, 42; transported by slaves, 38. *See also* African dances; Drumming; Ring dances; Songs
Dance bands, 67
Dance rhymes, 49
Dances: Americanized, 53; of white society danced by blacks, 67. *See also* African dances; Cakewalk; Dance, Drum, and Song; Ring dances
"Dancing in the Sun" (John W. Work), 240, 241–244
Davis, Miles: describes John Coltrane, 190; *George Gershwin's Porgy and Bess*, 164–165, 218–219; moves from hard bop, 182; and 1960s jazz style, 186–188; performs bebop, 180
Dawson, William (composer), 121, 132; *Negro Folk Symphony*, 120, 154
"Death Song, A" (Howard Swanson), 252, **252**
Dett, Robert Nathaniel (composer), 255–256, 266
Devil, as trickster, 74. *See also* Esu
Dinwiddie Quartet, 65
Diop, Birago (Senegalese poet), 16
"Dippermouth Blues," 124
Discrimination, as subject for song text, 162
"Dixie Flyer Blues" (DeFord Bailey), 216, 222
Dockery Plantation, Mississippi, 79
"Doggin' Around," 168
Don Degrate Delegation, 198
Dorsey, Thomas A.: comes to national attention, 128; compositions of, in *Songs of Zion*, 199; creates gospel blues, 126; and Pilgrim Baptist Church chorus, 129; relationship: with Ma Rainey, 127; with Mahalia Jackson, 127, 170; sets lyrics of Langston Hughes, 131
Dorze, 28
Dranes, Arizona (singer), 65
Drumming: as basis for minimalism, 206; derivation of patterns, 28; experiments in 1950s, 188n.8; in *Five Creole Songs*, 156; melodic, in jazz, 195; pitch changes in, 28n.3; to produce altered states, 21; recordings of, 28n.3. *See also* Dance, Drum, and Song
Du Bois, W. E. B., 103, 152n.13
Dutchman (play, Amiri Baraka), 185

"East St. Louis Toodle-oo" (Duke Ellington), 115–116

Ebenezer Church, Chicago, 129
8 Bold Souls (ensemble), 264
8 Bold Souls (recording, Edward Wilkerson), 264, 266
Electronic music, 206
Ellington, Duke, 114, 131; amalgamates musical styles, 168–170; collaboration of, with Mahalia Jackson, 170; compositional style of, reflected in free jazz, 195; fascination with trains, 221, 222; musical philosophy of, 222n.9
Emancipation, 66
Ennanga (William Grant Still), 162
Ensembles: Air, 194; American Syncopated Orchestra, 104–105; Art Ensemble of Chicago, 192; Beaux Arts String Quartet, 166; "Cannonball" Adderley Quintet, 181; 8 Bold Souls, 264; Experimental Band, 191; Harlem Symphony Orchestra, 107; "Hell Fighters" band, 105; Honeydrippers, 143; John Robichaux Orchestra, 84–85; Jones Boys Sing Band, 175; Memphis Students, 104; Miles Davis Band, 164–165; Modern Jazz Quartet, 165–166; Negro String Quartet, 107; New Life, 198; Rabbit Foot Minstrels, 108; Society Orchestra, 105; Southern Syncopated Orchestra, 101, 105; Sylvester Decker's Excelsior Brass Band, 82; Tympani Five, 143. *See also* Vocal ensembles
Esu (Esu-Elegbara) (African divinity): and African-American concert-hall music, 211; in African-American culture, 48; as divine trickster, 16, 24, 74; encourages erotic content of jazz, 85; as god of irony, 140; as interpreter of Signifyin(g), 96; as mythical figure, 7; in the person of Harriet Tubman, 223, 225; as personified by jazz composers, 196; symbolism of, 23; as teacher of the blues, 78; transformations of, 48, 73, 94
Europe, James Reese (band leader), 105
Evans, Gil (composer), 164, 218–219
Experimental Band, 191

"Faithful One" (Robert Owens), 244, **246**
Famous Blue Jay Singers, 172
Famous Ward Singers, 173
Fantasy Variations (Ulysses Kay), 207, 253
Fisk Jubilee Singers, 60–61, 103, 104, 107
Five Blind Boys of Alabama, 199
Five Creole Songs (Camille Nickerson), 156, 269
Fodet (Senegambian song), 75
Folk rags, 66, 69
Folk tales, 23. *See also* Trickster tales
Fon, 16, 38
"For You There Is No Song" (Leslie Adams), 239–240; **239–240**
Foundation instruments, and time line, 29. *See also* Time line
Franklin, Aretha, 197, 204
Free jazz, 193–195. *See also* Cool jazz; Jazz

311

315